1 Neville Chamberlᴀ Personality and Policy

The memory of Neville Chamberlain and the idea of 'appease-ment' go together. Yet he invented neither the policy nor the word. When Hitler came to power and during the early years of the Third Reich, even while Nazi Germany grew more and more threatening, almost everyone favoured the policy of 'appeasement', the search for peace by the redress of German grievances. Later, however, in 1938 and 1939, it became the personal policy of the Prime Minister. Mr Chamberlain applied it longer than most of his Cabinet colleagues and most of the British people would have done. After February 1938, he personally took the lead in the House of Commons in defend-ing appeasement while the Foreign Secretary spoke only in the less contentious atmosphere of the Lords. Above all, in Septem-ber 1938, his three visits to Hitler, without any other British minister, applied an adventurous and dramatic style in interna-tional affairs and brought him individual fame as the great appeaser. In that month he staked his reputation on success in pacifying the Third Reich. He did so willingly because he believed he could do it. The Munich agreement, he thought, justified his faith.

The policies that led him to Munich had rational grounds to support them; what distinguished Chamberlain was his con-fidence that those policies had succeeded. Thereafter he be-came the representative of a dwindling minority who believed that Munich meant peace rather than another in a series of ever more threatening crises. His hopes deceived him. His policy failed when war came in September 1939: 'Everything that I have worked for, everything that I have hoped for, everything that I have believed in during my public life, has crashed into ruins.'[1] In consequence writers and speakers have misunderstood and under-rated him. He was neither a coward nor a fool; he was neither ignorant nor idle. He was a culti-vated, highly intelligent, hard-working statesman, yet he has

1

been written off as a petty, narrow-minded, boring provincial.

Chamberlain's papers are, appropriately, in the library of the University of Birmingham. With them are those of Joseph and Austen Chamberlain, his father and brother, whose national and international importance makes absurd the suggestion that Neville's upbringing somehow imposed limited mental horizons. The papers at Birmingham make up a uniquely effective historical source. Sometimes they offer a moving intimacy of access to the Prime Minister's personal life. They show the breadth of his interests. His last diary, for 1940, is there. As always it contains the train times from Paddington to Snow Hill and Euston to New Street, the two Birmingham stations, neatly written out. The diary pocket holds his membership of the AA and of the National Art Collections Fund as well as a season ticket for the Leicester Gallery, known then for its exhibitions of 'Artists of Fame and Promise'.

Chamberlain liked pictures, although modernism aroused his hostility, even anger. As Chancellor of the Exchequer he extracted canvases from the National Gallery, for 11 Downing Street, after some difficulty in bringing the 'unruly Director to heel'. Kenneth Clark prevented his securing a Cuyp but he managed, enviably, to take examples of Hobbema, Ruysdael, Claude, Teniers and Bonington.[2] When he visited the Royal Academy, in May 1934, he looked for Stanley Spencer's latest works, having read *The Times* critic's admiring, and perceptive, words: 'It is reasonably certain that in 50 years' time he will be recognised as one of the very few contemporary painters who has really counted in the history of English art.' Chamberlain thought differently: 'I was not prepared for the hideous, sordid, grotesque productions which I saw at Burlington House. It rouses me to fury to think that impostors should have the impudence to fob off such stuff as "art" or that any otherwise intelligent person should be fool enough to try and admire it.' He was soothed, though, by a portrait by Gerald Kelly and by the elegant, flattering, pretty pictures of women by William de Glehn, an artist of the kind whose works came back into fashion in the anti-modernist reaction of the 1980s. In March 1935 he enjoyed the 'delightful', 'admirable', 'deliciously absurd', Sassetta panels just put on exhibition in the National Gallery. In the same week, when Hitler was responding angrily to the British White Paper on defence, he went to Agnews' exhibition of watercolours where he liked the de Wints, Varleys, and the rest of the early English school and 'there are some delightful drawings by Renoir' but also 'some hideous nudes by Mark Gertler. I don't know why Agnews have them'. Having condemned that mildly expressionist artist, he refused altogether to see Epstein's statue of Christ, a sculpture then thought to be highly provocative: 'He must have done it for the cynical satisfaction of hearing fools exhaust their vocabulary of admiration over it.'[3]

During the same week he went to a Royal Horticultural Society show, with 'spring flowers beyond words', and heard the Busch quartet playing a variety of composers from Haydn to Dvorak. 'Though the only quartet of Beethoven they played was an early one, rather immature from him, he knocked spots out of all the rest.' In 1935 and 1936 he went to piano recitals given by Edwin Fischer, Wilhelm Backhaus and by Rachmaninoff who, Chamberlain noted, aroused so much enthusiasm that he had to give five encores. After he attended a concert conducted by Sir Henry Wood, Sir Henry wrote to Chamberlain to say how pleased he had been to see him in the audience and the Chancellor promptly invited him to lunch as a prized guest. Opera, on the other hand, he did not care for: he commented on Verdi's *Otello*: 'I don't much care if I never hear it again. The fact is opera does not really appeal to me and with the exception of Mozart's I am not enthusiastic about any of them.' (The exception was characteristic of 1930s tastes.) Later Verdi's *Macbeth* got a gentler response, though he found 'the atmosphere of Mutual Admiration at Glyndebourne a little difficult to live up to', but that was in 1939 and thoughts of the problems of Poland and Danzig distracted him.[4]

Chamberlain preferred music to the theatre: 'I enjoy music much more than drama.' He showed eager interest just the same: he found Dover Wilson's book, *What Happens in 'Hamlet'*, 'so exciting that after finishing it I promptly read it all over again'. He went to see Shakespeare plays; he condemned John Gielgud whom he found 'much too noisy a Hamlet for my taste' but was charmed by Peggy Ashcroft as Juliet. Chamberlain, then, was not insensitive, even if his tastes were what might have been expected of an elderly and staid Conservative

in the 1930s.[5] He formed strong views on the arts and expressed them firmly and even cantankerously. So it was in his
political life. He dominated British Cabinets in the 1930s by his
strength of conviction and decisiveness. In MacDonald's
'National' government, and under Baldwin, Chamberlain
counted most. He thought so himself and others agreed. He
managed British policy at the Ottawa conference and at the
disarmament conference – 'It amuses me to find a new policy
for each of my colleagues in turn and though I can't imagine
that all my ideas are the best that can be found, most of them
seem to be adopted faute de mieux!' He could not help it: 'You
would be astonished if you knew how impossible it is to get any
decision taken unless I see that it is done myself and sometimes
I wonder what would happen to the Government [MacDo-
nald's] if I were to be smashed up in a taxi collision.' By 1935
he had 'become a sort of acting P.M.', working out defence and
foreign policy. Considering the Stresa conference that year, he
thought: 'I shall have to send [sic!] Baldwin as well as Eden
along with Simon.' Then, over the Ethiopian problem, 'I have
been very active and though my name will not appear I have as
usual greatly influenced policy and ... method also.' During
the Rhineland crisis 'It is true that I have supplied most of the
ideas in bringing the French to reason and taken the lead all
through' but he admitted some credit was due to 'both Edward
and Anthony' (Halifax and Eden) for 'each of them was most
helpful'. Sometimes things could go wrong. In January 1937
when he was working out a 'little scheme' for encouraging
restraint in Hitler, Eden made a speech which caused Hitler
'annoyance': 'it was very unfortunate that owing to my P.S.'s
[private secretary's] casualness A [Anthony] did not get my
comments on the passage about Germany. I didn't like it and
several of my colleagues also thought it unfortunately worded.
I was very sorry as up to then A had done well.'[6] In May 1937
Chamberlain became Prime Minister and he could manage
things more easily.

Lord Londonderry served with Chamberlain as Secretary for
Air throughout the Ramsay MacDonald coalition government
in 1931–5. He wrote to Halifax, in August 1939, a resentful
letter about Chamberlain: 'From 1931 he has always made
mistakes, and as the "Dictator" of our Administration from that

time he is responsible for all our troubles, and may take credit for our successes, if any. Ignorant people blame Ramsay and Baldwin, when the real villain of the piece is N.C.' Admittedly, to Charley Londonderry, Chamberlain's most prominent misdeed was that he 'got rid of me when I was absolutely on the right lines' (about air strengths). Ramsay MacDonald supports this testimony to Chamberlain's leading position. MacDonald was Prime Minister of the 'National Government' from 1931 until 1935 and remained in the Cabinet until 1937. When Baldwin succeeded MacDonald, the new Prime Minister, MacDonald complained, made Chamberlain 'adviser on everything' and 'sole confidant'. MacDonald found that Chamberlain 'is encouraged to take too much upon himself and holds the P.M. in his pocket'.[7]

Concentration and hard work rather than sociability and charm won personal influence for Chamberlain. Duff Cooper, who worked closely with Chamberlain for a year as Financial Secretary to the Treasury, and served with him subsequently for four years in the Cabinet, described him as 'not a man whom it was easy to know well. Ungregarious by nature, he never frequented the Smoking Room of the House of Commons.' Duff Cooper's clubs, White's, Buck's, the Beefsteak and the St James, contrast with Chamberlain's membership of the Carlton, compulsory for leaders of the Conservative Party, and of the rarefied Athenaeum. Neither did Chamberlain frequent the fashionable meeting places of the day such as the Savoy Grill. Chamberlain was not a diner-out; he explained why in a letter of March 1935, to Lady Stanhope, in which he opted for lunch: 'Dinner doesn't suit me very well, as I always have so much work to do in the evening, but I should be delighted to come to lunch.' Jock Colville, sent from the Foreign Office to act as a Downing Street secretary in 1939, found Chamberlain polite but 'austere': 'He seldom said to me anything not strictly related to business.' In 1938 and 1939, R. A. Butler regularly worked with Chamberlain and Lord Halifax, the Foreign Secretary, who spoke in the Lords, when they prepared answers to Parliamentary questions, the most important of which were handled in the Commons by the Prime Minister. In April 1938 Butler described a long session with them, preparing answers to 33 questions. Halifax took an interest in 'turns of phrase' but Chamberlain 'brings a most critical mind to bear not only upon the Office [Foreign Office] minutes which are attached to the questions, but to the answers themselves. These he frequently redrafts in pencil with very little hesitation ... he does not like vague and polite phrases but wishes to go straight at the opposition and express exactly what he means. The tradition of soothing Members by such phrases as "the honourable and gallant gentlemen will be aware" are usually erased.' Chamberlain, although pleasant to co-operators and subordinates ('Chips' Channon comments on 'his usual dazzling smile') hated opposition and criticism and found it difficult to be agreeable to their authors. Jock Colville, after a few months in Downing Street, decided that 'he likes to be set on a pedestal and adored, with suitable humility, by unquestioning admirers'.[8] Certainly he loved flattery more even than most politicians; part of his tragedy was that Hitler exploited this weakness.

Perhaps Chamberlain's comparative lack of sociability made it less necessary for him to cultivate that tolerance of disagreement that helps to make a successful dinner-table guest. He was not, however, hermit-like in his habits. He enjoyed country house weekends, especially shooting parties, and took a tolerably skilled part in the organised slaughter of pheasant and partridge. His favourite sport was more solitary; he was a serious angler. His greatest triumph, a trout of five and three-quarter pounds, he caught in Hampshire, staying with Sir Joseph Ball, 'a better fisherman than I'; photographs of Chamberlain and his catch appeared in the press, but Chamberlain's host, Sir Joseph Ball, shunned publicity and did not appear. Ball's contacts with Chamberlain concerned more than fish. Chamberlain took great care to keep informed of opinion within the Conservative Party. The Conservative Parliamentary chief whip, David Margesson, well-known, well-respected and well-liked, supervised Conservative MPs. Sir Joseph Ball, head of the 'Conservative Research Department' at Central Office, and a former member of MI5, supervised study of the outside world. Margesson concerned himself with party unity; for instance he wrote to Chamberlain to suggest that he might possibly bring Churchill into his government when he became Prime Minister. Ball supported Chamberlain, right or wrong.

He acted as a stealthy and furtive political manipulator as well as in the more avowable role of chief analyst of political trends. Chamberlain seems to have had no qualms about learning more than was publicly known about the deliberations of the Labour Party executive or about the control by the Conservative Party, through Ball, of a purportedly independent weekly journal.[9]

In Chamberlain's last diary there remains his card as Fellow of the Royal Horticultural Society. He found flowers, gardens and bird-life more congenial than colleagues and much more congenial than the casual acquaintances who impinge on active politicians. When he was Chancellor, he put up a nesting box and had a bird table made for the garden of No. 11 Downing Street. In mid-July 1939 with lowering crises in Europe and Asia he worried about the roses at Chequers, 'very poor this year compared to what they were last summer ... Only Caroline Testout retains her customary vigour.' Two weeks later he observed that 'The spotted flycatcher brood is almost ready to fly' and he reported that 'I have worked like a beaver in the gardens and woods and am busy planning new improvements as fast as I am able. I get an extraordinary amount of pleasure and satisfaction out of my outdoor amusements here [Chequers], especially in connection with trees.' But his dog, Spot, had had to go to the vet: 'I miss him dreadfully and keep looking for him and then remembering he is not here.' Most of all he enjoyed family weekends at Chequers. In 1938 and 1939 about one-third of his weekends were spent alone there with his wife, Annie. He planted trees including several tulip trees, red oak and other specimens. He even contributed a short note to *The Countryman* on 'Natural History in Downing Street' discussing the leopard moth and the conduct of a pair of blue tits, 'perhaps I should say black tits, for they were a grimy couple'.[10] To English minds these preoccupations, so far as they were known, implied reliability and wisdom and strengthened confidence in Chamberlain.

Neville Chamberlain's appearance also inspired a certain confidence. He had none of the dandyish affectation of his father or of Austen, his half-brother, who distinguished themselves by their monocles, their orchids and their elegance. Neville gave no hint of raffishness; his dark clothes and his stand-up starched Edwardian collars suggested the prudence of the managing director of an old-established bank or the senior partner of a large firm of solicitors specialising, perhaps, in family settlements. He was small and wiry, and assertively grey in aspect. He spoke clearly and carefully in unornamented, direct language. He had ample financial means for his modest, middle-class, way of life. He noted his capital in his diaries; in the 1930s he had £50,000 or more, enough to make him a millionaire in late-twentieth-century money. Apart from attacks of gout, he kept fit until overwhelmed by cancer in 1940. His weight, fluctuating around 10 st. (140 lbs or 63 kg), he recorded in his diary. He withstood the stress of his office; in 1939 he reached the age of 70 but in July he remarked 'fortunately I continue to sleep' and it was uncommon for him to resort to a sleeping pill. Even so he hated public speaking: 'the preparation ... fills me with gloom until it is over'.[11]

Chamberlain was never flippant and seldom light-hearted. However, he took part in that most popular of 1930s diversions: going to the cinema. Early in 1936 he saw Charlie Chaplin's latest film *Modern Times*: 'We laughed till we ached.' He admired *Moscow Nights*, a film with Laurence Olivier as the guardsman hero, for 'it was extremely well acted and entirely free from vulgarity'. Philip Sassoon took the Chamberlains to see *The Ghost goes West*, a René Clair whimsy, with Robert Donat as the main actor. 'We laughed consumedly' – no doubt Neville enjoyed in that film its condescending amusement at American naivety.[12]

In his methodical way Chamberlain noted down the books he read. He read literary criticism – among the books listed for 1939 is Mary Lascelles' scholarly and sensitive study of Jane Austen, still sought after by university students fifty years later. But biographies attracted him most, especially historical biographies. In 1939 he read Holland Rose on Napoleon; Rosebery on the younger Pitt, Brian Tunstall on Chatham and books on animal and bird painting and on fishing. He was sufficiently sensible not to stress the 'lessons of history', though he used H. W. V. Temperley's *Foreign Policy of Canning* to support his objections to warning Hitler that Britain would go to war in case of a German attack on Czechoslovakia in September 1938.

It is sad that Neville Chamberlain should have been denied

three or four years at a university, while his father sent his other son, Austen, to Cambridge. He would have enjoyed himself. Moreover his intellectual weaknesses which contributed to, and even explain, the failure of British policy towards Hitler's Germany might have been diminished or cured. He might have been trained to distinguish between things as he wished them to be and things as they were, he might have learned to consider unwelcome evidence, he might have been more ready to criticise himself and less sensitive towards the criticism of others.

In the years from 1931 to 1937 Chamberlain enjoyed a highly successful period in office as Chancellor of the Exchequer so that his prestige grew and his succession to Baldwin as Prime Minister became more certain. During his Chancellorship the numbers in work rose steadily, recorded unemployment fell below 10 per cent for the first time since 1929, before the world slump; exports rose and in 1935 industrial production was greater than in 1929. Chamberlain got the credit whether or not he influenced, or even understood, what was happening: 'I confess', he wrote in October 1934, 'I am puzzled to account for our continuous improvement, even in exports.' Low interest rates, low commodity prices, the realistic value of sterling, the reflationary effects of subsidised house-building, were not topics that took up much space in his correspondence; international affairs got more attention by far. As Chancellor of the Exchequer, Chamberlain did not limit himself to strictly financial matters. When he took up office international finance, through reparations, war debts, the Ottawa agreements for imperial preference, and the abortive World Economic Conference of 1933, led his department into some of the main issues in diplomacy. From there he extended his range to the whole of foreign policy, especially during the years when Ramsay MacDonald's grip slackened. Military spending and rearmament naturally concerned the Chancellor and Chamberlain smoothly took the lead.[13]

In 1937 Chamberlain seemed certain, as Prime Minister, to be able to conclude his career in triumph. Subsequent denigration has falsified interpretation of British policy towards Hitler by misunderstanding Chamberlain's interests and abilities. The disaster that befell him did not derive from stupidity or ignorance on his part. Posthumous libels have destroyed Chamberlain's reputation and falsified historical interpretation. Churchill began it. In conversation, during the war, he described Chamberlain as 'the narrowest, most ignorant, most ungenerous of men' and after the war he published his view. The first volume of Churchill's war memoirs, *The Gathering Storm*, came out in 1948. At once his eloquent, persuasive prose captured the public mind and no subsequent analysis, however scholarly, has lessened its intellectual hegemony. Chamberlain was pinned down and labelled. While 'an upright, competent, well-meaning man' he showed a 'lack of all sense of proportion and even of self-preservation'. He possessed a 'narrow sharp-edged efficiency', he had a 'limited outlook and inexperience of the European scene'. This depreciation is misleading; Chamberlain was not like that. Narrowness of mind, ignorance of Europe are not the explanations of what he did. In 1938 and after Chamberlain was probably wrong and Churchill probably right; but Chamberlain had good reasons for his moves into disaster. The coming of war was more complicated than Churchill claimed and Chamberlain's errors are less simply explained than by his alleged ignorance and stupidity.

Chamberlain's attachment to his family led to the accumulation of evidence of exceptional value to historians. Few letters, it is true, survive to his wife or children. Annie was subject to symptoms of stress and depression. She suffered, in the common 1930s word, from her 'nerves'. Perhaps this explains Chamberlain's reliance on the interest of his sisters in his work of influencing or deciding British policy. Once a week he wrote either to Hilda or Ida and once a week replies came from one or another of them. They supplied well-informed critical support and approval for their brother. Neville Chamberlain awarded them his commendation in slightly patronising words. 'My sisters are not mere "yes-women"; they have minds of their own and I know that if they approve what I am doing it is not because it is I who am doing it.' Hilda and Ida kept over 1200 letters from their brother. Contemporary gossip dismissed Annie Chamberlain as knowing nothing of foreign affairs; Neville, it was alleged, got all his mental stimulus and confidence from his sisters.[14] As a result historians can assess Neville Chamberlain's motives and the reasons for his actions with unusual precision. Through Hilda and Ida he presents his own weekly explanation and justification.

The letters, if dry, are readable. They show a warm, affectionate personality. They lack wit, although Chamberlain was given to a certain waggishness, and they show no capacity for self-criticism. Vanity, touchiness and obstinacy recur. These defects brought the tragedy of complete failure in foreign policy and have earned him posthumous derision. War with Germany and the disaster of enemy conquest of France and the Low Countries in 1940 were, arguably, the results of Chamberlain's faith in his own success. Until 1938 British policy towards Germany was dictated by the belief among the majority of the British public that Germany had real grievances which should be rectified, grievances which derived, in large part, from the alleged follies of French foreign policy. This view was reinforced by consciousness of British military inadequacies. At that time Chamberlain expressed and formed part of a consensus in foreign policy.

In 1938 came dissension and Chamberlain led one side in a growing dispute. In September he indelibly identified himself with 'appeasement'. Moreover he thought he had succeeded, by his own personal intervention, in making Hitler see reason. After Munich he attempted, tenaciously, but with varying degrees of concealment from increasingly disillusioned colleagues and from worried public opinion, to renew and extend his supposed success. He persisted even after the German occupation of Prague in March 1939. Whenever he was free to choose he opted for conciliation rather than confrontation towards Germany. It seemed impossible for him to think himself mistaken. No one can know what would have happened in Europe if Mr Chamberlain had been more flexible or if someone else had taken charge, but it is hard to imagine that any other foreign policy could have had a more disastrous outcome.

2 Rearmament and Reparations

Hitler used the Treaty of Versailles of 1919 to raise the European storms that Chamberlain and his colleagues hoped to calm. Hitler's demands for the destruction of Versailles won him support at home and disguised his ambitions both from the German people, and from foreign statesmen. Most Germans wished to change Versailles and many, therefore, sympathised with what they thought to be Hitler's international aims. In Britain, too, such demands might seem inconvenient, but not obviously unacceptable. If Hitler's only purpose outside Germany was to revise Versailles, then it seemed reasonable for British governments to continue, after he came to power, to try to change the treaty to make it more congenial to Germans. This the British had done ever since it was signed and Hitler's advent only made that policy appear more urgent. Since British observers attributed his rise in part to foreign, and especially French, obstinacy in maintaining Versailles, then to quieten him, or to lessen German support for him, required efforts to restrain foreign, especially French, hostility to Germany.

Hitler's hatred of Versailles, however, carried him, and eventually the German people, beyond mere modification. Hitler intended not only to reverse the defeat of the First World War but to make Germany safe from any similar defeat in future centuries. Hitler believed Germany lost the First World War because socialists who, he believed, were Jews or inspired by Jews, had used the privations caused by allied blockade to trick the imperial German military and civilian authorities into surrender. Hitler determined to create a Germany immune from blockade, to construct, that is to say, a completely self-sufficient German empire within which Germans could always be adequately fed and made able to defend it for a thousand years to come against any possible foe. These aims made futile the essential purpose of 'appeasement', to keep things broadly as they were, and in particular to keep the British Empire secure from military threat, by making limited concessions to Hitler.

Hitler wanted far more than Chamberlain and his associates would allow. The limited concessions of 'appeasement' could bring peace only if they reduced support inside Germany for Hitler and his warlike policies. They did not, however, succeed in strengthening opposition to Hitler because they seemed to be concessions made to Germany because of Hitler rather than in spite of him. If anything, they strengthened Hitler, because he seemed able to secure concessions by threats alone without bloodshed.

The grievances of Versailles which provided Hitler with the means to appeal to German support and foreign sympathy were reparations, disarmament, colonies, the demilitarisation of the Rhineland, the enforced independence of Austria, the frontiers of Czechoslovakia and the frontier of Poland. That is not a complete list, but grievances such as the internationalisation of German rivers counted for less.

Reparations made the greatest grievance of all, not only for their real effects but for what their effects were thought to be. The Treaty of Versailles required Germany to pay the victorious allied powers for the damage done to them by the war of 1914–18, a war, the treaty asserted, which Germany and her allies had brought about. Most Germans denied German guilt for the war and exaggerated the effect of the reparations deduced from it. German observers, including well-qualified economists, blamed the collapse of the currency in 1923 on reparations and it is true that the obligation to transfer resources abroad without payment tended to weaken the mark, while the French armed occupation of the Ruhr to enforce reparations set off a form of resistance, stoppages of production, which destroyed the mark. In September 1929, before the next economic calamity, Hitler, with the financial support of his new conservative nationalist ally, Hugenberg, denounced the 'traitors' in the government who were accepting 'the enslavement of the German people' in the newly negotiated Young plan for reparation payments.[1] His predictions were followed, and apparently justified, by the disasters of the great depression. Reparations, which ceased altogether in 1932, even in their closing stages reduced confidence in the mark and so forced even more severe deflation in Germany to maintain its value than would have been needed otherwise. This effect was, in fact, small compared with the impact of the great slump, but Hitler's ranting against foreigners and their alleged German accomplices, and the widespread belief in the evil effects of reparations, helped him to secure for the Nazis one-third of the electorate in 1932, the year when 6 million workers were unemployed.[2]

To British observers the history of reparations came to seem the history of a mistake. In 1919 Keynes, the most lucid of economists, persuasively denounced them and in 1932 Lloyd George, one of the three men most responsible for Versailles, tried to make out that they were not his fault. Hitler's accession to power in January 1933 was thought to be in great part a result of reparations. British opinion blamed the French for exacting them. Lloyd George denounced the clouded judgement of French politicians: 'The distrust and ruthlessness that swayed their judgement at all the conferences on reparations ... and even as recently as last year caused them to palter over-long with the Hoover moratorium proposal, are to a very high degree responsible for the continued unsettlement of Europe and the world-wide economic depression which has now supervened.' The moratorium proposed by President Hoover on 20 June 1931 suspended payments on debts between governments, including reparations. The French 'paltered' by delaying agreement for two weeks to force the reaffirmation of the principle of reparations payments. Many commentators, inside and outside Germany, attributed the collapse of the German banking system in mid-July 1931 to this French obstruction of Hoover's plan to restore confidence in the mark. In January 1932 Brüning, the tight-lipped, austere German Chancellor, announced that reparations payments could never be resumed; Keynes, visiting Germany that month, found that 'everyone naturally attributes all the miseries of the acute deflation which is occurring to reparations'. British opinion agreed that reparations should end.[3]

French politicians, especially on the Right, believed their electorate expected them vigilantly to uphold the treaty, which the French sacrifices of 1914–18 had gained. Their actions in delaying and obscuring the formal end of reparations, something the British thought essential to restore confidence and begin German economic recovery, stoked British anger. The first Prime Minister of the 'National' coalition government, Ramsay MacDonald, wrote to his new Foreign Secretary, Sir John Simon, in January 1932 that the 'whole situation is getting so bad owing to French delays that ... we shall be in precisely the same fix as we were after the French, by their delays, had destroyed all chance of the Hoover Moratorium having a sweeping effect on the European situation ... unless we show the French that they are not going to keep us twiddling our thumbs to play their game, they are going to pursue, under a cloak that looks more or less respectable, the policy which brought them into the Ruhr some time ago, and is now threatening the ruin of Europe.'

About the same time Sir Robert Vansittart, the verbosely brilliant official head of the Foreign Office, made a broader complaint, of 'the egotism and stupidity' not only of France but also of the USA. To British ministers and officials the solution of the reparations problem had long seemed obvious: the Germans owed reparations to the European allies of the First World War and the allies owed money to the United States that they had borrowed to fight the war. The United States should cancel the war debts and the ex-allies would cancel reparations. Not merely did American administrators and Congresses refuse, but, as the British complained, they also made difficult the payment of the war debts they demanded. Tariff barriers checked imports to the United States and so made it difficult for their debtors to earn dollars. This compelled payment in gold. French economic management aroused the same criticism by imposing similarly deterrent tariffs. The United States Congress pushed through in 1930 the Smoot–Hawley tariff law, which doubled already high tariff levels to an average of about 50 per cent on import values. France increased tariff rates in 1931, 1932 and 1933. By 1932 the value of United States gold stocks amounted to 4 billion dollars and French to 3 billions, doubled since 1929, while British gold reserves were only 590 million and German 250 million.[4]

Moreover, as Vansittart put it, the monetary authorities in France and the USA, with more than two-thirds of the world's gold between them, 'resolutely refused to play the gold standard game'. He meant that inflows of gold were supposed to stimulate an increase in bank credit and so increase demand inside the country gaining gold. The consequent stimulus to imports and weakening of exports should then act to check the inflow of gold. American and French central banks and finance ministers, on the contrary, were accused of 'sterilising' gold by intervening to hold down the money supply. Thus the gold movements of the early 1930s brought generalised deflation. By this process reparations and war debts, insisted on by greedy French and clumsy Americans, damaged France, the USA, the UK and most desperately of all, Germany, with its unstable and threatened democracy. Few British citizens followed these complicated arguments. Many, however, picked up from journalists and politicians the belief that the short-sighted meanness of selfish foreigners, especially the French, had driven Germany to despair, and so to Hitler. Ramsay MacDonald, whose domestic failures as Labour leader inclined him, especially now that he was the Prime Minister of a mainly Conservative government, to concern himself with foreign policy, recorded the following emotions in his diary: 'France has been playing its usual small-minded and selfish game over the Hoover proposal . . . To do a good thing for its own sake is not in accordance with French official nature. So Germany cracks while France bargains' (5 July 1931). 'The behaviour of the French has been inconceivably atrocious' (11 July 1931). 'Again and again be it said: France is the enemy' (22 July 1931). 'The French are still at war with Germany. They are afraid of its trade unless it is hobbled' (21 June 1932).[5]

German complaints against the disarmament clauses of Versailles provoked further British discontent with the conduct of the French. Reparations ended before Hitler came to power; attempts to win agreed arms limitations continued and roused more dispute between Britain and France on how to deal with Nazi Germany. The world disarmament conference opened at Geneva on 2 February 1932, after six years' work by the preparatory commission for disarmament, starting in December 1925. The delay made another German grievance. The Treaty of Versailles compelled German disarmament 'to make possible a general limitation of the armaments of every nation'; Germans, and their British sympathisers, among whom Lloyd George was one of the most fluent, blamed the French statesmen who 'declined to carry out that part of the Treaty which imposed a solemn obligation on France to follow the example Germany had been forced to set in respect of disarmament'.[6] German demands for 'equality of rights' dominated the disarmament conference. Versailles limited the German army to 100,000 men (who became a highly efficient long-service professional army); German governments under Hitler's immediate predecessors, and even more aggressively under Hitler, demanded numerical equality with the French metropolitan army. Successive French governments insisted on guarantees of security against aggression, preferably by collective action in support of the victim or, at least, by effective supervision of the application of any newly agreed limitation on armaments.

In September 1932 the German government, then headed by von Papen, withdrew from the disarmament conference, complaining that equality of rights had not been given; in December 1932, the month before Hitler became German Chancellor, Schleicher's government returned to the conference, after Britain, France and Italy had promised to grant to Germany 'equality of rights in a system which would provide security for all nations'. In October 1933 Hitler withdrew again, this time both from the Disarmament Conference and the League of Nations. He complained of humiliation imposed on Germany by the continued denial in practice of immediate equality in armaments. The British government at once set itself to work out an arms limitation agreement acceptable to Germany and to persuade Germany to come back to the League, to symbolise co-operative inclinations. Eden, the elegant, ambitious junior Foreign Office minister, then Lord Privy Seal, went to Berlin and conferred with Hitler on 21 and 22 February 1934. The Führer gave a first-class performance of the role of a concerned statesman eager for peace. 'It was his earnest wish to collaborate with other Powers ... He would recognise all obligations which Germany had undertaken of her own free will ... Germany earnestly desired to reach a solution.' He made himself out to be more moderate and conciliatory than his own Foreign Minister, von Neurath. He impressed his British audience. Eden thought Hitler to be 'sincere in desiring a disarmament convention, as he wished to be able to push on with a long programme of internal reconstruction' though he felt 'less sure' of those who surrounded Hitler.[7]

Eden found out what Hitler insisted on and the British incorporated his demands in an amended version of their proposals for disarmament of January 1934, itself a modified version of their proposals of March 1933. Germany would have an army of 300,000 men, an air force about half the size of the French; supervision would be arranged and any breach of the convention would lead to consultation among the signatories. The 'heavily armed powers' would destroy their more powerful weapons after five years. By this time the right-centre government of 'national union', brought into power by the riots of 6 February 1934, was in control in Paris. The British now asked the new Doumergue government to agree to German rearmament without effective guarantees of security for France. French acceptance would prevent French isolation but Germany would rearm and the proposed agreement provided only sanctions 'more theoretic than real', as Doumergue complained to Eden.[8]

On 17 April 1934 the Doumergue cabinet outvoted its lively Foreign Minister, Louis Barthou, and decided to reject British pleas for tolerance towards Hitler and of German illegal rearmament. 'France', they declared, 'must make the first of its preoccupations the conditions of its own security ... Its wish for peace must not be confused with the abdication of its defence.' That evening Barthou gave the statement to the British chargé d'affaires, Ronald Campbell. Barthou apologised for its disagreeable nature and Campbell agreed that it would cause great disappointment in England. It did. Nearly two years later Vansittart complained that 'whenever a compromise with Germany could be postponed, France was blind enough to think that other German demands would be more slowly developed. It was for this reason that one opportunity after another of coming to terms with Germany was lost.' Eric Phipps, the British ambassador to Berlin, wrote to Wigram, head of the Central Department, which dealt with Germany in the Foreign Office, in June 1935: 'I believe that Hitler would have kept to his offer once it had been accepted by the other side.' Another Foreign Office official, Orme Sargent, wrote: 'We always urged the French to make a bargain with the Germans while there was yet time. They refused to do so, namely when they rejected the German offer in April 1934.'

When Barthou gave the French rejection to Campbell he added that England need only say 'If Germany attacks France I shall be at your side.'[9] Barthou wanted Britain to be a reliable ally of France; only then could French governments agree to concessions to Germany.

British governments, however, would not make an alliance with France. Most British voters, and most British ministers, rejected any entangling alliance. Alliances might bring Britain into war because of the behaviour of unreliable and unstable foreign politicians. Barthou implied that the security provided by assured British support would make French governments less assertive; British opinion felt the reverse. The self-governing dominions, Canada, Australia, New Zealand and South Africa, also opposed United Kingdom commitments in Europe: they could themselves be dragged into war, or encounter fierce domestic dispute, in case Britain went to war. Continental European quarrels should either be ignored or, if Britain were to intervene, it should only be to help their solution, not to take sides. If Britain took sides it might exacerbate quarrels rather than calm them. In particular, to take sides against Germany might make Hitler even more resentful and unmanageable. Scholarly studies of the First World War increased the fear of alliances. Alliances, and the associated arms race, it was argued, had caused the First World War. The 'lessons of history' seemed clear: to prevent another great war, avoid alliances.

After the French refusal to discuss German rearmament the British did not know what to try next. Next day, 18 April, Simon circulated a despairing Foreign Office paper to ministers. It expected a Parliamentary enquiry on 'what we are going to do in the face of German rearmament ... The answer that we are going to do nothing will only encourage Germany further, though it is the truth and she knows it.' It seemed, of course, that the only hope of making an arms limitation agreement with Germany was by somehow finding concessions to the French desire for security to soften their opposition. Simon suggested an international agreement to forbid all bombing from the air; if any one country bombed another the rest should all bomb the guilty country. Baldwin objected; it went too far. As the leader of the Conservative Party, with its huge

majority in Parliament, he was the most powerful of all politicians, more influential than Ramsay MacDonald, the 'National
Labour' Prime Minister, who had been abandoned by nearly
everyone in his own party. Stanley Baldwin played a particular
role in politics, that of the simple, honest plain-spoken, coun-
try-loving Englishman, wise, slow and steady, and played it
well. He cleverly identified trends of opinion and captured
them for the Conservative Party. Now he complained to the
Cabinet of the risk of 'being dragged into some conflict in the
East' for instance because of some bombs dropped over Poland.
He wondered if 'it might not be best to state firmly to the world
that any hostile action against France and the Low Countries
would not leave us disinterested'. Baldwin himself did it with
more elegance than clarity. At the end of July he gave this
thought to the House of Commons: 'Since the day of the air
the old frontiers are gone. When you think of the defence of
England you no longer think of the chalk cliffs of Dover; you
think of the Rhine. That is where our frontier lies.'[10]

In those words Baldwin rejected complete isolation. The
Royal Navy alone could no longer make Britain safe. The First
World War showed that even in naval warfare flotillas in
enemy-occupied harbours on the other side of the Channel
endangered British ships. The menace of the bomber, especially with the range of 1930s machines, made it doubly imperative
to keep Germany at a safe distance from the Channel coast. It
would be better still if Hitler and his government agreed to
renounce bombers, or at least to limit their range and number,
and this became the main purpose of British 'appeasement'.
Meanwhile the 'security' of France and the Low Countries was
a British interest but it should be arranged tactfully, politely
and unaggressively. France should be kept safe from Germany
without provoking the anger of the Third Reich. Simon responded favourably to a Belgian suggestion that Britain should
promise automatic assistance to Belgium against invasion so as
to cover France without directly appearing to do so. Other
ministers, notably Chamberlain, Halifax and Runciman, checked him. The plan would imply military conversations and the
division of Europe into two groups. It was incompatible with
the balanced Locarno arrangement, made in 1925, in which
Britain guaranteed Germany against France and Belgium as

well as France and Belgium against Germany. All that happened, therefore, was that Simon made a restrained remark in Parliament: 'the integrity of the territory of Belgium is no less vital to the interests and safety of this country today than it has been in times past' and wrapped it in references to 'this collective system' and 'assurances ... mutual in expression and reciprocal in intention'.[11]

Chamberlain had his own scheme for security. It reconciled two conflicting needs: it was comprehensive, universal and collective, yet did not risk dragging Britain into an unwanted war. He suggested a mutual aid convention with limited forces pledged in advance by all the participants to a central agency. It would form an international police force to stop an aggressor. The Chiefs of Staff successfully opposed it. Though Chamberlain remained 'convinced that my plan offers the only chance of progress towards security' he soon involved himself in other topics: in British rearmament and the problem of Japan.[12] Barthou tried to make up for British caution by visiting Poland, Czechoslovakia, Romania and Yugoslavia to revitalise French alliances and understandings in eastern Europe. He worked towards yet more 'security' for France by seeking an entente with Italy and by evolving a plan for a grandiose eastern European pact which became known as the 'Eastern Locarno'. The Soviet Union, Germany, Poland, Czechoslovakia and the Baltic states were each to pledge themselves to come to the assistance of any of the others attacked by one of the signatories. France and the USSR would support each other against aggression. In September 1934 the Soviet Union joined the League of Nations, ready for 'collective' resistance to aggression.

Barthou asked for British support. Simon replied by insisting that the pact should be indisputably reciprocal, so that France should also guarantee Germany against Soviet attack and the USSR should guarantee Germany against French attack. Secondly, Simon asked for some advance towards 'equality of rights', that is towards legalising the rearmament of Germany. Simon told Barthou that 'he would not be able to satisfy the House of Commons and British public opinion merely by saying that the Eastern Locarno was on a reciprocal basis. He would have to show how it contributed to disarmament.' The

French therefore agreed, to please the British, to a joint assertion that the proposed reciprocal guarantee 'would afford the
best ground' for a 'reasonable application of the principle of
German equality of rights in a regime of security for all
nations'.[13]

The single-minded steadiness of British policy towards Germany had survived and would continue to survive many disappointments. At this stage, in the second half of 1934, the
French government still seemed the origin of the disappointments. Soon the composition of the French government
changed and consequently British hopes of an arms-limitation
agreement with Germany revived. Hitler rejected the 'Eastern
Locarno' on the pretext that the pact did not advance 'disarmament', that is, approve continued German rearmament. Nazi
activities in the summer of 1934 should have reduced belief in
the orderly, legalistic nature of the Third Reich. On 30 June
1934 Göring announced that Hitler had ordered the suppression of 'a clique of S.A. leaders' who 'wanted to start a second
revolution'. Hitler admitted the killing of 70 people including
the commander of the Nazi SA party militia, Röhm; many
more disappeared. The event marked a Hitlerian concession to
German 'moderates'. Phipps, the British ambassador in Berlin,
accordingly thought that if a disarmament agreement 'is still
desired the otherwise nauseating events of the weekend have
improved the prospects quite considerably'. On 25 July Austrian Nazis attempted to promote union with Germany by
seizing the Chancellery and Vienna radio; they killed the
Chancellor, Dollfuss. The Austrian army and police squashed
the coup but, a day later, Mussolini claimed that Italian forces
had at once moved to the Brenner frontier, a claim believed by
European statesmen. Chamberlain's attitude to Mussolini was
permanently affected by this apparently forceful display.[14]

At the end of 1934, Baldwin and Simon reaffirmed British
policy – to secure an agreement to limit armaments. In November, Baldwin looked ahead and pointed to 'grounds for very
grave anxiety' in the progress of German rearmament, in
defiance of Part V of Versailles, but declared that he had not
'given up hope either for the limitation or for the restriction of
some kind of arms'. Simon, in the same Commons debate,
declared afresh 'that we are for regulated limitation as opposed

to competitive unregulated armaments'. In December 1934, Simon set it for himself as 'the great task of 1935'. To carry it out 'we must first persuade the French – and pay the necessary price for such persuasion ... The legalisation of German rearmament and the cancelling of the armament clauses of Part V of the Treaty of Versailles are a bitter pill for the French to swallow; especially as they don't believe in any German promise. But the alternative is not the stopping of German rearmament but its continuation at an ever-increasing rate behind the screen.'[15]

To the British 'European appeasement' meant limits on the strength of the German air force and navy. The rest of British policy in Europe was made up of inducements to other countries to join in working for limits on German armed strength. Only in March 1939 did Chamberlain hesitantly turn to attempts to threaten Germany into arms limitation. The United Kingdom favoured the status quo, keeping things as they were, and wished to prevent disturbance to the British Empire. British responses to an arming and aggressive Germany could take one of four forms. One was not to respond at all, to do nothing to provoke or challenge Germany by interfering in Europe or by rearming; very few favoured this course which would lead to dependence on German good-will. A second was heavily armed isolation, an attractive option apart from the unlimited cost of defence without allies. The third choice, favoured by most of the varied domestic opponents of the government, was to seek strength for resistance to aggression from world-wide co-operation or from limited sets of collaborators. The objection was that that risked involving the United Kingdom in the defence of inconvenient and irrelevant parts of the status quo, such as Danzig or Memel or Transylvania. There remained 'appeasement', a word meaning originally nothing more than bringing peace to Europe, but one which came to mean the search for concession to Hitler to induce him, or enable him, to renounce armed force as a means for change. What is odd, in retrospect, about British appeasement, even when Chamberlain was in full control, is the parsimony in the concessions offered to Hitler. One explanation was that the British thought French obstinacy and folly to be the cause of German desire for greater power, another that Hitler was thought to be a comparatively moderate exponent of German discontents so that the more unquestioned his power the easier appeasement should be.

By the new year of 1935 the more 'reasonable' French government offered fresh hope. Flandin and Laval had replaced the intransigent Doumergue and Barthou, the latter gunned down in Marseille by Croat nationalists aiming at the King of Yugoslavia. Laval, the new Foreign Minister, gave priority, among Barthou's schemes for understandings to defend the status quo in Europe, to an understanding with Italy to support Austrian independence. To the delight of the British Cabinet he was ready, once he had made an agreement with Italy, to carry on negotiation for Barthou's eastern pact but simultaneously to engage in 'discussion with Germany of agreement about armaments'. British ministers invited Flandin and Laval to London to work out a plan for a 'general settlement'. New arms limitations would be evolved and the limitations on German armed strength imposed by Versailles abolished, thus 'legalising' the German rearmament which had already taken place. There should be a western European air pact, which would promise that if any one of Germany, France, Great Britain and Belgium attacked any one of the others from the air, all the rest should at once provide air force support to the victim. Britain would favour an 'eastern pact' of mutual guarantee. In these ways 'security' was offered to France. The Foreign Office took care to make sure that this Anglo-French plan, announced on 3 February 1935, could be reported in the Paris press as a victory for Laval and Flandin in their dealings with the notoriously pig-headed British. Thus it went out of its way to make sure that French ministers knew well in advance that there was no hope of their extracting any British commitment of ground troops; the French were warned not to ask for staff talks with their evocations of Sir Edward Grey's half-promises before 1914. The impact of British concession to France was not to be weakened by any public rejection of a French request.

On the other hand, there was nothing much in the 'Anglo-French plan' to appeal to Hitler. The Führer had a long conversation with Sir Eric Phipps a few days before the Anglo-French meeting. He advised the British Conservative Party,

Phipps recorded, to 'discard so unattainable an object as disarmament from their programme'. He made clear, as so often
in this decade, his own unchanging terms for Anglo-German
understanding. Germany would lead the world on land, Britain
at sea. He spoke of 'a certain fixed ratio between our respective
fleets'. He 'concluded by displaying an almost touching solici-
tude for the welfare of the British Empire'.[16] It is possible to
understand Hitler's mounting fury as every British government, MacDonald's, Baldwin's and, most energetically of all,
Chamberlain's, intruded themselves on his attention with unwanted schemes for European stability and peace. All Hitler
wanted from the British was that they should not interfere in
his concerns. This book is a history of British interference.

Two linked reasons for the British habit of intervention to
put things right should be added to the simple preservation of
a satisfactory status quo. Enlightened, progressively minded
British citizens felt a sense of duty to the world. This went, in a
way which is perhaps difficult for those living at the end of the
century fully to understand, with a long-established sense of
British power and influence. Seymour Cocks, Labour member
for Broxtowe, reminded the Commons in March 1935, 'The
prestige of this country is still high, thank God, and so is the
power of this country', and Lord Cranborne, the influential
and able Conservative, a little later observed 'We are far the
richest country in Europe, we are still far the most powerful
and respected nation in Europe.'[17] The year 1935 presented
one of the last of the great imperial spectacles, a triumphant
celebration, when London took up its role as the 'heart of the
greatest Empire the world has ever seen', with the Silver
Jubilee of King George V. At Spithead, ships of the Royal
Navy, for almost the last time, anchored as representatives of
the largest fleet in the world. That year the future of India
dominated Parliamentary proceedings: day after day Westminster legislated for the remote millions of the sub-continent.
It still seemed natural to believe that London could and should
organise the world.

After the Anglo-French communiqué of 3 February 1935,
Simon arranged for an invitation for him to go to meet Hitler
to advance the agreed plan for 'disarmament', or to find out if
it could be adapted to suit German wishes; Hitler apparently

welcomed the visit in order to push his own plan for Anglo-German friendship. The talks had to be postponed when Hitler became, as he claimed, literally speechless after the British government responded to German rearmament by publishing, on 4 March 1935, a White Paper, initialled by the Prime Minister, justifying measures to strengthen the British army, navy and, above all, the air force. New dates for the talks in Berlin were fixed for 25–26 March 1935. Before then the German Air Ministry announced the re-creation of a German Air Force, forbidden by Versailles, and on 16 March Hitler told Sir Eric Phipps of his decision once more to disregard Versailles by restoring conscription for the German armed forces and creating a peace-time army of about 500,000 men. He assured Phipps of 'his friendly feelings towards Great Britain with whom conflict would be quite unthinkable' and mentioned that he only needed a fleet equal to 35 per cent of the British. Phipps, as usual, reported contemptuously on the latest German outrage and went on to suggest renewed attempts at a disarmament convention: 'I seem to see bases for convention in Hitler's latest proposals.' For Phipps the Nazis were vulgar, pretentious, loutish, nouveaux-riches. From Berlin he sent amusing sneers at the Nazis; later in the 1930s, in Paris, he became disheartened and irritable. His elegantly expressed sense of superiority added credence to his assertions that bargains could be made with the Nazis.

On 18 March the British Cabinet assembled for an emergency meeting to decide what to do. Chamberlain, on his own account, determined the outcome, becoming 'a sort of acting P.M.'. He wrote to his sister the same afternoon. 'Hitler's Germany is the bully of Europe. Yet I don't despair.' Only firmness and clarity would make Germany behave reasonably. Chamberlain knew what was needed. Simon must ask if Hitler was still ready to discuss the Anglo-French plan of February. Then 'it would be necessary for Simon to talk plainly in Berlin'. Inspired by Chamberlain, the Cabinet agreed that Simon should face Hitler with an alternative. Either Germany would co-operate in regional collective arrangements for security or a structure of competing alliances would form.[18]

Hitler, as agreed, was asked if he still wished to talk to Simon. No one consulted the French. Corbin, the French ambassador in London, protested in a 'rather lively' conversation with Simon. The British Foreign Secretary countered with the reproach that the French refusal to discuss disarmament in April 1934 had caused all the trouble. However, something had to be done to keep the French and Italian governments from forcing a break with Germany in response to the open German defiance of Versailles. Laval suggested that Simon should first come to Paris to confer with the Italian Under-Secretary – Chamberlain insisted that only Eden should go; a junior minister rather than the Secretary of State. More important, Mussolini suggested a meeting in northern Italy of British, French and Italian ministers which he would attend.[19]

The Berlin meeting with Hitler disappointed Simon and the British Cabinet. Simon decided that while Germany 'greatly desires a good understanding with Britain' she was determined to rearm, get all Germans inside her borders, reject collective security and wanted colonies back. 'All this is pretty hopeless; for if Germany will not co-operate in confirming the solidarity of Europe, the rest of Europe will co-operate to preserve it in spite of Germany. This may not prevent an ultimate explosion, but it will delay it. We may see the curious spectacle of British Tories collaborating with Russian Communists while the League of Nations Union thunders applause. There may be no other course, but will it preserve peace? I most gravely doubt it.' Chamberlain complained of a series of negatives from Berlin and wondered 'what are we to do next?' Yet Hitler skilfully encouraged British hopes, even if he rejected their general settlement. His tentative offer of alliance: 'the British Empire might one day be glad to have Germany's help and Germany's forces at her disposal' was not likely to be welcome. On the other hand his readiness to discuss naval armaments and limit German claims to 35 per cent of the British navy at once led to a British invitation to join in preparations for the forthcoming naval conference. Hitler spoke favourably of the suggested air pact and did not rule out agreement on air force strengths. Moreover he suggested agreement on '(1) the prohibition of the use of gas and incendiary bombs; (2) the limitation of bombing to the fighting zones; (3) possibly the complete prohibition of all bombardment from the air'.[20]

Though Hitler did not appear ready to settle down in a

stable Europe, he seemed willing to renounce any naval challenge and even to forswear strategic bombing. In this way he strengthened the hope that his objects were not necessarily incompatible with the welfare and safety of the British Empire. When the Cabinet discussed policy before the Berlin visit Simon explained Hitler's objection to rejoining the League of Nations. 'He would say that the injustices of the Treaty of Versailles could not be rectified within the present structure of the League. Was it possible, for example, to imagine a unanimous vote by the League in favour of an alteration in the frontiers of Germany? Our reply to that ought to be to invite him to come back to the League and see what could be done to alter its constitution.'[21] Evidently the Cabinet did not fear alterations to the frontiers of Germany. What ministers supposed Hitler to want did not in itself threaten Britain's safety and independence. What might be dangerous, it seemed, was not Hitler's wishes but the way in which he might try to win them. In the process Germany might either become overwhelmingly strong or set off a European war which would involve Britain. Hitler's Germany must be induced to seek its objectives in a reasonable, peaceful way.

The Foreign Office stressed that the other important European powers, France, Italy, Poland and the Soviet Union, should join in the process. Hence Eden went on after Berlin, where he accompanied Simon, to Moscow, Warsaw and Prague. Hence the journey of MacDonald, Simon and Vansittart to Stresa to meet Flandin, Laval and Mussolini. Eden, in particular, emphasised the need to involve other powers in new security arrangements. This did not mean that Eden, or Foreign Office officials, intended to construct an anti-German coalition to restrain Hitler. Eden, on the contrary, looked for a framework of international co-operation in which Germany would be part. British ministers agreed on the need to restrain France and Italy from confrontation against Germany. They agreed that 'if asked by France and Italy to put an end to conversations with Germany and to do nothing more than indicate our intention to stand firm with France and Italy we should not agree to it: while we should frankly admit that there was much evidence to show that Germany could not be brought to acceptable agreement, we should make it clear that we were not finally convinced that this was the case until after further explorations' and that 'our general aim should be peace achieved by some system of collective security under the League of Nations, without an acceptance of new commitments'.[22]

The Stresa conference, in the Palazzo Borromeo on the Isola Bella, involved Mussolini's displaying his importance and Laval and Flandin displaying their concern for French security. The beauty of the scene perhaps helped MacDonald and Simon to secure their calming objective, as Chamberlain put it 'to keep the confidence of the French and Italians without being dragged at their tail'. The three powers agreed in a 'declaration' that they found themselves 'in complete agreement in opposing, by all practical means, any unilateral repudiation of treaties which may endanger the peace of Europe, and will act in close and cordial collaboration for this purpose'. On 2 May 1935 Ramsay MacDonald, in his last month as Prime Minister, spoke to the Commons, and boasted of Stresa as a sham; the so-called 'Stresa front' was nothing more than a verbal reproof to Germany for past misbehaviour combined with an empty threat for the future. A politician, MacDonald explained, has to decide whether 'he is now to abandon his attempts to build up, on general confidence, a peace system in Europe or seek refuge in those combinations of sheer force which have never saved him from war and never will.' He told the House that 'the instructions which we took with us to Stresa were not to make agreements which excluded any country on account of what has happened from taking part in further negotiation.' He ended his speech by asserting that 'the outlook – and I say this with great conviction and considerable intimacy of knowledge – has chances of appeasement as well as palpable dangers and it is the constant care of this country to help on the changes that must come by negotiated agreement and without disturbance to the peace of Europe or of the world.' Hitler's Germany, in spite of its uncontrolled rearming and its successful evasion of schemes for mutual assurances of security remained, in the opinion of the British Cabinet, a worthy partner in negotiation.[23]

The French government believed its public required a sterner attitude. A few days after the Stresa meeting they signed the new Franco-Soviet alliance, immediately followed by an alliance between Czechoslovakia and the USSR. British officials disliked these documents: they increased the risk of French, and therefore possible British, involvement in eastern European quarrels and made more likely the division of Europe into rival groupings. The British government, in contrast, continued its attempt to include Germany in negotiated agreements. The results of these British attempts settled into a pattern. Often they ran into the barrier of French reservations; if, on the other hand, Anglo-French agreement seemed imminent then the German government found reasons for delay. Hitler had at his disposal an experienced bureaucracy including an able foreign ministry and diplomatic service. They were skilled at maintaining negotiations or prospects of negotiation in the future. Hitler's line seems to have been, first, to avoid multilateral agreements because the less other powers cooperated with each other, the greater German relative strength, and, secondly, if possible, to avoid joining in new agreements to limit German actions, in case their breach aroused unnecessary excitement. The German foreign ministry, headed by the comparatively amiable Baron von Neurath, could safely be left to carry out these tasks. One negotiation in the summer of 1935, however, made a sharp exception to Hitlerian evasiveness, and led to the Anglo-German naval agreement. It was his own work, executed by his own favourite for foreign affairs, von Ribbentrop.

When Simon talked to Hitler in Berlin they had agreed on Anglo-German discussions on naval limitations. British ministers, officials and naval officers intended to bring Germany into preparations for the forthcoming naval conference at which they hoped limitations might be agreed by the USA, France, Italy and Japan. Talks began in London on 4 June 1935 and it was Ribbentrop who came. At once Ribbentrop demanded immediate recognition of the 35 per cent ratio between German and British naval strength 'as fixed and unalterable'. British ministers, eager to limit German strength and determined to try for continued limitation of the world's navies, gave way to Ribbentrop's peremptory proposal. Simon, in his last day as Foreign Secretary, suggested an attempt to bring limitation of air strengths into the Anglo-German talks and suggested other powers should be informed that the British intended to agree to Ribbentrop's demands and asked for their observations. Sir Bolton Eyres Monsell, the First Lord of the Admiralty, with the backing of Baldwin (who became Prime Minister next day) defeated the Foreign Secretary. Other powers should simply be told what the British intended to do. Simon predicted that the French would complain of a breach of Versailles; the First Lord replied that 'the maintenance of a rigid view of that Treaty had resulted in large German increases, both in the air and on land' so repeating the familiar point that the French were to blame for the growing German danger.[24]

Ribbentrop attributed the new agreement to Hitler's 'generous and far-sighted outlook ... Thus began a new chapter in the history of their countries and the foundation was laid for a future friendship of the two great countries.' Hitler 'was a very consistent man and thought in long historical periods'. The limitation of the German navy to 35 per cent of the British was accepted by the Germans 'because in their mind Great Britain was excluded for ever as a possible enemy'. Both sides were delighted. The German navy was pleased by the overthrow of the limitations of Versailles, although its commander, unlike Hitler, considered the treaty to be provisional; the British navy supposed that the Germans without the treaty would build more than the 35 per cent limit. The British supposed that they might now be able to cope simultaneously with the German and Japanese fleets; the Germans had secured British agreement, in effect, to their domination of the Baltic. The Germans relished the public demonstration that Stresa did not mean that Britain would trouble about French or Italian agreement before dealing with Germany. Hitler supposed that Anglo-German naval rivalry had brought Britain into the war of 1914; this danger had gone and Anglo-German understanding advanced. The British believed that it showed that 'realistic' diplomacy could prevent an arms race. Chamberlain considered it almost too good to be true: 'I am satisfied that we were right in clinching the agreement with the Germans, which ... looked so good as to make me suspicious.' Eden thought it possible that the naval agreement 'opened French eyes' and made them readier to consider an agreement on parity in the air. Craigie, then the

Foreign Office official responsible for naval issues, claimed it as an 'essential preparatory step in order to render possible that "general settlement" of outstanding problems which was outlined in the London Communiqué of February 3rd'.[25]

Thus encouraged, the new Foreign Secretary, Sir Samuel Hoare, and Eden, now brought into the Cabinet as the newly created minister for League of Nations affairs, and their officials eagerly resumed the search for limitation on air strengths. The French government insisted that land armaments should be included in negotiations, but objected to any proposal generous enough to be acceptable to Germany, and insisted that any air pact should permit bilateral arrangements between Britain and France to make it effective; this the Germans opposed. The Germans argued that air limitation would be impossible without the USSR and declared that they would not join the USSR in any understanding. Phipps, the British ambassador in Berlin, saw Hitler on 13 December 1935 and pressed for something to be done about an air pact and air limitation. Hitler seemed ignorant of earlier discussions and distinctly irritable. He rambled away from air limitation into repeated denunciation of those 'noxious microbes' the Russians. Phipps brought him back when he 'remarked that we were even now engaged in a race in air armaments'. Hitler replied that 'there could be no question of an air race between Great Britain and Germany' but suggested nothing except a secret exchange of information between the two air forces. 'War between England and Germany ever again was unthinkable: hence the Anglo-German Naval Agreement, which Herr Hitler would loyally respect for all time ... The two great "Germanic" peoples must never again fight one another; he had been pressed to demand 50 per cent of our fleet, but had declined, for he wished to show beyond doubt his determination to remain on the most friendly terms with us.' Hitler's proposal, Phipps commented, 'means in plain English that we should content ourselves with a modest air force representing only a mere fraction of Germany's. This would presumably be in response to Germany's noble gesture in only demanding a navy of 35% of ours.' Phipps had cornered Hitler into a clear revelation: he would readily leave the British navy dominant on the oceans of the world but he could not equip Germany with anything less than the strongest air force in Europe. It was impossible to make the Third Reich impregnable without forcing Britain into dependence on German good will.

In London, however, those who studied Phipps' report concluded that a settlement with Germany was difficult but not impossible. A senior British official, Wigram, who later became sceptical before his early death, minuted only that 'the moment is not ripe for negotiation'. Hitler's subordinates, more patient in manner than their chief, told the British that steps towards Anglo-German settlement must wait the resolution of the crisis over Ethiopia.[26]

3 British Policy and the League: Manchuria and Ethiopia

Chamberlain and his supporters, when they defended 'appeasement', stressed the threat of Japanese and Italian attacks on the British Empire if peace were not maintained with Germany. In the 1930s, the rulers of both Japan and Italy thought themselves obliged to express real, or imaginary, international economic and political grievances. Japanese and Italian remedies for their grievances, especially the Japanese, threatened British interests, and, in two confrontations, challenged the authority of the League of Nations. In both conflicts the League 'failed': collective action by the members of the League of Nations did not prevent Japanese and Italian conquests. In these confrontations League action aroused Japanese and Italian anger. The opponents of the British government at home accused it of causing the failures of the League. Some members of the government thought, on their side, that supporters of the League needlessly forced Britain to alienate Japan and Italy and increase the number of countries the Empire had to fear. The government, however, could not risk the domestic odium that open neglect of the League would bring. The first great League crisis of 1931–3, which led to complaints of British betrayal of the League, made it certain that the government would try more effectively to parade loyalty to the League of Nations in the Ethiopian crisis in 1935–6.

Japan suffered from over-population. In the 1920s the population increased by nearly one million a year. The Japanese home islands did not grow enough food, and imported food had to be paid for by industrial exports. Industrial exports needed imported raw materials and fuel; the only primary product exported on a large scale was raw silk. Emigration was restricted in the 1920s by, for instance, quotas imposed by United States legislation and by the 'White Australia' policy. The Japanese people, vulnerable to a slump in world trade, suffered hardship when demand in the United States for Japanese exports, especially silk, collapsed; their sufferings were exacerbated by the inappropriate free-market orthodoxy applied by the internationally minded Japanese governments then in power. After months of deflation, cuts in government spending, and restraint in the money supply, they returned to the gold standard in January 1930. More deflation, cuts in government spending and restraint in the money supply followed this ill-timed step until a new government gave up the gold standard again in December 1931. Now Japanese governments reversed the policies of the 1920s. In the 1920s they tried to co-operate in the development of a demilitarised, free-trading, world economy. Within Japanese administrations the representatives of the army and navy in the service ministries still tended to come from the more cautious and conservative upper ranks. In 1930 these moderates angered their younger comrades by agreeing to the Treaty of London, which extended the limit on Japanese warships, which had been fixed by the Washington Treaty of 1922 at three-fifths of the British or American levels, to include cruisers and destroyers as well as capital ships.

After 1931 Japanese governments increased public spending, especially on the army and navy, and allowed the yen to depreciate. Exports rose and production, especially of weapons, increased. At the end of 1934 Japan denounced the naval limitation treaties and Japanese admirals rejected proposals for their replacement which did not permit equality with the British and American fleets. The idea of a Japanese-controlled economic sphere, to assure essential imports and provide land for settlement, became the new orthodoxy. Younger officers called for military action to seize Japanese living space and to curb a growing Chinese nationalism directed against economically and legally privileged foreigners. Chinese nationalism opposed European power in China, especially that of the British, who controlled public utilities, transport, and the customs system, whose citizens enjoyed exemption from Chinese laws and jurisdiction, whose soldiers guarded their settlements and whose warships and gunboats patrolled Chinese rivers. In the 1920s Chinese nationalists led anti-British boycotts.

Japanese militarists claimed to the Chinese that they wished to liberate Asians from European exploitation; to the Europeans they claimed that they would defend the rights of all traders and investors.

The first violent expression of the developing anti-capitalist, anti-internationalist, militaristic Japanese line of thought came in Manchuria in 1931. In September the Japanese army in Manchuria began to take over the government of its three provinces, legally part of China, as a reply to Chinese challenges to Japanese control of the South Manchurian Railway. In March 1932 the Japanese set up a new state in Manchuria, under their control, and called it 'Manchukuo'. Chinese nationalists responded by boycotts of Japanese imports, successfully blocking half their total value.

Japanese armed forces struck back in Central China, at Shanghai, in January 1932. Thousands of British citizens lived there in semi-colonial fashion; the capital value of British enterprises in the area was put at about £60 million (£1.5 to £2 billion in 1990s values).[1] British newspapers reported fierce fighting near to the international settlement when Japanese military units tried to clear Chinese forces from around Shanghai. This action made the Far East an issue in British politics. In the second half of 1931, slump, unemployment, the defence and abandonment of the gold standard, the break-up of the Labour government, the appearance of the 'National Government', and its triumph at the general election, commanded attention. In international politics German reparations and war debts seemed to matter most. The Shanghai crisis advertised Japanese belligerence. Though a Shanghai cease-fire came in March, through the mediation of the British naval C-in-C, Admiral Kelly, on board the cruiser *Kent*, moored at Shanghai, Japanese aggression now became established as a prominent item on the list of British worries overseas.[2] Having subdued Chinese forces in Manchuria in 1932, the Japanese army invaded the adjacent Chinese province of Jehol and added it to 'Manchukuo'. At the end of May 1933 the Tangku truce suspended serious fighting for the time being. Japanese conquests in China concerned the United Kingdom in two ways: because the Chinese government invoked the League of Nations and because of the immediate threat to British trade and investment in China and the long-term threat to the British Empire in the east.

Two assumptions determined British policy; one was that the British Empire alone could not risk war with Japan, the second that the United States would not risk war with Japan. British naval strategy between the wars laid down that the battle fleet should be based in the United Kingdom and in the Mediterranean, at Malta. In case of any Japanese threat to Australia, New Zealand, Singapore, Malaya, Ceylon, Burma or India or to British trade and possessions in China the main fleet would concentrate and sail to Singapore and from that base dispute control of southern Pacific waters with the Japanese. Construction of the naval base at Singapore and of its defences against attack from a hostile sea-borne force had been stopped in the 1920s; in 1932, the doctrine, put in its final form in 1928, that there would be no major war for ten years from any given day, was cancelled and it was agreed, once again, that Singapore should be developed as a base for the battle fleet and made capable of defence against naval attack, for the time between the outbreak of a war and the arrival of the British fleet. Until Singapore was ready Britain lacked a fleet base east of Malta. In March 1932, the Chiefs of Staff reported their view that a Japanese attack might succeed in capturing or destroying the facilities on which the fleet would have to depend in the East and 'expose to depredation, for an inestimable period, British possessions and dependencies, trade and communications, including those of India, Australia and New Zealand'. Vansittart minuted that 'we are incapable of checking Japan in any way if she really means business' and concluded that 'we must eventually be done for in the Far East unless the United States are eventually prepared to use force'.[3]

Simon, as British Foreign Secretary, asked Stimson, the United States Secretary of State, if he contemplated any step to check Japan beyond protest. Simon wrote to MacDonald, the Prime Minister, that 'Stimson replied that he recognised that nothing but protest could be done'. Inconveniently, however, Stimson proved eager to launch public protests and maledictions and to press the British to do the same and to use their influence to organise at the League of Nations still more denunciations of Japan. Stimson 'felt', he told Simon, 'that, if

suitable occasions were chosen, the accumulated effect on public opinion was considerable and this would in the end influence Japan'.[4] Simon, and some of his advisers, thought, on
the contrary, that the denunciations would anger the Japanese,
strengthen the militarists and make them even more aggressive. Thus denied the assurance of support from the United
States the British government determined to avoid risking war
with Japan.

As a result British policy in the Far Eastern crisis in 1931–3
became simple in aim but difficult to carry out in practice: it
was to avoid incurring the hostility of any of the participants.
This suited John Simon's inclinations and talents. He was
ingratiating by nature, supremely competent at making the best
of any case he had to support and at giving a high-minded
flavour to the shiftiest evasion. His talents brought their penal-
ties. Simon longed to be liked and failed. Chamberlain commented 'the House detests him; he hasn't a friend even in his
own party and the cause is that, quite wrongly, they distrust his
sincerity'. Ramsay MacDonald thought much the same, noting
in his diary Simon's 'terrible manner and smile which robs him
of the appearance of sincerity'.[5] Simon now tried to maintain
the friendship of Japan, China and the United States while, for
the benefit of opinion at home, supporting the League of
Nations.

Stanley Baldwin set out part of Simon's brief when he wrote
to him in December 1932, 'I want to avoid a Chinese boycott or
a war with Japan. I have faith that you will avoid both.' Miles
Lampson, the British ambassador in China, warned that those
pro-Japanese British in China who believed that Japan was
upholding all foreign rights in China should 'look ahead and
bear in mind the Chinese will sooner or later have their tails up
again when undue anti-Chinese partisanship now may be remembered against us.' He looked back to the 1920s, when
Chinese nationalists aimed their boycotts against the British.
Simon set out another part of his brief when he minuted 'Good
relations with Japan are of the first order of requisites and
must be safeguarded: but we must, consistently with this, play
our part as a member of the League.' Moreover, as Simon told
the Cabinet, 'we cannot afford to upset the United States of
America over this and I do not mean to do so'. From Washing-

ton the British ambassador wrote to Simon 'about the choice between a Japanese and an American policy over China ... there can surely be no real danger of our choosing the Japanese rather than the American part if we have to make a choice'.[6] The Chinese nationalists, the United States, the supporters of the League, all demanded that Britain should denounce the aggressive disregard of their international obligations by Japan. From the British embassy in Tokyo, on the contrary, Sir Francis Lindley sent passionately worded despatches and telegrams pleading with the British government, 'whose stake and influence in the Far East far outweigh those of any other European country', not to alienate 'the most powerful nation in the Far East ... we now have the chance of gaining the friendship of the only nation in the Far East whose future is, as far as we can judge, reasonably assured and whose power to injure us is almost unbounded'. The value of the good-will of Japan should be weighed against 'that of a handful of Chinese politicians who are here today and gone tomorrow' and the government in London should 'examine critically the advantages likely to be gained by following a line laid down by America which, like England in the days of Palmerston, is so invulnerable that she can with perfect impunity indulge the loftiest sentiments of humanity where her own interests are not involved'. Lindley admired the Japanese people whom he did not think 'fundamentally militaristic'. He believed that hostile British gestures only served to prevent recovery of influence on the part of his 'liberal Japanese friends'. In London the senior official concerned in the Foreign Office, Sir Victor Wellesley, warmly supported Lindley. For him the British 'interest in the territorial status of Manchuria is infinitely less than their interest in maintaining cordial relations with Japan'.[7]

For Sir John Simon the greatest problem in all this was the League. The Chinese central government appealed to the League for assistance against Japanese action in Manchuria and Shanghai. What Simon wished to arrange was that the League should do enough to placate the Chinese and Americans without upsetting the Japanese. He had an even greater problem: how to do enough to content supporters of the League at home. What he did was to secure the appointment by the

League of a commission of enquiry, whose report, when accepted by the League Assembly, precipitated Japanese withdrawal from the League; to arrange a declaration by the League that territorial changes secured in breach of the Covenant would not be recognised, and to impose, but only for four weeks, in the spring of 1933, a unilateral British embargo on the sale of arms to China as well as to Japan. All this, though it meant much hard work and worry for Simon, Eden and their officials, frequent visits to Geneva and polite transatlantic telephone calls between Stimson and Simon, made no difference at all to the success of Japanese aggression against China.

British 'public opinion' in the first part of the 1930s seems overwhelmingly to have supported the League of Nations. The question arises, however, what was meant by support for the League? The outbreak of the Manchurian crisis coincided with the General Election following the formation of Ramsay MacDonald's 'National' government, an election which gave that government 'a greater majority than dreamland ever portrayed', in Churchill's words. The King's speech, at the opening of the new Parliament, made the usual pious reference to the League: 'My Government intend ... to continue their active interest in the work of the League of Nations' and went on to mention the disarmament conference but did not refer to the Far East at all. In the four-day debate on the Address only two speakers mentioned Manchuria: Lansbury, the pacifist leader of the shrunken Labour Party, who asked what steps the government were taking 'to bring that dispute to an end' and Geoffrey Mander. Mander, a Liberal, was the most persistent speaker and questioner on foreign affairs in the 1930s and a zealot for the League. (He was also active in praise of the works of William Morris and his circle.) Into a debate mainly devoted to currency, commerce, industry and tariffs he intruded Manchuria and put forward the 'League' position: 'It is a test question. We have to decide whether war is to be permitted ... We have the whole of the League plus America on the one side and Japan on the other.' He hoped the Council of the League would 'use all the moral force they possibly can' and if that were not enough 'use financial and economic pressure and, if that will not do, use pressure in the way of a blockade in preventing goods going into or coming out of Japan'. His peroration asserted that 'we have to take a bold and courageous view and, without using any physical force – that will not be necessary – mobilise all the different methods of economic, financial and moral pressure which are available to force Japan to realise that war is not going to be permitted to break out again ... There is no doubt that, if we fail in this issue, we are abandoning all the hope that arose out of the war, and the sacrifice of a million Englishmen, to say nothing of 9,000,000 others, who gave their lives for a great ideal will very largely have been in vain.'[8]

By early 1933 the Far East attracted much more attention. In February the opposition forced a debate on the Foreign Office estimates. Representatives of all parties supported the League. Lansbury, for the Labour remnant, wanted non-violent action. The supply of British arms to Japan should be forbidden and the British government should make another appeal to the Japanese people and the Japanese government 'to try to come to an understanding with the people of China'. Herbert Samuel, for the Liberals, thought that 'it may be that economic forces, combined with the moral pressure of world opinion, will after no long interval bring Japan to a more reasonable state of mind ... The Japanese are a proud, a sensitive and a great, people and they cannot be insensible to the opinion of the world.' Austen Chamberlain, in his role as (extraordinarily pompous) Conservative elder statesman, could not think 'that the verdict of the assembled world united at Geneva will count for nothing in the settlement of those issues when that settlement comes. There is no nation in the world today, however strong, however mighty, however powerful its arms, that can afford to neglect the judgements at Geneva.' However, the government should try 'to bring together the two parties in the Far East and to cause them to compose their differences'. Another Labour member thought that the situation could 'have been largely avoided if Britain had exercised in these international councils her enormous influence, and declared herself much more unequivocally than she has done in the last 18 months'. A 'National Liberal' expressed passionate opposition to any British involvement in war in the Far East but hoped that economic boycott might in the end force Japan out of Manchuria.[9]

Support for the League evidently meant desire for the organisation of 'world opinion' to bring to reason a warlike aggressor, followed, in extremity, by the organisation of economic pressure. The use of armed force against an aggressor would not be needed. In any case the League would make resort to aggression unlikely since it would encourage conciliation and the peaceful settlement of disputes. For its advocates, therefore, the League was not a means of organising armed resistance to aggression, it was a means of making the use of armed force unnecessary. Disarmament appeared both as a cause and a consequence of 'collective security'. Rejection of national armaments would remove the dangers of an arms race. In July 1934, when Labour moved a vote of censure on the government's plan to bring the RAF nearer to its approved strength, Clement Attlee, speaking for Labour, asked for the government to tell people 'that there is no such thing as national defence in an armed world and that they will have to work for a world organised for peace and for collective peace'. Herbert Samuel called for a 'supreme effort to secure international agreement' and accused the government of having so 'little faith in the success of the World Disarmament Conference that they must now, straight away, increase our air force and abandon hope of any effective result' and Stafford Cripps, the most lucid Labour speaker, proclaimed that 'the Covenant of the League is implicit with the belief that disarmament is the essential feature in the safety and security of the world'.[10]

It is not surprising that, in these years, before the crisis caused by German use of force in 1938, everyone agreed that attempts should be made to persuade Hitler to discuss German grievances and to limit German armaments: that is to say attempts at 'appeasement'. That consensus showed itself in the spontaneous reaction in the House of Commons from Herbert Samuel, the Liberal leader, when Simon interrupted the debate and told the House in the evening of 18 March 1935 that Hitler had agreed to see him to discuss the 'general settlement' in spite of his recent announcement of German conscription: Samuel observed that his statement 'will be received with general satisfaction', and commented that Simon went 'as the emissary of the nation' with 'the full force of combined national support'. Consensus came less easily over Japan. Ministers and the Chiefs of Staff worried about the general enthusiasm for the League because they believed that it brought danger of unnecessary conflict, in this case with Japan, which would surely resist blockade by war.

The Far Eastern crisis caused Neville Chamberlain to suggest a fundamental reconsideration of British foreign policy. He argued that Japanese friendship was more important for Britain than the friendship of the United States or the good-will of China and of the friends of the League. His attempt began with a memorandum by Sir Warren Fisher, Chamberlain's boisterous senior official at the Treasury, which Chamberlain circulated to the Cabinet in the spring of 1934. Though marred by that offensive sense of superiority towards Americans which the senior inhabitants of Whitehall in those days could seldom repress, it set out forcefully the argument that Germany was more dangerous to Britain than Japan and that Japanese friendship should be cultivated to free British strength to overwhelm the German menace. Chamberlain's interest grew after the Japanese Foreign Minister told the new British ambassador in Tokyo that he would welcome a non-aggression treaty with Britain.[11]

At the beginning of August 1934 Chamberlain went off on holiday to a house near Kinloch Rannoch: 'When I walked up the hill after our arrival on Wednesday and saw the heather and the rocks and the burn again I could have shouted for joy ... Even Annie declares that she is getting real delight out of the view.' Soon, though, he was 'composing memoranda about Defence and Foreign Policy'. His next letter revealed that 'it concerns Japan and the navy and defence policy generally ... as no-one else has any definite policy at all I may perhaps pick up some support'. Simon he found evasive, and there were two difficulties that Chamberlain never overcame: the 'lethargy of the F.O.' as well as the 'duplicity of the foreigner'. Chamberlain's view was clear. If the necessary defensive preparations against Germany were to be undertaken 'we certainly can't afford at the same time to rebuild our battle fleet. Therefore we ought to be making eyes at Japan instead of which we spend our time flirting with that detestable Norman Davis', who was President Roosevelt's special representative. Chamberlain resented obstacles created by American high-mindedness to 'realistic' understandings with powerful foreigners. He did not care for the United States or its citizens: 'We ought to know by this time that the U.S.A. will give us no undertaking to resist by force any action by Japan short of an attack on Hawaii or Honolulu. She will give us plenty of assurances of goodwill, especially if we will promise to do all the fighting, but the moment she is asked to contribute something she invariably takes refuge behind Congress.' When it came to the United States, 'We have the misfortune to be dealing with a nation of cads.'[12]

In October 1934, Chamberlain missed a day's shooting at Burghley House to enable him, he reported, 'to direct the proceedings of the Cabinet Committee on the Jap-Naval talks' (about the preliminary discussions on the attempt to renew the Washington and London naval limitation treaties) so as 'to prevent anything being done to spoil the more important talks. I am really beginning to entertain hopes at last of a successful issue on this vastly important bit of foreign policy.' Simon and he produced a joint memorandum for the Cabinet. Soon things began to go wrong. The Japanese acted tactlessly in Manchuria by asserting a monopoly of oil exploitation: 'it could hardly have come at a more inopportune moment and of course will provide splendid ammunition for Anti-Japs who include all the League of Nations Union fanatics, the pacifists, the Labour Party and the Samuelite Liberals.' (The 'Samuelites' were the Liberals who had gone into opposition to the National Government in protest against tariffs.) Just the same he thought 'we could easily make an agreement . . . if the USA were out of the picture. It is the Americans who are the difficulty . . . If I were working the thing I should feel more confident of success but I always have my doubts as to how far Simon is really convinced of the wisdom of what I persuade him to do.'

Simon, in fact, allowed the Foreign Office to smother the whole notion, helped by Japanese assertiveness in China, which fitted badly the amiable friendliness of the foreign ministry in Tokyo. Japan tightened control in Manchuria, notably by excluding British and American oil companies, and advanced the attack on Chinese integrity by supporting autonomy for the Chinese provinces adjoining Manchuria.[13] The British Foreign Office tamed Chamberlain's plan by extending his suggestion of an Anglo-Japanese understanding to a triple Anglo-Japanese-American pact. Since the United States firmly insisted on the principle of the 'open door', equal access for all traders and investors to China, and since this was precisely what the Japanese denied in practice, if not yet openly in theory, such a treaty would have no significance except as a means of blocking British impulses towards negotiating with Japan to create spheres of interest in China.

Chamberlain, therefore, failed in what would have been a direct challenge to the supporters of the League. Even as it was, however, the complete failure to do anything practical to check Japan aroused the suspicion that the British government did not base its actions on loyalty to the League.

Early in 1935 another act of aggression began to be prepared when Mussolini ordered the build-up of Italian forces on the frontiers of Ethiopia. The Fascist theories that justified Mussolini's claim to dictatorship subordinated both individualism and class conflict to united national effort. In the early 1930s, fascism faced difficulties. Italian unemployment stayed high after the depression beause of the over-valuation of the lira, so that the dictator needed some non-economic success and some distraction for discontented Fascist militants. Over-population, which had in the first place created the problems that brought the Fascists to power, created a demand for land to colonise. Now that the door to the United States was almost shut and movement to northern Italy from the south checked by economic stagnation, that meant territorial aggrandisement.

The Ethiopian crisis was made by British public opinion. Simon seemed to have been indecisive and shifty over the Far East and was widely held to have 'let down the League'. When Baldwin became Prime Minister, replacing the weary Ramsay MacDonald as head of the 'National Government', he moved Simon from the Foreign Secretaryship to the Home Office. He made further obeisance to the League by making Anthony Eden a minister for it, with a seat in the Cabinet, and introduced a new face as Secretary of State, Samuel Hoare, who had acquired some liberal patina through his association with Indian reform. They made an impressive team. Eden, young, carefully groomed, 'faultlessly' dressed, already skilled in international negotiation, made himself liked by his elaborate charm, though some of his English-speaking interlocutors disliked his habit of addressing them in conversation as 'my dear'. Hoare, industrious, prim and precise in manner, an experienced administrator, had survived a long Parliamentary duel with Churchill over India. He was perhaps the only Cabinet colleague able to treat Chamberlain as an equal.

Baldwin's increasing anxiety to 'support the League' is easily explained: in the first months of 1935 took place that extraordinary manifestation of public opinion in favour of the League, the 'Peace Ballot'. This was not a test of opinion; it did not involve collecting answers to neutrally worded questions from a representative sample of citizens or voters. It was a questionnaire answered, for the most part, by committed League supporters and therefore resembled a monster petition. The size of the response made it impressive. Over 11 million 'ballot papers' were returned, equal to half the total number of votes cast in the previous general elections, of 1929 and 1931. Over 10 million favoured non-military sanctions against an aggressor, and nearly 7 million accepted the principle of collective military measures. Baldwin received a League of Nations Union delegation, for a formal presentation of the figures, and assured its members that the League remained 'the sheet anchor of British policy'.[14]

When he became Prime Minister in 1935, Baldwin inherited the huge Parliamentary majority of 1931. Three million or more voters who voted Labour or Liberal in 1929 voted Conservative in 1931. As leader of the Conservative Party, Baldwin's task was to retain, or recover, these voters for the next election. He was well-suited for this task, as a conciliatory, mildly bumbling, political moderate, the natural leader of an uncombative 'national' coalition of 'men of goodwill'. There existed, in case he failed, an alternative type of Conservative leader, the committed anti-socialist, strike-breaker, eager to rearm and determined to maintain the Empire and its old ideals. Churchill, prowling out of office, with anti-socialist credentials firmly established in the 1920s, denouncing surrender to sedition in India, clamouring for armaments in 'the language of a Malay running amok', as the Liberal leader put it in 1934, stood ready. It is not surprising that in 1935 Baldwin suppressed his isolationist instincts and became a supporter of the League, eager to drown in humbug some inconvenient indiscretions such as his speech in November 1934: 'a collective peace system in my view is perfectly impracticable. It is hardly worth considering.' Baldwin opened the election campaign in 1935 in a speech including these words: 'See what you can do to bring the other nations in. "Hitch your wagon to a star". Above all, work for all you are worth for that collective peace which, difficult of attainment as it may be, hard as it may be to get, is yet the only alternative between a race in armaments and the risk of uncontrolled war breaking out some day in the world and lighting a fire that mankind will not be able to put out before it has destroyed them.'[15]

A politician must stay in office but few do so without caring what they do. Baldwin, as his later testimony convincingly suggests, at the time, like Chamberlain, believed rearmament to be overdue. As early as the end of 1934, Baldwin tried to make a connection between support for collective security and armed strength as a substitute for the standard bracketing of the League and disarmament.[16] It would be wrong, moreover, to think of ministers in 1935 as the puppets of a public opinion they did not in any way share; most of them, though much more sceptical than devoted supporters of the League, would, of course, have liked the League to be in some way able to prevent aggression. They thought of the League as admirable and desirable but unattainable in an imperfect world. Whatever they thought, in 1935, though, they had to try to make it work or at least make a convincing pretence of trying to make it work.

In 1935, before October, about 225,000 Italian troops moved south through the Suez Canal. At Stresa, a senior British official warned the head of the African department in the Italian Ministry for Foreign Affairs of the dangers of 'a possible forward military movement by the Italians against Abyssinia'. In the United Kingdom, he explained, 'we had a very vocal and humanitarian element in our public opinion who would not conceal their feelings'. The Italian replied that British 'public opinion had not taken very kindly to Japan's policy in Manchuria' and that it had made no difference. In fact, the lack of effective League action against Japan made it more urgent for Baldwin's government to rebuild its reputa-

tion as devotees of the League. In May 1935 Simon sent a
message, which the Cabinet had discussed, pointing out to
Mussolini the 'deep feeling that is entertained in the United
Kingdom in support of promoting the peaceful solution of
international disputes by or under the League of Nations'.
Italian forces began their attack on Ethiopia on 3 October.
Until then Britain and France tried to find a peaceful solution.
What that meant was something acceptable to Mussolini and to
the Ethiopian Emperor, Haile Selassie, which could then be
presented as a 'League solution'. All came to nothing. Mussolini
proposed to 'avenge' the Italian defeat at Adowa; he intended
to feature on the international, and domestic, scene as the
Dictator of a Great Power, the man of implacable, 'virile',
resolution; he did not wish to appear as the third member of a
partnership dominated by the 'effete' democracies and to have
control of Ethiopia furtively smuggled to him.[17]

Mussolini openly made ready to launch an attack on Ethiopia
once the rainy season was over. Everyone involved had ample
time before October to work out policies and strategies. The
British Cabinet reached these conclusions: direct British interests in north-east Africa would not seriously be jeopardised
by an Italian conquest of Ethiopia; public opinion, however,
forced Britain's support for some kind of League action against
Italy; if there were no such action it must appear that the
British government was not to blame; League action drastic
enough to foil Mussolini might provoke the Italian Duce into
war, starting with a sudden 'mad-dog act' against those mainly
responsible; the United Kingdom therefore must not take
action against Italy without the certain support of France,
assured and worked out in advance; if such French support
were given, Mussolini would, in any case, climb down and the
League 'succeed', if French support were not given, as was
more likely, the League would 'fail', but France could be
blamed. Baldwin came back specially from his annual holiday
at Aix-les-Bains to preside over a small meeting of key ministers (Ramsay MacDonald, Chamberlain, Simon, Hoare and
Eden) on 21 August and at an all-day special meeting of the
full Cabinet the next day. Chamberlain thought Baldwin need
not have bothered since his input was negligible. His own
contribution was, he thought, what mattered.[18]

In advance of these discussions Hoare and Eden talked to Austen Chamberlain and Winston Churchill, as the most influential Conservatives outside the government, Herbert Samuel, the leader of the Liberals, George Lansbury, the Labour leader, and Lloyd George. All insisted that the United Kingdom should express support for collective action by the League of Nations. Lloyd George made his belief clear that any failure to try out League procedure 'would bring down upon our heads the overwhelming mass of public opinion' and Hoare cited the Foreign Office press department in confirmation. Austen Chamberlain told Hoare, 'If we edged out of collective action ... a great wave of opinion would sweep the Government out of power.' Hoare reported to his colleagues this threat of 'a wave of public opinion against the government', so that 'it was absolutely clear that the only safe line for His Majesty's Government was to try out the regular League of Nations procedure'. Opinion pressed for collective action; the armed services, especially the admirals, resisted. Most naval officers disliked the League and disliked its supporters. Eagerness for disarmament among supporters of the League did not commend them to the navy. The League seemed to be a device for involving Britain in every international quarrel everywhere and so making the Royal Navy an international police force, disrupting its routines, endangering its ships and spoiling its strategies. Some naval officers saw no good reason for supporting Africans against colonising Europeans, especially if the result were, unnecessarily as they thought, to make the Mediterranean unsafe and extend naval commitments to the limit or beyond. Admiral Chatfield, the First Sea Lord, declared to the French Admiral Decoux that he saw no objection whatever to an Italian seizure of Ethiopia.[19]

British ministers did not expect anything to happen; they assumed that sanctions would not be imposed; either investigations would show them to be futile or Laval, the French premier, would block them. 'We shall now', wrote Chamberlain, 'always in concert with the French, explore the possibility of sanctions, the moment Mussolini begins his war. We shall, I expect, with France then find that, with Germany and U.S.A. declining to join us in our sanctions they would be utterly futile and we shall so inform the members of the League.' Two days after the Cabinet meeting Hoare wrote a personal letter to the British ambassador in Paris: 'You and I know ... that the presumptions that, firstly there will be collective action including full collective action by the French, and, secondly, that economic sanctions will be effective are, to say the least, very bold and sanguine. Nonetheless, whatever may develop, it is essential that we should play out the League hand in September ... We must, however, on no account assume the impracticability of sanctions until the League has made this investigation. It must be the League and not the British Government that declares that sanctions are impracticable and the British Government must on no account lay itself open to the charge that we have not done our utmost to make them practicable.'[20]

In September the British government acted its part. The audience, at home and abroad, astounded by displays of British vigour and power, responded as if the displays were meant seriously. In the Mediterranean the British assembled four battleships in the eastern Mediterranean, with another on its way, with two battle cruisers detached from the Home Fleet and sent to Gibraltar, against an Italian fleet led by only two battleships. These great grey ships of the line, going to sea from Grand Harbour in Valetta, or rounding Cape St Vincent as they sailed to the Rock of Gibraltar, were what British citizens, and foreigners, meant by British power. They did not share the worries in the Admiralty about anti-aircraft defences of ships at sea and in harbour at Malta or Alexandria. Then, on 11 September 1935, Hoare spoke to the assembly of the League. These words made a sensation: 'The League stands and my country stands with it for the collective maintenance of the Covenant in its entirety, and particularly for steady and collective resistance to all acts of unprovoked aggression.' Hoare and Vansittart thought this meant: the United Kingdom will act against Italy only as much as France does, and will do nothing at all about further German breaches of the treaties which do not involve crossing a frontier, such as sending troops into the Demilitarised Zone of the German Rhineland.[21]

The effect of Hoare's speech was not what its authors intended. It made Britain seem the leader in League action. Nearly all the other countries who were members of the League, surprised and delighted, supported what they saw to be the British lead. Laval conducted French policy with elegant evasiveness. Instead of flatly opposing League action against Italy, as the British had expected, he made a sustained attempt to avoid a clash with any of the forces involved. He had to consider the opposition of the French political Right to measures opposed to Italy, and of the army to any risk to the Gamelin–Badoglio understandings of June 1935 between the French and Italian army Chiefs of Staff. The two generals agreed then not to maintain forces on the frontier between France and Italy and to move troops to support whichever might be directly threatened by a German attack.[22] At the same time Laval needed the support of French Radicals and, for electoral purposes, they required obeisance to the League. Laval solved his problem by claiming to the British that he would agree to the maximum sanctions possible without provoking Italy into war, while at the same time telling Mussolini that he would agree only to the minimum sanctions necessary to prevent a public British denunciation of France. Thus Laval foiled the British Cabinet's hope that, by parading an expected French veto, the British government could 'support the League' without causing offence to anyone and without risk. Instead of providing a veto on action, the French skilfully prevaricated and postponed. So the British aroused Mussolini's wrath, which frightened Hoare and Vansittart, and, embarrassingly from their point of view, discovered that the French made demands that the British should promise in future 'to support the League' against Germany on behalf of France. The French did all this by publicly 'following the British lead' while privately making difficulties about supporting the British against a 'mad-dog attack by Mussolini'.

After the start of Mussolini's attack on Ethiopia in early October, Hoare and Eden, on behalf of the United Kingdom, found themselves, to their surprise, leading the League in imposing sanctions on Italy. The League's committees, instead of reporting the uselessness of sanctions, recommended an embargo on weapons, supplies and loans to Italy, which began in October, and then the banning of all imports from Italy and the prohibition of exports to Italy of rubber and metallic ores. These latter sanctions came into effect on 18 November 1935. The British electorate voted a few days earlier, on 14 November. In the middle of October Baldwin seized the chance offered by the nearly universal support for the government's new line in foreign policy and called a General Election.

As usual domestic issues, especially unemployment and housing, took first place in the electoral debate. Baldwin's stroke, however, removed opposition to the government's foreign policy as a motive to induce straying Liberals to join Labour. Candidates accused each other of 'war-mongering': government supporters attacked fanatical devotion to sanctions, the opposition attacked rearmament; but almost everyone paid homage to the League and praised it to the skies as a device for stopping wars. Following Hoare's speech and the votes for sanctions, Baldwin's government successfully proclaimed its attachment to the League.

Sir Archibald Sinclair, the new Independent Liberal leader in the Commons, spoke these words in the debate on the address when the new Parliament assembled in November 1935, 'The electors trusted the Prime Minister to see the new Geneva policy through', and Mander asserted 'It is undoubtedly the collective peace policy of the League of Nations which has brought the Government in again with their great majority' and 'as one who has in the past often criticised the foreign policy of the British Government I take pleasure at this moment in paying my tribute to the magnificent way in which during recent months they have been supporting the policy of the collective security of the League'.

The public voice had spoken out and the government had responded and won votes. Electoral victory, however, did not solve the problem of hostile Italians and lukewarm French. The government moved to end the war by working with Laval to provide a solution acceptable to Mussolini, which could then be foisted onto the Emperor of Ethiopia and the League. The Cabinet agreed to send Hoare and Vansittart to meet Laval and work out a peace plan. Later on it was claimed that Laval tricked Hoare, or that Hoare acted on individual impulse or that Vansittart misled Hoare. None of this was true. Hoare and Vansittart waited until after the elections, concealing, naturally, this evasiveness.[23] The Cabinet, having agreed to the attempt to make peace, was, of course, not surprised by the Hoare–Laval agreement; what did surprise it was the intense public hostility it aroused. British ministers, therefore, pretended surprise at the agreement and treated it as a personal eccentricity of an over-tired and ill Sir Samuel Hoare.

Hoare and Vansittart conferred with Laval on Saturday and Sunday 7 and 8 December 1935. They reviewed the situation. League members, and their British supporters, expected, as the decisive sanction, an embargo on oil exports to Italy to be declared. Hoare and Vansittart believed the oil sanction might provoke Mussolini into a 'mad-dog' attack on British forces in Malta and the eastern Mediterranean. They required categorical and detailed assurances of French military support. Laval made it a prior condition that a further attempt should be made to find a settlement acceptable to Mussolini. The resulting Hoare–Laval plan allotted for cession to Italy the part of Ethiopia Italian troops had so far conquered and a zone of about one-third of the rest, where Italy would have a monopoly of economic development, and direct the administration, under tenuous League supervision. In the next two weeks the Cabinet met five times to discuss the Hoare–Laval plan. Its attitude swung from support for the plan, though recognising that some League members might find it 'very distasteful', and a decision to press the Emperor of Ethiopia not to reject the terms on the one side, to a decision to abandon the plan and compel Hoare either to disavow it or resign. Baldwin once again led the government in submissiveness to 'public opinion'. Now, after the election, the opinion that mattered to Baldwin and the Cabinet was not that of the 'floating voter' but of the MPs of the Conservative Party. The new plan did not fit their recent election promises.[24]

Embarrassment was heightened by a French leak of the terms in time for the morning papers on Tuesday 10 December. That afternoon the speaker allowed Attlee, now Labour leader, to put a Private Notice question to Baldwin asking for full information. Baldwin squirmed with conciliatory evasion: 'I recognise the natural desire of the House for all the information it can have, but I cannot myself see – I will put it in this way, in my view a discussion at this moment might do very serious harm – I am not thinking of the Government but of the whole cause we have at heart – and I will undertake to the House that the moment that the proposals are agreed upon and have been submitted, and we are in a position to lay all the relevant papers, which we cannot do on our own account alone and in the middle of negotiations, I will lay them before the House . . .' Labour, however, forced a discussion and a division. Lees-Smith spoke for the opposition and denounced 'an abandonment of the foundation upon which the Government fought the last Election'. He set up a principle: 'A wanton aggressor shall not in any way or in any degree profit by the aggression.' Eden intervened to put the plan in a favourable perspective and Baldwin, closing the two-hour debate, retired into mystification. 'I have seldom spoken with greater regret, for my lips are not yet unsealed. Were these troubles over I would make a case and I guarantee not a man would go into the lobby against us.'[25]

Nine days later Samuel Hoare, hardly recovered from a fall when skating in Switzerland after the Paris talks, rose to explain his resignation. The Cabinet had deserted him, and their own policy, as a liability. Mark Patrick, his PPS, wrote to Hoare on 12 December to warn him. He had talked to scores of Members. 'I needn't bother you', he wrote, 'with the views of Socialists, or of people like Mander . . . the trouble lies with our own Party and with few exceptions a state of acute discomfort seems to prevail among them.' 'The more progressively minded' objected 'on League and ethical grounds'. The right-wing die-hards resented '"scuttle" before Mussolini'. Moreover many Conservative members 'complained to me that they will never be able to "get away with it" in their constituencies after what they have just been saying in the election'.[26] Cabinet ministers grew more and more uneasy. On 18 December the Cabinet had a 'very secret discussion'; Hankey, the Cabinet secretary, made only one copy of his record of the proceedings. Chamberlain reported that Hoare, at home recovering from his broken nose, intended to defend the plan in the Commons. In his pugnacious, confident way, Chamberlain took for granted, even then, that the Cabinet would support their Foreign Secretary. He was quite wrong. Simon, of all people, complained of the betrayal of the League. Lord Halifax, appearing in the high-minded role which he tended to assume provided it did not move him too far out of line with currently conventional opinion, believed 'the whole moral position of the

Government before the world was at stake' and 'thought the Foreign Secretary ought to resign'. As for Baldwin 'all he could say was that though he was not rattled, it was a worse situation in the House of Commons than he had ever known'. Hoare was told to resign or recant. A note in the Beaverbrook papers suggests that Baldwin sent Neville Chamberlain as a, sympathetic, emissary on another visit to Hoare and told Hoare that if he attributed to himself the responsibility for his plan and kept quiet about the Cabinet's prior assent he could be sure of an early return to high office. Moreover, according to this note, Baldwin called on the support of Austen Chamberlain by leading him to understand that he would become the new Foreign Secretary. The speeches from Hoare and Austen Chamberlain on 19 December certainly fit, and Beaverbrook was a close friend and patron of Hoare.[27]

Baldwin completed this effort to restore his reputation as a League of Nations man by making Eden Foreign Secretary on 22 December. Eden had not been to Paris with Hoare; he was especially associated with League action and, in his first Commons speech as Foreign Secretary, on 24 February 1936, he perfectly filled his role as the supporter of 'peace through collective security', effectively taking over two Labour Party points in urging the (meaningless) proposition that 'rearmament to strengthen collective security is the cheapest form of rearmament' and that while the government 'will take their full share in the policy of collective security they will have neither lot nor part in encirclement'. Everything was now going well. Italy appeared to be heading towards defeat by the League; sanctions caused serious shortage of foreign currency, exacerbating the difficulties of the over-valuation of the lira, and it seemed unlikely that the Italian invaders could conquer Ethiopia before the 1936 rainy season set in. Even ministers began to expect a 'League success'. Harold Macmillan, the most progressive of Conservatives, noted 'that the House, like the country, stands behind the Government in the policy of supporting the League' and that only extremists of Left or Right opposed.[28]

On 26 February the Cabinet met. Eden was worried as some signs suggested that Italy might win before the rains after all. In consequence he suggested that the League should impose the oil sanction, in spite of Italian threats of a 'mad-dog act'; if United States oil companies chose to support the sanction, it should be decisive. Baldwin asked every minister to speak. Baldwin himself continued to study the views of people at home: 'politically he thought that his own position as Prime Minister would be much affected ... a refusal to impose an oil sanction would have a disastrous effect both now and at the next General Election ... He also attached the utmost import- ance to the labour side of the question which was of vital importance to the Defence Requirements programmes.' Bald- win, cautiously, and Chamberlain, more vigorously, had brought rearmament into the election campaign; Baldwin wanted to make rearmament respectable by somehow associat- ing it with the League.[29] Thus the Cabinet agreed to propose a prohibition by the League of sales of oil to Italy.

In Geneva, Flandin, who had reappeared as French Foreign Minister, reacted with immediate anger. He insisted on a delay to enable a further attempt to make peace between Italy and Ethiopia and then extracted a high trump card from his hand. He put what he called 'a more serious question'. Britain must be 'ready to support France, even alone, in the maintenance of the Demilitarised Zone' in the Rhineland against Germany. The British government had no intention of doing anything of the kind. Their agitated discussions on how to evade Flandin's demand were interrupted by Hitler. On 7 March 1936 German troops entered the Demilitarised Zone.[30]

Hitler's action destroyed any chance of French assent to extra sanctions against Italy. A few weeks later organised Ethiopian resistance collapsed and the Emperor fled. The Cabinet toyed with the idea of trying to win some concession from Mussolini in return for a British proposal to lift sanctions; eventually Eden decided they should be lifted anyway. On 10 June Chamberlain, in an indecent display of his own decisive- ness, compared with Baldwin, demanded the end of sanctions in a public speech; the Cabinet agreed to raise them on 17 June.[31]

The League of Nations had 'failed'. It is hard not to regret that Laval and Flandin did not make the most of the opportun- ity to form an Anglo-French alliance under cover of League action against Italy. Then Mussolini would have been humbled or even overturned. Britain and France would, no doubt, have been able to recruit a humbled Italy into a partnership in attempting to cajole or even threaten Hitler's Germany into moderation. Blum's popular front government, if it had already been in power, might have supported the League, but it was not the style of the French Right which, faced with what it supposed to be a choice between Mussolini's displeasure or that of the British public, preferred to risk the latter. Even without French support the British government, under cover of the League, could probably have checked Mussolini and so heightened its influence as a force for peace. In retrospect it is even sadder that Britain did not try, since we know now that Mussolini had access to the information and instructions which reached the British embassy in Rome.[32] As things stood he knew it was safe to bully; if things had been different he would have had ample opportunities for graceful retreat.

However, it is the task of the historian to explain the past, not to indulge in inventive fantasies of what might have been. As it was, Baldwin and Eden managed to minimise the damage to the government's standing necessarily incurred by its failure successfully to 'support the League'. The oppositions discovered grounds for mistrust of the commitment to the League and collective security, but even though Hoare's return to the Cabinet on 6 June 1936 might feed scepticism, something of the national agreement on foreign policy sought by Baldwin remained, if somewhat bruised, and support for rearmament, looked for by Chamberlain, certainly widened. The Rhineland brought Germany back to the centre of discussion and on German issues consensus was easier to find.

4 The Rhineland Crisis and Colonies 1936–1937

The Rhineland was prominent in the list of German grievances provoked by the Treaty of Versailles. In that part of western Germany bounded by a line on the map running 50 kilometres to the east of the Rhine, the treaty prohibited all military activity; this part of the treaty infringed German sovereignty on German territory and involved unequal treatment of Germany. No one supposed that Hitler would tolerate the Demilitarised Zone for long and, in early 1936, diplomatists and journalists predicted an imminent challenge. In December 1935, after his turbulent talks with Hitler, Phipps reported: 'I fear that Zone will be re-occupied whenever a favourable excuse presents itself.'

In London the Foreign Office worked this prospect into its continuing study, how and when to get on with the effort to reach agreement with Germany, including arms limitation, especially in the air. At the end of 1935, the two senior officials in the Central Department of the Foreign Office, Sargent and Wigram, produced a long memorandum arguing for 'the active continuance of a policy which we have followed for 15 years – that of coming to terms with Germany' which might lead, even in eastern Europe, to a peaceful achievement of German aims 'so far as they have justice, logic and reason on their side'. Moreover, 'an Air Pact and Air limitation is still conceivable'. An attempt to come to terms would make it less likely that 'this dangerous question', of the Demilitarised Zone 'will be raised in an aggressive and threatening manner'. Early in 1936 Vansittart, the official head of the Foreign Office, wrote an even longer paper, rambling, hesitant and self-contradictory, but concluding that 'an early attempt to come to terms with Germany can only render it less likely that this dangerous question will be thrust forward in an aggressive and dangerous manner and so make possible a peaceful disappearance of the Demilitarised Zone'. In the end, though, he thought it essential to answer the 'colonial question' but 'we cannot answer it affirmatively except in return for an undertaking by Germany to return to the League, to agree to a serious measure of armament limitation, and to make no further territorial claims in Africa or in Europe'.

Vansittart's self-indulgent and verbose paper left unclear whether he hoped for a lasting settlement with Germany or a temporary and provisional agreement to gain time to rearm. Either way, he suggested the return of German colonies in order to meet another noisily expressed German grievance.[1] The Versailles Treaty took away all Germany's extra-European colonies. These territories were subsequently allotted to British, French, Belgian, Australian, New Zealand, South African or Japanese rule under League of Nations 'mandates', which prescribed conditions for their administration and made some ineffective provisions for their enforcement. The refusal to give mandates to Germany, the Nazis argued, taking up a grievance particularly cherished by the more conservative section of German society, imposed unequal treatment, insultingly justified by the 'colonial guilt lie', that is by the assertion that German treatment of indigenous populations had been especially harsh. Eden, as Foreign Secretary, passed Vansittart's paper on to Cabinet ministers together with compilations of threatening German utterances. How should British policy respond? Eden set out possible concessions to Germany: economic help through loans or trading concessions, the return of colonies or the abandonment of the Demilitarised Zone. There were dangers; easing economic strain on the rulers of Germany might only help them to prepare for war, and attempts to come to terms would make France and the Soviet Union suspicious and mistrustful. Such attempts might fail. But Eden approved the attempt; the British public would accept rearmament only if it were tried, and failure would strengthen the case for armaments. In what had become the orthodox Foreign Office attitude, all these papers set out gloomy forebodings about German intentions and growing German power and then went on to urge compromise and conciliation.

The careful mechanism of the British government moved in response to Eden's paper. Baldwin set up a committee on

Germany with MacDonald, Chamberlain, Eden, Halifax, Simon, Jimmy Thomas, the Cabinet's token proletarian and jester, and Runciman, a gloomy, ex-Liberal, isolationist. The Foreign Office proposed the drawing up of no fewer than fourteen memoranda to be worked out for this committee in consultation with the Board of Trade, the Treasury, the War Office, the Air Ministry, the Colonial Office, the Dominions Office, the India Office, and the Export Credits Guarantee Department. The League Council should be asked to set up an expert committee to look into access to colonial raw materials.[2] Flandin's reaction to Eden's demand for an oil sanction against Italy interrupted these careful procedures, which contrast so sharply with the disorganised energy of Nazi Germany's expansionist strivings for power. The oil sanction, according to Flandin, would cause Italy to resign from the League, seek a rapprochement with Germany, and refuse to apply the Locarno Treaty.

The western pact within the Locarno accords guaranteed France and Belgium against German attack (and vice versa) and Britain and Italy promised to assist the victim of aggression. Moreover a German occupation of the Demilitarised Zone, if it seemed a prelude to an immediate attack on France, committed the guarantors at once to assist any French riposte, while in any case of violation of the Zone, the French government would inform the League Council and Britain and Italy promised to act in accordance with the recommendations of the Council. Flandin told Eden that the French government 'counts on England being ready to support France, even alone, in the maintenance of the Demilitarised Zone' whatever Italy did or did not do, though he told Eden unofficially, in the evening of 3 March, that the French government would only act in common with the cosignatories of Locarno, but might take 'preparatory ... measures of a military character in anticipation of collective action'.[3]

Eden reported these French demands for action to a special meeting of a horrified Cabinet in Baldwin's room at the House of Commons on Thursday 5 March. Some ministers suggested that an Italian refusal to honour Locarno would absolve the United Kingdom. Baldwin and Chamberlain led the way in asserting the 'reality' that 'neither France nor England was really in a position to take effective military action'. The best solution was 'diplomatic action' to avoid the issue of British obligations under Locarno arising at all. Baldwin, to prevent 'a very difficult situation' for the government, supported Eden's suggestion that 'we should come to some arrangement with Germany'. Eden proposed that he should at once 'take up the question of an Air Pact with Germany . . . if this were done the question of the Demilitarised Zone was almost certain to be raised at an early stage'. Then the French could be drawn in and the question 'settled'. What this meant was that the German army would be let into the Rhineland in return for an Air Pact (which raised the hope of limitation of air forces). Next day Eden called in the German ambassador and suggested 'serious discussions on the Air Pact . . . I should like to secure air limitation also'. At the end of the conversation the ambassador asked for an interview the following morning so that he could bring an important message.[4] On Saturday 7 March, at 11 a.m., Herr von Hoesch brought his communication. 'He was afraid', Eden reported, 'that the first part of it would not be to my taste but the later portions contained an offer of greater importance than had been made at any time in recent history.' The Franco-Soviet pact, which Laval had signed in response to German conscription and which the Sarraut government ratified in early 1936, had, the German note announced, killed Locarno and troops were reoccupying the Rhineland, though only 'a few small German detachments'. There was, however, good news: Germany wanted to share in collective security and return to the League; Hitler would agree to a replacement for Locarno; Germany would sign non-aggression pacts with every state bordering the eastern frontier; Hitler would welcome an Air Pact.

Eden took the varied bait: 'I would have carefully to consider' all these offers 'but clearly the declaration in respect of Germany's attitude towards the League was most important.' That afternoon he saw the French ambassador, and, amidst expressions of deep regret, he condemned Hitler's action as 'deplorable'. However there was 'a very important memorandum', 'a contre partie was offered and that would undoubtedly have very considerable effect on public opinion'. So the French, Eden hoped, 'would not do anything to render the situation

more difficult . . . we must neither of us do anything to render
the situation more difficult outside' and 'there must be a steady
and calm examination of the situation'. Eden's reaction to
Hitler's breach of the Treaty of Versailles and of the freely
signed and repeatedly reaffirmed Treaty of Locarno was to try
for a new agreement with Germany. He had not yet seen the
Prime Minister or his other colleagues.[5]

He did not need to consult anyone. He knew well enough
what everyone, his colleagues and the public, would expect him
to do and his own point of view was exactly the same. He must
curb the French. 'Public opinion' is often difficult to delineate,
it is impalpable like some shifting formation of cloud and it is
hard to be precise about its effect. This time there is no
difficulty. The 'Rhineland crisis' spared Eden and the Cabinet
the subtle problems presented by Italian aggression in
Ethiopia. This time the solution was obvious; prevent the
French again spoiling the unexpected new opportunity of
coming to terms with Hitler. Corbin, the French ambassador,
described Eden, when he saw him after Hitler's coup, as 'a man
who was wondering what advantages could be drawn from a
new situation, not what barriers should be opposed to a hostile
threat'.[6]

In Britain few noticed the threat posed by the entry of
German troops into the Demilitarised Zone. Remilitarisation
pushed the German front line 50 or 100 miles to the east
onto the Dutch-Belgian and French frontiers. From now on the
German army could launch a surprise ground attack in the
west; from now on the French army could not move un-
opposed into Germany. Hardly anyone in Britain could yet
imagine a time when British statesmen might be eager for a
French attack on Germany to help an eastern European state,
like Czechoslovakia or Poland; on the contrary, France should
be held back from any such venture. On 7 March 1936 Hitler
seized, in part, the aim of his foreign policy: the free hand in
the East.

Two facts determined the course of the so-called 'Rhineland
crisis'. One was the French decision to take counteraction only
in collaboration with the British; the other the, entirely predict-
able, British decision to do nothing to damage a renewed
attempt to come to terms with Germany. The real crisis lay in

Franco-British diplomacy. The French Foreign Minister, Flandin, needed to show that he had been firm with the evasive British and had compelled them to do something serious to resist Germany: the British government needed to show most of its public the reverse, that it did not intend to risk a quarrel with Germany.[7]

On Monday 9 March, at the end of Questions, Eden read a long statement to the House of Commons. That morning the Cabinet, in a special meeting, had approved its text. It included reproaches. German actions 'have profoundly shaken confidence in any engagement into which the Government of Germany may in future enter' and it included a reassertion of the Locarno Treaty with respect to aggression on France or Belgium. Yet 'if peace is to be secured there is a manifest duty to rebuild. It is in that spirit that we must approach the new proposals of the German Chancellor.' By coincidence there began that afternoon a debate on the 1936 Defence White Paper. Baldwin added to his speech a passage on the latest events and showed his usual sensitive response to prevailing 'respectable' opinion. He treated the remilitarisation as a mere incident in an ancient dispute; 'a historical cleavage which goes back to the partition of Charlemagne's Empire'. He was patiently impartial: 'our best hopes have been blighted time after time, sometimes by the French, in our view, missing an opportunity of accepting some offer or, on the other side, by Germany doing some act to liberate herself as in the breaking of a treaty which has shocked our conscience' but 'we have no more desire than to keep calm, to keep our heads and to continue to try to bring France and Germany together in a friendship with ourselves'. Later, Hugh Dalton, now the Labour Parliamentary expert on foreign affairs, followed: 'It is true that Herr Hitler has broken treaty after treaty. It is also true that the French Government have thrown away opportunity after opportunity of coming to terms with him.'[8]

Eden and Halifax, who now held the sinecure Cabinet office of Lord Privy Seal, went over to Paris to win French and Belgian support for the policy 'of condemning the German action and then developing a constructive policy to re-establish the European situation'. To the Cabinet on 11 March they reported serious difficulty in pacifying the French government.

The French wanted 'firm action'. The German challenge should be taken up now when 'the risk of war' was 'remote'. Their attitude frightened Eden much more than it frightened Hitler. Eden 'thought it inevitable', unless they were 'confronted with some new factor', by which he meant a German concession such as a withdrawal of some or all of their troops from the Zone, that the French 'would proceed to military measures and ask us to do the same'. The Cabinet meditated on British public opinion 'which was strongly opposed to any military action against the Germans in the Demilitarised Zone. In particular, the ex-Service men were very anti-French. Moreover, many people, perhaps most people, were saying openly that they did not see why the Germans should not re-occupy the Rhineland.' Baldwin, blaming the victim, complained that 'it seemed very unfriendly' of the French government 'to put us in the present dilemma' of risking war or breaking Locarno.

An attempt followed, characteristic of the appeasement years, to persuade Hitler to make a practical, as distinct from a verbal, gesture of conciliation to make it easier for the British government to embark on negotiation with Germany and to avoid confrontation. Eden asked for a 'spontaneous' German gesture of a partial withdrawal of troops; the German government replied only that they would not send in more. When discussions between the Locarno powers and the members of the Council of the League shifted to London, the British negotiators continued to look for concessions to quieten the French, either to be requested from Hitler or to be offered by the British. Chamberlain hit on one: that an international military force, mainly British, should be stationed between the German and the French armies in the Rhineland. Flandin suggested another, the prohibition of German fortification in the Rhineland and added a possible British concession: staff talks. By 15 March, Flandin openly accepted defeat of his attempt to win 'action' from the British and listened passively to Eden's assertion: 'We were convinced that it would not be possible to secure German withdrawal from the Rhineland, and that to make an attempt to do so was to court certain failure and a grave risk of war.'[9]

In the end British ministers triumphed and the crisis dispersed in talk. On 19 March, the representatives of Belgium, France, Britain and Italy agreed on a windy document. It asserted the need for respect for international law. It 'invited' the German government to send no more troops into the Rhineland and not to build fortifications of air fields there. An international force would go to the Rhineland with the agreement of all the governments concerned (it never went there). Then it proposed negotiation with Germany on Hitler's proposals of 7 March, on 'revision of the status of the Rhineland' and on new mutual assistance pacts to replace Locarno. This was 'the effort of conciliation'. All the French got were assurances that if 'the effort of conciliation' should fail, the British (and the Italian) government 'will immediately come to the assistance' of the French or Belgian government 'in respect of any measures which shall be jointly decided upon'. Meanwhile Locarno was held still to apply in case of unprovoked aggression and the governments involved, including the British, agreed to staff talks to arrange the 'technical conditions' of assistance to the victim of such attack.

Attlee welcomed Eden's account of these proposals on 20 March 1936 and when they were debated on 26 March the speech Eden presented in their defence won him general applause. His speech cleverly blunted the dilemma of the Rhineland crisis, that the United Kingdom must break its promises to France under Locarno, or risk war. He claimed both to have honoured Locarno and to have won peace: 'I am not prepared to be the first British Foreign Secretary to go back on a British signature. And yet our objective throughout this difficult period has been to seek a peaceful and agreed solution.' 'It is', he declared, 'the appeasement of Europe as a whole that we have constantly before us.' He emphasised the unimportance of the British concession of staff conversations. He believed the situation when 'our neighbours', which of course, meant France, 'may become involved in conflict and may call for help in a quarrel that is not ours ... to be a general apprehension. The people of this country are determined that that shall not happen and that is the view of the Government.' The staff conversations were strictly limited to dealing with unprovoked German attack on France and Belgium.

Eden was a consensus politician, who widened his political

appeal at the expense of lack of definition. Now he received
abundant praise. Robert Boothby called for 'a resolute line'
towards Germany, while agreeing 'that the moment has not
come now. Nobody feels that we can apply very strong or
stringent measures against Germany because she has put
troops into the Rhineland', and he found resolution in Eden's
'magnificent speech'. Churchill, though producing sombre
warnings, pointed to 'an overwhelming consensus of opinion.
We owe a good deal of that fact to the speech of the Secretary
of State for Foreign Affairs. It was a great speech.' Even the
one Communist MP, the strident Scot, Willie Gallacher, supported Eden. 'Let me say, strange as it may seem, that I
honestly believe the Foreign Secretary, as distinct from some of
his associates, is earnestly and energetically desirous of maintaining peace and of bringing together the circumstances that
make for peace.' Sinclair 'as a political opponent' thought Eden
had 'handled a perilously critical situation ... with patience,
resource and a sincere and resolute devotion to peace'. Austen
Chamberlain ranked Eden's speech 'with the finest Parliamentary performances' and Neville Chamberlain, closing the debate for the government, was 'struck, and perhaps a little
surprised, at the general consensus of opinion' and thought
Eden 'must indeed have been gratified by the tributes which
have come to him from all sides of the House'. Eden did it by
professing peace and renouncing dangerous action while claiming that this went with efforts to strengthen the League. It was
only later, in retrospect, that March 1936 was picked out as the
moment when Hitler could have been 'stopped'. At that time it
never occurred to anyone, even to those whose minds were
beginning to take up ideas of 'stopping Hitler'.

Even those who thought the German problem to be more
and more threatening, wanted greater efforts only in the
future. Chamberlain did not share Eden's eagerness to please
by praising the League, which made Eden so valued a member
of Baldwin's government. Though Chamberlain could refer to
the League as the 'keystone' of British policy, he was more
inclined to stress 'not only the difficulties but the dangers which
are inseparable from a policy of collective security for the
purpose of obtaining collective action by States of unequal size,
of different views, of different degrees of armaments and,

above all, running very different risks'.[10]

After the excitement of the 'Rhineland crisis', the Germans did what they liked in the former Demilitarised Zone, rejecting or ignoring all 'invitations' to restrict their freedom there. Anglo-French staff talks took place, strictly limited to logistics; operations were not discussed. At the end of March, Ribbentrop, soon to become German ambassador in London (where he became renowned for tactless arrogance) presented a revised version of Hitler's peace proposal. Amidst much rhetorical self-justification, and complaints of unequal treatment, he suggested, in elaborately numbered paragraphs and subparagraphs, a 25 year pact of non-aggression among the western powers; in the next four months German reinforcements would not enter the Rhineland provided the French did not increase their forces in the frontier regions. There would follow negotiations on an air pact, and supervision of history lessons and historical writing in France and Germany by a mixed commission at Geneva to avoid mutual venom. Germany would offer non-aggression pacts to neighbouring states in the East, discuss arms limitation, the humanisation of war, German entry into the League (associated with equalisation of rights in the colonial sphere, an arbitration court and so on).[11]

Eden told Ribbentrop, he reported to the House of Commons, that he regarded the proposals 'as most important and deserving of careful study'. Spurred on by Flandin to reassure the French of British good sense and earnestness, the Foreign Office hit on the pertinent notion of asking Hitler to explain the principles on which the German government would decide to keep any treaties or agreements they made and not simply to disregard them. Remarks such as those of Dr Goebbels in January 1936 'if a treaty has once become intolerable there are higher laws than those written in ink' justified this question. In spite of pleadings from London, Hitler never bothered to reply.[12] This fitted the relaxed indifference of the German government towards the negotiations for new western pacts. Sometimes the German authorities picked on accidental excuses for delay – the French elections and the Spanish Civil War served them well in 1936 – or they simply demanded 'careful preparations'. At other times they raised their persistent obstacle, never overcome, to successful negotiation: the

French insisted on maintaining their commitments to help Czechoslovakia, Poland and the USSR against aggression, the Germans claimed that these commitments invalidated in advance any French pledge not to attack Germany and so, Hitler claimed, made pointless any western pacts of mutual guarantee.[13]

From the British point of view it was, in one way, better that talk about negotiating should continue rather than to admit that the negotiations, if they took place at all (which they did not) would never give any result. If the British government admitted failure in the 'effort of conciliation' they became, theoretically, committed to agreeing with the French on measures to counter the German military occupation of the Rhineland. As late as February 1938 they were still discussing whether or not the obviously futile 'effort' should be admitted to have 'failed'. Long before that, of course, the attempt to set going a 'general settlement', through new five-power pacts with arms limitations, security pacts and Germany's return to the League, was clearly wending its way, through memoranda and committees and repeated German evasions, to nothing. On 24 August 1936, making a contrast with this diplomatic procrastination, Hitler signed an order extending compulsory military service to two years.

Belatedly, some British officials and ministers began to ask if their attempts to settle with Germany had any chance of success. In the Foreign Office, the Central Department started to think that negotiations would be more likely to succeed, if ever, after more time enabled British rearmament to show results. Delay became desirable. At the end of 1936 Vansittart wrote a rambling and sometimes opaque paper to bring in the new year and entitled it 'The World Situation and British Rearmament'. If, he wrote, and underlined these words, 'we can stabilise the position till 1939, we shall have more than a fair chance of turning the corner, and turning it for good.' Therefore 'time is the material commodity the Foreign Office has to provide'. This policy of 'cunctation' went with that of 'keeping Germany guessing'.[14]

In the summer of 1936, the British government felt depressed and defeated. Mussolini had made the King of Italy into the 'Emperor of Ethiopia', in spite of the League: when Eden told the House that League sanctions would end, Lloyd George spat at him that he had 'never before heard a British Minister . . . come down to the House of Commons and say that Britain was beaten, Britain and her Empire beaten, and that we must abandon an enterprise we had taken in hand . . . It is a unique occasion and may God never repeat it for this Empire.' Then in May the Popular Front won the elections in France and at the beginning of June 1936 Leon Blum formed a government, relying on the Communists for part of his majority in the Chamber of Deputies. The British government contemplated with fearful incredulity the workers' demonstrations, strikes, and occupations of factories and the acceptance by alarmed employers of immediate rises in wages, of paid holidays and of negotiating rights for trade unions. Blum later claimed that he taught French workers to sing the *Marseillaise*; to British Conservatives and their 'National Liberal' and 'National Labour' hangers-on in the Cabinet, France seemed to sink into socialistic ruin.

At a depressed Cabinet meeting on 6 July 1936 'it was suggested our policy ought to be framed on the basis that we could not help Eastern Europe. We ought, however, to resist by force any attempt against our own Empire or Flanders.' This is as near as the British government ever came to granting Germany a free hand in eastern Europe; the Cabinet moved on to the view 'that while the Government should make up its own mind to reduce its commitments in Eastern Europe we should not announce that we were unwilling or unable to help in Eastern Europe'. That, of course, meant upholding the now vague obligations of the League Covenant and, in particular, continuing to tolerate French commitments to help eastern Europe and to try, if possible, to incorporate them in the general settlement with Germany.

An alternative to gaining time, or 'drifting', until Germany could be intimidated into peacefulness, was to find some concession to attract Hitler into moderation and the pursuit of peaceful development. Hitler's 'proposals' which accompanied the entry of German troops into the Demilitarised Zone of the Rhineland on 7 March 1936, included the 'expectation' in connection with German re-entry to the League that 'the question of colonial equality of rights . . . may be clarified through friendly negotiations'.[15] Eden wrote to Baldwin suggesting a committee to look into the possible return of colonies to Germany. The Prime Minister acted at once and established the Plymouth Committee on 9 March. It reported three months later.

Government spokesmen repeatedly denied any suggestion that the strident German demand for the return of colonies should be met. On 6 April, with the Plymouth Committee hard at work considering the return of colonies to Germany, Baldwin answered a question from Duncan Sandys asking whether the declaration made on 12 February by the Colonial Secretary that the government 'had not considered and were not considering the handing over of British mandated territory to any other power still represents the policy of His Majesty's Government'. The Prime Minister, producing that sort of well-crafted lie which passes for honesty in the House of Commons, replied: 'There has been no change in the attitude of His Majesty's Government in this matter.' Baldwin knew the British public would dislike returning colonies. The Plymouth Committee itself having observed, as any historian would agree, that public opinion in any country is hard to estimate, discovered four types of opponents: 'diehards' who would never give up an acre of territory governed by Britain; those who recognised a 'sacred trust' to promote the welfare of colonial peoples who should not be bandied about; those who felt that giving Germany any colonies would lead to demands for more; those who objected to any concession at all to the Nazi regime – British public opinion, the Committee thought, 'has very little sympathy with National Socialism and a definite dislike of dictatorships'. Opinion in favour of retrocession they found among those who felt Germany was unjustly discriminated against, those who were for 'peace at any price' and those who would pay 'a considerable price . . . to secure a general settlement with a good chance of permanency'.

Of the former German colonies most were held by South Africa, Australia, New Zealand, Japan and France. Those allotted to Great Britain were Tanganyika, one-third part of pre-1914 Togoland and less than one-fifth of pre-1914 Cameroons, the rest having gone to France. Only Tanganyika suited white settlers. The Committee foresaw possible armed resistance on the part of the two or three thousand British settlers there: 'We visualise a situation in which the officers of the King's African Rifles might be called upon to lead their native troops against the white settlers' to subject them to German rule. South Africa and Southern Rhodesia (i.e. the whites) would object to the return of Tanganyika and its loss would spoil the British 'all-red' air route from Cairo to the Cape. (To the British, red was, on properly made maps, the colour of the British Empire.) 'Its surrender should not be entertained.'

The Committee pointed out the silliness of the whole idea of returning colonies; even the return of all Germany's colonies 'would not improve her economic position to anything approaching the extent she expects'. And in any case it concluded that Britain, in combination with France, could return only the Cameroons and Togoland. This promised little effect on German economic difficulties. Those difficulties came from the priority given to German armament production which necessarily reduced exports and so created a shortage of foreign currency to finance imports. From German colonies, Germany could secure some imports without foreign currency but the Plymouth Committee recognised that the effect would be small. 'Economic appeasement', the idea of improving Germany's economic situation, in order to persuade Hitler to take up peaceful policies and limit armaments, involved the problem that peaceful policies and the limitation of armaments were precisely what was needed to improve Germany's economic situation. 'Economic appeasement' therefore, in practice, meant attempting to persuade Hitler, through lessons in elementary economics, that peaceful policies were best. Even to British politicians, something more seemed necessary to persuade Hitler, or to persuade other Germans to persuade or compel Hitler into peaceful ways and to abandon the belief that the welfare of the German nation could be secured only by military power. In August 1936, Neville Chamberlain, as Chancellor of the Exchequer, signed a somewhat tetchy letter from the Treasury to Eden, making the point that 'if the German Government chose, they could find ample scope for encouraging capital expenditure otherwise than on armaments'.

The Plymouth Committee's report led to a decision announced to the House of Commons on 27 July 1936: 'The question of any transfer of mandated territories would inevitably raise great difficulties – moral, political and legal – of which His Majesty's Government must frankly say they have been unable to find any solution.' The Conservative Party conference reinforced this rejection in October, voting by a large majority that cession of British mandates 'was not a discussable question'.[16] A colonial bargain, however, soon returned to a prominent place on ministerial agendas. One man put it there: Dr Hjalmar Schacht, President of the Reichsbank in the 1920s and again since March 1933, and Minister of Economics since August 1934, who had been responsible for managing the financial consequences of adventurous Nazi economics. He had applied stringent exchange controls and exploited the weakness of primary producing countries in south-eastern Europe to secure food in exchange for marks tied to specified German exports. The purpose was to meet the inflationary consequences of public works and armament programmes financed by expanded credit.

In 1936 the limits of what could be done by ingenious finance came in sight and Hitler approved the Four-Year Plan, designed to develop import-substitution to reduce the need for exports and to strengthen Germany for war. Göring took command of the Four-Year Plan. By comparison, Schacht represented normality and the theoretical hope of an eventual return to unobstructed international trade. He offered a fine example of the 'moderate' in German politics, the sort of person who, the British hoped, would persuade Hitler into rational courses. While in London the British government had given up the idea of bargaining with colonies, Schacht talked to Blum in Paris in August 1936. It took many months for the British to get clear reports of what happened. Blum, it seems, encouraged Schacht to think that he would be very willing to discuss colonies and that he would ask the British to join in. The French foreign ministry enquired what the British attitude to a colonial bargain would be without explaining that Blum had promised sympathy. Eden and the Foreign Office produced their standard reply, that it was difficult. Blum seems to have caused Schacht to understand that the British had vetoed a negotiation he himself would have welcomed. In consequence an angry Schacht complained of British obstruction. At the end of 1936 these complaints reached Sir Frederick Leith-Ross, who, as the Chief Economic Adviser to the government, was a Treasury official responsible to Chamberlain, the Chancellor of the Exchequer.

Soon Chamberlain, hoping German economic problems might impose a 'restraining influence on Hitler', told his sister, 'I have got a little scheme in hand for establishing a contact with Schacht which may or may not lead further in the same direction.' Leith-Ross heard the full story from Schacht in early 1937. Schacht again promised that colonial concessions would enable him to keep Hitler reasonable and to induce him to behave peacefully.[17]

Chamberlain wanted to get on with it, to work out what Britain might ask from Germany, by way of Schacht, in return for giving to Germany, say, Togoland and the Cameroons. The Foreign Office, and Eden, wanted to work out, first of all, whether or not Britain should offer colonies and, if the question were to be discussed at all, to take it away from Schacht and Leith-Ross, the Treasury (and Chamberlain) and bring it into the hands of von Neurath, the German Foreign Minister, the British ambassador in Berlin, the Foreign Office (and Eden). By this time the Foreign Office, interested in 'gaining time', were not worried by any delay that might result. Ministers considered the issue in the Committee on Foreign Policy and supported Chamberlain against Eden. British ministers decided to go for a bargain in which Schacht would arrange for guarantees of a peaceful Germany in exchange for the return of colonies mandated to France. In an elaborate and carefully argued despatch to Sir Eric Phipps (now transferred from the bleakness of Nazi Berlin to the diplomatist's ultimate reward, Paris, the most beautiful and exciting of capitals), he was instructed to tell Blum that 'every advantage should be taken of these overtures on the part of Dr. Schacht in order to explore the possibilities of a general agreement with Germany'. The British government would therefore be interested 'to learn whether the French Government would be disposed . . . to contemplate the transfer of their mandates in the West African area'. Phipps had a 'very friendly luncheon' with Blum and Delbos, the French Foreign Minister; they replied, courteously, with a clear 'no': French opinion would not stand it and

German airfields in West Africa would threaten French North Africa. Both these French ministers wished to work with their British colleagues, they valued British support more than their predecessors had done so they were obviously not merely making bargaining points in the manner of Flandin or Laval.[18]

The British Cabinet accepted the French veto with surprising calm. It was partly that Blum's obvious merit and honesty calmed the fears his coming to power originally inspired. For instance Chamberlain 'was very favourably impressed by him as I sat next him at lunch. He seems straightforward and sincere.' Moreover the British thought Schacht's influence over Hitler to be declining. Chamberlain told the Dominion representatives at the Imperial Conference in June 1937 that he had asked Lord Lothian when he visited Hitler to find out Dr Schacht's status. 'Lord Lothian had been told that Dr. Schacht had all possible authority in financial and economic questions, but not in political matters. Since then other indications had been received that the German government was rather dissatisfied with Dr. Schacht's proceedings, and more especially with the emphasis which he had laid on German colonies.'

Mr Chamberlain, who had just become Prime Minister, went on to answer a question from the Prime Minister of Canada on German policy. Speaking to a friendly audience from distant societies, who possessed comparatively limited knowledge of the European scene, he exposed his assumptions more carefully than he might have done to his immediate colleagues. 'He thought that what Germany regarded as most urgent was an easement of the internal situation in Germany ... What the German Government would probably like, though they were afraid to say so, was some assistance of a financial and economic character, including the waiving of some of the rights and advantages obtained in such matters by other nations. Probably also they desired some political appeasement which would enable them to make some progress – not, of course, by force – with neighbouring countries containing considerable numbers of persons of German race.'[19]

Hitler's Germany had smashed the Versailles restraints on German armament, which now went forward without any limits, and on the Rhineland zone, where German armed forces moved with complete freedom. Chamberlain correctly summarised the remaining grievances from Versailles: the independence of Austria, and the large number of Germans living under Czechoslovakian or Polish rule and in Danzig and Memel. What is striking about Chamberlain's remark to the Imperial Conference is the relaxed casualness the record attributes to him. Two things surprise. One is that he still thought possible a peaceful destruction of Versailles; the other that he supposed that moderate revision would satisfy Hitler's ambitions. This went with the obstinate belief in Hitler as a 'moderate' among Nazis: a triumph for the author of *Mein Kampf*. It took Chamberlain until September 1939, long after most of his colleagues and admirers, to abandon his faith. That is the theme of his Prime Ministership.

Chamberlain thus set out the agenda of the next two years: Austria, Czechoslovakia, Memel, Danzig, Poland. The peacemakers of Paris obliged the German-speaking population of what was left of the Austrian part of the old Hapsburg monarchy, after Italy, and the newly invented Czechoslovakia and Yugoslavia had been allotted their parts, to remain independent of Germany unless the Council of the newly invented League unanimously decided otherwise. In July 1934, Austrian Nazis attempted to seize power and murdered the Italian-sponsored anti-socialist dictator, Dollfuss. Austrian forces suppressed them. In July 1936 the German government recognised Austrian sovereignty in return for a promise that the Austrian government would act as a 'German State'. The British government, most portentously at Stresa in 1935, asserted their desire for the maintenance of Austrian independence.

In fact, they cared little about it. Eden made the point in the summer of 1937 when he commented on a suggestion by Sargent in the Foreign Office that the German Foreign Minister should be told that Britain would object to German annexation of Austria and 'that H.M. Government would view the consequent increase in Germany's material, strategic and political strength in Europe as inimical to general peace and therefore to British interests'. Eden wrote 'I am not entirely convinced of the truth of this.'[20]

Czechoslovakia, a state imagined during the First World War and created in its aftermath, contained the largest group of ethnic Germans under foreign rule. Over 3 million, more than one-fifth of the total population of Czechoslovakia, were German, most in the frontier regions of Bohemia and Moravia, but with a colony in Prague, where a German university continued side by side with the Czech university as a remnant of the time, a century before, when Prague had been dominated by German language and culture. The Germans in the Sudeten areas of Czechoslovakia had not been part of Bismarck's Reich and they did not have the associations with the Reich possessed by Germans in western Poland. In the 1920s, therefore, German attitudes to Czechoslovakia were comparatively benign and most of the political representatives of the Germans in Czechoslovakia became ready to accept the new state even though they found themselves in a country where Czechs dominated Germans rather than the other way round.

In the 1930s things changed for the worse. Hitler's background made him more interested in Czechoslovakia than his predecessors in Berlin. The depression hit the German-speaking areas of Czechoslovakia hard. Exporting industries endured high levels of unemployment and the return of Hitler's Germany to full employment caused the Sudeten German Party, led by Henlein, helped by German subsidies and growing intimidation, to secure the votes of most Sudeten Germans, to the dismay of Social Democrats and Jews. In 1936 and 1937 Henlein established himself in British eyes as a 'moderate' who hoped for political and economic concessions to Germans inside the existing frontiers of Czechoslovakia. He successfully induced the British Foreign Office, and British ministers, to think of the Czechs, especially Beneš, as obstacles to agreed reforms to tranquillise Czechoslovakia.

Early in 1937, Hadow, temporarily in charge in the British legation in Prague, sent to London a long memorandum on points at issue between Germany and Czechoslovakia. It denounced discrimination against the Sudeten Germans. Czech 'Chauvinists', the 'extreme left', 'the petty Czech official and politician' and the 'activist' Germans who favoured co-operation with Czechs and Slovaks to run the Czechoslovakian state combined, Hadow claimed, to slander Henlein's Sudeten German Party. Hadow confidently set out two (false) assumptions. 'The Sudetendeutsche Partei are not nearly as anxious as is commonly believed to be incorporated in the German Reich. It may even be doubted if they are particularly enamoured of the National Socialist doctrines ... Their leaders repeatedly affirm that they are fighting only for the right to live on an equal footing with the Czechs as loyal citizens of the Czechoslovak Republic. For two years no single concrete proof that they are not honest in this claim has been afforded, either publicly or privately by their opponents.' The second assumption had still wider implications: 'The German Government – and its head Herr Hitler – would be satisfied with face-saving concessions on the part of the Czechoslovak Government such as would enable Germany to claim – for home consumption – that the "part of the great German family" which marches with the Reich on its Southern borders had, thanks to the Führer, been granted their full rights and privileges as Czechoslovak citizens with the material and economic benefits that must accompany this change.'[21]

Hitler's rule made German claims on Poland and demands in Danzig, for a while, less urgent than in the 1920s. Versailles deprived Germany of the port of Danzig, internationalised under the League of Nations, and of territory lived in by Germans and ceded to Poland, which formed the 'Polish Corridor' to the port of Danzig and separated Germany from East Prussia. Poland received other lands which had belonged to Prussia since the partition of eighteenth-century Poland. German and Polish populations were intermingled but, as the Poles pointed out, many Germans had been encouraged to settle by deliberate Prussian policies after 1815. Unlike Czechoslovakia, Poland did not include whole regions largely populated by Germans. Apart from Danzig, then an overwhelmingly German city, there existed only one substantial German town lost to the Reich by the Peace of Paris. What Germans found hard to accept was the reversal of roles in the lost territories. The German inhabitants tended to be richer and felt themselves to be more 'orderly' and 'cultured' than the Poles, who outnumbered them except in some neat, German-dominated, villages. In the 1930s, Poland included about 700,000 German-speaking inhabitants – the number had fallen since 1913, partly through emigration, more because many prudently minded inhabitants changed national allegiance with changes in political control, a phenomenon less marked in the more homogeneously German areas of Czechoslovakia.

In the later 1920s, Poland felt less and less confident that France could be counted on to resist German challenges to Versailles; the tolerance towards possible revision of the treaty shown by France in 1933 inclined Pilsudski, the populist Polish military dictator, to take advantage of Hitler's lack of Prussian prejudices, and of Nazi hostility to the USSR, to secure seeming friendship with Germany. His Polish-German non-aggression treaty of 1934 made Poland rank as a friend of Nazi Germany. Indeed Poland seemed to be a 'revisionist' power and even claimed colonies. Danzig remained an awkward source of tension. Hitler showed reluctance to discourage 'patriotic' Germans there and Nazi agents took over political power. But the pact prevented direct Polish-German quarrels and in 1937 there seemed no danger of conflict.

Memel town was another of the culturally and linguistically German Hanseatic ports whose hinterland was not German. In this case Memel provided the only port for the newly independent state of Lithuania and the population of the Memel district, outside the town, was mainly Lithuanian. The Memel territory, about 70 miles long and 10–20 miles broad, had a population of about 150,000 in all. Lithuanians forcefully asserted their sovereignty over Memel in 1923, although they allowed a degree of autonomy for the port. In the 1930s the Nazis secured control of the town, effectively appealing, as usual, to Germans who considered themselves threatened by foreign tribes. The conflicts and recriminations that followed, although watched by the Foreign Office, did not attract much attention from British Cabinets; Memel never ranked high among their preoccupations.

A review of the problems he thought needed solution explains the relaxed confidence Mr Chamberlain displayed to the Imperial Conference in 1937. Austria could be permitted to join Germany if Austrians wished it; a few gestures would calm Hitler's worries about Czechoslovakia; German-Polish friendship would lead to amicable solutions over Danzig and stop oppression of Germans in Poland; Memel would not block Anglo-German understanding. It explains why Chamberlain did not worry about a problem that, in retrospect, seems insoluble. His object was a satisfied Germany and a peaceful Hitler. To satisfy Germany required concessions from its neighbours. But only fear of German force could extract such concessions, given the League of Nations' inability to secure treaty revision without unanimous votes. How then could Chamberlain hope for peaceful change and German disarmament? At first, Chamberlain supposed German grievances to be easily curable. When, in the summer of 1938, the cure proved more difficult, because, he thought, of Czech obstinacy, Chamberlain applied, in September 1938, a new mechanism of his own construction. He tolerated German armed intimidation in pursuit of an object he approved, and agreed to a solution of a German grievance on a basis negotiated with him by Hitler. The apparent triumph of this method came at Munich. Thereafter Chamberlain tried to repeat that success and win the reward of German disarmament.

5 The Spanish Civil War: British Opinion and Policy

On 18 July 1936 a group of generals seized power in Spain. After hesitating, the legal government, whose authority rested on democratic elections, fought back. It relied on the section of the armed forces, and the civil guards, who remained loyal, together with the assault guards and, increasingly, hastily formed and armed militias. On the other side, Hitler and Mussolini decided within days to send aircraft to help to transport the army in Spanish Africa to mainland Spain. These troops, Moroccans, foreign legionaries and the most efficient Spanish formations, under the command of General Franco, proved the best soldiers in the war and Franco soon became the commander-in-chief of the rebel forces and 'chief of the Spanish state'. Many British people accepted one of two simplified versions of the issues at stake in the Spanish civil war. One version had a would-be military dictator, supported by rich landowners and capitalists and a reactionary and intolerant branch of the Roman Catholic Church, making war on a progressive, reformist, democratic government, which, on its side, found support from workers in industry and agriculture and from the enlightened and educated liberal members of the middle class. A rival version pictured a powerless government presiding over a violent, disorderly, brutal association of Communists and lawless anarchists who attacked property, burned churches in fits of atheistic ferocity, and who acquired a thin cover of respectability from a few powerless liberal intellectuals, a fearsome coalition from whom Spain would be rescued by the forces of order and decency.

The Spanish civil war was a less important step towards European war than many people thought at the time. The reason was that the British and French governments successfully reduced it to a noisy, emotive and cruel sideshow. They chose to treat the war as an issue which, despite Italian and

German intervention in favour of Franco, need not and should not make their countries risk war with Italy and Germany. Both governments preferred a victory for Franco to the chance of escalation of the Spanish civil war into war between the great powers. Moreover, in the end, the victory of the Italian and German side did not change the European balance of power sufficiently to change the prospects of war for the democracies or for the Dictators. Only after the fall of France in 1940, an event for which he had no blame, did Franco's victory significantly weaken the British, and even then, Franco judged it imprudent to enter the war.

As often in these years, what France might do worried the British government. Blum's ministry, like the Spanish government, rested on support from portions of the political centre, the socialist Left and Communists. Most of Blum's supporters wished France to help the Spanish government against the military revolt. To French republicans, Spain presented analogies with familiar political conflicts; an anti-parliamentary right-wing with military sympathies and the support of a Catholic Church wishing to restore its grip on education, marriage laws and the press, represented a threat they could recognise. The British Cabinet, therefore, felt immense relief when it discovered that Blum, on his side, thought that French intervention in Spain might lead to a military coup in France or, more convincingly if less avowably, to the desertion of Radicals from his parliamentary majority. Moreover, if the French helped the Spanish government, and Hitler and Mussolini helped the rebels, the conflict in Spain might lead to ideological war on a European scale.

Eden and the British Cabinet enthusiastically welcomed Blum's solution, to evade pressure for French intervention by proposing a general agreement to the effect that none of the powers should intervene in Spain. So fervently did the British government espouse this proposal for a non-intervention agreement that Blum, conveniently for him, could blame the British for French failure to give all-out aid to Spain, while the British government sometimes cited the French initiative in defence of their own support for non-intervention.[1]

Early in August, however, two French admirals, in plain clothes, descended on the Admiralty, escorted by the naval attaché. They were Darlan and Decoux, the heads of the French naval staff. They feared that Spain, weakened by conflict, might be unable to resist predatory acts by Italy or Germany. They feared a German occupation of the Canary Islands and an Italian seizure of the Balearics, under cover of aid to Franco. What did the British naval command think? The First Sea Lord, Admiral Chatfield, was politely unhelpful: 'The Admiralty had no policy', and the First Lord, Samuel Hoare, in a letter to the Foreign Office, expressed himself more decisively. 'We should continue our existing policy of neutrality ... I mean strict neutrality, that is to say a situation in which the Russians neither officially nor unofficially give help to the Communists. On no account must we do anything to bolster up Communism in Spain.' Hoare favoured a neutrality biased against the Spanish government (when Churchill sent him off, in 1940, to be ambassador to the victorious Franco, he became the right man in the right place).[2] Thus the British Admiralty brushed off a proposal for Anglo-French intervention, made by people who had no sympathy for 'Communists', and lost a chance of a show of Anglo-French vigour.

Inside the British Cabinet there was as yet no occasion to worry much about Spain, for, in the second half of 1936, ministers expected a speedy victory for Franco. The problems caused by German and Italian and, a little later, by Soviet intervention would soon, therefore, disappear and worries about French reactions come to an end. So, for a time, the Cabinet could allow itself to be distracted by the embarrassing conduct of King Edward VIII. However, after the first few months, it became clear that the Spanish war might be a long drawn-out problem. At the start of the revolt in Spain the plotters failed in Barcelona, and in the whole of Catalonia, Valencia, Madrid and the northern Basque country, where Bilbao remained in government hands. In Catalonia and much of the Basque region the hostility to the revolt felt by the industrial working class was reinforced by cultural and linguistic separatism opposed to the unifying, centralising doctrines of Franco's supporters. Indeed, many Basque clergy, unusually among devout Catholics, supported the government. The government, therefore, at the end of 1936 held most of the industrially developed regions of Spain. There the army revolt provoked democratic and egalitarian manifestations of a type which confirmed the impression among the French and British political left and centre that the Spanish government stood for enlightenment against brutal reaction. The policy and propaganda of the Communist Party, internationally and in Spain, reinforced the model of good against evil. The outbreak of the Spanish military rebellion coincided with the full flowering of the latest Moscow-inspired party line, that of solidarity among all anti-Fascists, including bourgeois democrats and even the formerly detested non-communist socialists. The Spanish Communist Party now came forward as the party of order, discipline and legality, against precipitate social change. Its extremely effective propaganda machine emphasised the (real) liberal and democratic socialist aspects of the Spanish government and understated the growing influence of the Spanish Communists. The Communists in Spain helped, too, to check the unorganised, murderous atrocities, which sometimes accompanied socially revolutionary manifestations on the government side.

Many British Labour and Liberal supporters felt that the Spanish struggle was their struggle, part of a general contest between democracy and fascism, between freedom and dictatorship. The British government, and most of its supporters, inclined to leave the Spanish war to Spaniards and not to risk involvement in a war for the sake of their liberty. It was not true that many British progressives wished to go to war over Spain or that many Conservatives strongly favoured Franco. Labour and Liberal supporters, however, suspected that the government favoured Franco; government supporters thought their opponents ready to risk an ideological war unjustified by direct British concerns. The issue between the British government and its opponents came to this: did the way in which the government applied the policy of non-intervention favour Franco? The Labour and Liberal oppositions asserted that it did. Within the Cabinet itself a different debate sometimes broke out: would Franco's victory injure British interests? The Cabinet decided that it would not, or that it would not do so sufficiently to justify the abandonment of 'non-intervention'.

It proved easy to secure agreement from the European powers to the principle of non-intervention in Spain. All the

European powers soon asserted their readiness to prohibit the export of aircraft, warships and weapons to either of the two sides in Spain. However, although a committee to apply the non-intervention agreement assembled on 9 September 1936,[3] it never successfully enforced non-intervention. Italy and Germany supplied weapons, soldiers and airmen (known, misleadingly, as 'volunteers') to General Franco. The Soviet Union followed suit on behalf of the Spanish government. The French government tried to keep going the pretence of non-intervention to avoid itself being forced into giving all-out help for the Spanish government. Among the main European powers only the United Kingdom seriously and effectively tried to carry out its promises.

The outcome was that the British government in order to stop competitive interventions, leading to European war, effectively prevented the Spanish government from procuring arms from British suppliers. Since Germany and Italy continued to supply Franco's forces, non-intervention could be said to favour the military revolt. While the Spanish crisis seemed likely to settle itself quickly, by victory for Franco, British ministers could keep calm. Franco's failure to capture Madrid changed the outlook for 1937. The war in Spain dragged on. That meant that Franco depended more and more on Italy and Germany.

Abruptly, early in the new year, Eden asked for a special meeting of ministers at very short notice. They assembled on 8 January. The Spanish civil war, Eden told them, 'has become an international battle-ground. The character of the future Government of Spain has now become less important to the peace of Europe than that the dictators should not be victorious in that country.' If Franco owed eventual victory to Hitler and Mussolini 'moderating influences' in Germany would have no chance of checking 'aggressive tendencies'. Eden even declared 'that if we did not stand up to the dictator powers now it would bring war nearer. In addition we should lose the support of our friends in Europe if war came.' Eden hoped to extend non-intervention by persuading Germany and Italy to prohibit the departure of 'volunteers' to Spain, that is, to persuade them not to order troops to Spain. The way to do that, he explained, was set to up effective controls over the supply of war material to Spain, already theoretically prohibited, which could be extended to 'volunteers'. For this purpose the government, Eden's paper suggested, should 'be ready to offer the services of His Majesty's Fleet for the purposes of supervision by sea of all approaches to Spanish ports both in Spain and in Spanish overseas possessions with a view to preventing access to their territories either of volunteers from foreign countries or of war material.'

The assembled Cabinet ministers blocked this plan, led by Samuel Hoare, the First Lord, who was obviously irritated that he and the Admiralty had first seen Eden's proposals only that morning: 'Some preliminary discussion, at any rate, would have been desirable.' Moreover, Samuel Hoare, a not especially generous personality, probably resented Eden's popularity as the glamorous young Foreign Secretary after the Cabinet had ditched Hoare himself as the scapegoat for its attempted bargain with Mussolini over Ethiopia. He went on to say that the Left wanted to stop Franco 'but there were others, including perhaps some members of the Cabinet, who were very anxious that the Soviet should not win in Spain'. He, and several others, argued that if other European countries really wanted nonintervention to work the plan was unnecessary, and if they did not, then it 'was liable to embroil us with other powers'.[4]

Hoare and the others saw that Eden's proposal, if it had any point at all, would reverse the policy the Cabinet had taken up – that is, of joining in a pretence of making 'non-intervention' work in order to enable the French government to resist pressures from inside France to intervene in support of the Spanish government.

At the beginning of March 1937 Eden again called for drastic action. Franco had requisitioned some copper, sulphur and pyrites belonging to British firms in Spain, and they had been dispatched to Italy and Germany. The Foreign Secretary suggested that the navy should intercept the ships carrying these cargoes. This time it was Chamberlain who took the lead in restraining him, patiently pointing out the danger of starting a war with Germany and Italy. Instead Franco's government was approached and two weeks later Eden told the Cabinet that they had promised 'they would interfere as little as possible with the business of the mining companies and the United

Kingdom should receive all the minerals it requires ... they appeared to desire to retain their old customers and not to let German and Italian influence become too strong.' Franco did not lack prudence.[5]

Next month government orders, inspired by Hoare and the Admiralty, drew violent attacks in the House of Commons and outside. In April, Franco's insurgent forces began their attack on the Basque country in north-eastern Spain, which was important for its industries and minerals. The Basques also provided good publicity for the government side. Their ethnic motives for resistance to Franco carried support from all classes, and from the Church, and therefore nullified Francoist propaganda that government supporters were all godless 'reds'. Soon Franco's naval commanders announced that they were blockading the port of Bilbao in support of his land attacks. On 7 April 1937 Hoare told the Cabinet that Admiral Cunningham, the C-in-C, Mediterranean, reported 'that the blockade of Bilbao was in fact effective'. A signal from HMS *Blanche* confirmed this. Hoare assured the Cabinet that the navy could force a passage for British merchant ships into any Spanish port but firmly opposed what he argued would be a violent breach of non-intervention. On the contrary, the Cabinet decided to warn British ships that to sail in the neighbourhood of the Basque coast was dangerous. On 10 April General Franco conveyed a message to the British ambassador to Spain (who was now established in Hendaye, just over the French border). He threatened that if the four British merchant ships at St Jean de Luz attempted to enter Bilbao his warships would attack.[6]

Baldwin called a crisis Cabinet meeting for the next day, Sunday. The Cabinet decided to tell Franco that Britain would not tolerate any interference with British ships at sea, but allowed Hoare to tell the naval authorities that all naval protection was to be withdrawn from British merchant ships which disregarded the government's wishes and proceeded through territorial waters to Bilbao. On Monday 12 April Baldwin answered a private notice question from Sinclair in the Commons about protection for 'peaceful British shipping' approaching Bilbao. Baldwin read out the reply agreed by the Cabinet: 'Shipping should not, for practical reasons, and in view of risks against which it is at present impossible to protect them, go into that area.' He announced that interference with British shipping on the high seas, as distinct from coastal waters, would not be tolerated and that HMS *Hood* (then the largest warship in the world) had been sent to the north coast of Spain. However, when Shinwell asked what the government would do if British vessels took the risk of sailing to Bilbao, Baldwin evaded: 'I do not propose to answer at this moment any hypothetical question.' The 'blockade' of Bilbao, the opposition claimed, was imposed by British prohibitions, resulting from intimidatory bluff from Franco's side, rather than by his forces.[7]

On Wednesday 14 April Labour forced a debate which Attlee opened with unusual passion and venom. 'On Sunday the Cabinet met: the British Government met, the Government of the greatest maritime country in the world, the Government of the country which keeps a great fleet for the express purpose of protecting British shipping ... the Prime Minister comes down to the House and makes a firm declaration that we cannot tolerate any interference with British shipping at sea. The White Ensign is hoisted and then the White Flag is run up. British ships are warned that the Government cannot protect them. They are to all intents and purposes told that they must not go to Bilbao. General Franco may not be able to make an effective blockade but the British Government will oblige him by doing so.' For the government, there followed Sir John Simon, always brought in to expound an awkward case. He put the point, amidst constant interruption, that the best information, that from British warships, suggested Bilbao harbour to be blocked within territorial waters and that naval protection outside the three-mile limit would not therefore ensure safe passage. The opposition complained that the navy relied on information coming from Franco's side and disregarded the assurances of the Basque authorities that the immediate approaches to Bilbao were safe. What Churchill called 'violent hostilities' broke out in the House and, even for him, the Speaker felt obliged to intervene to secure a hearing. The Labour member, Lt-Cdr Fletcher, explained the anger of his party, and of Liberals. 'The Government are certainly showing no fondness for democracy in Spain at the present time ... It is clear that the Government have a foot in Franco's camp.'[8]

Franco's attempted blockade soon caused the government even greater embarrassment. The four ships waiting in St Jean de Luz became individually celebrated through the press. Three of the four turned out to have captains named Jones, who became distinguished as 'Potato' Jones, 'Ham and Egg' Jones and 'Corn-cob' Jones after their cargoes. 'Potato' Jones gained special publicity. He told a reporter that he would not sail for the Spanish coast: 'I can't go there can I? I can't go against Admiralty orders.' Others could and did. The first ship into Bilbao was the *Seven Seas Spray*. The ship was cheered into the port by tens of thousands of Basques with cries of 'Vivan los marineros ingleses' and 'Viva la libertad'. The Basque authorities gave a ceremonial dinner for Captain Roberts and gave him a cigarette case inscribed with the thanks of the Basque people and presented to Fifi, his daughter, a bracelet with the Basque flag. Basque claims that the approaches to Bilbao were safe proved correct; the British Admiralty's accept-ance of Franco's assertions was proved wrong.[9]

Franco's attack on the Vizcaya province, Santander, and the Asturias, with its iron ore and heavy industry, slowly led to complete victory. Bilbao fell in June, Santander in August and Gijon in October. The government maintained its refusal to send the navy into territorial waters to help British vessels there or to rescue fugitives from Franco's forces and, especially when desperate refugees were left stranded on shore, the Labour and Liberal oppositions denounced its conduct. In the spring of 1938 Franco's forces advanced to the sea between Valencia and Barcelona and split government-held Spain in two. In spite of government victory on the river Ebro in the summer, Franco's victory became certain. However it was not until January 1939 that Franco's forces took Barcelona and they entered Madrid in March 1939, amid internal quarrels in the disintegrating republican armies.

The struggle in Spain stirred more emotion in Britain than any other episode in international history between the wars. It did not divide the country. Support for Franco, so far as it existed, was generally tepid except from a few right-wing extremists, including the comparatively amiable Arthur Bryant, who believed Franco to be 'a man of liberal sympathies', or Roman Catholics of particularly authoritarian inclinations, or

from a few people naturally inclined to affect minority attitudes. The Conservative Party conferences of 1936 and 1937
noticed Spain only to include non-intervention there among
the benefits conferred by a wise government, and Franco
hardly rated a mention. (The emotion of the delegates in those
conferences was reserved for effective and tumultuously
acclaimed protests against any notion of the cession of British-
ruled territory in any part of the world.)

Conservatives favoured detached support for non-
intervention. Even Hoare, at the Sunday Cabinet, remembered
to say that he 'had no desire that General Franco – or the other
side – should win'. Sir Henry Page Croft, in 'Spain: the Truth
at Last', a pamphlet published by the *Bournemouth Guardian* in
June 1937, regretted the 'lazy indifference of Conservatives
and other National Government supporters to events in Spain
where everything that we hold most dear is being assailed,
whether it be law and order, liberty of conscience or the right
to worship God', that is, of course, by the 'Spanish Reds'. At the
1936 and 1937 Conservative conferences, however, he did not
speak about Spain and his interventions were confined to a
vigorous defence of the British Empire.[10] A more accurate
reflection of Conservative feeling came from the Marquis of
Zetland, a Cabinet minister as Secretary for India. Writing with
the latest news for the Viceroy, he observed, in favour of
'non-intervention', that 'a new world war because one set of
Spanish desperadoes insists on cutting the throats of the other
set of ditto, would, indeed, show the human race to have
become bankrupt in intelligence'. The Conservative Party, in
fact, produced a highly effective advocate for the Spanish
government, the Duchess of Atholl, MP for Kinross and West
Perthshire, author of *Searchlight on Spain*, a best-selling 'Pen-
guin Special'. Gallup polls suggest limited support for Franco
and widespread indifference. In October 1938 57 per cent of
those questioned favoured the Spanish government, 9 per cent
Franco, and the other 34 per cent had no opinion.[11]

By contrast to the Conservatives, Spain aroused turbulent
emotions in the Labour Party. The leadership, made up of that
section of the articulate politicians elected by constituency
Labour parties to the National Executive which enjoyed the
support of the larger trade unions, which meant the more

moderate among them, supported non-intervention. This proved hard to sustain. The left-wing party intelligentsia, Stafford Cripps, Harold Laski, G. D. H. Cole, for example, advocated co-operation with all anti-Fascist forces in a popular front to fight European fascism. The 'united front', involving co-operation with Communists, brought the standard hostile response to 'entryism' from the party leadership. To Attlee, Greenwood, Morrison and Dalton, its most prominent members, the Spanish war was an embarrassment. They disliked the way that united action in providing aid for Spain by fund-raising for medical supplies or in demonstrating for the end of non-intervention gave respectability to the 'united front' pressure groups.

At the Labour Party conference in Edinburgh in October 1936, Greenwood sheepishly defended non-intervention; it was, he admitted, 'a very, very bad second best' which, he claimed, resulted from Blum's initiative. Next morning visiting Spanish comrades spoke to the conference, which received them rapturously: Senor de Azua and then, speaking in English, Isabel de Palencia. At the end of her speech 'Conference rose and sang enthusiastically "The Red Flag"'. Attlee and Greenwood promptly went off to London from Edinburgh to discuss Spain with Chamberlain, then deputising for Baldwin, in order to forestall demands from the conference for immediate support for Spain. On their return, Attlee declared that the National Executive of the Labour Party intended to demand strict investigation of the workings of non-intervention and, if it were found ineffective, to call upon the French and British governments to give it up and to restore to the Spanish government 'their right to purchase the arms necessary to maintain the authority of the Constitutional Government in Spain'. Pushed by pressure groups such as the Labour Spain Committee, the Labour leadership slowly gave way and moved from unsuccessful demands that non-intervention be strictly applied to demands, equally unsuccessful, that the 'farce of non-intervention' be ended and the Spanish government be allowed to purchase arms from any available supplier. By July 1937 the party adopted the new line and, at the conference in October 1937, a motion for 'a nation-wide campaign to compel the government to abandon the so-called Non-Intervention Agreement' was carried unanimously.[12] It made no difference and the government continued the futile struggle to make 'non-intervention' work, in spite of the evident determination of Italy and Germany to intervene until Franco had won; the real object of the British government, of course, was to avoid the risks to European peace that French intervention would bring.

The clamorously expressed opposition view smashed the cross-party approach to foreign policy which Baldwin and Eden achieved on the Rhineland crisis in March 1936. For what it set out to do 'non-intervention' succeeded. Spain did not bring general war and Lloyd George was wrong. The war, he proclaimed, 'may decide the fate of Europe. It may decide the issue of whether Europe is going to be controlled by democracy or dictatorships.'[13] The Spanish civil war neither caused the Second World War nor determined its outcome. 'Non-intervention', however, aroused anguished debate and acrimony between the government and its opponents. It provided a bitter background to Chamberlain's debut as Prime Minister and made him more contentious. It caused restlessness on Eden's part and the beginnings of a rift between him and the new Prime Minister. It helped to generate the inaccurate belief that, as Lloyd George went on to say, 'with the change in the Premiership, there is a change in policy'.

Even Baldwin might have found it difficult to cool the emotions aroused by the Spanish civil war; Chamberlain did not try. He did not share Baldwin's skill in evading or countering accusations of sympathy for fascism, and of class bias. In consequence trade union leaders had a ready-made excuse for refusal to risk the interests of their members in accelerating rearmament. They could claim that the government's foreign policy did not justify sacrifices of sectional interest. The Amalgamated Engineering Union included a high proportion of the skilled workmen whose acquiescence in relaxing their rulebook could help to accelerate rearmament. Their leaders once explicitly objected to co-operation in a wrongheaded foreign policy and objected to the refusal to supply British-made arms to the Spanish government; the Spanish conflict inhibited effective appeals to the whole nation on the part of the British government.[14]

One of the most opaque aspects of the Spanish tragedy is the policy of the USSR. Their help to the Spanish government began vigorously but then declined. It is possible that Stalin and his associates tried out the policy of co-operation with the bourgeois democracies of the west in an anti-Fascist coalition and concluded that the British and French governments were unreliable partners and that their domestic oppositions lacked strength to coerce them. It may be that 'non-intervention' contributed to the prickly suspicion with which Stalin and his associates treated Britain and France in the summer of 1939 and so to the diplomatic revolution which gave Hitler his opening for war.

6 Chamberlain and Eden

Neville Chamberlain became Prime Minister on 28 May 1937. His elevation made no abrupt break. He had dominated Baldwin's Cabinet when it considered international issues. Characteristically, he was fully aware of his own importance: in January 1936 he wrote that defence policy 'has been guided by me'. His colleagues, he reported, waited on his judgements: 'When I am silent everyone else is also.' Now, Chamberlain set himself to secure peace and prosperity and believed he could do it. On coming to office he told his ministers to work out two-year programmes for their departments, which he would make effective, while arranging to leave something over to offer the electorate at the next General Election. He did not demur when Stanley Baldwin said to him, 'It will be a wonderful thing for you if you can bring about European peace. I hadn't got the energy to do it during my last two years.' Chamberlain had the energy. Now the policy of the Chamberlain–Eden team, sustainable rearmament and the search for German assent to arms limitation and a European settlement, would be pursued with extra vigour. Within a few weeks of taking over, Chamberlain 'saw and took an opportunity . . . to say a few kind words to Germany which may have a far-reaching effect'. Simon, ever-ready with soft words, assured Chamberlain that the House of Commons 'liked your manner of . . . telling them what they ought to think. Very different from S.B. fumbling with his papers.'[1] Now rearmament would continue to be kept compatible with 'stability' and opportunities for international conciliation even more thoroughly explored.

Chamberlain felt no need to be authoritarian, confident in his capacity for sound argument and in his ability to point out the folly of disagreement, and he scrupulously followed correct procedures of debate and discussion in the Cabinet and its committees. Chamberlain was a strong Prime Minister. He worked hard, read relevant papers and spoke with ordered

clarity. He expected to be able to persuade colleagues, foreigners, and, most difficult of all, excitable dictators, to be
reasonable in their conduct. Disagreement, unexpected as it
was, made him irritable and contemptuous. Hence the exceptional dislike he aroused in the Parliamentary oppositions. He
readily used provocative debating points to clinch his arguments. He was admired, respected, or feared, rather than
loved, except by a few who worked closely with him. The
closest of these was Sir Horace Wilson, an eminent civil servant,
expert in industrial disputes, who had been attached to the
Prime Minister's personal staff by Baldwin, kept on by Chamberlain, and who became the most devoted assistant of his new
chief. He left a sympathetic portrait. 'The Prime Minister was
always ready to consider carefully views and arguments put
before him and he took time before making up his mind what
course to follow. When that course was settled he did not
wonder whether it was right and whether it would have been
better to decide to try something else.'[2] He did not easily
change his mind.

It is not surprising that a clash eventually came with his
Foreign Secretary; it is surprising that it did not come sooner.
Anthony Eden lacked Chamberlain's complacent obstinacy; on
the contrary he worried and doubted. Outbursts of anger
symptomatic of a temperament strained by mental stress sometimes broke through his habitual charm. He showed sensitivity
to the feelings and opinions of others, treated political opponents with tactful courtesy and refused to dismiss the concerns
of potential foreign friends and allies as tiresome irrationalities.
Underneath an appearance of languid self-confidence, characteristic of the English upper class to which he belonged by birth
and education, although he was not rich, he was vain, touchy
and jealous of his official position and prerogatives.

Two reasons brought initial harmony between the new Prime
Minister and his Foreign Secretary. For each of them, at first,
collaboration seemed inevitable. Both enjoyed high political
standing. Other senior members of the government, either
discredited or obscure, offered no challenge to Chamberlain's
predominance. On his side Eden enjoyed wider popularity
than any other British politician. The Ethiopian crisis and
Hoare's resignation established Eden's reputation as the lead-

ing exponent of 'collective security through the League of Nations'. He found himself praised by outsiders for anything they thought the government to do well while his colleagues were blamed for everything unsuccessful or unpopular. He seemed indispensable to the government as a talisman of international virtue whose presence protected it from the high-minded; weakened the Labour and Liberal positions; and helped to keep Churchill in political isolation. In practice, Eden and Chamberlain agreed wholeheartedly on the most important issue in foreign policy: that Britain could and should avoid war with Germany. At the beginning of 1937 Eden told the Cabinet that 'this year would determine Germany in following a policy alternatively of co-operation or foreign adventure' and, a year later, he still thought, as he wrote to Chamberlain on 9 January 1938, that an agreement with Germany 'might have a chance of a reasonable life, especially if Hitler's own position were engaged'. On 31 January he told Chamberlain 'I entirely agree that we must make every effort to come to terms with Germany.'[3]

As they worked together, Chamberlain and Eden differed over methods and tactics. Chamberlain, irritated by what he regarded as the insensitivity and obstructiveness of the Foreign Office, eventually concluded that Eden, although he did not think him to share those defects, did not try sufficiently hard and steadily to overcome them. About Mussolini they disagreed more fundamentally. Chamberlain felt it worth making sacrifices to secure Mussolini's good will; Eden did not think it possible to gain Mussolini's friendship and, in any case, thought it not worth having. Early in 1938 Chamberlain decided, at last, that he could more easily attempt to win better relations with Germany, Italy and Japan, the potential enemies of the British Empire, without Eden. All of these countries posed new problems in the second half of 1937. Italian intervention in Spain became even more aggressive; Japan took up arms in China and Germany remained threateningly enigmatic: as Chamberlain put it in the summer, 'present situation (or situation before August) Germany holding aloof from conversations, continuing rearmament, still vaguely talking of injustice and inequality, but unable or unwilling to specify what she wants. In the mean time plays up to Italy and Japan.'[4] This chapter deals

with the Eden–Chamberlain relationship in making policy towards Germany, their main concern, and then towards Japan
and towards Italy, potential foes whose enmity could be deadly
if conflict ever came with Germany, and, underlying British
foreign policy, the nursing of United States support.

The Foreign Office clarified its view of British policy towards
Germany before the expected arrival in London of Neurath,
the German Foreign Minister, for a planned visit that never
took place. In June 1937 Strang, of the Central Department,
pointed to the difficulty of Anglo-German agreement. 'Germany is in favour of change, and of drastic change. She has
strengthened herself in order to secure that change should take
place to her advantage, by peaceful means if possible, but by
war if necessary.' The British, on the contrary, hoped 'to
preserve the status quo even against peaceful change (if the
change should be to Germany's benefit) as long as possible'.
Germany would 'like to obtain from us an assurance that we
should disinterest ourselves in events in those parts of Europe
where our vital interests are not concerned . . . we cannot give
any such assurance.' Even so, however, 'we cannot make any
promise that we shall intervene by force of arms in any part of
Europe other than western Europe'.[5]

Britain refused a free hand to Germany in central and
eastern Europe; but would not promise to resist German
aggression there. Britain accepted peaceful change in theory
but would not specify any in practice, or ask Germany to set
out its demands; because the Foreign Office thought it best to
keep things quiet as long as possible, while Britain grew militarily stronger.

At first Neville Chamberlain seems to have regarded the
Foreign Office as an obstacle to Eden's good intentions. Eventually he came to regard Eden himself as an obstacle to agreement with dictators. Somehow nothing got done; Eden agreed
in theory but nothing happened in practice. Chamberlain recorded his confidence, and his fears, in July 1937: 'I believe the
double policy of rearmament and better relations with Germany and Italy will carry us safely through the danger period,
if only the F.O. will play up. I see indications that they are
inclined to be jealous.' In October he exclaimed: 'But really,

that F.O.! I am only waiting my opportunity to stir it up with a long pole.'[6]

Vansittart, the official head of the Foreign Office, upset the Prime Minister by his initial hostility to the proposed visit by Lord Halifax to Germany to attend a slightly absurd hunting exhibition to be held in Berlin. Lord Halifax, a Cabinet minister as Lord President, who deputised at the Foreign Office for Eden when the latter was ill or on holiday, received the invitation through the editor of *The Field*, as Master of the Middleton foxhounds. Chamberlain hoped he would go and seize the opportunity to talk to German potentates, including Hitler himself, and find out how, at last, to track down the elusive general settlement, end the arms race and secure world peace. The Foreign Office, and Eden, showed more reticence. On 27 October 1937, Eden talked to Halifax and Sir Nevile Henderson, visiting London from his embassy in Berlin. He noted that 'the former will listen and confine himself to warning comment on Austria and Czecho-Slovakia . . . I have impressed on Sir N. Henderson the need for doing all we can to *discourage* German initiative in these two states. We must keep Germany guessing as to our attitude. It is all we can do until we are strong enough to talk to Germany.' Chamberlain wanted to 'talk to Germany' now. Halifax wrote to Eden that evening: 'After leaving you tonight I went to see the P.M. He was very strong that I ought to manage to see Hitler – even if it meant going to Berchtergarten [*sic*] – or whatever the place is. He truly observed . . . that we might as well get all the contacts we could. I agree – and therefore would be grateful, if you do not disagree, if this could be communicated to Henderson before he leaves.'[7]

Before he went back to Berlin, an 'enthusiastic' Henderson wrote direct to Halifax promising to arrange for him to meet Hitler. From Berlin he wrote again 'if Germany will undertake to be "satiated" by the concessions we make her, we should be generous . . . if we are not too niggardly, Germany will keep her word, at any rate for a foreseeable period. And particularly so, if we take it for granted that she will keep her word . . . We should not oppose peaceful evolution any more than we could condone forcible expansion.' On 8 November Halifax sent to Chamberlain some rough notes on the line he would take in

Germany. 'I haven't yet shown Anthony either Henderson's letter or my notes. I am not happy over the F.O. attitude over Czecho S. or Austria. [Halifax scored out 'our' attitude and substituted 'the F.O.' attitude] ... I hope that we should not feel bound to (in Henderson's words) oppose "peaceful Evolution" – rather liberally interpreted, perhaps.' This light-hearted cynicism, unthinkable from Eden or Chamberlain, shows Halifax moving towards the 'appeasement' policy (which he and Chamberlain pursued in 1938) in its fully developed form.

Hitler wanted to rearrange eastern Europe to suit Nazi theories of German needs without interference from Britain; the British opposed chances in eastern Europe brought by threats or by force, while approving peaceful change. These British and German aims were irreconcilable. In 1937 the irreconcilable nature of their policies expressed itself in German evasions: refusal to explain what Germany wanted or to join in efforts to make European peace more secure. Most British officials concluded that attempts at the elusive general settlement with Germany would not succeed until increased British military strength made Hitler more pliable; Halifax and Chamberlain decided that only greater tolerance of German bullying could make Anglo-German agreement possible. Eden dithered between the two positions. From Brussels he wrote to the Prime Minister: 'Our strength in armaments within the next twelve months may be decisive for peace and, therefore, the financial consideration appears to be secondary.' (This was not Chamberlain's emphasis at that moment.) Eden insisted 'that we have got to meet the challenges of the dictators and that to do so we have to be strong in armaments'.[8] Meanwhile Halifax wrote again to the Prime Minister to warn him that, in Eden's absence at the Brussels conference on the Far East, the Foreign Office might ruin the chances of reconciliation offered by his visit to Germany and to urge the Prime Minister to take a close interest. His 'rough notes' were subjected to a close commentary by Vansittart, Sargent and Strang, in the Foreign Office, and considered at a meeting after Eden's return between Chamberlain, Halifax, Eden and Vansittart on 14 November. Vinegar was added to Halifax's oil: Halifax noted for his talks in Germany, 'Wrong to think that there was not growing will and capacity to understand German viewpoint in

England' and the commentary pointed out that 'it is not perhaps so certain that there is an equal will and capacity in Germany to understand the British viewpoint'. Once again, it was a difference of tactics and timing: Halifax thought 'we would do our best to help towards peaceful solutions by counsel to Czechoslovakia' and the officials commented 'if a successful solution is to be reached, things will have to move a good deal more slowly than Herr Hitler would suggest ... The French government still takes a very rigid view of the Sudetendeutschen question, and we have hardly yet begun to educate them.' The Foreign Office supposed delay would facilitate a 'solution'; Chamberlain and Halifax thought delay might mean missed opportunities and, in the end, make matters worse.[9]

It is premature to write of Chamberlain and Halifax as the managers of British foreign policy in 1937. However, the future team was already finding itself harmonious and Eden discordant. Eden had telephoned from Brussels to urge that the Halifax visit should be cancelled on the grounds of Hitler's apparent lack of enthusiasm for a conversation; Chamberlain 'stressed the fact that he was most anxious that the conversation should take place', and Eden, when he came back, complained to Halifax and Chamberlain of press exaggeration of the importance of Halifax's excursion.[10] Halifax left for Germany the next day. He saw Neurath, Göring, Goebbels, Schacht and Blomberg in Berlin and went to Berchtesgaden to see Hitler for a three-hour conversation.

Halifax's conclusions ran contrary to the evidence he set out in his own report. Evidently he found what he had hoped to find: on 12 November, three days before he left, he wrote 'I have a feeling that if we could once convince them that we wanted to be friends we might find many questions less intractable than they now appear.' Hitler showed no interest in disarmament, objected to the 'Versailles mentality' and the status quo, and declared it 'impossible to imagine peaceful revision with the consent of all'. Göring put things even more clearly. 'He welcomed the existence of the British Empire, which he thought a great and stabilising influence for world peace – and thought we ought on our side to have no difficulty in recognising that Germany was entitled to have special

spheres of influence, in quarters that were vital to her interest
and wellbeing.' As Halifax put it, Göring 'does definitely look
forward to readjustments in central Europe, so brought about
as not to give an excuse – or probably opportunity – for any
outside power to intervene.' Yet Halifax suggested that the
British should attempt a colonial settlement and use it 'as a
lever upon which to pursue a policy of real reassurance in
Europe: in other words, instead of trying to do a bargain on
the line of getting him [Hitler] to drop colonies as a return for
a free hand in Europe, to try for the more difficult but possibly
sounder bargain of a colonial settlement at the price of being a
good European'. A free hand in Europe was what Hitler
wanted; instead the Halifax visit started the British government
on a renewed effort to establish 'good relations' with Hitler by
an offer of colonies and then to persuade Hitler to become 'a
good European', that is to limit his ambitions to those that
could be achieved peacefully. Halifax even told the Cabinet
that 'the basis of an understanding might not be too difficult as
regards Central and Eastern Europe'.[11]

Chamberlain, also finding what he hoped to find, thought
the Halifax visit 'a great success because it achieved its object,
that of creating an atmosphere in which it was possible to
discuss with Germany the practical questions involved in a
European settlement'. With surprising confidence, he set out
German policy,

> they want to dominate Eastern Europe; they want as close a
> union with Austria as they can get without incorporating her
> in the Reich and they want much the same thing for the
> *Sudetendeutsche* as we did for the Uitlanders in the Transvaal.
> They want Togoland and Kameruns. I am not quite sure
> where they stand about S.W. Africa, but they will not insist
> on Tanganyika if they can be given some reasonably equiva-
> lent territory of the W. coast possibly to be carved out of
> Belgian Congo and Angola. I think they would be prepared
> to come back to the League if it were shorn of its compulsory
> powers now clearly shown to be ineffective and though
> Hitler was rather non-committal about disarmament he did
> declare himself in favour of the abolition of bombing aero-
> planes.

Now here it seems to me is a fair basis for discussion though no doubt all these points bristle with difficulties.

But I don't see why we shouldn't say to Germany, give us satisfactory assurances that you won't use force to deal with the Austrians and Czecho-Slovakians and we will give you similar assurances that we won't use force to prevent the changes you want if you can get them by peaceful means.

The Prime Minister went on to explain how Portugal could be squared over Angola; the League reformed; and general disarmament brought about by limiting the size of tanks, aircraft and guns. 'In short I see clearly enough the lines on which we should aim at progress but the time required to arrive at satisfactory conclusions will be long and we must expect setbacks. All the same the obstacles don't look insuperable.'

On the same day that Chamberlain wrote those cheerful words to his sister, Eden approved a Foreign Office paper based on views expressed by Laurence Collier, the official most sceptical of the possibility of Anglo-German understanding. It would be a mistake 'to risk opening the floodgates of territorial change by open and express acquiescence in German, Italian or Japanese expansion before it occurs'. It would be safer 'to tolerate, for the time being at any rate, the present state of armed truce'. The paper advocated 'the unheroic policy of so-called "cunctation". For periods in the past, Europe has managed to exist, under armed truce, without a general settlement, but without war.' On the contrary, Chamberlain was determined to win a general settlement and end the 'arms race'. Eden did not directly oppose him. At a Cabinet meeting he emphasised the main problem: 'if the Cabinet's attitude was, as his was, that colonial concessions could only be contemplated in return for a general settlement, this was clearly not Germany's view', but, according to the minutes 'he did not say that on this account the attempt should not be made, but the difficulties should be realised'. Towards Germany Chamberlain was an optimistic appeaser, Eden an appeaser, too, but more pessimistic.[12]

After Halifax's return, Eden and Chamberlain settled back into easy agreement on policy towards Germany. Halifax showed tact and his usual self-effacing modesty, which was not entirely affectation, telling the Cabinet that 'he might have been deceived, or his judgement might have been at fault, or the German attitude might change'. He avoided further injury to Eden's *amour-propre*. Morever, it turned out that he had not committed himself or the government to anything specific in his conversations in Germany. On 29 November 1937, a week after Halifax's return from Germany, French ministers, Chautemps, Prime Minister, and Delbos, Foreign Minister, came to Downing Street to meet Chamberlain, Eden and Halifax. The meeting pleased everyone. The French ministers were pleased at British involvement in central Europe and mistakenly felt reassured that the British would not go further with Germany without full Anglo-French discussions in advance; Chamberlain found the French surprisingly amenable, although Delbos carefully emphasised 'that the two governments were in agreement ... that European appeasement was not to be achieved at the price of a free hand for aggression'. Halifax said little, while Eden took a prominent part. Corbin, the French ambassador in London, who was present, noted that 'the facts show to be untrue the tendentious rumours spread about for some time about the so-called strained relations between Mr Chamberlain and the Secretary of State'.[13]

Oliver Harvey, Eden's devoted Foreign Office private secretary, wrote in his diary on 5 December, that Eden had told him that the Prime Minister now shared his policy: 'A.E. found himself in agreement on main lines with P.M.' On Germany 'they were in absolute agreement'. Eden put aside any thoughts of leaving the government. Now he and Chamberlain worked together towards the 'general settlement' in which a contented Hitler would agree to limit the armed strength of the Third Reich in return for colonial concessions in Africa and some peaceful reforms in central Europe in favour of Germans outside the Reich. Chamberlain arranged, as he thought, to make Eden less worried and easier for him to work with through a device for shifting Vansittart out of his position as the permanent official at the head of the Foreign Office. This was something Eden had hoped to do, and failed to bring about. Eden disliked Vansittart, whose overbearing brilliance he resented. Chamberlain thought that Sir Alexander Cadogan, Eden's own choice for Vansittart's post, would reduce

Eden's preoccupation with the dangers of every possible course of action. Cadogan's calm good sense, Chamberlain believed, would tranquillise Eden and steady his impulsiveness.

At the end of 1937 and the beginning of 1938 Eden, on his side, seemed to be content with his position. He wrote to the Prime Minister: 'I really find it hard to express how much I have appreciated your readiness at all times to listen to my problems and help in their solution, despite your many other preoccupations.' He went out of his way to insist that his sensibilities were unruffled: 'I do hope that you will never for an instant feel that any interest you take in foreign affairs, however close, could ever be resented by me' and he wrote of 'close collaboration between Foreign Secretary and Prime Minister which, I am sure, is the only way that foreign affairs can be run in our country'. Evidently Eden, whatever his private thoughts, did not then wish to challenge Chamberlain.[14]

Together, they led the government's search for a peaceful Germany. They studied what should be offered to Germany and what required in return. When Halifax came back from Germany, Chamberlain began to think of a revived colonial offer. Portugal might give up some territory in Africa (in exchange for 'money or territory elsewhere', as he put it) to make it unnecessary for Britain to give up Tanganyika. Germany should promise not to use force against Austria or Czechoslovakia and should agree to discuss disarmament. Discussions on Anglo-German matters and smooth relations between Eden and Chamberlain were soon interrupted by crisis over British relations with the other potential enemies, Italy and Japan, and over the handling of the greatest but most elusive of possible friends, the United States.

In the second half of 1937, the active, articulate, Eden–Chamberlain partnership grappled with threats to the Empire from the three hostile powers: in November 1937 the Chiefs of Staff repeated their familiar warning. 'We cannot foresee the time when our defence forces will be strong enough to safeguard our territory, trade and vital interests against Germany, Italy and Japan simultaneously.' Relations with all these powers might be affected by the attitude of the United States, potentially the strongest power of all.

That attitude the British found difficult to assess. The British ambassador could not easily arrange conversations with the President since any hint of British influence on him would embarrass him. In any case Roosevelt, however friendly his tone, sometimes disguised his thoughts, or avoided thinking, by falling into what Sir Ronald Lindsay, the British ambassador, called his 'inspirational' mood. Cordell Hull, the Secretary of State, ran into 'lengthy disquisitions of a general and abstract character' while Norman Davis, 'ambassador-at-large', was 'a profuse rather than a clear thinker'. Only Sumner Welles, Under-Secretary of State, was rated a 'highly competent diplomatist' but Lindsay did not 'trust his estimates of public opinion'.[15]

On 8 July 1937, Japanese troops exchanged shots with the Chinese garrison at Lukouchiao, west of Peking. Japanese reinforcements soon arrived in northern China and further skirmishes led to sustained Japanese attempts to make secure and extend their existing areas of control. Chinese agreement to this process proved more difficult to obtain than the Japanese hoped and their military operations consequently grew in scope. In August fighting spread to Shanghai. Here the value of British investment exceeded that of any comparable area outside the United Kingdom. Through Shanghai passed the trade of the whole Yangtse valley. Sir John Pratt, the expert on China in the Foreign Office, asserted that Japanese victory here or even stalemate would be 'a complete disaster from which British interests in China from the Yangtse valley northwards might never recover', but unless 'we are prepared to issue an ultimatum to Japan and back it with sufficient force ... there is nothing we can do to protect British interests'. Mr Chamberlain put his view with his usual clarity: 'He could not imagine anything more suicidal than to pick a quarrel with Japan at the present moment when the European situation had become so serious. If this country were to become involved in the Far East the temptation to the dictator states to take action whether in eastern Europe or in Spain, might be irresistible.'

If the United States gave full support to British action against Japan, then the situation would change. British policy towards Japan therefore went with attempts to win that support. They proved unrewarding. The American administration feared isolationist and anti-British opinion and therefore disliked taking the lead in any action in the Far East, objected to seeming to follow a British lead, refused joint action and was uneasy even about separate but 'parallel' actions.

Eden accepted greater risks in courting United States approval than Chamberlain wished to do. In September Chamberlain altered a telegram to Washington which Eden had approved. It asked what the American government thought about 'some form of economic boycott of Japan'. Chamberlain put in what Eden regarded as an invitation to the United States to reject the idea: 'We are not convinced that the sort of action suggested here would be effective.' When Eden discovered the change he directed the British embassy to 'make it quite plain' to the US State Department 'that the question of whether or not the kind of action suggested here would in fact prove effective clearly requires further examination. We should be very glad to undertake such an examination with [the] United States government if the latter felt able to join with us in doing so.' On 1 November Eden departed for the Brussels conference of the nine powers committed under the Washington Treaty of 1922 to maintain the status quo in the Pacific. There he found Norman Davis ready to speculate about economic sanctions against Japan. Briefly returning from the conference to London, Eden talked to Chamberlain who objected to sanctions. From Brussels Eden told the Foreign Office to send a telegram to Washington expressing willingness to join with the United States in sanctions provided the United States would join in defending British Far Eastern territories against any Japanese riposte: 'I naturally wish to take all possible steps which may lead to closer Anglo-American co-operation, whether in Europe or the Far East. Any suggestion that we are lukewarm in the matter of joint action might fatally impair the good will of President Roosevelt.' Eden told Vansittart not to let this telegram be seen outside the Foreign Office and later confirmed that the Prime Minister should not be given a copy. On 13 November, however, Sumner Welles made it clear that Norman Davis had no authority to talk of boycotts and that nothing would happen.

Next month Japanese forces set off a first-class international incident on the Yangtse river. Even Mr Chamberlain began to hope for active Anglo-American co-operation against Japan. On 17 December he wrote to his sister: 'It is always best and safest to count on *nothing* from the Americans except words but at this moment they are nearer to "doing something" than I have ever known them.' Four days earlier news came that the gunboat HMS *Ladybird* had been hit by Japanese artillery fire and that Japanese aircraft had sunk the United States gunboat *Panay* and set fire to three ships belonging to Standard Oil; HMS *Bee* had picked up American survivors. 'It seems to me just a heaven-sent opportunity and you can bet your bottom dollar I am making the most of it.'[16]

The British Cabinet had already decided that firm action must be taken to curb Japanese interference in the management of the Chinese Maritime Customs – which serviced Chinese foreign debts. At Shanghai the Japanese had seized all the customs vessels. Eden 'thought the time might come when we should have to approach the United States Government and ask if they would send ships to the Far East if we would do the same'. Chamberlain did not object but 'felt sure that the reply would be that American interests were not sufficient to justify a despatch of ships and that American public opinion was not much concerned'. On 27 November a telegram went to Washington that the British thought it time to show the Japanese 'that our two Governments are prepared in the last resort to support representations by an overwhelming display of naval force' and suggested staff conversations. On 30 November Cordell Hull, 'more than usually difficult to understand', appeared to refuse and Sumner Welles confirmed that that was what Hull meant to do. However, after the Yangtse incident the British Cabinet tried again to secure American co-operation and agreed to despatch most of the Royal Navy to the Far East, 'a fleet of eight or nine capital ships with the necessary accompaniment of other units if the United States Government would make at least an equivalent effort'.

On 17 December, after a diplomatic reception at the White House, Sir R. Lindsay had a secret interview with President Roosevelt. The President sparkled. He favoured Anglo-American naval staff conversations. They should work out a blockade of Japan. The American navy should control a line from the Aleutian islands, through Hawaii to north of the

Philippines, and the British navy should take over from there to Hong Kong. He proposed that a squadron of US navy cruisers should visit Singapore. Eden suggested trying 'to tie Roosevelt down to present movement of ships rather than future blockade'. In London the China experts in the Foreign Office enjoyed themselves in working out details of what should be taken away from the Japanese. Captain Ingersoll, USN, arrived in London on 31 December to begin staff talks; it soon turned out that he intended to discuss hypothetical circumstances rather than immediate action. On 10 January Welles brought everyone down to earth when he told Lindsay that the visit of cruisers to Singapore and other mild gestures were all that the President intended; everything else represented eventual possibilities which might be considered only after outrageous conduct from the Japanese had continued long enough to arouse American opinion. Chamberlain felt disappointed. On 9 January he wrote of his efforts to 'jolly along' the USA. Two days later, having received the news from Washington, his tone changed: 'It is evident that the Americans feel themselves obliged to act with the greatest caution and to take only one step at a time ... I feel that this would be a most unfortunate moment to sail the fleet away.' Soon after Chamberlain wrote those words, Welles made a call on the British embassy in Washington, in the evening, carefully avoiding publicity, to present a remarkable proposal. It concerned every aspect of British policy, towards Germany and Italy as well as towards Japan.[17]

The worse British relations with Japan, the more important relations with Italy. For Britain to defend its economic and imperial interests in the East would require the bulk of the fleet to sail to Singapore. Italian enmity made unsafe the Mediterranean, the shortest and best equipped route. In 1937, therefore, British policy towards Italy acquired redoubled importance, the more so because in that year Mussolini displayed new symptoms of aggressive irresponsibility. The main occasion remained the Spanish civil war. Unabashed Italian support for Franco, anti-British propaganda in the Near East, Mussolini's own journalistic fulminations in the *Popolo d'Italia* came together to alarm the Foreign Office. Early in 1937 the Cabinet approved a minute of the Committee of Imperial Defence that

'Italy cannot be counted as a reliable friend but in present circumstances need not be regarded as a probable enemy'. In June Eden presented a Foreign Office paper urging a new assumption for defence planning that 'Italy cannot be considered as a reliable friend and must for an indefinite period be regarded as a possible enemy'. Chamberlain persuaded the CID, and the Cabinet, to reject this formula. Italy should not, he conceded, 'be considered as a reliable friend' and should not be included with the United States and France as a country against which no special measures of defence were needed, but was not categorised as an 'enemy'.[18]

A reader of these debates within the Committee of Imperial Defence and the Cabinet would be wrong to find them narrow and unreal. The collective responsibility of British Cabinet ministers required them to accept joint policy decisions. Where there were serious disagreements, individual ministers tried to win over opponents by setting out their positions as unprovocatively as they could, and, almost by stealth, to win a satisfactory minute, or 'conclusion', which then went to government departments as a guide-line for action. Paradoxically, therefore, sharp disagreement sometimes produced bland and opaque discussion. Towards Italy Eden favoured intimidation, Chamberlain conciliation. The careful courtesy of colleagues, itself a dialectical weapon, further shrouded the sharpness of dispute. There was another reason for lack of clarity: Eden's indecision. He worried uneasily about the Prime Minister's policies yet had no thought-out alternative to offer and seldom felt confident enough even of his objections on points of detail to challenge them directly. When officials criticised policies of conciliation, Eden responded; when the Prime Minister and other ministers urged conciliation he assented. His indecision in disagreement is not surprising: if the Prime Minister was wrong, then war or indefinitely prolonged heavily armed confrontation must be the alternative.

Soon Italian conduct shifted the balance of argument first to Chamberlain's side then to Eden's and it went back and forth until both men agreed to part. On 7 July 1937, Eden read to the Cabinet a letter from Drummond, the British ambassador in Rome, suggesting that Mussolini might be 'working up his public opinion for an eventual war with us'. He had, however, no action to suggest and left the way open to Chamberlain to convince the Cabinet that 'the real counter to Italy's disquieting attitude was to get on better terms with Germany'. We shall find Chamberlain sometimes using this argument, that any difficulty with one European dictator required above all the riposte of conciliating the other, in reverse: when Hitler seemed especially dangerous Mussolini's favour should be won.

The Prime Minister persuaded the Cabinet to do nothing combative to counter Italy's 'disquieting attitude'. A week later, on the contrary, Eden asked for British military reinforcement in the Mediterranean. Then Chamberlain delayed matters until 23 July by switching discussion to the Committee of Imperial Defence. By that time Mussolini had turned conciliatory. Count Grandi, the voluble Italian ambassador in London, told Eden that the Duce really wanted friendly relations, had no ambitions in Spain and would like to discuss understandings defining close Anglo-Italian relations. He had a message from Mussolini to give to Mr Chamberlain expressing these points. Chamberlain argued that until he had seen Count Grandi 'we should do nothing which could arouse Italian suspicions or be construed as provocative'.

On 27 July 1937, Grandi saw Chamberlain and conveyed Mussolini's message. The Duce wanted *de jure* recognition of the Italian Empire in Ethiopia. Chamberlain replied that this could only be given as part of 'a great scheme of reconciliation'. Chamberlain composed a letter to Mussolini expressing British willingness to start conversations to remove 'all causes of suspicion or misunderstanding'. Mussolini replied at once agreeing to conversations and Grandi brought his letter to 10 Downing Street on 2 August.[19]

By that time Eden had gone on holiday near Southampton Water. He left a letter for Halifax, who took charge of the Foreign Office in his absence. Eden thought we should 'go slow about Anglo-Italian rapprochement'. At the last Cabinet meeting before the recess the Prime Minister went out of his way to be agreeable to Eden: he 'paid a tribute to the skill, patience and ability with which he had dealt with the situation, and expressed the hope that he would be able to take some holiday'. Eden's tranquillity was soon disturbed. Chamberlain was at work. On 7 August he sent to Halifax his ideas on talks with

Italy designed to win 'the full return of the Italian attitude to the pre-Abyssinian position when we could exclude her from the list of possible enemies'. He concluded with a significant 'last word': 'these Dictators are men of moods. Catch them in the right mood and they will give you anything you ask for.' So Mussolini must 'feel that things are moving all the time'. On 10 August Halifax conferred in the Foreign Office with Drummond, the British ambassador to Italy, Vansittart and six other officials. They worked out a programme for the talks with Italy. Next day Halifax wrote to Eden, 'I hope you won't be too much shocked'. Eden replied 'You will probably not be surprised to hear that I disagree with it . . . we should decline to be rushed into these conversations.'

Halifax wrote to Vansittart 'this letter from Anthony disquiets me . . . it is, as I see it, rather dangerously divergent from what the P.M. contemplated and what he has been trying to do.' Halifax added 'I am not saying anything about Anthony's attitude to the P.M. at present.' It seems he changed his mind, for on the same day, 15 August, perhaps because Eden had come to London to protest, he wrote to Chamberlain 'entre nous, Anthony is rather unhappy' and 'seemed inclined to contemplate "marking time" '. Meanwhile Italian support for General Franco took a new form. Early in August Franco asked Mussolini to prevent Soviet Russian shipments of weapons and supplies reaching Spanish government ports from the Black Sea. Italian surface ships sank a Spanish tanker off Tunisia on 11 August. The British ambassador learned that Italian submarines had been ordered to attack without warning Spanish government vessels, or ships of any nationality believed to be bound for Spanish government territory. On 12 August Vansittart warned the Italian chargé d'affaires but the Admiralty, presumably from intercepted and decoded signals, discovered, as the First Lord, Duff Cooper, told a hastily assembled group of ministers on 17 August, that 'submarine attack upon British ships approaching Spanish government ports was contemplated and that such attack might take place at any moment'. At once the order went out, and was made public, 'that if any British merchant ship is attacked by a submarine without warning, His Majesty's ships are authorised to counter-attack'.

Mussolini continued to strut and shout, on August 27 he congratulated Franco on the capture of Santander and boasted of the 'powerful' Italian contribution: 'this already close brotherhood in arms is a guarantee of the final victory which will free Spain in the Mediterranean from every threat to our common civilisation'. On the same day Chamberlain told Drummond, now Earl of Perth, of his anxiety 'that the Italians should not ... think we were trying to draw back in any way – rather that we were proceeding with preparations for the talks' for Anglo-Italian détente. Within a few days Italian submarines, or, as they were referred to so that speaking terms could be maintained with Mussolini, 'unidentified' or 'pirate' submarines, went too far. They sank the SS *Woodford*, a British-registered tanker, and, worst of all, one of them fired a torpedo which narrowly missed a British destroyer, HMS *Havock*. Mussolini realised that he had lost control and on 4 September stopped Italian attacks. The French government threatened to abandon 'non-intervention' unless the British agreed to a conference to work out action to suppress 'piracy' in the Mediterranean. Chamberlain assented and, telephoning to Eden from Scotland, admitted that 'a friendly message from Signor Mussolini could not be held to justify indulgence in the conduct of which the Italians were now apparently guilty in the Mediterranean'. Eden busied himself with the organisation of the conference at Nyon, near Geneva. The British insisted on invitations to Germany and Italy, who declined, the French on inviting the Soviet Union, which accepted.[20]

Disagreement between Eden and Chamberlain reappears at a Cabinet meeting on 8 September. Eden argued that Italy 'was unstable and untrustworthy' so that, 'even if our relations with Italy could be much improved it would make very little, if any, difference to our military preparations'. For Chamberlain, on the contrary, the purpose of talks was to make it unnecessary to prepare for war with Italy. He thought that defence preparations against Italy 'could be reduced, but he agreed that this could not be done rapidly'. The Nyon conference, to suppress the 'pirates', went well. Indeed it succeeded before it began. The British Admiralty learned from decrypted signals that the Italian submarines had been directed to cease their offensive patrols before the conference began on 10 September. However,

Anglo-French destroyer patrols began to protect shipping lanes and the Italian navy itself joined in.

At this stage the British and French worked together to stop the Italians torpedoing ships in the Mediterranean. Italian violence, real and rhetorical, made it more likely that a substantial body of French opinion, and the French military, both anxious to prevent the emergence of an Italian satellite state ruled by Franco, would force French intervention on the side of the Spanish government against Franco's rebel nationalists. In order to avoid the risk of consequent escalation of the Spanish civil war into war between France and Italy, or between France, on the one side, and Italy and Germany on the other, in which the United Kingdom would be entangled, the British government had to try again to restore some minimum plausibility to 'non-intervention', or, at least, to continued discussions of non-intervention. The British began to press for the granting of 'belligerent rights' to Franco and to the Spanish government, while arranging for withdrawal of foreign 'volunteers' from Spain. Belligerent rights would give to both sides in the Spanish conflict the right, in international law, to proclaim blockades of hostile ports and to intercept ships sailing towards them and confiscate 'contraband', that is to say weapons and military supplies. Since the majority of Spanish naval officers supported Franco, his ships, though numerically inferior, were likely to be better at blockading, so that belligerent rights would benefit his cause. In return, Italy and Germany might agree to join in a general withdrawal of 'volunteers' which, though it might not equally benefit the Spanish government's forces, would help to isolate the Spanish civil war, reduce foreign backing for each side, enable the French government to continue to keep out and so reduce the risk of escalation into European war.

Meanwhile the British government, keeping the potentially inconvenient French in the background, would assure Mussolini of its friendly feelings. It knew, however, that what Mussolini most wanted was full British recognition of his new empire in Abyssinia. The British government wanted prior permission from the League of Nations to give international respectability to this gesture and had to explain to the Italians that flagrant Italian intervention in Spain made it difficult to secure this permission, especially because it made it more embarrassing for the French to use their influence among League members. Whatever his hesitations Eden joined in the pursuit of this double-sided (even two-faced) policy. Within the Prime Minister's immediate circle Eden was, in effect, on probation. Would he try to block useful conversations with Italy or permit the suspect Foreign Office to do so? His popularity, charm and negotiating skill would help if he could be persuaded to bring them to bear. In Sir Horace Wilson's papers is preserved a copy of a letter from Hankey, the Cabinet secretary, to Vansittart in the Foreign Office, urging efforts to win good relations with Italy and British recognition of the Italian empire in Abyssinia. 'The Prime Minister asked me privately to do anything I could with the Foreign Office in this direction.' The Prime Minister saw Hankey's letter. Horace Wilson also filed a letter from Lord Tyrell enclosing a memorandum discussing Eden and Italy. 'It seems to me a chance to put Eden "on trial" to clear up the past increasing bad relations with Italy . . . Eden would have justified Chamberlain's support should the above results be achieved but if through Eden there was failure through personal prejudice, it is difficult to see how Chamberlain would not have to take some action.' In the autumn of 1937 Chamberlain still thought Eden worthy of his support. The Cabinet minutes record his telling ministers on 29 September that 'he thought that the Foreign Secretary fully realised and shared the feelings of his colleagues in the Cabinet and that the latter could endorse the Foreign Secretary's policy'. In mid-September Chamberlain, worrying about the Foreign Office, thought Eden docile enough. 'I must say A.E. is awfully good in accepting my suggestions but it is wearing to have always to begin at the beginning again and sometimes even to re-write their despatches for them. I am terribly afraid lest we should let the Anglo-Italian situation slip back to where it was before I intervened.'

However, the Anglo-Italian talks did not start. The main Italian demand was for recognition of their sovereignty over Ethiopia; this the British government could not give without the approval of the League which it would be difficult to secure while the Italian dictator continued well-advertised support for a military rebellion against a member-state of the League.

Pro-League opinion at home objected to *de jure* recognition especially without League approval; imperially minded opinion objected to Italian anti-British propaganda broadcast to the Arab Middle East by high-powered transmitters at Bari.[21]

Into this deadlock there stepped a loquacious widow, Lady Chamberlain, wife of the recently deceased former Foreign Secretary Sir Austen Chamberlain, Neville's half-brother. For Mussolini she was a reminder of happier days when no great rival dictator cumbered Europe. She visited Rome in December and Mussolini invited her to see him in the Palazzo Venezia. Ivy Chamberlain reported home that the Duce had declared 'We do want friendship ... Why therefore can we not commence conversations?' Lord Perth, from Rome, argued that

> we have come to a point in Anglo-Italian relations which may well represent Signor Mussolini's last effort to achieve his desire of re-establishing friendship between the two countries. If we refuse conversations or adduce reasons even if they are good, against opening discussions now he will come to the definite conclusion that we do not wish for an understanding with him and that we are waiting till we are sufficiently rearmed for our 'revenge'.

Chamberlain spoke to Eden just before Christmas and on New Year's Day 1938 Eden sent him suggestions for exploiting *de jure* recognition of Italian rule in Ethiopia as a negotiating asset. Then he departed for a holiday in the South of France.[22]

This time Mr Chamberlain himself took charge of the Foreign Office and the direct management of his world policy for peace: joint action with the United States navy in the Pacific to chasten Japan, following up the Halifax visit by a general settlement with Germany, restoring Anglo-Italian friendship by *de jure* recognition of the King of Italy as Emperor of Ethiopia. His exchange of letters with Eden on the last topic was abruptly interrupted. Early on 12 January 1938 four 'immediate and most secret' telegrams arrived from Washington conveying a highly confidential message from the President to the Prime Minister. Roosevelt had been worrying for some time about the possibility of another world war, from which the United States might not be able to keep out. He wished to involve the United

States in the search for peace but feared isolationist opinion. Fortunately, from this point of view, as far as Europe was concerned he saw the way to do it not in entangling alliances but, like Halifax and Chamberlain, in encouraging peaceful change. Contemplating the world scene at the end of 1936 and in early 1937 he took up a plan. The plan, inspired and worked out by Sumner Welles, the Assistant Secretary of State, a man especially trusted by Roosevelt, was 'to make an appeal for a conference to deal with the fundamental economic problems, which are behind all the unrest'. Even this degree of involvement in world affairs might arouse inhibiting opposition. Only on 11 January 1938 did the President try to launch his plan when Sumner Welles came under cover of darkness to the British embassy in Washington.

In essence the President's idea was to buy arms limitation (which the dictators would concede) by promising equal access to raw materials (a concession to Germany and Italy). In advance the 'nations of the earth' were to agree on 'norms of international conduct'. Roosevelt asked for the support of the British government as an essential condition. He set a close time limit perhaps to keep the secret to help to amaze American opinion into acquiescence by a dramatic and unexpected innovation. Only if the British government agreed by 17 January would he proceed to warn France, Germany and Italy on 20 January and then announce the plan to the diplomatic body in Washington on 22 January. He had dropped the idea of a world conference and intended to request a few other governments to join the USA in elaborating proposals to be submitted to all governments. After that a lasting peace might require further changes. In discussing those the United States would take no part. Sweden, the Netherlands, Belgium, Switzerland, Hungary, Yugoslavia, Turkey and three Latin American governments would make up the committee for world appeasement so that every view would be represented except, Chamberlain observed, 'that of the people who matter'. The President's initiative he intended, Sumner Welles explained, to work 'parallel' to the British effort and to lend it 'powerful support'. Sir R. Lindsay, the experienced and effective British ambassador, sent his own recommendation, and urged 'respectfully but very earnestly . . . a very quick and cordial acceptance'.[23]

In the afternoon of 12 January, Cadogan sent the messages to the Prime Minister and next morning discussed them with Horace Wilson; Chamberlain came back to London that evening and sent off a telegram to Washington. Wilson and Chamberlain disliked Roosevelt's plan. It would annoy the dictators and interfere with their own schemes for disarming Hitler and Mussolini. Cadogan responded by drafting a message to Washington suggesting that Roosevelt should defer the launch of his plan but promising that if he wished to launch it at once the British government would give him wholehearted support. Chamberlain deleted this promise of support and ordered the despatch of the truncated telegram. The telegrams were sent by messenger to Eden and he was told by telephone to return at once from the South of France. Eden, therefore, got back to England, delayed by bad weather, and found that the Prime Minister had clearly rejected Roosevelt's plan.

This confronted him with a central issue in British policy. The government intended to settle legitimate Italian and German grievances in return for their ceasing to prepare for war. This, the government thought, required direct Anglo-German and Anglo-Italian contacts. In the process, however, friends might be lost whose help would be needed if things went wrong. Easily the most important friend would be the United States. Without United States support the defence of British interests in the Far East was impossible if Germany and Italy simultaneously threatened war in Europe. However, the idea of granting *de jure* recognition to Mussolini's conquest of Abyssinia was unattractive to the American administration, committed as it was to refuse to accept the legality of territorial changes made by force. Chamberlain and Eden recognised that this recognition was essential if any serious attempt were to be made to win Italian good-will. British negotiations with Germany moved towards concessions over African colonies to make Germany moderate in Europe; Roosevelt's plan might, Chamberlain thought, cause Germany to lose interest in British offers. Eden thought those disadvantages acceptable in order to make every effort to secure Roosevelt's good-will and American co-operation while Chamberlain thought the disadvantages excessive for what seemed to him uncertain results in American good-will. Chamberlain did not think it worthwhile to reduce what seemed to him good chances of success in Europe. Eden thought any chance of increasing American good-will should be seized because he was much less confident in the success of British policy in Europe. The talks with Ingersoll in London, embodying a hope of eventual American naval support against Japan, strengthened his belief.[24]

For the first time Eden clearly opposed the Prime Minister and fought for his view. He won. It was a hard fight, carried on through a two-hour dialogue with Chamberlain on 18 January and through four meetings of the Cabinet Foreign Policy Committee on 19, 20 and 21 January. Eden, his private secretary recorded, 'saw his way clear ... we must drop any idea of proceeding with *de jure* recognition in deference to Roosevelt and we must tell him that we would back his initiative in the fullest possible measure'. Eden wrote down his thoughts and took them over to No. 10: 'What we have to choose between is Anglo-American co-operation in an attempt to ensure world peace and a piece-meal settlement approached by way of problematical agreement with Mussolini.' Eden did not believe that 'this initiative need injure the prospects of our negotiations with Germany'.

Roosevelt rendered Eden's victory pointless. From Washington there emerged confusing and contradictory views on *de jure* recognition of Mussolini's empire which, in the end, suggested that the President did not care provided recognition was the outcome of decently protracted negotiation. As for what Chamberlain called his 'rather preposterous proposals' Roosevelt first said, through Welles, on 15 January, that he would delay 'for a while', after which the message agreed in London went out from a beaten Prime Minister: 'I warmly welcome the President's initiative and will do my best to contribute to the success of his scheme whenever he decides to launch it.' Then on 24 January Roosevelt explained that he would 'probably' send another message, and on 2 February that the British should 'hold back their horses' for a few days yet, on 9 February that the President had decided to postpone 'for a matter of days and not weeks', on 16 February that he would launch his plan soon after the 23rd but on the 25th Welles reported Roosevelt as thinking Chamberlain's diplomatic initiative as described in Parliament to be 'entirely right' and that he had decided 'to hold his plan in abeyance for the present'. A delighted Chamberlain wrote on this latest telegram from Washington, 'This is excellent.'[25] In his memoirs Churchill expressed contempt for Chamberlain's handling of the Roosevelt 'offer':

> No event could have been more likely to stave off, or even prevent, war than the arrival of the United States in the circle of European hates and fears. To Britain it was a matter almost of life and death ... We must regard its rejection – for such it was – as the loss of the last frail chance to save the world from tyranny otherwise than by war. That Mr. Chamberlain, with his limited outlook and inexperience of the European scene, should have possessed the self-sufficiency to wave away the proffered hand stretched out across the Atlantic leaves one, even at this date [1948], breathless with amazement.[26]

Yet the timing of Roosevelt's moves suggests that he was genuinely trying to support Chamberlain's efforts and perhaps even that he wished to help Chamberlain to overcome Eden's hesitations. Thus the 'offer' came when Eden was out of the way and it was specifically addressed to the Prime Minister. Moreover Roosevelt dropped it at once when news came that Chamberlain had forced Eden out of his government. We cannot be certain what Roosevelt thought, but Sumner Welles acted as his spokesman throughout this episode. The French chargé reported to Paris on 24 February that Welles had told him that he thought Eden's policy difficult if not impossible to carry out. 'That of Mr Chamberlain, much more realistic, opens, on the contrary, interesting possibilities from the point of view of the establishment of European peace ... the United States therefore hopes that the Prime Minister will succeed.'[27]

Whatever its motives it was not the 'Roosevelt offer' that caused Eden's resignation. After the victorious battle Eden fought over the British response, friendly relations revived between himself and Chamberlain. On Sunday 13 February Chamberlain wrote to Hilda: 'I saw Anthony on Friday morning and we were in complete agreement, more complete perhaps than we have sometimes been in the past.' He and Eden worked harmoniously together on German policy and

Eden seemed reconciled to the attempt to get on with the long anticipated 'talks' between Ciano and Lord Perth in Rome. A week later, however, Eden gave up his post as Foreign Secretary. Until almost the last minute Chamberlain tried to keep Eden. Ivy Chamberlain provoked an angry letter from Eden to the Prime Minister on 8 February. She had read to Ciano, and later to Mussolini, a letter from her brother-in-law expressing his eagerness to start the 'talks' with the Italian government. Eden disliked the expression of eagerness which weakened the British position and this episode, he wrote to Chamberlain, caused him 'considerable apprehension which is not allayed by this morning's news that Lady Chamberlain was to stay for another month in Rome'. The result was an immediate apology from Neville and a promise to tell Ivy to keep quiet. In truth, however, the Prime Minister was delighted by the 'magical' effect of Ivy's action. At last, he wrote, Ciano and Mussolini were 'convinced of my sincerity' in seeking Italian friendship.[28]

Soon Hitler strengthened Chamberlain's belief that the time had come for Anglo-Italian rapprochement and simultaneously confirmed Eden's hesitations. On 12 February the Austrian Chancellor, Schuschnigg, drove from Salzburg to visit Hitler at Berchtesgaden. Schuschnigg hoped for a confirmation of the German recognition of Austrian independence embodied in the Austro-German agreement of July 1936. Instead Hitler bullied and shouted and, under the threat of armed attack, drove Schuschnigg into arrangements to enable the progressive nazification of Austria including the appointment of a Nazi, Seyss-Inquart, as Minister of the Interior. On 15 February the Foreign Office learned of Schuschnigg's comments: 'Herr Hitler had talked like a madman and had openly declared his intention of absorbing Austria. Dr. Schuschnigg said he could not have believed a responsible European statesman could be so unscrupulous and so violent.' Next day Ciano told Perth, the British ambassador in Rome, that 'an early start should be made with Anglo-Italian conversations in view of possibility of certain future happenings'. He would say no more but this cryptic telegram from Perth was soon supported by another one, this time from Ivy Chamberlain who had had lunch with Ciano. She reported, in a telegram sent to Eden for transmission to the Prime Minister, that Ciano had declared 'time is everything. Today an agreement will be easy but things are happening in Europe which will make it impossible tomorrow.' More stimulus to Chamberlain's eagerness came from (anonymous) notes given to Wilson on 16 February, presumably by Sir Joseph Ball, who was in touch with Adrian Dingli at the Italian embassy. Downing Street was assured that if Anglo-Italian talks had started before Schuschnigg was bullied at Berchtesgaden, Mussolini would

> undoubtedly have taken a very strong line with Hitler and have despatched troops to the Brenner Pass ... D feels, however, that all is not lost and that a remarkable improvement could be effected in the situation even at this stage provided that action is taken immediately ... He thinks that Mussolini would certainly stiffen his back immediately against Hitler and that he might even at this late stage feel it necessary to send troops to the Brenner Pass.

Neville Chamberlain concluded that the conversations must start at once. The news from Austria caused Eden, on the other hand, to hesitate. He wrote to Chamberlain late on 17 February that 'we must be very careful not to commit ourselves ... until we have had time to go carefully into all the implications'. He suspected 'some kind of arrangement between Rome and Berlin'. Even Vansittart, he reported, thought that Mussolini might be 'playing us along'.[29]

Horace Wilson wrote later that he was called to the House of Commons about 11 p.m. 'and found the Prime Minister most dejectedly looking at a letter from Eden in which once more he said he doubted whether anything ought to done. The Prime Minister felt more and more depressed.' Wilson still supposed that Chamberlain wished to keep Eden, who after all was the most widely admired politician in the country, and next morning submitted suggestions to Mr Chamberlain for compromise with Eden. Chamberlain, however, had had enough. He decided to make no concession and to appeal to the Cabinet against Eden and insist on the immediate opening of conversations with Italy. Later that morning, Friday 18 February, Grandi, the Italian ambassador, came to 10 Downing Street to confer with Chamberlain and Eden, and according to his own report he found them in the role of 'two enemies confronting each other, like two cocks in true fighting posture'. Grandi encouraged Chamberlain to believe that Mussolini would try to restrain Hitler from violence towards Austria if the talks began. After some discussion the Prime Minister told Grandi to come back in the afternoon and then rounded on Eden when he again objected to immediate formal negotiations with Italy. Chamberlain recorded his reproaches: Eden 'had missed one opportunity after another of advancing towards peace; he had one more chance, probably the last; and was wanting to throw it away'. When Grandi returned he was told to come back on Monday. Next afternoon, Eden and Chamberlain set out their positions to a special Cabinet meeting and Chamberlain made every minister speak. Fourteen ministers supported him, three backed Eden. Then Eden announced that he would resign. Chamberlain insisted on his position and suggested the Cabinet meet again on Sunday afternoon.[30]

Chamberlain stressed, indeed exaggerated, his differences with Eden. He wanted no more compromise. He told the Sunday Cabinet that there existed 'a fundamental difference of outlook' in that Eden 'did not really agree with the attempt to get on terms with Germany and Italy'. The surprise expressed by several ministers seems genuine, yet, as we have seen, there were real differences. The German and Italian governments were delighted by Eden's departure; on the face of it, they perceived the differences between Eden and Chamberlain more clearly than their own Cabinet colleagues. In Cabinet discussions both Eden and Chamberlain had searched for common ground except over Roosevelt's communication when Chamberlain had given way. Eden was skilled at negotiating for consensus; Chamberlain had, so far, thought Eden's presence in the government worth the trouble of working for agreement. Eden's departure weakened the Chamberlain government's claim to speak for the nation. Opposition to its foreign policy had involved demands for greater emphasis on the League and, with rapidly diminishing emphasis, for disarmament, from Labour and Liberal spokesmen and a demand for accelerated rearmament from a few Conservatives. Eden had given the impression of sympathy for all these causes. Now without him, Chamberlain's combativeness made foreign policy more sharply controversial. Eden's resignation led to a Labour Party motion of censure in the House of Commons. In the debate Lloyd George accused the government of giving way to an Italian threat that it was now or never for an Anglo-Italian understanding. Chamberlain took the trouble to get the Cabinet to acquiesce in his concealing from the public the documents that justified this accusation: 'In view of their clear reference to the Austrian situation it was impossible to publish these papers ánd on that he intended to stand firm' and to agree to authorise him to tell the House of Commons that every member of the Cabinet had agreed that they had not felt 'under any sense of duress, compulsion, bullying or blackmail of any kind'. Chamberlain's reply to the debate included an open and combative dismissal of the value of the League of Nations as a means of preserving peace, thus emphasising his divergence from Eden's rhetorical attitudes. For the vote on the Labour motion, the Conservative Party whips worked hard to minimise abstentions in support of Eden among Conservative MPs. Numerically they succeeded but, as the French embassy reported to Paris, the great majority of the 330 Members who voted for Chamberlain were 'obscure members who have never spoken ... if quantity was on Chamberlain's side, quality was in Eden's camp'. The small number of abstainers were mostly MPs who had shown interest in and knowledge of international affairs. However, Chamberlain had successfully asserted his dominance both of the Cabinet and of the House of Commons.[31]

Chamberlain's choice of successor to Eden emphasised and reinforced his control over British foreign policy. After a few days as acting Foreign Secretary, Lord Halifax took over. R. A. Butler succeeded Cranborne, who had resigned with Eden, as Parliamentary Under-Secretary. With the Foreign Secretary in the House of Lords, Chamberlain himself acted as the main Parliamentary spokesman for the government on foreign affairs, leaving routine questions to Butler. Until September 1938, Halifax fully shared the Prime Minister's attitudes to foreign affairs and from those attitudes Butler never deviated. Halifax restored to the government some of the appeal to the high-minded that Eden had provided. He could hardly pretend to Eden's enthusiasm for the League but he was distinctively Christian and decidedly a gentleman. His manner was modest and self-deprecating. His public and private utterances were emollient and conciliatory. He even appealed to left-wing anti-imperialists as a result of his comparative courtesy, when Viceroy, to Gandhi, which had earned him the accolade of an attack from Churchill. Moreover he had a then widely acceptable skill in field sports, as an MFH, and a benignly patrician interest in village cricket. Deafness lent him a pleasantly abstracted air while he tried courteously to agree with everyone he spoke to, saw many sides of most arguments and expressed his own opinions as mild reservations. In another respect he differed from Chamberlain, in seeming comfortably lazy. He was liked and respected, and under-estimated.

Soon after Anthony Eden's resignation, Chamberlain wrote 'To me it was really a relief that the peace makers [between Eden and himself] were unsuccessful. A. would never have been able to carry through the negotiations with any conviction and in his hands they might well have failed. Now at least they have a fair prospect of success.' By forcing Eden's departure, Chamberlain had staked his reputation on his success.[32]

7 Chamberlain and Halifax: March–August 1938

Emancipated from the hesitations and doubts of Eden, Chamberlain's confidence continued to grow. During the next months, Halifax reinforced it. He weighed matters sagaciously and then came down on Chamberlain's side. After a few weeks Chamberlain purred 'I thank God for a steady unruffled Foreign Secretary who never causes me any worry.'[1] Cadogan, at the Foreign Office, discounted the worries and reservations often expressed by Vansittart. Together Halifax and Chamberlain led Cabinet discussion on foreign affairs, the one reflective, rather dry and solemn in tone, the other sharp and decisive. Two diplomatic manoeuvres moved forward, one in search of renewed friendship with Italy, the other of a settlement with Germany. Then, at last, there could be an agreement to disarm.

Chamberlain would have liked to extend British peacemaking to the Far East. He insisted that no chance of mediation between the Japanese and the Chinese authorities should be missed. However, overwhelming evidence showed their positions to be irreconcilable. The Prime Minister reluctantly rejected the opinion, widespread among the military, that the United Kingdom should support Japan against the Chinese Nationalists and Communists and revive the Anglo-Japanese alliance. Such a policy would alienate the United States administration, attached to its doctrine of non-recognition of changes brought by force, and, in any case, it could only have succeeded if Britain and Japan had had compatible economic interests in China. The Japanese, however, wanted monopoly rights, the British to defend their mercantile investment and maintain the Open Door. The outcome was that the British government helped Chinese resistance, hoping that Chiang could hold out long enough to force Japan to compromise, while at the same time the British tried not to upset Japanese opinion, especially that of the, now somewhat subdued, internationally minded moderates. The policy of helping China, eloquently advocated by Sir Archibald Clark-Kerr, the British ambassador to China, involved help in building the Burma Road as a new means of contact between the outside world and nationalist China. The second policy, of conciliating Japan, tenaciously advocated by Sir Robert Craigie, the British ambassador in Tokyo, led to the rejection of government support for a loan to China. This ambiguous policy was taken up because, without United States support, the British government felt it could not try to halt Japanese expansion and therefore had to wait for the Chinese conflict to end in stalemate.[2]

But it was for the sake of restoring Anglo-Italian friendship that Chamberlain had endured the 'blood and tears', as he put it, of Eden's departure. The morning after Eden resigned, Chamberlain sent a telegram to summon Lord Perth from Rome to join in planning the much-disputed conversations Perth was to conduct with the Italian Foreign Minister, the bumptious Ciano. In retrospect, their futility should have been obvious from the start. What Chamberlain wanted was a reliable, trustworthy, friendly Italy. Under Mussolini (as Eden correctly pointed out) this was not available. Chamberlain took the conversations seriously, but we need not do so except in so far as their 'success' affected Chamberlain's later attitudes and conduct. Their formal outcome was that Britain promised to recognise the Italian Empire in Ethiopia, once the League had given permission, while Italy agreed, for the benefit of British opinion, to 'a settlement of the Spanish question'. What that amounted to was that Mussolini, while continuing to work to ensure Franco's victory, repeated former disclaimers of any designs on Spanish territory and reasserted pledges to maintain the status quo in the Mediterranean in general. 'Volunteers' would be withdrawn from Spain. The agreement would 'come into force' only when progress had been made, that is some 'volunteers' withdrawn; Mussolini promised that all Italian 'volunteers' would leave Spain after the war. Mussolini also promised to reduce the Italian garrison in Libya and it was agreed that the British and Italians should exchange information about any substantial military movements in their colonies, territories and protectorates in the Mediterranean, the Red

Sea, and north-east Africa. The Italian government pledged itself to cease anti-British propaganda in the Middle East. The essential bargain was that the British gave Mussolini added prestige in exchange for British hopes, never fulfilled, of a return to the days when British strategic planners could count on Italian neutrality in any British war. Chamberlain, moreover, thought that the agreement would secure Italian support in persuading, or even compelling, Hitler to keep the peace. He came to believe, encouraged by Grandi and his spokesmen, that Mussolini might have prevented German absorption of Austria if Eden had not delayed the agreement with Italy: 'It is tragic to think that very possibly this [the Anschluss] might have been prevented if I had had Halifax at the Foreign Office instead of Anthony at the time I wrote my letter to Mussolini' (that is in July 1937). The agreement 'came into effect' on 16 November 1938 on the basis of a partial withdrawal of Italian forces from Spain.[3]

However, the most important task for the newly liberated Chamberlain–Halifax partnership was to continue the search for the elusive general settlement with Germany, the latest episode of which had begun with the Halifax visit. In the weeks before his resignation Eden had worked with Chamberlain to assemble new British offers to Hitler. The plan, which Halifax suggested, of persuading Hitler to be a 'good European' in return for a 'colonial settlement' should have seemed doomed from the start. Henderson reported from Berlin that the German government was 'in no hurry' over its claim to the return of former German colonies and 'was not in the least expecting an early communication on the subject'. On 1 December, however, the Cabinet agreed that the Committee on Foreign Policy should study the colonial issue and a month later Eden circulated to members of this committee a paper on the next steps towards a general settlement with Germany. In the Foreign Office, some officials welcomed German readiness to delay: 'The longer Germany is prepared to wait, the longer is the time allowed for H.M. Government to pursue their rearmament undisturbed.' Halifax and Chamberlain thought differently: Halifax told Henderson in November that 'the PM is taking the matter up with great determination and I greatly hope that we may see early progress' and in January 1938 he found Chamberlain 'quite determined to make progress'. Chamberlain told Sir Thomas Inskip, the Minister for Co-ordination of Defence, 'to go into the technical aspects of the question of limitation of bomber aeroplanes as well as other forms of qualitative disarmament'. Thus he hoped that the Germans would agree to render their air force incapable of a 'knock-out blow' against the UK. Chamberlain brooded about colonial concessions to Germany. There appeared the outlines of a possible bargain to be wrapped up in a 'general settlement', that is, a promise from Hitler to seek only 'peaceful change'. Halifax felt 'the real difficulty about a general settlement arose from our doubts as to whether the Germans were reliable ... we must probably rely upon (a) the better relations we might hope to create through an all-round discussion and settlement; and (b) the self-interest of the Germans not being for war.'[4]

Halifax applied himself to creating 'better relations' with Hitler. When he went to Berchtesgaden in November 1937, he found Hitler 'quiet and restrained, except now and again when he got excited: over Russia or the press'. In Berlin, Goebbels told him that 'nothing would do more for better relations than if our Press could be induced to stop attacking Hitler personally'. To avoid irritation to Hitler, Halifax and Chamberlain kept the USSR out of Anglo-German diplomacy. As for the press, Halifax, on his return from Germany, tried to influence proprietors and editors. On 1 December 1937, for instance, he followed up a conversation with Lord Southwood, part-proprietor of the *Daily Herald*, with a letter angrily complaining about a cartoon by Will Dyson published in the paper that day – evidently Halifax was keeping watch. The drawing accurately represented the government's ideas: perhaps that helped to enrage Halifax. It showed a symbolic female figure, representing Europe, proffering her baby, representing colonial peoples, to a menacing Hitler: 'Take my child, but spare, oh spare me!' Halifax reproached Southwood in offensively moralistic tones: 'I think you were disposed to take the view that the temper in which we all wished to see cartoonists portraying public characters was that of humour without cruelty. I am bound to say that I think the cartoon in today's issue is a long way from this, and, it seems to me, if you don't mind my being frank, malevolently and I think unjustly cruel. It is exactly this kind of approach to international problems that appears to me to make advance so difficult, and I therefore deplore it.' It may well have been correct that the British press irritated Hitler, who found it difficult to understand why British friendship eluded him. This unwelcome fact he readily ascribed to Jewish influence and it is known that his press secretary kept Hitler well informed of the contents of the press of the world. Hitler, indeed, exploited the alleged press conspiracy against him as an excuse for spurning attempts at appeasement and in his speech on 20 February paid tribute to the power of the press by announcing the creation of three additional army corps to counter it.[5]

The British authorities had to circumvent another possible obstacle to appeasement: calls made by the French government for firm action. In December 1937 Eden, who sympathised, since the suggestion might help to make unnecessary a desperate pursuit of reconciliation with Italy, passed on to the Chiefs of Staff a proposal from the French ambassador in London for close Anglo-French staff conversations. On 4 February 1938 Admiral Chatfield, Air Marshal Newall and General Gort answered with a stark 'no', in a paper in which they tried, and failed, to discover military reasons to conceal their hatred of any idea of collaboration with the French. The army, they claimed, had too few forces available to make discussion worthwhile, the navy would need the help of the French if the British fleet went to the Far East but if France seemed to be allied with Britain against Italy, German intervention might be provoked 'with the consequent risk of a world conflagration' while as for the air, 'from the purely military point of view the French attitude is admittedly logical' but 'we feel certain that the opportunity of turning such conversations to their own political advantage would be seized upon by the French with avidity'. They 'would flaunt an Anglo-French accord in the face of Germany. Apart from the deplorable effect of such a leakage upon our present efforts to reach a détente with Germany, it is most important', they went on, somewhat lamely, 'from the military standpoint, that at the present time we should not appear to have both feet in the French Camp. We consider, therefore [sic], that the military advantages of closer collaboration with the French regarding concerted measures against Germany, however logical they may appear, would be outweighed by the grave risk of precipitating the very situation which we wish to avoid, namely, the irreconcilable suspicion and hostility of Germany.'[6]

On 18 February the French ambassador gave a memorandum to Eden, now in his last days as Foreign Secretary. It asked that the British and French should threaten Hitler with concerted opposition 'to any *coup de main* or act of war likely to bring into question the territorial status quo in Central Europe'. Eden had already approved a telegram to Paris that 'we should deprecate any Anglo-French warning or protest in Berlin' over Austria or central Europe. In the Foreign Office Strang condemned the new French memorandum as 'a rather typical French production. They put up proposals which go well beyond what they themselves are willing (or in a position) to perform, and will place the responsibility for inaction upon us.' The Cabinet approved the reply that the British government 'feel that the steps which they hoped to take in Berlin are more likely to create conditions favourable to peaceful development and the restoration of confidence in central Europe'.[7]

The British took those 'steps' only on 3 March, delayed first by the ominous changes in the leadership of the Third Reich: the suppression of the office of Minister of War, which Hitler took for himself, combined with the supreme command of the armed forces, the substitution as Foreign Minister of the egregious Ribbentrop for the better-mannered Neurath, the promotion of Göring to the rank of Reichsmarschall, changes which reduced possibly moderating influences on Hitler. Now, Sir O. Sargent minuted in the Foreign Office 'We may have to look to Hitler personally for any moderating influence': an unlikely possibility which was still widely believed.[8]

On 14 January Horace Wilson told Cadogan that the Prime Minister was on the point of 'getting down closely to the Colonies question' and he requested suggestions for 'contributions' towards 'appeasement' to be asked from the Germans. A week later Chamberlain had 'an idea . . . which does seem to me to open up a hopeful prospect'. He presented it to the Foreign Policy Committee on 24 January, who accepted it 'promptly and even enthusiastically', as the Prime Minister wrote, and Henderson was sent for to discuss it. It was 'an entirely new method . . . the opening of an entirely new chapter in the

history of African colonial development'. Central African territories would be subjected to a uniform set of rules voluntarily
accepted by existing colonial powers. Within this area Germany, obeying the new rules, would have its own territory to
govern and exploit, subject to provisos for the protection and
betterment of native populations, free trade, and demilitarisation; compensation of some kind would be found for those
powers, France, Portugal and Belgium, who would assign territory to Germany. 'The proposals', the Prime Minister thought,
'should have a good reception in Berlin.' The Committee met
again on 3 February with a paper from the Foreign Office on
possible German contributions towards appeasement. Sir
Nevile Henderson, who was present, warned that 'the German
government would not be greatly thrilled by what was now
proposed'. Just the same the Cabinet hoped, as Eden put it, to
secure 'some substantial measure of air disarmament, and, in
the political sphere, some satisfactory solution of Germany's
controversies with Czecho-Slovakia'. Henderson was more encouraging on disarmament than on colonies: 'Herr Hitler held
very strong views on the question of the bombing of the civil
population, and had expressed himself in favour of some
arrangement under which bombing should be prohibited in
places over thirty miles behind military front lines.' Chamberlain was practical: he called for a definition of a bombing
aeroplane and an agreement 'that all such aeroplanes should be
abolished and that no more should be constructed'. The
Cabinet showed much more interest in this point than in
Czechoslovakia.[9]

Henderson eventually talked to Hitler, and Ribbentrop, with
Schmidt, the interpreter, in the Reichschancellery in Berlin.
Henderson effectively represented some aspects of the English
governing class; his suits assertive only through their elegance,
his manner that of someone born effortlessly to command. His
slightly excessive jauntiness, the carefully trimmed moustache,
the carnation in his buttonhole, the hint of the modish bound-
er, his unflurried incompetence in speaking German, the self-
confidence given by substantial private means, all seem to have
increased the anger aroused in Hitler by what he had to say.
Hitler wanted the British not to interfere in the European
continent while he reconstructed it to create an economically

self-sufficient Greater Germany capable of fighting protracted and victorious wars against all possible rivals. Henderson, on the contrary, urged that German armed strength should be limited, especially any weapon which might threaten the United Kingdom, and proposed that European changes should take place only as the result of general agreement. As a reward for Hitler's renunciation of Hitlerism, Henderson talked vaguely about reintroducing limited German rule to some restricted part of tropical Africa. Hitler, 'glowering in his chair', first complained angrily of the 'sensationalist press . . . numerously represented in England' and then, in two or three sentences, waved aside British policy. 'Germany would not allow third parties to interfere in the settlement of her relationship with countries of the same nationality or countries with large German populations' and, moreover, 'if in Austria or in Czechoslovakia internal explosions took place, Germany would not remain neutral, but would act like lightning'. As for colonies, he 'could easily wait four, six, eight or ten years'. As for aerial disarmament 'German armaments were conditioned by Russia . . . in an armaments discussion the British must therefore start with Russia'.[10]

Halifax explained the response he proposed to the Cabinet on 9 March 1938. 'The German government . . . did not want to tie their hands by talks, and still less by undertakings to ourselves . . . The moral he drew was that all this emphasised the importance of the conversations with the Italian government. There was some reason to believe that Signor Mussolini was annoyed with the Germans.' Halifax went on to explain what he intended to say to Ribbentrop, who had returned to London to make his farewells on becoming Foreign Minister. 'He proposed that his remarks should be composed of a mixture of disappointment, reproach and warning. His warning would not take the form of threats', but rather of putting 'the objections to Herr Hitler's statements'. The Home Secretary, Sir Samuel Hoare, suggested saying that 'if Germany invaded Austria or Czechoslovakia they raised dangers in Europe of which the end could not be foreseen'.[11]

Two days later, when Chamberlain and Halifax gave lunch to Ribbentrop and when, after lunch, Halifax spoke to the German Foreign Minister about German conduct, the German army was invading Austria. A few days earlier, the Austrian Chancellor, Dr von Schuschnigg, announced a plebiscite on Austrian independence; most Austrians were expected to vote for the existing state of affairs. In response, Hitler and Göring intervened to destroy the existing state of affairs. They ordered Schuschnigg to cancel the plebiscite under threat of invasion. Then they told him to resign and hand over governing powers to the Nazi Interior Minister, Seyss-Inquart. The President of Austria refused to make Seyss-Inquart Chancellor, and instead Göring told Seyss-Inquart, as Austrian Minister of the Interior, to ask for the help of German troops 'to maintain order' in Austria: a process hastened by Göring's decision that Seyss-Inquart need not bother to work out the text of an appeal, but simply express agreement. Schuschnigg's final act, before the President at last gave way on 12 March, was to order that German forces entering Austria should not be resisted; apart from Jews and socialists, most Austrians seem to have welcomed the abrupt creation, announced on 13 March, of the Anschluss with Germany and the creation of 'Great Germany'. Meanwhile Hitler sent Prince Philip of Hesse to Rome with a propitiatory message for Mussolini; Hitler welcomed Mussolini's acquiescence with excited gratitude. Mussolini and Ciano, in spite of the launching of the Anglo-Italian talks, declined even to discuss the German coup with the French or British ambassadors in Rome.

The German union with Austria, forcibly and brutally imposed, represented 'peaceful evolution' only on a very liberal interpretation indeed. Neither Chamberlain nor Halifax was much perturbed by the union itself: most Austrians seemed to acquiesce in it or even welcome it. The alarming German display of armed strength in the invasion of Austria suggested to Chamberlain and Halifax only that the British government should have made greater efforts to get on terms with the dictators. Of course they felt reproachful towards Hitler and his associates, whose actions made it more difficult for them to keep British policy peaceful and friendly. They disliked Hitler's rude treatment of Henderson and the violent reaction to what Chamberlain agreed to be Schuschnigg's 'folly' in ordering the Austrian plebiscite. Chamberlain decided to 'say something like this' to Hitler: 'We gave you fair warning that if you used violence to Austria you would shock public opinion to such an extent as to give rise to the most disagreeable repercussions. Yet you obstinately went your way and now you can see for yourself how right we were . . . but it is of no use crying over spilt milk and what we have to do now is to consider how we can restore the confidence you have shattered.' There was no question of Chamberlain's abandoning the search for understanding with Germany. He told the Cabinet's Foreign Policy Committee on 15 March that 'he did not think anything that had happened should cause the government to alter their present policy, on the contrary, recent events had confirmed him in his opinion that the policy was the right one and he only regretted that it had not been adopted earlier.' However, 'recent events had greatly disturbed public opinion . . . the government's policy would have to be explained and justified to public opinion even more carefully and thoroughly than would otherwise have been necessary.'[12] As time went on Chamberlain stuck to his policy but, understandably, found it more and more difficult to 'explain and justify'.

Chamberlain and Halifax felt it necessary to go through the motions of a formal reassessment of British policy. There was no doubt of the outcome. Now that Chamberlain had survived Eden's departure and successfully installed the like-minded Halifax, those two ministers easily dominated the Cabinet, but so important a decision required the full use of the mechanism of government discussion. Halifax presented essays on policy, written by Foreign Office officials, to the Foreign Policy Committee of the Cabinet, which considered, too, a formal report from the Chiefs of Staff before producing conclusions to the full Cabinet for final debate. In the process the doubts and hesitations of other ministers could be quietened and their own confidence reaffirmed. Halifax wrote a 'semi-official letter' to Nevile Henderson on 19 March and set out his own thoughts. 'We are being very heavily pressed to make all kinds of firm declarations.' Halifax had in mind the French, the Labour and Liberal oppositions, together with some well-informed Conservatives, notably Winston Churchill, who argued in the House of Commons on 14 March that Hitler could be stopped from further expansion only by definite warnings that Britain would join in resisting future German aggression.

On 13 March Chamberlain explained to his sister his immediate reactions to the Anschluss. He denied the efficacy of the League in dealing with the German problem: 'it is perfectly evident, surely, now that force is the only argument that Germany understands, and that collective security cannot offer any prospect of preventing such events until it can show a visible force of overwhelming strength, backed by determination to use it.' He went on that 'such force and determination are most effectively mobilised by alliances, which don't require meetings at Geneva, and resolutions by dozens of small nations'. At this point, Hilda may have supposed that her brother had abandoned hopes of the appeasement of Europe, but the next sentences would have reassured her: 'Heaven knows, I don't want to get back to alliances but if Germany continues to behave as she has done lately, she may drive us to it ... However I am not going to take the situation too tragically ... For the moment we must abandon conversations with Germany, we must show our determination not to be bullied by announcing some increase or acceleration in rearmament, and we must quietly and steadily pursue our conversations with Italy. If we can avoid another violent coup in Czechoslovakia, which ought to be feasible, it may be possible for Europe to settle down again, and some day for us to start peace talks again with the Germans.' Two weeks later he told Hilda that he had 'weighed up the situation and decided quite definitely what was the right course and to my great satisfaction I found Halifax had come independently to the same conclusion'.[13]

In Hitler's Reichstag speech of 20 February, and in his conversation with Henderson, he had announced that he intended to force changes in the position of Germans in Austria and Czechoslovakia. Now that Hitler had dealt with Austria, his attention, the British government assumed, would turn to Czechoslovakia, whose western provinces were now encircled by the Great German Reich. Unease increased when the German government, through Göring, denied that Czechoslovakia was threatened. A German attack on Czechoslovakia would, by treaty, set off a great European war. France had promised to help Czechoslovakia against German aggression and the USSR had promised to join with France in helping Czechoslovakia. Hence the Anschluss, the German union with Austria, precipitated a careful reassessment prior to a reassertion of British policy.

Halifax set out his views to the Foreign Policy Committee of the Cabinet on Friday 18 March. By that time, he had been able to study a series of papers from Foreign Office officials. On 17 March, Sir Orme Sargent, evidently disillusioned by the Anschluss, asserted that the British government must choose between trying to secure the safety of the British Empire by co-operating with Hitler in building a German world empire or, alternatively, by organising defence against Germany by military co-operation with France and Belgium, strengthening ties with Greece and Turkey, cultivating Poland and Russia to preserve them 'as friendly neutrals in the day of trouble', resisting German and Italian domination in Spain, buying off Japan and 'above all, we should, with infinite patience and tact, continue to humour, cultivate, interest and educate the United States Government and the United States people'. Sargent expressed what turned out to be the choice facing the United Kingdom in the 1930s and 1940s: between German or American dominance of the world. (There could be no doubt what the British choice would be, if it came to that.) Cadogan, the new Permanent Under-Secretary in the Foreign Office, denied that it need come to that: 'I am quite prepared to believe that the incorporation in the Reich of Austrian and Sudetendeutsch may be only the first step in a German expansion eastwards. But I do submit that this is not necessarily so, and that we should not rush to hasty conclusions.'[14]

Halifax spoke to the Foreign Policy Committee when it met on Friday 18 March. He handed round and read out a Foreign Office paper, based on an analysis by William Strang, which set out the possibility of promising, conditionally, to assist France, if the latter were attacked by Germany after France had gone to the help of Czechoslovakia defending itself against invasion. The condition would be that the Czechoslovak government had satisfied the British of their good treatment of the Sudeten German minority. Halifax produced a sceptical commentary on this paper. He thought Germany would object to any interference on the part of other powers in German-Czech questions and that Britain would risk war in trying to deter Germany from imposing its own solution. He believed that refusal to commit Britain to action would keep both France and Germany 'guessing' and so restrain them both. He rejected the assumption that, when Germany had 'secured the hegemony over Central Europe, she would then pick a quarrel with France and ourselves'. Moreover 'the more closely we associated ourselves with France and Russia the more we produced in German minds the impression that we were plotting to encircle Germany and the more difficult would it be to make any real settlement with Germany'. And 'a new commitment to France in respect of Czechoslovakia might involve us in war in the very near future when in certain respects, e.g. supply of A.A. [anti-aircraft] guns we were very unprepared.' The Prime Minister supported Halifax. He did not believe that Germany wished to absorb all Czechoslovakia and he insisted that the only permanent settlement would be one acceptable to Germany. Czechoslovakia was militarily indefensible, but if Germany could get 'her *desiderata* by peaceful methods there was no reason to suppose that she would reject such a procedure in favour of one based on violence': in other words, give Hitler what he wanted and he wouldn't snatch it.

Among the other members of the committee, Simon (Chancellor of the Exchequer), Hailsham (Lord President) and Malcolm MacDonald (Dominions) supported Halifax and Chamberlain, the latter pointing out that South Africa and Canada would not join Britain in a war for Czechoslovakia. Ormsby-Gore (Colonies) thought a new commitment would split public opinion from top to bottom and Inskip (Co-ordination of Defence) anticipated the views of the military by asserting that Germany could easily conquer Czechoslovakia, and that only a long war would get Germany out of Czechoslovakia again. Only Hoare (Home Secretary), who thought a new commitment to France might increase feelings of urgency over rearmament, and Oliver Stanley (Board of Trade) showed any interest in announcing support for France. Stanley suggested that it might deter Germany and help to win French support for the Anglo-Italian rapprochement but then changed sides by declaring that the preservation of Czechoslovakia as it stood was not a vital British interest. The committee did not demand 'a clear, decided, bold and unmistakable lead ... and all the rest of the twaddle' as Chamberlain put it. The record of its proceedings does not suggest that it was with reluctance that Chamberlain gave up the idea of a declaration of support for France, or that he did so only because of British military weakness. Indeed the committee meeting on 18 March deliberated and formed its view without waiting for the reply of the Chiefs of Staff who were urged 'to meet as early as practicable' to get their report out in time for the committee meeting on 21 March. This later meeting ratified the decision of the earlier meeting, but made Halifax sugar the pill for the French of the British refusal to announce support for the Franco-Czech alliance. Halifax, for his part, showed no sign of concern for French susceptibilities: 'No doubt France would be shocked but he could not see how in any case this could be avoided. Because France would be shocked was no reason why we should refrain from pursuing a policy of the correctness of which we were fully satisfied . . . his impression was that the French were never ready to face up to realities, they delighted in vain words and protestations . . . France had been told over and over again that we could and would not enter into any fresh commitments.' Halifax, however, was forced to withdraw draft statements to be presented in Paris and to the House of Commons and to insert warmer references to France.[15]

When the full Cabinet met on 22 March they had in front of them the report of the Chiefs of Staff on the military implications of German aggression against Czechoslovakia and Halifax and Chamberlain exploited it to secure agreement to their policy of concession to Germany. The report insisted that German forces could overrun Bohemia and Moravia within weeks or days and that no outside pressure could stop them; 'we can do nothing to prevent the dog getting the bone, and we have no means of making him give it up, except by killing him by the slow process of attrition and starvation'. Britain and France could liberate Czechoslovakia only by a long and painful war, which might begin with an attempt at a knock-out blow from the German air force against a weakly defended United Kingdom. If Japan and Italy joined Germany then the military implications would arouse 'the deepest misgivings'. Halifax told the Cabinet that he and Chamberlain had examined the proposals that Britain should guarantee Czechoslovakia or guarantee support to France if France took action in accordance with her treaty 'with some sympathy towards the idea of a guarantee'. Halifax was suggesting, therefore, that he and the Prime Minister felt reluctantly compelled by military exigencies to renounce their preferred policy of calling a halt to German advance. As we have seen, the evidence suggests that Chamberlain and Halifax believed a peaceful and acceptable settlement with Germany to be obtainable and therefore wished in any case to work for it. The Chiefs of Staff provided a justification, not an explanation, for their actions. One consequence of this justification was that the government decided that steps to speed up rearmament should be announced. In the Cabinet discussion, it was agreed 'that there was an underlying resentment at the idea of constantly having to knuckle under to the dictators for lack of sufficient strength'. After the Anschluss Cabinet ministers believed rearmament to have the support of the public; henceforward the government emphasised rather than understated its efforts to rearm.[16]

Potential opponents of Chamberlain's wishes in the Cabinet, what the Prime Minister called 'weak-kneed colleagues', appear to have been won over to acquiescence mainly by the redrafting of the statement to be given to the House of Commons to make it friendlier to France. Duff Cooper, for instance, wrote at the time that the statement 'quite clearly implied that if France went to war we should go too. This was all that I wanted. It was perhaps wiser in the long run to imply than to state it. Our own public opinion is reluctant to accept the unpleasant necessity.' In the end Duff Cooper proved the most determined opponent of Chamberlain in the Cabinet but he was ineffective. He was notoriously lazy or perhaps, more accurately, he distributed his energies more widely than an effective Cabinet minister can allow himself to do. He was a talented writer of elegant biographies as well as highly sociable. Hoare once priggishly expressed 'the lowest opinion of him' to Chamberlain apparently because 'he was mixed up with bad company and was drinking far too much champagne'. For some time he was taken in and outmanoeuvred by Chamberlain's superior political skills. In fact, the statement made by the Prime Minister added nothing to British commitments:[17]

Should we forthwith give assurance to France that, in the

event of her being called upon by reason of German aggression on Czechoslovakia to implement her obligations under the Franco-Czechoslovak Treaty, we would immediately employ our full military force on her behalf? Or, alternatively, should we at once declare our readiness to take military action in resistance to any forcible interference with the independence and integrity of Czechoslovakia, and invite any other nation, which might so desire, to associate themselves with us in such a declaration?

. . .

His Majesty's Government feel themselves unable to give the prior guarantees suggested. But while plainly stating this decision, I would add this: Where peace and war are concerned, legal obligations are not alone involved, and, if war broke out, it would be unlikely to be confined to those who have assumed such obligations. It would be quite impossible to say where it might end and what governments might become involved. The inexorable pressure of facts might well prove more powerful than formal pronouncements, and in that event it would be well within the bounds of probability that other countries, besides those which were parties to the original dispute, would almost immediately be involved. This is especially true in the case of two countries like Great Britain and France, with long associations of friendship, with interests closely interwoven, devoted to the same ideals of democratic liberty and determined to uphold them.

Chamberlain and Halifax had turned down a French suggestion that the British and French governments should discuss the European situation before settling their policy. They imposed their views – the French were given advance notice of Chamberlain's statement (as was Winston Churchill) but no chance to modify it. On 17 March Litvinov, the Soviet Foreign Minister, publicly announced the willingness of the USSR to discuss 'practical measures called for by the present circumstances . . . Tomorrow it may be too late, but today the time has not yet passed if all the States and especially the Great Powers will adopt a firm and unequivocal stand in regard to the problem of the collective salvation of peace.' Maisky, the Soviet ambassador in London, presented the proposal to the Foreign

Office. Without discussion Halifax replied, on 24 March, that the British preferred 'the settlement of outstanding problems' to the organisation of 'concerted action against aggression'.[18]

Czechoslovakia presented the most urgent outstanding problem. Chamberlain and Halifax now put their policy into effect. They would press the Czechoslovak government to satisfy the grievances of Germans inside Czechoslovakia. The Czechs must understand that if they failed they could not expect protection from Britain or from France against armed incursion from Germany. They would restrain French governments from encouraging Czechoslovakia to resist German demands and they would prevent the French from promising armed support to Czechoslovakia against German aggression: the French would be restrained by the British refusal to promise British aid to France. At the same time German violence would be restrained by the possibility that Britain might be involved in a subsequent war. The French and Czechs would be restrained by what the British might not do; the Germans by what the British might do. In speeches on 20 February and 28 March Hitler threatened German action if the grievances of Germans living in Czechoslovakia were not put right. This Halifax and Chamberlain were very ready to do: from the earliest moment they regarded transfer of the Sudeten territory to Germany and the neutralisation of Czechoslovakia as a possibility in the last resort, if the Czechoslovak government could not, or would not, satisfy the demands of the Germans in Czechoslovakia, as expressed by the Sudeten German Party, led by Konrad Henlein.[19]

At first Halifax worried most of all about the French government. After the Anschluss, Leon Blum had returned to power in France, attempting, but failing, to form a great national government. Halifax, and those of like mind, regarded his Foreign Minister, Paul-Boncour, as, in the words of Sir Eric Phipps, British ambassador in Paris, 'a positive danger to the peace of Europe'. Paul-Boncour reasserted French pledges to Czechoslovakia, spoke up for the League, favoured intervention in Spain against Franco and had, once, memorably, discovered a suitable label for Mussolini: 'ce César de carnaval'. Paul-Boncour showed signs of refusal to 'face the realities', he was to be reminded that there was no pledge of support in the

Prime Minister's statement of 24 March. Moreover Paul-Boncour wished to assert the 'common determination of France and Great Britain to unite in order to ensure respect for international law and for the right of nations to be independent'. He hearkened to dangerous British visitors. Lloyd George visited Paris with two 'enormous rolled maps of Europe' and urged that France should take the lead in meeting the European crisis, and then Britain would be compelled to follow. Next Churchill came over to Paris and preached 'a solid Anglo-French bloc against Germany' as a preliminary to a European 'Grand Alliance'. Phipps intervened to persuade Daladier not to keep Paul-Boncour as Foreign Minister in the government he formed after Blum's fall on 8 April 1938.

Now Georges Bonnet, a right-wing Radical, became Foreign Minister. Phipps and Chamberlain would have preferred the amenable Chautemps but felt pleased that the Daladier–Bonnet team at least brought relief from Paul-Boncour. Phipps suggested that Halifax and Chamberlain should go to Paris 'if Daladier does well and Bonnet shows himself to be sound . . . to fortify them'.[20] They did better: they invited Daladier and Bonnet to England and arranged for them to dine and stay with the King and Queen at Windsor Castle. Since Chamberlain and Halifax had already determined British policy, they set out to persuade the French ministers to accept it and to apply it. They needed the French to secure Czechoslovak concessions. They wanted them to threaten to withhold French support in case of German aggression against Czechoslovakia, rather than to encourage Czechoslovak resistance and so risk a European war in which the British would have to intervene to prevent a French defeat.

British and French ministers met during two days, 28 and 29 April 1938, at 10 Downing Street. Twelve men assembled. Four spoke at length, the two Prime Ministers and the ministers for foreign affairs. The others were silent, apart from a few remarks by Corbin, the sombre, dignified French ambassador in London. Chamberlain, in familiar territory, led the discussions. His headmasterly style and appearance reinforced the impression of authority conveyed by the confidence and clarity of his statements. Halifax supported Chamberlain's commanding competence with his imperturbability and reflective slowness emphasised by the speech impediment which was so common an outcome of the ferocious upbringing given to male children of the English upper class. Halifax tended to disguise disagreement and avoid the direct bluntness that Chamberlain preferred. Daladier seemed blunt and direct; small, thickset and tough-looking, in appearance neither an intellectual nor a prosperous bourgeois, his political support rested on his appeal to the ordinary French voter. He played the role of the strong, decisive leader, a part which his increasingly worried, hangdog look did not fit. Few trusted or liked Bonnet, the new French Foreign Minister, whose large nose went with a distinctly shifty appearance, but he was clever and moved confidently in Parisian financial circles. Among the officials, Vansittart attended, remaining at the centre of events, well-informed but less able to influence decisions than Cadogan, his successor as Permanent Under-Secretary. Cadogan seemed the ideally dispassionate, calm civil servant, but his diaries show how much emotion he repressed in public. A strong supporter, at this stage, of the Chamberlain–Halifax policy, he wrote in his diary at this time that the 'parrot-cry of "rearmament" is mere confession of failure of foreign policy. We *must* reach a modus vivendi with Germany.'[21] From Paris there came the enigmatic, reserved, official head of the French Foreign Office, Alexis Léger, otherwise the poet St John Perse, whose *Anabase* had been translated into English by T. S. Eliot, and who won the Nobel Prize for Literature after the war, and Charles Rochat, head of the European Division at the Quai d'Orsay. From the French embassy in London the French team was completed by the junior and well-liked official, Roland de Margerie. From the Foreign Office were present Orme Sargent, sceptical, acerbic, disillusioned by long experience of attempts to get on terms with Germany, William Strang, an exceptionally able official, and Frank Roberts, who has survived into the television age charmingly, and loyally, to defend the pre-war Foreign Office.

On the first day the British suggested low-level contacts, through attachés, between the two air staffs, but, at first, opposed army and naval talks but then accepted contacts between military attachés to discuss the movement to French territory of two British divisions which might, or might not, go to France in case of war. The British tried to persuade the

French to join in improving relations with Italy and did not encounter much opposition. The most interesting and critical discussions concerned policy towards Czechoslovakia on the second day, 29 April. Halifax set out the British line: Britain and France should press Beneš urgently to negotiate a settlement of the German minority problem with representatives of that minority. In reply Daladier insisted that Henlein, the leader of the Sudeten German Party, intended to destroy the present Czechoslovak state. If Henlein declined to accept reasonable offers, then Britain should openly join France in promising to support the Czechoslovak government and prevent the dismemberment of Czechoslovakia. Daladier declared that German policy aimed to tear up treaties and destroy the equilibrium of Europe. Eventually Germany, having first secured the petrol and wheat resources of Romania, would turn against the western powers. War could only be avoided if Great Britain and France showed that they were ready to stop Hitler's advance by taking action to save the independence of Czechoslovakia.

Chamberlain responded with every argument at his disposal. Militarily Germany could destroy Czechoslovakia whatever the other powers might do and it would need a long and arduous war, whose outcome would be uncertain, to re-create Czechoslovakia, should the allies, if they won, still wish to do so. But he did not believe Germany intended to destroy Czechoslovakia. What seemed to be German expansionism might only be 'preparations against encirclement which Germany undoubtedly thought she had to guard against and against which she required to take every possible precaution'. Reducing Italian suspicion of Great Britain had led to a reduction in Italian hostility. Bonnet and Halifax supported their principals and then Daladier, with mounting eloquence, restated the French plea: 'if we submitted on every occasion before violent measures and the use of force, the only result would be to precipitate renewed violence and ensure further success for the use of forceful methods'. He denied that Germany was worried about encirclement. If Germany were allowed to win 'all the resources of central and eastern Europe, how could any effective military resistance be opposed to her?' Daladier closed his appeal by declaring that 'if there were no signs of a determined policy . . .

we should then have decided the fate of Europe, and he could only regard the future with the greatest pessimism'.

This 'awful rubbish' (in Cadogan's phrase) appalled Chamberlain. 'Fortunately the papers have no hint of how near we came to a break over Czechoslovakia. By one o'clock on Friday we had reached a deadlock. Daladier was saying to his own people that it was no use going on.' Chamberlain changed the places at lunch, put Daladier next to him and exploited his schoolboy French to lay the basis for the afternoon's compromise. Chamberlain opened the afternoon session by agreeing, in principle, to Anglo-French naval staff talks, which the Admiralty opposed for fear of provoking the Germans into denouncing the Anglo-German naval agreement. Halifax followed by promising British intervention in Berlin to ask what Germany wanted in Czechoslovakia and, if need be, to draw the German government's attention to the passages of Chamberlain's speech of 24 March about its being within the bounds of probability that Britain would be drawn into a war involving France. Halifax claimed that 'it would be going a long way if ... we were to report direct to Herr Hitler the words which Mr Chamberlain had already pronounced ... there was a great difference between repeating such words direct to the German government and so giving it a particular application, and pronouncing it in the House of Commons primarily for our own people.' Thus Halifax made out that the British ministers were coming as close as they dared to the French position. (He hastened to make it clear to the Germans that they were not – a few minutes after the talks had ended he asked the German chargé in a 'markedly cordial and friendly manner' to tell Ribbentrop that Britain had undertaken no new military commitment.[22]) This Daladier and Bonnet accepted and so abandoned their own arguments.

How are we to interpret this Anglo-French conference? The effect was clear – to draw Britain further into the Czechoslovak issue; the British could hardly risk leaving it in the provocative hands of the French. Perhaps Chamberlain was correct to suppose that Daladier genuinely wanted Anglo-French co-operation in helping Czechoslovakia to resist any German demands that threatened its future independence. Perhaps Daladier reluctantly gave up only when he found it impossible to

persuade the British that German expansion should be resisted. More likely Daladier never expected to persuade the
British to promise resistance to Germany and hoped only to get
the British to take the lead in the negotiations that British
refusal would make essential. There is a third possibility, that
Daladier and Bonnet were speaking for the record, to show
that they had done their best to carry out the repeatedly
proclaimed French policy of defending Czechoslovakia against
German aggression, while themselves hoping that the British
would impose their veto and remove all risk that the French
government might actually have to follow the policy it advocated. Perhaps Daladier and Bonnet thought any risk of war
in 1938 unacceptable or even believed, like Halifax and Chamberlain, that a stable and acceptable European settlement could
be secured by peaceful negotiation. A British journalist,
Maurice Gerothwohl, former diplomatic correspondent of the
Daily Telegraph, spoke briefly to Daladier just after Daladier's
arrival in London, before the conference began. Gerothwohl
told the German embassy in London that Daladier had said to
him: 'Are you [that is the British] going to put pressure on
Prague? Are you going to give the Czechs pressing counsels of
wisdom? . . . We are bound, bound in honour to Czechoslovakia
by treaty . . . But you are free . . . The Germans themselves
want the Czechoslovak question settled now – summer. And we
must assume they mean it . . . Germany is in a dangerous
mood. She is terribly strong . . . The peace of Europe probably
depends at this moment on the Czechoslovak issue and on what
your government and especially Mr. Chamberlain will do.' This
journalist spoke also to the Comte de Brinon. He was one of
the leading organisers of pro-German opinion in France. He
had known Daladier for some years and had been used by
Daladier and other French ministers for unofficial contacts
with the rulers of Nazi Germany. Brinon, as Gerothwohl reported to the German embassy, explained that Daladier hoped
'that Chamberlain and Halifax would themselves suggest that
pressure should be put on Prague so that Daladier could
acquiesce without seeming to have taken the initiative . . .
Bonnet was, if anything, even keener than Daladier on steering
clear of France's obligation to fight for Czechoslovakia.'[23]

Years later, in 1967, Daladier was questioned about these

documents. He claimed to have no recollection of this conversation with Gerothwohl. The report, he wrote, attributed to
him 'ideas which he had resisted'. Probably Daladier felt that
concession to Germany to keep the peace could not be avoided
in 1938, not least because he could not expect British support
for the defence of Czechoslovakia. If he used the words attributed to him in the German documents, he may well have been
expressing anxiety to persuade the British to take the diplomatic lead and so to win as much help from Britain as he could.
This fits his apparent satisfaction at the outcome of the Anglo-
French discussions.[24]

British policy-makers now began to act. Britain put pressure
on Beneš, the Czechoslovak President, Hodza, the Prime Minister and Krofta, the Foreign Minister, to reach agreement with
the Sudeten German Party (SDP) and Henlein, its leader, by
offering concessions to the demands of the Germans in
Czechoslovakia. Britain pressed France to apply pressure to
Beneš, Hodza and Krofta. The British began to make tactful
enquiries in Berlin to find out what the German government
might find acceptable, to urge the German government to be
patient and to help instil patience into the SDP. The Czech
government was told that there was no question of any British
support for Czechoslovakian independence until agreement
had been reached with the Sudeten Germans. If Beneš and the
Czech authorities were reasonable, and could be bullied into
sense and if Hitler were patient, and vague prophecies of the
disastrous consequences of impatience could restrain him, all
should be well. Eventually Anglo-German negotiations for a
general settlement and an arms limitation agreement could be
resumed.

British policy in the spring and summer of 1938 rested on two
assumptions: that Henlein would work for agreement with the
Czechoslovak government and that Hitler could be prevailed
upon to tolerate the continued existence of a Czechoslovakia,
provided that state was speedily modified in a way
acceptable to Henlein and the Sudeten Germans. Both assumptions were false. Hitler's words and his conduct show that he
intended, as soon as possible, to wipe Czechoslovakia off the
map. In May 1938 Hitler told his commanders to be ready to
attack Czechoslovakia by 1 October, at the latest: 'It is my

unalterable decision to smash Czechoslovakia by military action in the near future.' As for Henlein, he saw Hitler at the end of March. Hitler told him 'that demands should be made by the Sudeten German Party which are unacceptable to the Czech government . . . Henlein summarised his view to the Führer as follows: We must always demand so much that we can never be satisfied. The Führer approved this view.'[25] Whatever his personal opinion, Henlein had to obey. Hitler's displeasure would destroy his political support among Sudeten German nationalists.

At this interview Hitler congratulated Henlein on his success in England and asked him to go there again as soon as possible. Henlein deserved Hitler's praise. Group Captain Christie, a businessman, former air attaché in Berlin, who knew Germany intimately and spoke fluent German, arranged for Henlein to visit London for the first time in August 1935. Henlein lectured to the Royal Institute of International Affairs, a 'respectable' institution before which he acted the part of the moderate and reasonable statesman. Christie knew Vansittart well and acted as chief of an unofficial intelligence network which reported to him. Christie arranged for Vansittart, then the official head of the Foreign Office, to meet Henlein whom Vansittart found 'moderate, honest and clear-sighted'. Apparently Henlein possessed the knack of winning the confidence of British interlocutors which he exploited during frequent visits to London. In 1938 he excelled himself when he came to London in May. Vansittart explained that 'I have been on very friendly terms with Herr Henlein for some years past and have seen him frequently during his visits to London' before asserting that in his latest conversation he had shown himself 'a wise and reasonable man'. On 27 April 1938, Halifax told the Cabinet that 'Henlein was more and more coming under the influence of Herr Hitler'; on 18 May after Henlein's visit, he gave the Cabinet a different view: 'Sir Robert Vansittart had formed two conclusions from his conversation, first that Dr Henlein had no instructions from Berlin, and second that Dr Beneš could get an agreement of a useful character if he would only act quickly.'[26]

There is no point in analysing the foredoomed attempts made by the Czechoslovakian government to reach an under-

standing with the Sudeten German Party. Their only possible
hope of success would have been in persuading the British
government that the Czechoslovak authorities had done their
best. Henlein's work, however, made the British think that
Beneš and his ministers were not really trying, since, on his
side, Henlein, they thought, was able and willing to work for a
settlement of Sudeten grievances within the existing frontiers
of Czechoslovakia. Beneš and the Czechoslovakian government
were inhibited in seeking British and French approval and
support, by offering concessions to the Sudeten Germans, by
their need to maintain the morale of the loyal supporters of the
Czechoslovak state. In consequence, to the British government,
Henlein seemed reasonable and moderate; Beneš to be ob-
structing a peaceful solution.[27]

On 19 May 1938 several reports came in to the Foreign
Office of German troop concentrations near the Czechoslovak
border and on the next day the Ministry of Foreign Affairs in
Prague told the British of information, which they thought
'well founded', of German troop concentrations in Saxony. In
Czechoslovakia elections approached and the British ambassador in Berlin raised fears in London by commenting 'that if
there were a really serious incident on Sunday during the
elections I have no doubt myself but that Herr Hitler would
give orders for the German troops to cross the frontier immediately'. Newton, the British minister in Prague, told London that the Czech Chief of Staff was reported to favour
immediate mobilisation. Early on 21 May the Prague government called up one class of reservists, arousing a protest 'in
threatening language' from the German military attaché. That
afternoon Halifax despatched a telegram to Henderson directing him to warn Ribbentrop that if a conflict arose the British
'could not guarantee that they would not be forced by circumstances to become involved also'. Halifax went on to remind
Ribbentrop of the closing passages of Chamberlain's speech of
24 March (see above, p. 139). About the same time the Berlin
embassy telephoned a message from Henderson. Ribbentrop
had told him that two Sudeten Germans had just been killed by
a Czech officer. 'Germany could not sit by and allow Germans
to be murdered.' Henderson regarded the 'position as extremely critical'. At the end of that day Halifax sent another warning

as a 'personal message' to Ribbentrop: 'I would beg him not to count upon this country being able to stand aside if from any precipitate action there should start a European conflagration.'

Nothing happened. German troops did not cross the frontier. Chamberlain shared the general satisfaction, believing that the German government had abstained from an armed coup because 'they decided after getting our warning that the risks were too great'. In Berlin, however, Henderson soon decided that there had been no threat of German military action and the military attaché there, Mason MacFarlane, agreed.[28]

Halifax and the Foreign Office made sure that British policy maintained its careful balance: on 22 May Halifax directed Phipps, British ambassador in Paris, to tell the Foreign Minister that France should not assume that Britain would help France to defend Czechoslovakia and on 25 May Halifax told Masaryk, the Czechoslovak minister in London, that the least Prague could 'get away with' would be autonomy on 'the Swiss model' combined with neutrality in foreign policy. To minimise Hitler's possible resentment at a blow to his prestige, Halifax saw 'all the British press' on Sunday evening, 22 May, and told them that the 'last thing he desired' was that it should be said 'that the present corner had been turned owing to British firmness'. Henderson and the British military attaché in Berlin quickly decided that there had been no threat of German military action. Czech exaggeration and over-reaction, therefore, had manufactured the 'crisis'. However, the British government for a time believed that there had been a crisis and that firmness had some effect. Moderate counsels had prevailed in Germany: a reassuring conclusion. On 25 May when the Cabinet reviewed the Czechoslovakian problem Chamberlain is reported to have told his colleagues 'the Sudeten Deutsch should remain in Czechoslovakia but as contented people'. If Czechoslovakia became a neutral state 'it might be possible to get a settlement in Europe'. The Prime Minister cited as evidence Hitler's talk to the Aga Khan, months before, in October 1937. To the rotund holy man, the hero of English flat racing (he won the Derby five times and in 1935 his racehorse, Bahram, won the Two Thousand Guineas, the Derby and the St Leger), the Führer suggested that he might guarantee Czechoslovakian independence if the Sudeten regions became autonomous, a word of uncertain implications. A week later Halifax had good news for the Cabinet: 'certain secret information which Sir Robert Vansittart had received emphasised the willingness of Herr Henlein to adhere to the proposals he had made in London if he could get a quick result'. Halifax therefore pressed Beneš harder; 'at the moment Germany was not making trouble'. Three weeks later he had disquieting news for the Cabinet: he conveyed 'impressions from a secret source to the effect that Dr. Beneš was holding back'. So 'he intended to keep on putting pressure on Dr. Beneš. If Czech-Sudeten negotiations broke down 'he proposed to have a wise British subject available to slip off quickly to central Europe'. On 29 June, Halifax again encouraged the Cabinet: Henlein 'reported that Herr Hitler would not upset any settlement he might reach nor demand a plebiscite'. In mid-July Halifax worried that time might be running out. He had 'heard disquieting hints to the effect that Germany was working up for a rapid *coup* at the end of August'. As usual 'He felt that the only thing to be done was to continue to maintain pressure on Dr. Beneš.' Chamberlain spoke more cheerfully. He 'uttered a *caveat* against giving too much credence to unchecked reports from non-official sources.' He had seen Henderson 'who gave an account of the attitude of the German government that was not discouraging'.[29]

Then Hitler encouraged him even further by sending to London one of his war-time officers, Captain Wiedemann. He talked to Halifax on 18 July. He suggested that Göring might come to discuss Anglo-German relations – Chamberlain thought, and Halifax agreed, he told the Cabinet, 'that the opportunity of such a visit ought not to be missed'. Moreover Wiedemann, amidst the usual statements of Hitler's eagerness for British friendship, gave 'the most binding assurance' and later repeated 'most emphatically that the German Government was planning no resort to force', and said the German government might give a formal promise 'limited to a definite period'. The Prime Minister, reporting to the Cabinet, left out Wiedemann's provisos of no 'unforeseen and serious incident', and suggested the definite period might be a year. He believed therefore that it was possible that the attitude of the German government to British efforts to break the deadlock in Czechoslovak-Sudeten German negotiations 'might not be unfavourable'. Chamberlain told the House of Commons on 26 July, shortly before Parliament adjourned until 1 November, 'I believe we all feel that the atmosphere is lighter, and that throughout the Continent there is a relaxation of that state of tension which six months ago was present.'[30]

On that occasion Chamberlain told the House of Commons that, 'in response to a request from the Czechoslovak government', an experienced person would go out from Britain to investigate the Sudeten problem 'and endeavour if need be to suggest means for bringing negotiations to success'. It was Lord Runciman, a former Cabinet minister, cold and reserved in manner, rich, from a family of north-east coast ironmasters and shipbuilders, a man who shared Chamberlain's liking for music. Next day, Halifax, recently returned from accompanying King George VI and Queen Elizabeth on their state visit to Paris, a pleasant substitute for an Anglo-French alliance, repeated the news to the Cabinet with more frankness. After consulting the Prime Minister, and considering a list of suitable names, he had suggested a British mediator to break the deadlock he saw in Czechoslovakia.[31] His task, of course, was to tell Beneš what to concede to the Sudeten Germans. His nomination evoked a characteristic comment from Sir Nevile Henderson. 'I do not envy Lord Runciman the difficult and thankless job which he is undertaking. The Czechs are a pig-headed race and Beneš not the least pig-headed among them. And with it all, a master of words and formulae, which sound magnificent but are really empty.' Halifax felt 'slightly disposed to hope that R. may pull it off' but wanted Henderson to keep on trying to 'get into the very stupid heads of the Germans that if they insisted on stepping on the spring, the gun was awfully likely to go off'; the Germans should not believe 'that the danger of British intervention is negligible' if they started a European war.[32]

Runciman, the British government hoped, would help to protract Hitler's 'patience'. They hoped he would produce an agreed settlement in Czechoslovakia before Hitler set about imposing one by force. Ominous signs soon accumulated. From the end of July reports came from the ambassador and the military attaché in Berlin of large-scale military exercises planned for September and, on 3 August, came news of 'a partial test mobilisation in September' affecting seven or eight divisions in Germany proper and all formations in Austria. Henderson wrote personally to Halifax and admitted to being 'extremely perturbed'. Chamberlain had gone on holiday to Scotland but returned to London early in August to secure treatment for severe sinusitis. It turned out, he wrote, to be fortunate 'as things have been very difficult in central Europe and Halifax and I have been able to discuss it and decide on our own policy by conversation instead of by correspondence'.[33]

They faced what became a frequent issue: should they be firm and warn Hitler of dire consequences in case he broke the peace? Henderson wrote that 'we are more likely in my opinion to strengthen the Chancellor's hand against extremists if we show belief in his good faith', warnings, therefore, would make Hitler more dangerous, more inclined to listen to the 'extremists', whom Henderson assumed to be struggling with the 'moderates' for influence over the Führer. On 8 August the Foreign Office suggested the Prime Minister should send a personal letter to Hitler. On 10 August Halifax had a series of conferences with his advisers, including Vansittart, Christie and the British military attaché in Berlin. Meanwhile Chamberlain received a paper from Vansittart whose German informants believed Hitler intended to attack Czechoslovakia between the end of September and mid-October. Vansittart urged that Runciman should before then propose a plebiscite in the Sudeten territories and that Britain should threaten to aid France and Czechoslovakia in case of German attack. In the evening Chamberlain and Halifax decided that Horace Wilson should draft a communication for Hitler. Next morning Halifax and Horace Wilson, together with three Foreign Office officials, discussed his draft; Halifax and Chamberlain worked out a final version and it went to Berlin on 11 August by messenger. It contained a delicately-worded warning: 'a situation might rapidly arise in which it is no exaggeration to say that the peace of every one of the Great Powers of Europe might be endangered.' Hitler was asked 'whether it is really necessary to run such grave and incalculable risks, and, incidentally, to endanger and perhaps even destroy the prospects for a resumption before long of the conversations between our two Governments.' Ribbentrop complained angrily at being bypassed; Hitler did not trouble to reply. Military preparations continued.[34]

More messages disturbed what should have been shooting-and-fishing-time for Halifax and Chamberlain; the latter's recovery from his sinus trouble, however, made him feel 'more able to cope' with the European situation. On 19 August the Prime Minister wrote to Halifax to say he had just read Vansittart's account of a conversation with Ewald von Kleist-Schmenzin, an emissary of the moderates in the German army General Staff. Von Kleist described himself to Vansittart as a conservative, a Prussian and a Christian. He spoke forcefully and clearly. Hitler had decided to invade Czechoslovakia at the end of September. All the German generals opposed the risk of European war but could prevent it only with encouragement and help from abroad. Britain must proclaim its determination to resist German aggression. Von Kleist contradicted the notion that 'extremists' and 'moderates' were struggling for influence over Hitler. Vansittart quoted his words: 'There is only one real extremist and that is Hitler himself. He is the great danger and he is doing this entirely on his own.' Chamberlain received Vansittart's record just before leaving Downing Street to spend the weekend at Chequers and took it with him 'to think over it'. That same morning, General Lord Hutchison asked to see him and told the Prime Minister of his contacts with Germans, especially one acquainted with 'various generals'. His information ran counter to Kleist's. It suggested that Hitler had not yet made up his mind for war and if he were to be stopped from deciding on war the British should 'approach him and come to some understanding with him forthwith'.[35]

Thus Chamberlain took to Chequers the dilemma of British policy: should Britain threaten Hitler or negotiate with him? A decision was urgent. That evening the Prime Minister wrote to Halifax, who had gone to his country house in Yorkshire. Chamberlain inclined to the Hutchison view. Chamberlain thought von Kleist exaggerated the strength of German opposition to Hitler: 'he reminds me of the Jacobites at the court of France in King William's time and I think we must discount a good deal of what he says'. Nevertheless Chamberlain wrote 'I confess to some feeling of uneasiness and I don't feel sure that we ought not to do something.' Halifax replied on Sunday that he intended to renounce grouse-shooting for the moment and return to London on Tuesday. Very hesitantly, he, too, thought something should perhaps be done, though not 'a commitment' and only something capable of 'the most innocent interpretation, to keep H. guessing and strengthen the hand of his generals – if that sort of thing is really true'. He agreed to summon Henderson to London; the ambassador came to London on Sunday 28 August for three days. On Friday Halifax returned to Yorkshire, having arranged to see Henderson on Monday morning in London and to bring him over to 10 Downing Street in the afternoon together with Sir John Simon. Cabinet ministers were asked to break their holidays to come to Downing Street for a meeting on Tuesday 30 August to consider and ratify the continued British refusal to promise to fight Germany in case of a German invasion of Czechoslovakia.[36]

Before this meeting of ministers Chamberlain meditated about the continued failure of Runciman, in spite of his intermittent bursts of hopefulness, to obtain an agreement between the Czechoslovak government and the Sudeten Germans. In the absence of such an agreement, Hitler, it seemed, would soon use force to settle the issue; he was expected to announce his decision during the Nuremberg party rally in a speech on 12 September. Should Hitler be threatened or placated? If placated, how? Late in August efforts were made to persuade Runciman to ask for a meeting with Hitler. Runciman refused, objecting either to the task of inducing Hitler to accept his own conclusions as 'impartial mediator' or to that of listening to Hitler's solutions and passing them on to Beneš. A day or two before the Cabinet meeting on 30 August Chamberlain had a new idea. He would go to see Hitler himself. According to Horace Wilson's account, written a few years later, he and Chamberlain 'talked over the situation' late one night in the Prime Minister's study at No. 10 and 'came to the conclusion that there was one more step that might be taken when the Runciman breakdown became inevitable, namely that the Prime Minister should propose a personal meeting between himself and Hitler'.

By the time Cabinet ministers met on 30 August, only Halifax and Simon had been told. Chamberlain wrote that his 'unconventional and daring' idea 'rather took Halifax's breath away ... though I hope all the time that it won't be necessary to try it'.[37]

8 Munich

Eighteen ministers, nearly the complete Cabinet, met at Downing Street in the morning of 30 August 1938. Nevile Henderson joined them, at Mr Chamberlain's suggestion. Edward Bridges, now with several months' experience in the post of Cabinet Secretary in succession to Hankey, made his usual full record of their discussion. They debated once again the main issue in British foreign policy: how to prevent a war with Germany. One possibility was to threaten that Britain would go to war to oppose German aggression and so deter Hitler. The other was to try peacefully to solve German grievances by discussion to make it unnecessary for Hitler to go to war. In theory British policy was to do both. In practice, however, a choice had to be made. To threaten Hitler might make negotiation more difficult. To negotiate with Hitler would discourage possible anti-German allies and encourage other enemies to add their own demands to Hitler's.

Halifax first set out the evidence and concluded that if Hitler had decided on war, 'the only deterrent which would be likely to be effective would be an announcement that if Germany invaded Czechoslovakia we should declare war upon her. He thought that this might well prove an effective deterrent.' He then argued against it. Public opinion in Britain and the Empire would be divided. It would be difficult to carry out such a threat. In war Czechoslovakia could not be defended and would not be re-created as it was at the end even of a victorious war. If it were argued that it was a question of curbing the dictators he 'asked himself whether it was justifiable to fight a certain war now in order to forestall a possible war later'. In fact, Halifax, having suggested a deterrent, then argued on the assumption that the deterrent would fail to deter. Chamberlain did the same. According to the record, he told the ministers: 'Many people in this country and in Germany took the view that if we made it clear now that, if Germany used force, we should come in on the side of

Czechoslovakia, there would be no war. Many people of this way of thinking also thought that such a statement would probably be followed by revolution which would upset Herr Hitler.' He then proceeded to explain the disadvantages of going to war. He concluded by suggesting that even if Hitler were deterred from war, this apparent success for British policy might produce in Hitler 'a feeling of being thwarted' and therefore make him even more dangerous: evidently Chamberlain did not take seriously the prospect of Hitler's overthrow. Henderson supported the argument that a threat would make Hitler more difficult and, therefore, in the end make war more likely: it 'would strengthen the position of the extremists rather than the moderates'. Chamberlain asked every minister present to express his opinion and then summed up: 'The Cabinet was unanimous in the view that we should not utter a threat to Herr Hitler that if he went into Czechoslovakia we should declare war upon him.'

This meeting typifies the workings of the Cabinet in the months when Chamberlain's power was at its height. Before a Cabinet met the Prime Minister discussed the issues with Halifax and often with his two senior colleagues, Simon, Chancellor of the Exchequer, and Hoare, Home Secretary, both former Foreign Secretaries. The other senior member of the Cabinet, the Lord Chancellor, counted much less, but Lord Chancellor Maugham, as the most isolationist in the Cabinet, could be relied on to back proposals for restraint. Simon knew how to support a case, and once his mind had been made up for him, contributed skilled advocacy. Hoare usually expressed some doubts before coming down in support of Halifax and Chamberlain. Chamberlain was an authoritarian, directing, head of government. Yet he dominated, so long as he could, with the consent of the Cabinet, after long debates, not by circumventing it. On this occasion the 'weaker brethren', as Chamberlain privately named those who disagreed with him, raised only tentative difficulties. Together with Duff Cooper, the First Lord of the Admiralty, 'Buck' de la Warr, the Lord Privy Seal, Walter Elliot, Minister of Health, and Lord Winterton, the Chancellor of the Duchy, expressed doubt. Earl de la Warr became a political anomaly as a hereditary peer who supported Labour, when he entered the Lords as a young man. However, he followed MacDonald into the 'National' government of 1931, where, with the rest of his small group, his political position rested on Tory tolerance. Walter Elliot, a qualified doctor from Glasgow University, was a popular and moderate conservative, respected and trusted in Scotland, although prosaic and prosy. Eddie Winterton, an erratic, irascible, very tall, landowner, farmer and foxhunter, who had hunted with more than forty packs, had done badly in 1938 as the spokesman for the Air Ministry in the Commons (he was an Irish peer). Chamberlain brought him into his government, and kept him, perhaps because of his early association with Joseph Chamberlain. They, and probably other members of the Cabinet, seem to have been inhibited by the way the question was put: Chamberlain insisted that there was no need to decide what would be done if France went to war with Germany until it actually happened. Chamberlain said that the immediate issue was whether directly to promise help to Czechoslovakia in case of German attack. That put the prospect of intervention in a less attractive way from the point of view of the British Cabinet than a pledge to France would have been. The ministers who expressed unease made no stronger demand than that, as Duff Cooper put it, 'we ought to show that we were thinking of the possibilities of using force'. The Prime Minister successfully smothered this point in his summing up in which he said 'he thought it was very important not to exacerbate feeling in Berlin against us', and this thought was included in the formal Cabinet conclusions.[1] Moreover the Cabinet obviously still believed it possible, even probable, that the Sudeten Germans and the Czechoslovak government would reach agreement, provided Beneš were willing.

Chamberlain did not tell the assembled ministers of his plan to see Hitler to settle the Czechoslovakian problem in case Runciman failed to win an agreement between the Sudetens and Beneš and a German attack seemed likely. The Prime Minister went to Balmoral and informed King George VI who, according to Horace Wilson, gave his 'cordial concurrence' to his plan. Back in London, after a brief stay in Forfarshire, from which he was summoned back by Wilson on 6 September, he told Vansittart who 'fought the idea tooth and nail' and talked of 'Henry IV going to Canossa', Samuel Hoare, the Home

Secretary, Kingsley Wood, the Secretary for Air, and Tom Inskip, the Minister for Co-ordination of Defence. When the full Cabinet next met on 12 September, Chamberlain continued to keep his secret: Inskip remarked that Horace Wilson told him to be careful not to mention it 'either in or out of the Cabinet'.[2]

During the first days of September 1938, Halifax and Chamberlain waited tensely for Hitler's Nuremberg speech due on the 12th. Unless a Czech-German settlement was made by then, they supposed, Hitler would proclaim the need to invade Czechoslovakia. They arranged to bully Beneš but worried about whether or not to warn Hitler of the possibility of war with Britain. Repeated discussions between Chamberlain, Wilson, Halifax, Vansittart and Cadogan, back from a month in Le Touquet away from the Foreign Office telegrams, found Chamberlain still hostile to a warning and inclined to rely on his own proposed airborne descent on Hitler. Halifax, however, became 'unsettled', as the Prime Minister put it, perhaps under the influence of Vansittart, and insisted on working out a note of warning to Hitler, which was despatched on Friday 9 September by telephone to Berlin and then taken overnight by an embassy secretary to Henderson in Nuremberg. At once Henderson wrote to Wilson in his increasingly overwrought style: 'The form of Hitler's genius is on the borderline of madness ... an official démarche will drive him to greater violence or greater menaces.' Then Henderson sent back two more messages to Berlin which were telephoned from the British embassy to London, one for Cadogan, one for Halifax. They made the same point, a warning would 'drive Herr Hitler straight off the deep end' and be 'likely to be fatal to prospects of peace'. The first message came by air, after Cadogan had arranged for an aircraft to leave London to pick up the messenger in Cologne. In consequence Chamberlain, supported by Simon and Hoare, overruled Halifax, who was compelled to send a message, which was telephoned direct to Nuremberg that Henderson need not 'convey ... what you were instructed to say'.[3] The meeting of the Cabinet on 12 September again agreed not to issue a formal warning to Hitler; only Duff Cooper objected to reliance on Sir Nevile Henderson's advice against such a warning.[4]

In the first week of September Beneš, at last, won Runciman's approval by accepting virtually the whole of Henlein's original demands. The Sudeten German party promptly broke off negotiations, on 7 September, on the excuse of an incident at Moravská Ostrava (Mährisch Ostrau) where Sudeten Germans had set off a riot. Hitler spoke at Nuremberg on 12 September. He denounced Beneš and the Czechs and uttered vague but alarming threats of intervention in case of further incidents. Fresh outbreaks of rioting in the Sudeten areas followed the speech. On 13 September the Prague government declared martial law in some parts of the Sudetenland. From Paris, Phipps, the British ambassador, reported at midday that Bonnet felt 'that the whole question of peace or war may now be only a matter of minutes instead of days'. From Berlin Henderson insisted that Hitler was about to attack, 'failing immediate grant of autonomy to Sudetens'. He recommended the 'severest' pressure on Beneš to stop him continuing 'to haggle'. By early evening Bonnet was 'very upset' and wanted peace at any price. Daladier suggested a conference of Germany, France and Great Britain to secure peace.[5]

Chamberlain, of course, did not want the French to spoil his masterstroke. At 10 p.m. Chamberlain, Halifax, Cadogan and Horace Wilson agreed to launch 'Z'. Horace Wilson consulted Simon, 'do you think it would be well to summon the Cabinet before doing this?' Simon did *not* think it necessary and noted that Hoare agreed. Later that evening, therefore, the signal, drafted by Chamberlain himself, went by telephone to Berlin to be delivered to Hitler. 'I propose to come over at once to see you with a view to try to find a peaceful solution. I propose to come across by air and am ready to start tomorrow.' No one told Daladier or Bonnet. Daladier's suggestion of a conference of Britain, France and Germany evoked the reply that the Prime Minister was exploring another possibility. It was only after Hitler's answer had arrived, agreeing to meet Chamberlain, that Phipps was instructed to inform the French government. According to Phipps, Daladier 'did not look very pleased' and went on to say that he had refused suggestions that he himself should meet Hitler 'as he had felt a representative of Great Britain should be present'. Bonnet, on the other hand, demonstrated unmitigated delight. He had two reasons for satisfaction: Chamberlain's action postponed the risk that France might have to honour its commitments to Czechoslovakia and further entangled the British in grappling with the problem of Nazi Germany.[6]

The British Cabinet met at 11 a.m. on Wednesday 14 September. The majority of ministers now heard for the first time of Chamberlain's theatrical gesture. None protested. The Cabinet heard Chamberlain justify it by the panic shown by Daladier and Bonnet after Henlein had broken off negotiations with the government in Prague and then ministers settled down to discuss Chamberlain's proposals for his talk with Hitler. He would accept a plebiscite, at least in the predominantly German areas of Czechoslovakia. Everyone knew that that almost certainly meant eventual transfer of territory to Germany, though it was remotely possible that, given time, a constitutionally remodelled Czechoslovakia might make itself acceptable to a sufficient number of its German citizens to survive intact. Secondly the Prime Minister explained that Czechoslovakia, left defenceless by the loss of its frontier districts, might have to be given an international guarantee in which Britain should join. It is evident that Chamberlain already took for granted an early transfer of territory. The Cabinet did not discuss the suggested guarantee but concentrated on the question of the plebiscite. Ministers thought a plebiscite acceptable only if carefully prepared, well-conducted and delayed. Simon hoped for a period of autonomy to precede any plebiscite. Oliver Stanley, according to the record, wanted to insist on delay: 'immediate acceptance of a plebiscite would give Herr Hitler everything which he was now demanding by force and would be a complete surrender. In his view no government which proposed such a suggestion would stand for long. Nor would it deserve to.' De la Warr agreed. Winterton and Hailsham, whose son Quintin Hogg, fighting a by-election in Oxford, evidently conveyed the hostility forcibly expressed there towards sacrificing Czechoslovakia, opposed a plebiscite altogether. Duff Cooper insisted that war with Germany was inevitable, yet, oddly, approved Chamberlain's proposed visit to Hitler. In the end Simon proposed, and the Cabinet agreed, that Chamberlain should 'confer' with Hitler 'on the general lines indicated in the discussion'. The government, therefore, this meeting shows, would agree to the dismemberment of Czechoslovakia but wished it to take place in a slow and orderly fashion.[7]

Neville Chamberlain flew to Munich, with Horace Wilson and Strang from the Foreign Office, early on 15 September. Thence he continued by special train to Berchtesgaden where the Führer received him at his mountain retreat in the Obersalzberg. Chamberlain planned high drama. He succeeded. For two weeks to come he took the lead on the diplomatic stage. The French embassies in London and Berlin sourly pictured the journey as a humiliation. François-Poncet, the French ambassador in Berlin, commented that 'the fact that the head of the greatest empire in the world should have asked for an audience of the Chancellor of the Reich and agreed to go in person, not even to the German capital, but as far as Berchtesgaden, is considered by Hitler himself, his entourage and by German opinion as an immense success'. So it was, yet Chamberlain's personal dignity and, above all, the nature of his mission, to demand peace from the head of the most ferociously warlike state in the world, caused many, even of those who thought his adventure replete with folly, to recognise a certain nobility in the first flight of the grey, 69-year-old statesman.[8]

Hitler met him on the steps of his house. 'He looks entirely undistinguished', Chamberlain wrote to his sister, but the Führer won a friend. 'I heard from Hitler himself and it was confirmed by others who were with him that he was struck all of a heap' (by Chamberlain's proposal to visit him) 'and exclaimed "I can't possibly let a man of his age come all this way" ... it shows a side of Hitler that would surprise many people in this country.' Hitler played on Chamberlain's vanity. 'H.W. heard from various people who were with Hitler after my interview that he had been very favourably impressed. I have had a conversation with a *man*, he said, and one with whom I can do business and he liked the rapidity with which I had grasped the essentials. In short I had established a certain confidence, which was my aim, and in spite of the hardness and ruthlessness I thought I saw in his face I got the impression that here was a man who could be relied upon when he had given his word.'

Chamberlain came back well satisfied, then, although the

content of his conversation with Hitler differed from what he had hoped. He attempted to begin a discussion on Anglo-German relations and peace; Hitler demanded instead an 'instant solution' to the Sudeten problem, complaining that 300 Sudeten Germans had been killed and many more injured. As for most of his visitors, Hitler then launched a historical diatribe, 'a long account of what he had done' as Chamberlain put it. Eventually Chamberlain put to Hitler his own theory of Hitler's objects – that Hitler wanted the Sudeten Germans in Germany, not Czechs, and that he wished to destroy the treaty relations between Czechoslovakia and the USSR, and Hitler assented. Hitler, however, then got down to 'realities': 'the thing has got to be settled at once. I am determined to settle it. I do not care whether there is a world war or not. I have determined to settle it and to settle it soon and I am prepared to risk a world war rather than allow this to drag on.' Chamberlain then asked Hitler why he had let him come to Germany at all if he was not ready to negotiate and extracted a specific demand from Hitler: 'if the British government were prepared to accept the idea of secession in principle and to say so, there might be a chance then to have a talk.' The Prime Minister closed on this. He had nothing against the transfer of Czech territory, he told Hitler, but he would have to consult his colleagues, the French government and Lord Runciman (he did not mention the Czechoslovak government) and he and Hitler should meet again. The communiqué announced that 'in the course of a few days a further conversation will take place'.[9]

Chamberlain returned to London on Friday 16 September and at 6.30 p.m. met the now habitual group of ministers, becoming known as 'the inner Cabinet', Simon, Hoare and Halifax, in a meeting where, as usual, Vansittart, Cadogan and Horace Wilson were also present. Runciman, just returned from Prague, joined them and explained how he had told Dr Beneš that if he had been less dilatory 'he would not now be in his present fix'. The Prime Minister reported that Hitler wanted immediate self-determination. Mr Chamberlain thought it wrong to go to war to prevent it. Next morning he and Runciman made the same points to an emergency Saturday meeting of the full Cabinet. Runciman showed himself disillusioned about Henlein. He said that the Sudeten Germans and the Czechoslovak government had come very close two weeks earlier 'but at that time he had not fully realised the close connection between the Sudeten German leaders and Berlin'. Just the same 'the Czechs were, in fact, themselves responsible for most of the trouble'. The Prime Minister followed. He 'had formed the impression that Herr Hitler's objectives were strictly limited'; he thought Hitler was telling the truth when he said he only wanted a solution of the Sudeten problem. The Cabinet adjourned at 1.30 p.m. and met again at 3. Halifax sent off a belated invitation to Daladier and Bonnet to come to London immediately. The Cabinet gave Chamberlain no difficulty. Stanley, Elliot and Winterton wanted time to think about immediate self-determination for the Sudeten Germans but kept quiet thereafter except to insist that the principle should be applied in an orderly way. Duff Cooper feared in the morning that 'we might be led into a complete surrender' but after lunch thought it best to avoid war now because something might later occur to upset the rule of the Nazi Party. After lunch the Cabinet considered the possibility of guaranteeing the new frontiers of Czechoslovakia. No one objected. British involvement grew apace. The Prime Minister had in effect made the British the arbiters of what the Germans would be permitted to impose on Czechoslovakia; now the Cabinet acquiesced in the principle of setting a limit to German actions beyond which Britain would go to war. These tendencies did not, as yet, reach fruition. But the interfering, potentially belligerent, qualities of British 'appeasement' were increasingly evident. Peace, however, was in Chamberlain's mind and another hard but successful day ended with an encouraging telegram from Henderson. Göring had spoken 'in a very admiring and respectful manner' of Chamberlain. 'His language was undoubtedly based on impression created on Herr Hitler.'[10]

Next day, Sunday, Daladier and Bonnet, accompanied by Léger, Rochat and Jules Henry flew to England; Chamberlain went to Croydon to meet them, to begin an even harder day. Formal talks began at Downing Street at 11 a.m. Chamberlain told his story again and Daladier set out a series of reasons for resistance to Hitler's demands. At 2.45 the British 'inner Cabinet' met and agreed to a guarantee and to transfer territory without a plebiscite, since the French disliked plebiscites. After the lunch interval, Daladier, in spite of his earlier remarks, agreed to the cession of Czechoslovak territory provided Britain joined in guaranteeing what was left. At 5 p.m. the British left, pretending they were going to discuss the guarantee, thus emphasising to the French the generosity of British acceptance, and, in fact, drafted a communication to Beneš to bully him into acceptance of the cession to Germany of those parts of Czechoslovakia where more than half the inhabitants were German. At 7.30 Chamberlain gave this draft to the French to consider over dinner. He pointed out that it incorporated a guarantee in which the British would join. The conference met again at 10.30 p.m. Daladier agreed to Chamberlain's suggestion that the Anglo-French proposals should be sent at once to Prague and that the agreement of the British and French Cabinets to their delivery to the Czechoslovak government should be secured next morning. The meeting ended soon after midnight.

On Monday the full Cabinet met again and Chamberlain explained that a British guarantee of Czechoslovakia had been offered to the French the day before. All was going well for the Prime Minister. Even the Labour Opposition, he told the Cabinet, had begun to soften its attacks after he had explained to Citrine, Dalton and Morrison, representing the National Council of Labour – the joint Party–TUC committee – the ambiguous conduct of the French and the lack of clarity on the part of the USSR in explaining how it would carry out its pledge to help France in defending Czechoslovakia. The Cabinet agreed without hesitation to the Anglo-French plan. Duff Cooper, in unusually pacific mood, thought 'the prospect of war so appalling that he agreed that postponement of the evil day was the right course'. Winterton even expressed 'great satisfaction that there had been no disagreement in the Cabinet in regard to the action to be taken during the present crisis', though there was perhaps a difference in opinion about Germany's ultimate aims and Duff Cooper thought the difference 'one of emphasis only'. Chamberlain, therefore, as it seemed, had overwhelming British support for his solution of the Czechoslovak-Sudeten German dispute. The assent of the French government came at the end of the Cabinet meeting.[11]

Now, apparently, only the Czechoslovak government remained. It needed intense bullying to win Czechoslovak agreement. The British and French ministers in Prague formally delivered the Anglo-French plan to Beneš at 2 p.m. on 19 September. Before then the German government was told that Chamberlain expected to have the Czech reply that day and hoped to come to Germany again on 21 September to discuss it with Hitler, whose patience must not be tried too far. He did not meet his deadline: it took two days to force Czechoslovak acceptance. The French told the Czechs they would not honour their pledge to help Czechoslovakia if a German attack followed Czech refusal of the Anglo-French terms. Their justification was that their help would be ineffective without British support. The British and French ministers in Prague combined to make clear that Britain would not support France if France helped Czechoslovakia. The Czechoslovak government rejected this pressure to cede the frontier regions. At the same time, however, the British and French ministers reported that Beneš and his ministers would give way to a clear and final declaration that Britain and France would abandon Czechoslovakia to its fate if the Anglo-French proposals for cession of the Sudetenland were rejected. Perhaps the Czechs hoped that British and French opinion might, at the last moment, compel their governments to change their course or even bring about their fall. Perhaps, after all, Britain and France might threaten Germany and enable Czechoslovakia to limit or prevent loss of territory. Half an hour after midnight, 20/21 September, Bonnet telephoned to the French legation in Prague refusing French aid since the Czech government's action would break Franco-British solidarity and so 'remove all practical effect from French assistance' and at 1.20 a.m. Cadogan told the British minister to join the French minister in telling the Czechs to expect 'immediate German invasion ... a situation for which we could take no responsibility' and to act immediately 'at whatever hour'. Shortly after 2 a.m. the British and French ministers confronted Beneš, and stayed with him until nearly 4 a.m. Even so the Czech government continued to show hesitation after daybreak, and the British and French promptly repeated their nocturnal warnings in writing. At 5 p.m. on 21 September the Czech Foreign Minister conveyed

Czechoslovakian acceptance to the British and French ministers.[12]

Next morning Chamberlain flew to Germany to meet Hitler at Godesberg, on the Rhine, just south of Bonn: 'European peace is what I am aiming at, and I hope this journey may open the way to get it.' That afternoon, 22 September, Chamberlain suggested to Hitler an international commission to work out new frontiers for Czechoslovakia on the basis of self-determination for the German inhabitants. With a perfunctory apology, Hitler rejected Chamberlain's hard-won concessions. For Hitler no delay was possible. 'A solution must be found one way or another, either by agreement or by force ... the problem must be settled definitely and completely by the 1st of October.' He swept aside Chamberlain's suggestions for orderly and peaceful change. Once again, as at Berchtesgaden, the Prime Minister found that Hitler intended immediate war rather than calm consideration of the means to secure permanent peace. Hitler announced that German troops would start to invade Czechoslovakia and occupy the Sudetenland on 28 September. Chamberlain spoke frankly: 'He had induced his colleagues, the French and the Czechs, to agree to the principle of self-determination, in fact he had got exactly what the Führer wanted and without the expenditure of a drop of German blood. In doing so, he had been obliged to take his political life into his hands ... he was accused of selling the Czechs, yielding to dictators, capitulating, and so on. He had actually been booed on his departure today.'[13]

Chamberlain telephoned to Halifax that evening and told him that 'his interview with Hitler had been most unsatisfactory'. Hitler's demands 'would not do'. Yet the letter Chamberlain sent to Hitler next morning was amenable and conciliatory. Moreover Chamberlain and Horace Wilson tried to restrain the combativeness provoked in London by Hitler's bullying. Friday saw an exchange of letters, sent across the Rhine, between Chamberlain and Hitler and ended with a second conversation between them. The Prime Minister endeavoured unsuccessfully to persuade Hitler to soften his demands. The Führer substituted the word 'proposals' for 'demands' and insisted that the document setting out his wishes was a 'memorandum' and not an 'ultimatum' but changed nothing apart from stipulating

1 October rather than 28 September for the German occupation of the Sudetenland. However, Chamberlain and Horace
Wilson tried to stop the Czechs mobilising (that is they tried to
prevent the withdrawal of the existing British and French
advice to Prague not to mobilise). Wilson noted that the Foreign Office telegram reporting the decision taken by ministers in
London to permit Czechoslovak mobilisation 'spoilt our lunch'.
Until then Wilson seems to have been in relaxed mood. He
telephoned Downing Street about 11.30 a.m. to explain that
two coded telegrams were on their way from Godesberg, the
first of which, Wilson explained, presumably referring to
Simon, Hoare, Halifax and their advisers, would 'enable the
boys to go on playing marbles'. That day, Friday 23 September,
Chamberlain, communing with Horace Wilson, had to decide
between two courses of action. He could reject Hitler's demands and threaten war if Hitler attempted to enforce them or
he could take Hitler's 'memorandum' back to London and try
to persuade his British colleagues, the French government and
the Czechs to accept the Führer's new demands.[14]

The meeting with Chamberlain, when Hitler presented his
'memorandum', began about 11 p.m. on Friday. It ended after
midnight, at about 1.45 a.m. on Saturday 24 September. Before departing Chamberlain expressed, according to the German record, 'the feeling that a relationship of confidence had
grown up between himself and the Führer as a result of the
conversations of the last few days ... he did not cease to hope
that the present difficult crisis would be overcome, and then he
would be glad to discuss other problems still outstanding with
the Führer in the same spirit,' Hitler said 'he had similar hopes
... the Czech problem was the last territorial demand which he
had to make in Europe'. Chamberlain 'took his leave with a
hearty "auf Wiedersehen"'. His mind was made up; he would
not accept the failure of his policy, of working for peace with
Hitler, a policy now irrevocably linked with his name and
person: Chamberlain flew back to London in time to have
lunch with Halifax. In the afternoon he reported to the group
of ministers and officials, the 'inner Cabinet', that met repeatedly in September to manage the crisis. He advocated the
acceptance of Hitler's Godesberg memorandum. He spoke with
eloquence. What were Hitler's aims? 'The Prime Minister was

satisfied that Herr Hitler was speaking the truth when he said he regarded the question as a racial question': Hitler's objects were limited to the incorporation of Sudeten Germans in the Reich. Chamberlain told the committee – Simon, Hoare and Halifax with Vansittart, Horace Wilson, Cadogan and Strang present – that he had acquired some degree of personal influence over Hitler. There was no dissent.[15]

The full Cabinet met at 5.30 p.m. Mr Chamberlain again reported his meetings with Hitler at Godesberg and offered his conclusions.

Herr Hitler had a narrow mind and was violently prejudiced on certain subjects; but he would not deliberately deceive a man whom he respected and with whom he had been in negotiation, and he was sure that Herr Hitler now felt some respect for him ... The Prime Minister was sure that Herr Hitler was extremely anxious to secure the friendship of Great Britain. The crucial question was whether Herr Hitler was speaking the truth when he said that he regarded the Sudeten question as a racial question which must be settled, and that the object of his policy was racial unity and not the domination of Europe. Much depends on the answer to this question. The Prime Minister believed that Herr Hitler was speaking the truth ... The Prime Minister said that he thought it would be a great tragedy if we lost this opportunity of reaching an understanding with Germany on all points of difference between the two countries. A peaceful settlement of Europe depended on an Anglo-German understanding. He thought that he had now established an influence over Herr Hitler, and that the latter trusted him and was willing to work with him. If this was so, it was a wonderful opportunity to put an end to the horrible nightmare of the present armament race. That seemed to him to be the big thing in the present issue.

In any case, switching to a different line of argument, Mr Chamberlain insisted that this was not a good time to risk a war since defence against German bombing would become more effective in the future. The Cabinet adjourned at 7.30 p.m. and agreed to meet again next morning, Sunday 25 September, at

10.30 a.m. The French were urged to come over for discussion on Sunday afternoon and Daladier and Bonnet agreed to be in London by 5 p.m.[16]

That evening marked the limit of Chamberlainite 'appeasement' in British policy. Practically everyone involved in deciding policy and, it seems, most British opinion, apart from a few isolationists or pacifists, supported a policy of combining coercion and conciliation. Britain should seek peaceful change but simultaneously build up military strength to help in negotiating peace and to deter German aggression. Disputes came over the correct balance between concession and containment. How far should Hitler's Germany be placated by peaceful change, how far intimidated by British force or that of British allies? During the Godesberg meetings, Mr Chamberlain's position became less representative than it had been of British views on the correct balance between force and reasonableness in dealings with the Third Reich. Halifax warned Chamberlain at Godesberg by telephone that the 'great mass of public opinion seems to be hardening in sense of feeling that we have gone to limit of concession'. That Czech surrender to the Anglo-French plan led only to more strident German bullying at Godesberg provoked resentment and suspicions in Britain. The German embassy in London reported to Berlin that 'if we digressed from our present policy of wiping out the consequences of the sins of Versailles, and instead advocated imperialist ideas, we must reckon with the fact that the British nation as a whole will be ready to go to war against Germany'.[17] On Sunday 25 September the British Cabinet overrode Chamberlain's desire to persuade the French and the Czechs to accept Hitler's Godesberg terms.

The Prime Minister defended the Godesberg 'memorandum': its essential feature, immediate German military occupation of the Sudeten area, was to make sure that the Czechs had no time to make it 'a desert'. No goods or cattle might be removed before German troops arrived but what happened after the occupation 'was another matter which would be dealt with by the proposed German-Czech commission'. Sir Samuel Hoare expressed doubt: 'it would be a tremendous responsibility to advise the Czechoslovak Government to accept Herr Hitler's terms'. Then Halifax spoke. His hesitant conclusions transformed British foreign policy. From now on the Prime Minister had to reckon with a potentially dissenting voice in the Cabinet which he could not override or ignore. Halifax held a political position of unique strength. He was thought to stand for a high-minded, Christian, conservatism. Most politicians respected him, few disliked him. Unlike the Prime Minister he minimised disagreement and habitually claimed to agree with much of what his interlocutors put forward. His manner, his skill in field sports, his frequently expressed love of rural pursuits, made him seem, in everything except his high intellectual ability, a pure specimen of the English aristocracy, and he spoke with the voice of conscience. In every way he inspired confidence among the deferentially inclined Conservatives of the 1930s. Chamberlain must have known that he could not treat dissent from Halifax in the way that he had dealt with Eden's hesitations.

The Cabinet secretary recorded Halifax's tentative and reluctant disagreement with the Prime Minister. He told the Cabinet 'that he found his position changing somewhat in the last day or so, and even now he was not too certain of his view'. Cadogan had spoken to him late the previous evening and argued that Hitler had gone too far. Now Halifax thought Hitler 'was dictating terms, just as though he had won a war . . . he did not feel that it would be right to put pressure on Czechoslovakia to accept. We should lay the case before them. If they rejected it he imagined France would join in, and if France went in we should join with them.' Halifax thus found himself preferring the risk of war to acceptance of the Godesberg memorandum. Though he qualified his remarks 'he did not put this forward as a final conclusion, but his reflection through the night had provisionally led him to think that the present proposals involved a difference in principle [from the Anglo-French plan] and that pointed tentatively to the conclusion that it would be very difficult to put any pressure on Czechoslovakia.' This was a direct challenge to the Prime Minister. Chamberlain, taken aback by this overnight transformation, protested sadly in a note to Halifax 'your complete change of view since I saw you last night is a horrible blow to me, but of course you must form your opinions for yourself. It remains to be seen what the French say.' His note continued, 'If they say that they will go in, thereby dragging us in I do not think I could accept responsibility for the decision.'[18] The Prime Minister began to hope, on the other hand, that French reluctance to risk war would curb the discouragingly bellicose members of his Cabinet.

Later that day he tried to get Daladier to say that the French government would not or could not do anything to help Czechoslovakia when Hitler attacked. A telegram from Phipps, the British ambassador to Paris, which the Prime Minister had read to the Cabinet the previous evening, must have strengthened his confidence in French readiness to accept Hitler's Godesberg terms and so to help him to recover control of his restless Cabinet. To the surprise of senior officials in the Foreign Office, Phipps asserted that the British 'should realise the extreme danger of even appearing to encourage small, but noisy and corrupt, war group here. All that is best in France is against war, almost at any price.'

The Cabinet continued its discussions late into Sunday afternoon; several ministers suggested immediate Anglo-French military discussions to which Russian representatives should be invited. At about 5 p.m. Masaryk, the Czech minister, gave Chamberlain and Halifax a letter rejecting, with passion, the Godesberg terms. Daladier and Bonnet, with the French ambassador and four officials, met the 'inner Cabinet' together with Vansittart, Wilson and Cadogan and three officials at Downing Street at 9.25 p.m. on this crowded day. The French leaders came from a council of ministers in Paris that afternoon which had determined to reject the memorandum. Chamberlain countered with a sympathetic exegesis of Hitler's demands which, on his account, were merely arrangements for the effective preservation of law and order in the Sudetenland. He then proceeded to ask a series of questions on what the French intended to do if Germany invaded Czechoslovakia. Then Sir John Simon took up this cross-examination of Daladier. Both failed to shake Daladier from insistence 'that each of us would have to do his duty', 'each of us would do what was incumbent on him', 'that he would not return to France having agreed to the strangulation of a people'. At 11.40 p.m. the Anglo-French meeting adjourned, having agreed that General Gamelin, the French chief of defence staff, should come to London next morning to explain French military intentions. The British ministers then returned to the third meeting of the Cabinet that Sunday, a midnight meeting. Chamberlain tried, but failed, to persuade the Cabinet that Daladier and Bonnet had exhibited complete indecision. Their statements of their military plans, he said, had been 'evasive' and he thought it 'significant' that they had 'never once ... put the question "if we go to war with Germany will you come in, too?"' The Cabinet, however, showed no sign of changing its earlier view and, indeed, Halifax came near to contradicting the Prime Minister's account of the French attitude.[19] Now only a minority of the Cabinet definitely supported Chamberlain. Open disagreement came from Elliot, Duff Cooper, de la Warr, Winterton, Hailsham, Hore-Belisha and Oliver Stanley. Stanley, younger son of Lord Derby, had all the wit and charm of his family, was well-liked and admired in the Conservative Party and at dinner parties, and he shared the family influence in north-west England. Chamberlain could not survive the resignations of many such colleagues.

Chamberlain then put a new suggestion. In spite of the intense strain of the last few days his mind worked with its usual lucid concentration in pursuit of the object which he had persuaded himself was within reach: a peaceful settlement of the Czechoslovakian issue followed by an Anglo-German understanding which would secure the independence of Britain and the British Empire by voluntarily accepted restrictions on Germany's armed striking power. His most trusted collaborator, Sir Horace Wilson, should fly to Berlin. There he was to present a letter from Chamberlain containing an appeal to Hitler to help Chamberlain by making some concession in the demands he had made at Godesberg. The letter would suggest a commission, with German and Czech members and a British representative, to find ways for orderly transfer of Czech territory to Germany. If this written appeal failed, Wilson should orally warn Hitler that a German invasion of Czechoslovakia, if followed by active measures taken by the French in support of Czechoslovakia, would bring Britain into war with Germany. Chamberlain believed that it was the appeal, rather than the warning, that could prevent the impending war; probably the warning was included in Wilson's instructions only to secure the agreement of the Cabinet, and of the French, to his mission. For the moment it reunited the Cabinet. At the time, Duff Cooper recorded, 'I could hardly believe my ears. It was after all a complete reversal of what he himself had advised us to do the day before.' He missed the significance of the Prime Minister's response to his own suggestion that the warning should accompany the appeal. 'To do so would rule out all chance of acceptance of the appeal', Chamberlain replied, and later he repeated that 'he did not propose that anything should be included in his letter to Herr Hitler which looked like a threat. Anything in the form of a threat would destroy any chance of acceptance of the appeal'. Chamberlain believed that conciliation rather than coercion would make Hitler peaceful. This balance of emphasis between persuasion and threat made him a member of a minority in his own Cabinet and forced him to manoeuvre to put his convictions into effect. Later that day Henderson telephoned to the German foreign ministry in Berlin, 'not acting on instructions', he claimed, 'but from his own personal knowledge, that Chamberlain's position and policy were threatened by increasing difficulties', a point that must have been made to him by Horace Wilson who had telephoned to ask Henderson to tell the Germans that they should disregard any statements on the crisis not emanating from Chamberlain himself.[20] Thus Wilson attempted to nullify the Foreign Office and unreliable ministers, including Halifax.

Next morning, Monday 26 September, the full British team, headed by Chamberlain, again met Daladier and Bonnet. Gamelin talked first to Chamberlain and Inskip, the Minister for Co-ordination of Defence, and then conferred with civilian and military heads of the British army and air force. At midday the Cabinet met and was told that Daladier had agreed to Horace Wilson's mission to Hitler and to the messages he had been instructed to convey. Gamelin left the impression that the French army would do something active to honour the commitment to assist Czechoslovakia and not remain wholly on the defensive.

After lunch Churchill came to Downing Street and had half an hour with Chamberlain and Halifax. Parliament had been summoned to meet on Wednesday; Churchill's acquiescence in the government's moves would help avoid embarrassment. The conversation seems to have been amiable enough (though, as we shall see, Chamberlain felt no friendly feelings). After it, about 4 p.m., Halifax went over to the Foreign Office and telephoned a 'most immediate' message 'from the Prime Minister' to Wilson who had just arrived in Berlin: 'Since you left, French have definitely stated their intention of supporting Czechoslovakia by offensive measures if latter is attacked. This would bring us in: and it should be made plain to Chancellor [Hitler] that this is inevitable alternative to a peaceful solution.' Halifax's next action angered Chamberlain, whom he did not consult. Rex Leeper, head of the Foreign Office press department, came to see him and proposed to issue a communiqué: 'If in spite of all efforts made by the British Prime Minister a German attack is made upon Czechoslovakia the immediate result must be that France will be bound to come to her assistance, and Great Britain and Russia will certainly stand by France.' Halifax approved. This statement was the clearest and strongest threat made by the British government during the month of the Munich crisis. For Chamberlain it was unwelcome because he believed threats, especially public threats, made Hitler dangerous; some of his colleagues felt that threats were the only means of restraining Hitler.[21] The outbreak of war in 1914 continued to haunt their minds, when, it was alleged, Germany had gone to war because Britain had not made sufficiently plain the likelihood of British involvement. The threat Chamberlain had entrusted to Wilson to deliver to Hitler he knew that Wilson would do his best to soften and disguise.

At 5 p.m., Berlin time, Sir Horace Wilson, embodying the secretive virtues of the Home Civil Service, confronted the brutal genius of demagoguery and violence. Throughout Germany the authorities had ordered everyone to listen to the speech Hitler was about to make that evening in the Sportpalast. For those without their own radio receivers, public loudspeakers on the streets would enable them to hear their master's voice. Hitler tried out the substance of his speech on the imperturbably polite Wilson: gratitude for Chamberlain's efforts, denunciations and threats for Beneš and the Czechs. 'On the 1st October I shall have Czechoslovakia where I want her.' He demanded acceptance of his terms by 2 p.m. on Wednesday. Wilson reported home, through the Foreign

Office, a 'very violent hour'. Hitler was 'most impatient' and interposed 'insane interruptions' when he read Chamberlain's message to him. Wilson did not present the 'warning' to Hitler 'in view of intense emotion' but arranged to see the Führer again next morning. After Hitler's speech, in which ranting demands for Czech surrender enclosed soothing assurances to Chamberlain, Horace Wilson suggested that the warning message should be abandoned altogether. The Prime Minister replied that the special message must be delivered 'in view of what we said to the French' but 'should be given more in sorrow than in anger'. Sir Horace Wilson visited Hitler again soon after midday on 27 September. He delivered the warning 'in what I hope was the tone you would wish', as he reported to the Prime Minister. Hitler's tone remained vociferous: 'We should all be at war in six days. He would, unless the Czechs accepted his memorandum, smash Czechoslovakia.' Wilson softened the impact for Chamberlain: Hitler 'sent thanks again to you for your efforts, could not believe we and Germany could fall out over such a question, and finally begged that you would do all you possibly could to induce the Czechs to accept.' Wilson promised Hitler to do what he could: 'I will still try to make those Czechos sensible'.[22]

In London the Prime Minister issued to the press early that morning a statement promising that, if Germany agreed not to use force, the British government would ensure that Czechoslovak promises 'are carried out fairly and fully and ... with all reasonable promptitude'. Some ministers and the Chiefs of Staff met in the afternoon to discuss what to do after news came in of Hitler's intransigent attitude in his exchange with Wilson. They agreed to call up reservists in order to mobilise the British fleet. However, Chamberlain vetoed any publicity, though Duff Cooper, First Lord of the Admiralty, expected him to announce it in his speech to be broadcast at 8 p.m. This the Prime Minister did not do – on the contrary, his speech, delivered with understandable weariness, consisted of an appeal to Hitler and to German opinion to give time for a peaceful transfer of Sudeten German territory. Though he stigmatised the Godesberg demands as 'unreasonable', his tone was unaggressive and he stressed that the calling-up of men for the anti-aircraft defences or for ships were 'only precautionary measures ... which do not necessarily mean that we have determined on war'. He declared his readiness 'to pay even a third visit to Germany if I thought it would do any good'.[23]

The full Cabinet met to hear Horace Wilson's account of his visits to Hitler. As a preliminary the Prime Minister gave depressing news and opinions. He read a telegram from Henderson in Berlin suggesting that the Cabinet should advise Czechoslovakia to make the best terms she could with Germany, quoted the military attaché in Berlin on Czechoslovak moral and material weaknesses and invited Malcolm MacDonald to give a discouraging account of the attitude of the Dominions Wilson urged that the Cabinet should recommend to the Czechoslovak government to withdraw their troops and to allow Germany to occupy at once the areas Hitler had demanded; later on the final frontier could be determined. Chamberlain supported him. Duff Cooper immediately denounced the proposal. Chamberlain replied, claiming that the proposal 'was perhaps the last opportunity for avoiding war'. Once again Halifax disagreed: 'the suggestion amounted to complete capitulation to Germany'. Chamberlain gave way.

Now European war seemed imminent. The German government had demanded that Czechoslovakia should accept the Godesberg memorandum by 2 p.m. the next day, 28 September. The Czech government categorically refused. The French government had announced that it would take active steps to honour its commitment to support Czechoslovakia against German attack. The British government had declared publicly, and privately to Hitler, that Britain would then go to war. The last days of September, after Godesberg, were fraught with growing menace. After the late Cabinet meeting on 27 September, Duff Cooper, as First Lord, telephoned to the press section of the Admiralty to release the news of the mobilisation of the fleet. In the morning newspapers of 28 September this evocative announcement brought tension to its height. The previous weekend the issue of gas-masks to the entire population began (except for babies: provision for them came only in 1939). Mobile loudspeakers toured the streets of towns to tell the population to attend at depots to try on gas-masks. Early in the week the Home Office posted to every house in the country a handbook on protection against air raids. Local authority employees dug trenches in parks, for instance in Cardiff, where nine miles of trenches to take 24,000 men, women and children were begun, and in the royal parks in London. In Birmingham and Swansea private cellars were listed in order to use them to supplement trenches, and hastily built shelters were provided for those whose normal dwellings were specially vulnerable or who might be caught by air raids away from home. Plans for the evacuation of children from large towns were brought up to date and in London meetings of parents assembled on Saturday. Searchlights were set up on Horse Guards Parade and anti-aircraft guns mounted there and on the Embankment. On the morning of 28 September the inhabitants of British cities expected to endure German bombing within days or even hours.

Chamberlain assured his wireless audience on 27 September: 'You *know* that I am going to work for peace till the last moment.' Later that evening Lord Perth, the British ambassador in Rome, was told to carry out his own suggestion that he should ask the Italian Foreign Minister to persuade Mussolini to use his influence to moderate Hitler's impatience. Perth called on Ciano at 10.30 a.m. and Ciano at once went to Mussolini, who instructed the Italian ambassador in Berlin to ask Hitler to delay the mobilisation orders allegedly due to go out at 2 p.m. At 11.30 a.m. the Foreign Office despatched two messages from the Prime Minister drafted by himself, one for Hitler, 'I am ready to come to Berlin myself at once to discuss arrangements for transfer with you and representatives of the Czech government together with representatives of France and Italy if you desire', and one for Mussolini begging him to urge Hitler to agree. Horace Wilson, bypassing Halifax, told the Germans, through Ribbentrop's agent in London, that the Führer's demands should be put in a different form to enable Chamberlain to get them accepted in substance. About 2.30 p.m. word came to London from Rome: 'At Signor Mussolini's request Herr Hitler has accepted to postpone mobilisation for 24 hours.'[24]

That afternoon Parliament met. At 3 p.m. the Prime Minister opened what was planned as a two-day debate in the House of Commons on the European situation. Instead the House adjourned at 4.30 p.m. after an exciting end to Mr Chamberlain's speech. Chamberlain gave a careful, documented account of events and had reached the point at which he reported Hitler's agreement to delay until the next day his alleged intention to order German mobilisation. Then a note which Cadogan had brought, almost, but not quite, running from the Foreign Office, reached Sir John Simon who was sitting next to Mr Chamberlain. At a suitable pause Simon showed him the note: Hitler invited Mussolini, Daladier and Chamberlain to confer the following morning at Munich. 'I need not say what my answer will be', Chamberlain concluded amid tumultuous cheering joined, once Attlee had pronounced himself 'absolutely certain that everyone in this House will have welcomed the statement of the Prime Minister', by members from every side. Even Churchill added his good wishes. Chamberlain did not assemble the Cabinet that evening, or even the 'inner Cabinet'; no doubt he wished to avoid pressure on him to insist on conditions for agreement.[25]

Next morning, the members of the Cabinet, at Simon's suggestion, went to Heston to see off the Prime Minister who flew to Munich accompanied by Sir Horace Wilson and Lord Dunglass. The conference began soon after midday, 29 September. Ribbentrop met the Prime Minister at the airport; Hitler went to meet Mussolini at Kufstein, a station just across the old Austro-German frontier about an hour's journey from Munich. The Germans exaggerated Mussolini's role: probably Hitler thought it best to attribute the tactical retreat of calling the conference to Mussolini's intervention. In fact, Hitler never allowed himself to be influenced by Mussolini's opinions or wishes, however much he referred to his feelings of friendship and admiration for this 'great man'. Hitler liked to have an independent head of government as a sycophant.

The Germans arranged that Mussolini should present as his own the proposals that formed the basis of the Munich agreement. Provided Hitler made some concession, and agreed to relax his Godesberg demands to enable Chamberlain to argue that the settlement was negotiated rather than dictated, the terms mattered little. They extended the period during which German military occupation of the area in Czechoslovakia inhabited by a majority of Germans should take place. Instead of occupation being scheduled for one day, 1 October, it was to be spread over the period from 1 to 10 October. Plebiscites were to be held under the supervision of a commission of British, French, Italian, German and Czechoslovak representatives and this commission should determine detailed frontiers of the territories to be ceded at once and of the plebiscite areas. There should be a right for individuals to opt into or out of the transferred territories. (In fact, the plebiscites were never held and the option to leave German-ruled territory never came into effect.[26]) What mattered to Chamberlain was to advance the process of Anglo-German understanding and to press on towards agreement on arms limitation.

About 1 a.m. on 30 September Chamberlain asked Hitler for a private talk. He did not inform Daladier. Hitler readily agreed, probably feeling that Chamberlain needed encouragement and support if he were to give Hitler the much-sought free hand in eastern Europe, something in fact beyond Chamberlain's power or desire to give. Later that morning they met in Hitler's private flat. This, it seemed, was the climax of Chamberlain's career, his moment of triumph. He urged joint action by the 'Four Great Powers' to end the Spanish civil war. He suggested the abolition of bombing and bomber aircraft. He argued for reduction of restrictions on trade. To all this Hitler replied amenably if vaguely. Then Chamberlain produced two copies of a joint statement he and Wilson had prepared in advance. Hitler seemed ready enough to sign anything. They put their names to these words: 'We regard the agreement signed last night and the Anglo-German Naval Agreement as symbolic of the desire of our two peoples never to go to war again. We are resolved that the method of consultation shall be the method adopted to deal with any other questions that may concern our two countries, and we are determined to continue our efforts to remove possible sources of difference and thus to contribute to assure the peace of Europe.'

Chamberlain had won! He had brought peace! A tired but contented Prime Minister, having acknowledged grateful applause from the Munich populace, returned to London. At Heston, beaming, he emerged from his aircraft and spoke to the waiting crowds. 'The settlement of the Czechoslovakian problem which has now been achieved is, in my view, only the prelude to a larger settlement in which all Europe may find peace.' Then he waved 'the paper which bears his [Hitler's] name upon it as well as mine' and read out its contents. Then he motored to Buckingham Palace through the crowds braving the rain to cheer him. With heavy rain still falling, he appeared on the balcony with King George VI and Queen Elizabeth to the cheers of another bedraggled but enormous crowd. Then, at last, he returned to 10 Downing Street and more crowds. With a little encouragement from his associates, he appeared at a first-floor window to tell them that it was 'the second time in our history that there has come back from Germany to Downing Street peace with honour. I believe it is peace for our time.' Then he thanked the British people (presumably for supporting him) 'from the bottom of a proud heart' and suggested, sensibly, that everyone should go to bed and sleep peacefully. The records of Mr Chamberlain's voice and appearance made on film and in recorded sound, make evident his pleasure and sense of achievement. His first, and excellent, biographer, K. G. Feiling, suggested that Chamberlain came back doubting the success of his effort for peace: 'All this will be over in three months' he reports him, presumably on evidence from Halifax, as saying to the Foreign Secretary in the car from Heston. After the war Halifax wrote to *The Times* categorically denying that his remark meant that Chamberlain lacked confidence in Munich. Chamberlain, he explained, was speaking of the unreliability of the British electorate rather than that of Hitler.[27] Chamberlain believed his policy meant peace and was determined to carry it on.

9 From Munich to Prague

More than 20,000 letters and telegrams, the Prime Minister told the House of Commons, came to 10 Downing Street in late September and early October 1938. Gifts, he wrote to his sister, came 'in embarrassing profusion', but, he went on, 'we are very little nearer to the time when we can put all thoughts of war out of our minds and settle down to make the world a better place. And unhappily there are a great many people who have no faith that we can ever arrive at such a time.' Halifax recorded that Chamberlain agreed 'that while hoping for the best it is also necessary to prepare for the worst'. Chamberlain showed faith and hope; most others, including several Cabinet ministers, were more concerned to increase and accelerate preparations for the worst. On Sunday 2 October he had a quiet day at Chequers replying to his more important correspondents. Among them he wrote to Maurice Hankey, recently retired after serving as Cabinet secretary for more than twenty years: 'I believe with you', the Prime Minister wrote, 'that we have at last laid the foundations of a stable peace, though it still remains to build the superstructure.' In spite of admirers like Hankey and the plaudits of the public, Chamberlain sensed a growing isolation. In the Cabinet, as he told his sister, 'what I want is more support for my policy and not more strengthening of those who don't believe in it, or at any rate are harassed by constant doubts'.[1]

The 'weaker brethren' in the Cabinet wanted to accelerate and increase rearmament. Buck de la Warr wrote to the Prime Minister on 4 October. He felt strongly 'that we should immediately take new and drastic steps both to strengthen our defences and – almost equally important – to make it clear to the world that we are doing so'. Moreover he opposed any lessening of 'contact with Russia and the small nations of Europe'. Chamberlain replied evasively: 'I do not think we are very far apart, if at all, on what we should do now, but I do not want to pledge myself to any particular programme of arma-

ments till we have had a chance to review the situation in the
light of recent events.' Among Cabinet ministers, Oliver Stanley, he told his sister, gave him most trouble. He, too, wrote to
Chamberlain that he thought Munich 'an uneasy truce, which
can only be converted into a lasting peace if the interval is used
drastically and energetically for the increase of our power'. At
the first Cabinet meeting after the Prime Minister's return on 3
October from his brief visit to Chequers, Walter Elliot pointed
to the view 'strongly held in certain quarters ... that every
effort should be made to intensify our rearmament programme' and Halifax urged that ministers should not make speeches
'which would preclude consideration of the need for such
intensification'. The Prime Minister spoke, according to the
record,[2] with some emotion.

> He had been oppressed with the sense that the burden of
> armaments might break our backs. This had been one of the
> factors which had led him to the view that it was necessary to
> try and resolve the causes which were responsible for the
> armament race.
>
> He thought that we were now in a more hopeful position,
> and that the contacts which had been established with the
> Dictator Powers opened up the possibility that we might be
> able to reach some agreement with them which would stop
> the armament race. It was clear, however, that it would be
> madness for the country to stop rearming until we were
> convinced that other countries would act in the same way.
> For the time being, therefore, we should relax no particle of
> effort until our deficiencies had been made good. That,
> however, was not the same thing as to say that as a thank-
> offering for the present *détente*, we should at once embark
> on a great increase in our armaments programme.

That afternoon a four-day debate on Munich in the House
of Commons began with the personal explanation of his resignation from the government given by Duff Cooper, until
then First Lord of the Admiralty. Though some of the other
dissidents had been expected to go with him, he resigned
alone. It meant a sacrifice for him. The Admiralty provided a
beautiful house and a comfortable yacht; he was not rich and

he was extravagant and generous. He made an elegant speech. He ended by pointing out that 'the Prime Minister believes that he can rely upon the good faith of Hitler' but, he added, 'how are we to justify the extra burden laid upon the people of Great Britain' in increasing or accelerating rearmament 'if we are told at the same time that there is no fear of war with Germany and that, in the opinion of the Prime Minister, this settlement means peace in our time?' The debate was not enjoyable for the Prime Minister: 'a pretty trying ordeal especially as I had to fight all the time against the defection of weaker brethren and Winston was carrying on a regular campaign against me with the aid of Masaryk the Czech Minister. They, of course, are totally unaware of my knowledge of their proceedings' – evidently Chamberlain was getting intercepts from tapped telephones. 'All the world seemed to be full of my praises except the House of Commons.' It became clear that many, even of the Prime Minister's supporters, were less confident in the permanence of peace than he was. At the end of the debate, Chamberlain felt compelled partially to disavow his own hopefulness.

> I am told that the policy which I have tried to describe ['of personal contact with the dictators'] is inconsistent with the continuance, and much more inconsistent with the acceleration of our present programme of arms. I am asked how I can reconcile an appeal to this country to support the continuance of this programme with the words which I used when I came back from Munich the other day and spoke of my belief that we might have peace for our time. I hope hon. Members will not be disposed to read into words used in a moment of some emotion, after a long and exhausting day, after I had driven through miles of excited, enthusiastic, cheering people – I hope they will not read into those words more than they were intended to convey. I do indeed believe that we may yet secure peace for our time, but I never meant to suggest that we should do that by disarmament, until we can induce others to disarm, too.

Chamberlain hoped soon to induce others to disarm to make it unnecessary for Britain to arm. Cadogan told Corbin, the

French ambassador in London, on 6 October that the only
immediate consequence that Chamberlain expected from the
declaration he brought back from Munich was negotiation on
the abolition of aerial bombardment and, if possible, the suppression of bomber aircraft. About the same time Chamberlain
spoke to Halifax to suggest 'an approach to Russia with regard
to the abolition of bomber aircraft ... on the strength', Halifax
wrote to him in reply, 'of what Hitler said to you at Munich on
September 30th'; evidently Chamberlain took seriously Hitler's
concern for the humanisation of aerial warfare and hoped,
astonishingly, to persuade the Soviet Union to join in and so to
reassure Hitler of its practicability.[3]

During the Commons debate Eden made what became his
usual call for 'a national effort in the sphere of defence very
much greater than anything that has been attempted hitherto
... a call for a united effort by a united nation'. A week later he
had a long talk with Halifax, who told Chamberlain that Eden
'was all out on the tack of the necessity of increasing our
industrial production, which he did not believe could be done
without something like special wartime powers, and this again
he did not believe could be done without your widening the
basis of your government'. Halifax strongly supported
Anthony Eden's suggestion. 'One of my colleagues, and a very
important one', Chamberlain wrote, 'is pressing me to broaden
the base of the Cabinet by taking in, or offering to take in,
Labour, and also Anthony.' Chamberlain, resting after the
Commons debate with the Douglas Homes at the Hirsel, set out
his objections much more clearly to his sister than he could
have done to anyone else. In his view Eden did not understand
'that the conciliation part of the policy is just as important as
the rearming ... And, if we had Labour men in I see them
forming a group with him which would keep up a constant
running fight over every move in the international game. That
would soon make my position intolerable. I have had trouble
enough with my present Cabinet.' He wanted a quite different
solution, not 'to take as partners men who would sooner or
later wreck the policy with which I am identified. I could not
have a General Election at this moment; I am convinced it
would have been bad tactics. But I don't believe I shall settle
down comfortably here or succeed in establishing confidence

abroad in the continuity of the policy till I have got a mandate on that policy from the country, and accordingly I shall watch eagerly for an opportunity to seek it.' Hoare, too, favoured an election, though even he wanted Eden back: 'I would get him in if and when you can', he urged Chamberlain.[4]

The opportunity for a General Election never came. Chamberlain knew that his policy of peace through conciliation of Hitler and Mussolini was less popular than he thought it should have been. He knew that most of those who applauded Munich did so because they thought he had bought time to enable the United Kingdom to grow militarily stronger and to be able to resist threats of violence, not because they thought it the first of a series of agreements with the European Dictators. During the House of Commons debate after Munich, the Italian Foreign Minister sent a bullying message to London that the British government should agree within two days to bring the Anglo-Italian agreement into operation when Italian troops returning from Spain arrived at Naples, or else Mussolini would make a military alliance with Germany. Chamberlain 'on merits' wanted to give in to this characteristic piece of Fascist diplomacy. But 'I could not bring myself to make an announcement to that effect to the House at that moment . . . Moreover I did not feel certain that any further step towards agreement with the Dictators at this moment might not precipitate further resignations from the Govt.'

Chamberlain needed a tangible gain from his policy, some definite concession from Germany. So far he had helped Hitler to secure his publicly stated demands without resort to force. Chamberlain needed some more tangible benefit to the United Kingdom than what Churchill called 'promises of good-will for the future'. Early in October the Prime Minister's press secretary set out the position to Dr Hesse, who worked in the German embassy in London. In general, the German government should express friendship towards Britain and confidence in Chamberlain. In particular, something ought to be done with respect to armaments in order to strengthen Chamberlain's political position. Hesse reported that the Downing Street press secretary had explained that 'if Chamberlain had success in the disarmament question, he would find an opportunity to go to the country for a general election. By giving Chamberlain

success in the disarmament question we had it in our power to
stabilise or not to stabilise pro-German tendencies in Great
Britain.' It was not that Chamberlain's position as Prime Minister was threatened: he commanded an enormous majority in
the House of Commons. After the Munich debate the government had a majority of 222. On 17 November 1938 Churchill
urged that 50 Conservative members should vote against the
government on an amendment to the Address in favour of a
Ministry of Supply: only three did so, Churchill himself,
Harold Macmillan and Brendan Bracken, and the government
secured a majority of 196. As Prime Minister and leader of the
Conservative Party Chamberlain could count on the votes of
the immense flock of generally not very well-informed Conservative Members of Parliament. Yet Chamberlain could detect an underlying resentment at Hitlerian bullying. Conviction
among his supporters in the rightness of the search for compromise with Hitler and his own authority in pursuing it
needed reinforcement. For Chamberlain, Eden presented a
bigger problem than Churchill. Most Conservatives thought
Eden cautious and constructive and he carefully maintained
this attitude. In his speeches he did not denounce the government; on 17 November he voted with the government on the
Ministry of Supply. Many Conservatives might press Chamberlain to strengthen his position by bringing Eden back in advance
of the General Election; as we have seen, Chamberlain
did not wish to do so. Chamberlain, therefore, found himself
compelled to engage in rearmament sufficient to quieten such
voices while trying to retain his freedom of action to conciliate
and appease. On 31 October, Chamberlain insisted that Germany and Italy suspected that British rearmament 'was
directed against them, and it was important that we should not
encourage their suspicions'. He attacked the 'false' view that
'one result of the Munich agreement had been that it would be
necessary for us to add to our rearmament programme. Acceleration of existing programmes was one thing but increases in
the scope of our programme which would lead to a new arms
race were a different proposition.' However, when, in a
Cabinet discussion on 7 November Chamberlain showed hesitation in accepting an Admiralty proposal to build twenty more
convoy escort vessels he could do no more than win agreement

that the decision should be reconsidered later in the light of foreign policy developments. In fact, the proposal was soon fully justified by the German decision, notified to the British on 10 December, to treble the German submarine fleet.[5]

Hitler and the German government did not help. For Chamberlain the months from Munich to February 1939 brought disappointment after disappointment. Hitler spoke at Saarbrücken on 9 October 1938. He did not celebrate the coming of peace. He did not intend to disarm. He thanked Mussolini, Germany's 'one true friend', but as for the two other statesmen who worked for peace at Munich, they might lose their offices at any time. In England, Duff Cooper or Eden or Churchill might come to power and, of course, they would immediately try to begin a new world war. Together with 'the menacing figure of the Jewish-international foe', and the world press, they obliged Germany to be ready to defend itself. He had decided to accelerate work on German fortifications in the west. The British should abandon the attitudes of the Versailles epoch; Germany had had enough interference from governesses. At Weimar on 6 November, having made a tactlessly derogatory reference to 'umbrella-carrying' bourgeois (Chamberlain was everywhere associated with umbrellas), he proclaimed a 'fundamental principle': 'The German is either the first soldier in the world or he is no soldier at all.' Outside Germany, Hitler alleged, incitement to war persisted: 'When the rest of the world speaks of disarmament, then we too are ready for disarmament, but under one condition: the war agitation must first be disarmed.' On 8 November, in the hallowed beer-cellar in Munich where Hitler started the Putsch of 1923, he summoned his old fellow-fighters, and the whole German people, to watchfulness against those in France and England who wanted war. While Germany wanted nothing from Britain and France except former colonies, 'that is, of course, no occasion for war'. But elsewhere attempts to gain rights by negotiation had proved futile: 'There should be no surprise that we secure for ourselves our rights by another way if we cannot gain them by the normal way.' This series of speeches suggested that, for Hitler, Munich had not shown the way to a peaceful, disarmed Europe.[6]

That same day vom Rath, a secretary at the German embassy

in Paris, died of wounds from a revolver fired by a Polish Jew as a protest against German persecution. On the night of 9–10 November Nazis unleashed destruction and terror against Jews throughout Germany. Synagogues were attacked and burnt, Jewish shops and offices broken into, looted and smashed. Jews were threatened, assaulted and turned out of their homes; there were suicides and murders. The police stood aside. Hundreds of Jews were arrested and sent to concentration camps. Jewish-held insurance was voided and the community fined the equivalent of nearly £100 million. The government forbade Jews to engage in any skilled work and excluded them from all places of entertainment or culture and from certain streets. The acting head of the British embassy, Sir George Ogilvie-Forbes, reported that he had 'not met a single German of whatever class who in varying measure does not, to say the least, disapprove of what has occurred. But I fear it does not follow that even the outspoken condemnation of professed National Socialists or of senior officers in the army will have any influence over the insensate gang in present control of Nazi Germany.' These people did not seem possible partners in the pursuit of peace.[7]

Hitler's failure to proclaim the coming of peace contributed to the weakening of Chamberlain's support among the electorate at large from the high point achieved when the flight to Munich was announced. None of the eight Parliamentary by-elections in October, November and December 1938 reflected the awed gratitude for the saviour of the world that Chamberlain seems to have hoped for. In two of them the Conservatives lost the seat; Bridgwater was the most striking setback where Vernon Bartlett, standing as an independent, won the seat with 6000 more votes than the combined Labour and Liberal votes at the previous election, turning an overall Conservative lead of 4500 votes into a deficit of over 2000. At the end of November a member of the Research Department in Conservative Central Office sent to its director, Sir Joseph Ball, an urgent message: 'The outlook is far less promising than it was a few months ago, and there are a large number of seats held by only small majorities, so that only a small turnover of votes would defeat the Government.' He advised that a General Election should be postponed. In December 1938, Chamberlain's relief was evi-

dent at the defeat of the Duchess of Atholl in Kinross and West
Perthshire where she resigned her seat, to which she had been
elected as a Conservative, to stand, unsuccessfully, as an independent against a newly chosen Conservative candidate; she
was an expert on the iniquities of General Franco and the
deficiencies of Chamberlain's attitude to Hitler, he an expert
on Shorthorn cattle. Chamberlain wrote to Margesson, the
Conservative chief whip, 'I was overjoyed at the result of the
Perth election which was far better than I ventured to hope. It
is a grand wind up to a very difficult session.'[8]

Late in November 1938 Ogilvie-Forbes sent to London a
brief appreciation of Hitler's views.

Herr Hitler accepted the Munich agreement with relative ill
grace. Nevertheless he hoped that the Munich declaration
would have the effect of slowing down British rearmament
and leaving him militarily supreme in Europe. This hope has
been dashed by the insistence of all parties in England on
accelerated rearmament. On top of this came widespread
criticism in England of the Munich agreement and finally the
storm of indignation over the treatment of the Jews. In
consequence Herr Hitler considers that there is now nothing
to be gained by taking British public opinion into consideration and he feels free to give expression to the intense
resentment which the slightest breath of opposition or criticism now arouse in him.

Hitler's restlessness soon led to more ominous news and
reports. After Munich rumours that his interest was turning to
encouragement of Ukrainian nationalism caused little fear in
London; western rearmament or agreement with Germany on
selective arms limitation, would, it was thought, safeguard
British interests in case of German expansion, whether by
peaceful means or threats, in eastern Europe. In contrast,
reports that Hitler contemplated attacking Switzerland or the
Low Countries or Holland, or even the United Kingdom,
aroused excitement and alarm. The Cabinet, the Foreign Policy
Committee and the Chiefs of Staff discussed these threats
during three weeks in January 1939. Cabinet ministers considered the state of the German economy, above all German

shortage of foreign currency. The level of German arms production, with the consequent decline in civilian output, meant
that German exports could not finance German imports, in
spite of the maintenance through elaborate structures of exchange control of an artificially high foreign exchange value of
the mark. Hitler must therefore soon choose between reducing
arms production or making immediate war, to solve by conquest German shortages of food, raw material and labour.
Hitler, it was reported, had been angered rather than satisifed
by British intervention culminating in Munich. Chamberlain
was 'a long way from accepting all this information' and 'also
thought it was somewhat curious that the Führer should now
be described as intensely irritated at the result of Munich'
though, if true, it showed how dangerous it was that a dictator
should be 'baulked'.

However, Chamberlain joined in a series of important decisions. If Germany attacked the Netherlands the Cabinet agreed
that Britain must go to war. It was not only that such an attack
might be the prelude to an attack on Britain. German occupation of the Netherlands would make Britain less easy to defend.
Therefore, as the Chiefs of Staff put it, 'failure to intervene
would have such moral and other repercussions as would
seriously undermine our position in the eyes of the Dominions
and the world in general. We might thus be deprived of
support in a subsequent struggle between Germany and the
British Empire.' They accepted the possibility of war, and the
Cabinet followed them, even though Italy and Japan might join
with Germany and 'if we were compelled to enter such a war in
the near future we should be confronted with a position more
serious than the Empire had ever faced before. The ultimate
outcome of the conflict might well depend upon the intervention of other Powers, in particular of the United States of
America.' Once again, as on 25 September 1938, the British
government decided it would go to war to prevent so substantial a growth in German power as to threaten British independence. This decision of January 1939 differed from that of
September 1938 because the impending German threat this
time was in the west, close to Britain. This time, therefore,
France should be encouraged to go to war. So the Cabinet
agreed, if the French government enquired, to promise to fight

if France did so in reply to an invasion of Switzerland; to seek full staff conversations with the French and Belgian governments even though this would bring 'a far more binding commitment than had hitherto been contemplated' and was 'almost tantamount to an alliance'. Soon the Cabinet considered other concessions to the French.

At the beginning of 1938 the Cabinet had decided that only two divisions should be equipped and trained for a continental European campaign; now, early in 1939, the British army began to rebuild an expeditionary force. After the loss of the Czechoslovak army to the possible strength of an anti-German coalition, the French army felt the need for early and substantial reinforcement in war. Moreover the open British assumption that the next war would be fought by the British at sea and in the air, leaving the French the high casualties of combat between mass armies, began to raise French protests. Daladier put the point directly to Chamberlain in November 1938, speaking of 'the need for greater support from Great Britain in the event of German attack on Great Britain or France. It was not enough to send two divisions after three weeks. More divisions should be sent and as far as possible they should be motorised.' Already hostile observers of British policy pointed to British military preparation to fight to the last Frenchman.[9]

Chamberlain was interested in French policy for other motives than to secure French help in a defensive war against Germany. His first motive, as usual, was to prevent war rather than to prepare to fight a war. As Hitler became disappointingly difficult to deal with after Munich, he turned, as he had done at the end of September 1938, to Mussolini. He told the Cabinet on 30 November 1938 that he and Halifax had reached the conclusion some weeks ago 'that, as the prospects for appeasement were not very bright in Berlin, it might be useful that they should visit Rome'. Mussolini might encourage Hitler to pursue peace: Chamberlain hoped 'that Signor Mussolini could be persuaded to prevent Herr Hitler from carrying out some "mad dog" act'. With some embarrassment the British government brought the Anglo-Italian agreement of 16 April 1938 'into effect' on 16 November. The agreement stipulated 'a settlement of the Spanish question as a prerequisite'. Now Chamberlain and the government argued that a withdrawal of about half the Italian infantry from Spain was enough and that the Spanish civil war was no longer a danger to the peace of Europe. The process was accompanied by a successful attempt to secure an invitation to Rome for early January 1939; Mussolini, of course, was delighted to have the British Prime Minister and Foreign Secretary come to seek his favour.[10]

Soon, however, a bizarre episode in Rome complicated British courtship of the supposedly influential Italian dictator. In November 1938 the Daladier government despatched François-Poncet as ambassador to Rome, thus unconditionally recognising the Italian conquest of Ethiopia. The new ambassador was to try to end the Franco-Italian hostility inspired by the Spanish civil war and to mark the French government's movement away from the doctrinal anti-fascism of the Popular Front governments of 1936 and 1937. However, on 30 November, Ciano, the Italian Foreign Minister, in the presence of Mussolini, spoke to the Chamber of Deputies, a powerless body, and referred to the natural aspirations of the Italian people. This remark provoked cries from the Deputies and the public galleries, variously reported, including 'Tunis', 'Jibuti', 'Corsica', 'Nice'. Similar shouts, apparently from civil servants and plain-clothes police, greeted the Deputies in Piazza Venezia, whither they had marched in formation along the Corso. More realistic Italian demands were those for the preservation of the position as Italian citizens of Italians in Tunisia, who made up the majority of the non-indigenous population there, and for arrangements to give Italians some control over the direction of the French railway from the capital of Ethiopia to the French-controlled port of Jibuti. The wilder demands implied wholesale territorial changes: the transfer of those territories from decadent, democratic France to virile, militarised Fascist Italy. The new French ambassador to Rome, François-Poncet, suggested that Italian propaganda was trying to 'make of the Italians of Tunisia the Sudetens of Italy' and that the Italian government, encouraged by the Anglo-Italian agreement, might perhaps ask the British to 'give a new mission to Lord Runciman'.

On his side, Chamberlain insisted that his visit to Rome should go ahead, that the Italian government had disavowed the shouts of 30 November, and that the Anglo-Italian agreement provided for the status quo in the Mediterranean and covered Tunisia, Corsica and Nice. The French government reacted with fury to the Italian pretensions. Daladier made it clear to Chamberlain on his way to Rome 'that the French government would not make any concessions at all to Italy', and two weeks later he visited Corsica and North Africa and announced that he 'would not cede an acre' of the French Empire. In order to keep what he imagined to be Mussolini's friendship, Chamberlain wanted to show some sympathy at least for some of the milder Italian claims. To be able to persuade his colleagues to let him do so, and to enable him to press the French into some less brutal rejection, he had to agree to the sweeping concessions to French military demands that marked British military policy in 1939. The most he dared suggest to his Cabinet, before going to Rome, by way of concession to the Duce was that he should tell Mussolini that the British 'would not encourage the French to refuse to discuss such matters' as the position of Italian residents in Tunisia and the regulation of the French-controlled railway from Addis Ababa to Jibuti. Another worry that afflicted Chamberlain was the continuing danger of an Italian-French quarrel over Spain for 'unless and until the affair is settled ... the road to appeasement will be blocked' yet he could not risk the effect on British opinion of agreeing to 'belligerent rights', which would mean that Franco's ships could blockade ports still remaining to the tottering Spanish government, in order to help Franco and his Italian allies to finish the war. For the rest of 1939 Chamberlain continued to seek Italian friendship and to fret about the obstacles the French put in the way.[11]

At the end of 1938 and the beginning of 1939, then, Chamberlain felt gloomy. Hitler did not show any friendliness. Ministers produced threats of resignation. Many Conservatives showed doubts about his foreign policy. The Perthshire by-election cheered him; then in mid-January, during his visit to Rome, he persuaded himself, with his agility in hoping for the best, that Mussolini wanted peace and disarmament and would help him to get them from Hitler. On 16 January 1939, Inskip, still Minister for Co-ordination of Defence, left a paper in 10 Downing Street discussing the possible preparation by the Committee of Imperial Defence of a plan for disarmament.

Kingsley Wood, he reported, had expressed the disapproving view of the CID: 'In his opinion, the country would, in its present temper, resent any proposal for disarmament. Moreover, every member of the Committee was overwhelmed with very responsible duties and it was a waste of time to draw up proposals which could only be of academic value.' Back from Rome, Horace Wilson thought differently. 'When Sir Thomas Inskip wrote this note he did not know how the conversations in Rome had proceeded as regards possible limitation of bombing etc. . . . we ought to be ready if – as may well be the case – Mussolini follows up the hint you gave him.' Chamberlain commented, 'I agree and will speak to Inskip about it tomorrow.' Chamberlain had put to Mussolini, and repeated the point, that Hitler should curb German armaments; Mussolini's casual signs of interest gave Chamberlain disproportionate encouragement.[12]

Soon Chamberlain grew still more hopeful. On 28 January 1939 he spoke in Birmingham. He conveyed an appeal to Hitler. Having spoken of the strictly defensive nature of British rearmament and proclaimed his hope that at last the government might secure international peace, he emphasised these words: 'I feel that the time has now come when others should make their contribution.' Horace Wilson arranged for the text of this speech to be sent in advance to Berchtesgaden for Hitler to read while he was preparing his own speech. Hitler gave this speech on 30 January. Wilson believed it to be comparatively restrained as a response to his gesture. Moreover, as Halifax told the Cabinet, the Berlin embassy reported that Hitler's reference to a 'long peace' had been a last-minute interpolation. Chamberlain believed Hitler had responded to his appeal: 'In my Birmingham speech I said it was time someone else made a contribution. Thereafter Hitler altered his speech at the last moment and made it more pacific.' Then on 15 February a dinner of the Anglo-German Fellowship took place in Germany where Henderson was the guest of honour, flanked at table by the Duke of Coburg and by SS Obergruppenführer Lorenz. Henderson reported that he had submitted an advance copy of his own conciliatory speech to Coburg, who was to reply, and the Duke's speech, he claimed, 'was then completely re-written under higher direction'. Chamberlain declared himself 'much struck' by Coburg's speech with its references to 'close and friendly relations between Germany and England'. Chamberlain thought this might be the long-awaited 'response' to his own friendly gestures towards Germany. Chamberlain asked Henderson to let it be known in Berlin that he had 'noticed' the Duke's speech and in his next speech at Blackburn on 23 February he tried to signal his approval.[13]

Chamberlain concluded from the international flirtation he supposed to be taking place that Hitler was again responding to his advances as in that great moment in Munich when Hitler had agreed to their joint declaration of mutual esteem. He thought, correctly, that the pace and scale of German armaments production had created urgent balance of payments problems. Hitler's speech of 30 January gave public expression to German difficulties in paying for imports of food and raw materials. The only solution, apart from armed conquest of foreign resources, must be to cut rearmament and increase exports. Chamberlain, and indeed all those in London who knew something about the German economic situation, recognised that the rulers of Germany must soon decide between peace or war. The Prime Minister proposed to make smooth Hitler's path to peace. Britain would make it easier for Germany to join in re-creating a world economy, less hampered by the exchange controls and bilateral bargains in which Nazi Germany had come to specialise. Britain would try to further German access to raw materials and food by loans of convertible currency in order to bridge the gap until civilian exports recovered. The possibility of colonial concessions would be reopened. Arms limitation would follow as an inevitable consequence of the return of the German economy to civilian competitiveness. So attractive was this prospect, one which 'would overflow with benefits for all' that Chamberlain seems to have found it impossible to imagine a government which could reject it. The rapid increase in the defensive power of the RAF and the corresponding reduction in the vulnerability of the United Kingdom contributed to his growing confidence that Hitler would not choose to risk a great war. As we have seen, in January 1939 some thought that the weakness of the German economy would precipitate a violent German outbreak; Chamberlain thought it would bring peace.

British businessmen had already set in motion talks with German industrialists principally to establish market-sharing arrangements in south-eastern Europe. In mid-February Ashton-Gwatkin, from the economic section of the Foreign Office, went off to Germany under instructions from Halifax to 'exchange views . . . on the economic situation in Germany and in the world'. He concluded that economic facts would compel Germany into a policy of peace, though he noted that Ribbentrop had told him 'that there was some further task for Germany to do in Central Europe "where England must not mix herself in"'. On this Vansittart minuted for Halifax on 8 March that 'the Germans have practically told him what I foretold to you some weeks ago, i.e. that they are going to destroy the remains of Czechoslovakia'.[14] From Berlin the British military attaché asserted that economic assistance to Germany would merely sustain an increase in existing German armaments production. Henderson disagreed with his military attaché. Though Halifax warned him that the Prime Minister was becoming 'rather optimistic' and that his 'German friends' must 'show more than smooth words as evidence of friendly hearts', Henderson encouraged Chamberlain's confidence. Chamberlain's private correspondence shows mounting complacency. 'All the information I get', he wrote to his sister on 19 February, 'seems to point in the direction of peace.' Early in March he put his hopes before the public, anonymously, in a talk to lobby correspondents. He went so far as to predict the assembly of a disarmament conference in the remaining months of 1939. Halifax sent him a firm rebuke, insisting that the Prime Minister should consult his Foreign Secretary before making statements on foreign affairs.[15] That was on 10 March; on that day ominous news arrived. The Czechoslovak President had dismissed the Slovak government in order to halt a developing movement, encouraged by Germany, to secure independence for Slovakia.

The Nazi government, it seems, felt Munich had, or should have, represented a British and French grant of a free hand to Germany in central and eastern Europe and certainly felt Czechoslovakia to have become part of the German sphere. The French government and, still more firmly, the British government and public, felt the Munich agreement meant or ought to mean German acceptance of peaceful discussion to bring European changes. As early as November 1938 Hitler had explained that he would intervene violently in Czechoslovakia if the latter fell under unsound 'influences'. In February more threats began to be expressed; apparently Hitler had determined to destroy what little independence Czechoslovakia still possessed. Perhaps German economic constraints made urgent the seizure of Czech gold reserves and Czech economic resources. That month anti-Czech propaganda began to be directed to Slovakia from Vienna radio, of what the French minister in Prague called an 'extremely violent and especially odious' nature. Jews and Czechs were denounced. Each day Jews living in Slovakia were individually named, accused of exploiting the people and denounced, and then the question was posed, 'When will he be sent to a concentration camp?'[16] On 13 March the German press adopted its usual crisis style by denouncing a new Czech 'reign of terror' against Germans; Father Tiso, the Slovak leader, obeyed a summons to Berlin where he was ordered to secure a declaration of Slovak independence, which was done the next day. Hacha, the Czechoslovakian President, asked to be received by Hitler, presumably to discover German terms for the continued existence of his state. He arrived in Berlin on 14 March and, later that night, received the news that German troops were invading Czechoslovakia; he was ordered to ask for German protection and told that any Czech resistance would lead to the immediate bombing of Prague. That evening, before the outcome of Hacha's visit was known, Halifax had instructed Henderson to present to the German government a mild admonition, the tone and content of which adequately summarise the British way of dealing with Hitler at that time.

His Majesty's Government had no desire to interfere unnecessarily ... They are, however ... deeply concerned for the success of all efforts to restore confidence and a relaxation of tension in Europe. This seems to them more particularly desirable when a start is being made with discussions on economic subjects to which, as His Majesty's Government believes, the German Government attach no less importance than they do themselves, and the fruitful development of which depends so directly upon general state of confidence.

From that point of view they would deplore any action in Central Europe which would cause a setback to the growth of this general confidence on which all improvement in the economic situation depends and to which such improvement might in its turn contribute.[17]

By the time this message reached Ribbentrop, a fast-moving German army reconnaissance detachment had entered the presidential palace in Prague.

10 Guarantee to Poland

The Cabinet met every Wednesday morning. On Wednesday 15 March 1939, therefore, it could think promptly about the news of the destruction of Czechoslovakia. Ministers easily agreed that Britain should not use force to counter the German invasion. Embarrassingly, the British and French governments had promised at Munich to join in a guarantee of the new frontiers of Czechoslovakia and on 4 October 1938 Sir Thomas Inskip told the House of Commons that the British government felt that the guarantee was already morally binding. Halifax now suggested to the Cabinet that they could argue that Inskip's statement was intended only to cover a short period before the great powers worked out a joint guarantee. Months had elapsed and the joint guarantee had not been agreed. Therefore no guarantee existed. Chamberlain preferred to argue that Czechoslovakia had, as it were, spontaneously fallen apart: 'It might, no doubt, be true that the disruption of Czechoslovakia had been largely engineered by Germany, but our guarantee was not a guarantee against the exercise of moral pressure.' Moreover, the Prime Minister seemed reluctant to believe that Germany had destroyed Czechoslovakia by force of arms: later in the meeting he told ministers that he 'thought the military occupation was symbolic, more than perhaps appeared on the surface'.

Only Leslie Hore-Belisha, the Secretary of State for War, argued that the German move was the beginning of a process of eastern expansion and colonisation. The Cabinet's search for, in Halifax's words, 'some overt action to show our disapproval of Germany's action' led only to a decision to postpone the visit to Berlin of the President of the Board of Trade to continue negotiations for Anglo-German economic understandings, to recall Henderson from Berlin 'to report' and to cease payments of the British grant made to the Czechoslovakian government after Munich. That afternoon the House of Commons debated Czechoslovakia. Chamberlain opened with a speech, using a Foreign Office draft which took into account the decisions of the morning's Cabinet. However, he added to the prepared draft a short concluding passage of his own.

> It is natural that I should bitterly regret what has now occurred. But do not let us on that account be deflected from our course. Let us remember that the desire of all the peoples of the world still remains concentrated on the hopes of peace and a return to the atmosphere of understanding and goodwill which has so often been disturbed. The aim of this government is now, as it has always been, to promote that desire and to substitute the method of discussion for the method of force in the settlement of differences. Though we may have to suffer checks and disappointments, from time to time, the object that we have in mind is of too great significance to the happiness of mankind for us lightly to give it up or set it on one side.

Seven hours later, winding up the debate for the government, Sir John Simon repeated 'that while I join ... in deploring these recent events – and I do not mince words about it – there is no justification for jumping from that deplorable fact to the conclusion that it is a basis on which my right hon. Friend's policy may be condemned. As he said at the beginning of the Debate, he intends to pursue that policy and so do his colleagues.'[1]

Two days later, on Friday 17 March, the Prime Minister spoke differently. He had previously arranged to speak to the Birmingham Conservative Association that day and they provided him with a perfect, loyal, audience. The discredit into which Chamberlain has fallen has obscured the political skill with which his speeches were devised as well as their oratorical force; the Birmingham speech of March 1939, hurriedly prepared as it must have been, was a model of argumentative skill. He opened by declaring that he would carry on: 'Tomorrow I shall attain my seventieth birthday ... as I am still sound in wind and limb, I hope that I may have a few more years before me to give what service I can to the state.' In effect he disowned his speech to the House of Commons. Now he understood how widespread dissatisfaction had become with the policy that had culminated in the Munich agreement and he had been told, not least by Halifax, that something more must be done to counter Hitler's latest piece of bullying, if his government were to survive it. With incredulous indignation in his voice, he set out his version of the case against him and, to polite applause, devoted half his speech to refuting it.

> It has been suggested that this occupation of Czechoslovakia was the direct consequence of the visits which I paid to Germany last autumn and that since the result of those events has been to tear up the settlement that we arrived at at Munich that proves that the whole circumstances of those visits was wrong and it is said that as this was the personal policy of the Prime Minister the blame for the fate of Czechoslovakia must rest upon his shoulders.

Enthusiastic applause came, however, when in ringing tones that concealed the caution of the utterance, he referred to a previous speech:

> I pointed out that any demand to dominate the world by force was one which the democracies must resist but I added that I could not believe such a challenge was intended because no government with the interests of its people at heart could expose them for such a claim to the horrors of modern war. And indeed with the lessons of history for all to read it seems incredible that we should see such a challenge. But I feel bound to repeat that while I am not prepared to engage this country by new unspecified commitments, operating under conditions which cannot now be foreseen, yet no greater mistake could be made than to suppose that, because it believes war to be a senseless and cruel thing, this nation has so lost its fibre that it will not take part to the utmost of its power in resisting such a challenge if it ever were made.[2]

In the spring and summer of 1939 Hitler's impatience and British hostility to further concessions forced Chamberlain into more bellicose positions than he wished. Increasing confidence in British defensive strength only confirmed his own belief that conciliation could succeed. Reasonable Germans, even perhaps

Hitler himself, would see that no lightning military strike could any longer brush aside British opposition to change forced by German armed strength and prevent the eventual mobilisation of overwhelming force on the side of the democracies. Such British opposition, if expressed tactfully and unprovocatively, and combined with sympathetic readiness for peaceful change, would bring peace. The German occupation of Prague did not change Chamberlain's policy but it made it much more difficult for him to put it into effect. Many Members of Parliament, some of his own Cabinet, Foreign Office officials, even sometimes Halifax himself, favoured sabre-rattling threats. Chamberlain's continued struggle for peace involved restraining combativeness at home as an essential part of the process of curbing it abroad.

The effects of German shortage of foreign earnings set off more excitement while Mr Chamberlain was on his way to Birmingham that Friday. German pressure for economic concessions brought the Romanian minister in London, Tilea, to the Foreign Office where he alleged that the Romanian government had received a German ultimatum demanding privileged rights to Romanian exports, including oil and grain. Tilea asked what Britain would do if Germany attacked Romania. Halifax told the Prime Minister and that evening the Foreign Office sent enquiries to Moscow, Warsaw, Ankara, Athens, Belgrade and Paris asking the opinion of the respective governments in those capitals. The Cabinet assembled on Saturday afternoon although that morning the British representative in Bucharest sent a message to London denying any immediate threat to Romania.[3] Romania provided an opportunity for the reassertion of the interest of Britain and France in the tranquillity of central Europe, and then, as Chamberlain hoped and believed, to re-create the spirit of Munich and to resume the search for rational solutions for international problems; or, as most of those he worked with assumed, to begin to establish barriers to the rising arrogance of the Third Reich. The record of the Saturday afternoon Cabinet shows Halifax thinking that it 'would be an advantage if the Cabinet took this opportunity of considering what our position would be if a situation such as had been envisaged were to arise in the future' and going on to suggest that, 'if Germany committed an act of naked aggression in Roumania, it would be very difficult for this country not to take all the action in her power to rally resistance against that aggression and to take part in that resistance herself'. At this meeting Chamberlain came as close as he ever did to saying that he had been wrong, and had changed his mind. 'The Prime Minister said that up till a week ago we had proceeded on the assumption that we should be able to continue with our policy of getting onto better terms with the Dictator Powers, and that although those powers had aims, those aims were limited. We had all along had at the back of our minds the reservation that this might not prove to be the case but we had felt that it was right to try out the possibilities of this course ... he had now come definitely to the conclusion that Herr Hitler's attitude made it impossible to continue to negotiate on the old basis with the Nazi regime. This did not mean that negotiations with the German people were impossible. No reliance could be placed on any of the assurances given by the Nazi leaders.' Hence his speech the previous evening. 'The Cabinet', the record says, 'indicated their warm approval of the Prime Minister's speech ... He said he regarded his speech as a challenge to Germany on the issue whether or not Germany intended to dominate Europe by force. It followed that if Germany took another step in the direction of dominating Europe, she would be accepting the challenge.'[4]

What did Chamberlain mean? How novel were the attitudes and policies he now proclaimed? He did not think that war was certain. It could be, and probably would be, prevented. This he would do, but not by assembling the maximum number of states and peoples to use force to frustrate German aggression. This process might frighten Germans into an immediate armed struggle against encircling foes and so cause, rather than prevent, a great war. He would not insist that every European frontier should be defended and maintained as it was. He would certainly not oppose peaceful change brought about by rational discussion. He believed, as strongly as ever, that he could persuade Mussolini to restrain Hitler. This belief implied continued faith that Hitler might be cajoled or bullied into moderation. It was on this point that the post-Prague Prime Minister showed most uncertainty: was the Führer compatible with peace? Sometimes he seemed to share the view of a

Labour Member of Parliament that 'the only restraint upon him is the limit of his power' or even that of Duff Cooper: 'while that thrice-perjured traitor is at the head of the German State, I consider any agreement he signs is not worth the paper it is written on'. On other occasions, after the characteristic resentment that he felt whenever the dictators failed him had subsided, he showed more tolerance. On Hitler he wrote in July 1939, 'I can't help thinking that he is not such a fool as some hysterical people make out and that he would not be sorry to compromise if he could do so without what he would feel to be humiliation.' Sir John Simon, replying to the debate in the House of Commons on 3 April 1939, pointed to the change in attitudes brought about by German conduct and spoke of the Prime Minister as 'the man who was prepared to go furthest in giving credit to German declarations'. Among those in power Chamberlain remained that man.[5]

Did Chamberlain, then, survive March 1939 unmodified? Two changes occurred. First he became more ready to warn Hitler. However, he remained anxious not to provoke him. Orators should not be rude about dictators. On 29 March 1939 Halifax drew attention to some points that ministers should bear in mind when considering public speeches and the Prime Minister 'suggested a further point, namely, that it was desirable that ministers should abstain from personal attacks on Herr Hitler and Signor Mussolini'. But, tactfully, carefully, although effectively, Hitler could be warned that armed aggression anywhere, including eastern Europe, might lead to war with the British Empire. Moreover Chamberlain became more suspicious of Hitler's good faith; in future bargains with Hitler he would require more solid guarantees than mere assertions of good-will in exchange for concessions to Germany. In March 1939 all British policy-makers became less inclined to trust dictators; like everyone else Chamberlain became more cautious than he had been, but he remained the most hopeful, the most credulous of British statesmen. Whenever there remained a choice between belligerence or restraint, Chamberlain continued to choose restraint. As Dirksen, the German ambassador in London, put it the day after the Birmingham speech: 'As long as Chamberlain is at the helm, a relatively moderate course is assured.'[6]

Chamberlain's first essay in tactful deterrence came in his proposal for a four-power declaration. He worked it out himself, since the Foreign Office, he explained, was 'as usual barren of suggestions': 'it is pretty bold and startling, but I feel that something of the kind is needed ... I am also preparing another appeal to the same quarter as before ... in the hope of putting on a brake. As always, I want to gain time, for I never accept that war is inevitable.' He intended, that is to say, simultaneously to employ his favourite device, that of asking Mussolini to calm Hitler.

On 20 March Cadogan, the Permanent Under-Secretary, read the draft declaration to Corbin, the French ambassador in London. The British, French, Soviet and Polish governments would pledge themselves 'immediately to consult together in the event of any action being taken which appears to constitute a threat to the security or independence' of any European state. The proposal horrified Corbin. He said that a promise merely to talk about future aggression would actually encourage it. Helped by this intervention, with which he evidently agreed, Cadogan consulted Halifax, and the Foreign Secretary, together with the Prime Minister and Horace Wilson, agreed that the four governments would undertake 'immediately to consult together as to what steps should be taken to offer joint resistance to any such action'.[7] The proposal for the declaration went to Paris, Moscow and Warsaw later that day. At the same time Chamberlain carried out his own diplomatic manoeuvre. He sent a personal letter to Mussolini. He did not send the letter prepared for him by the Foreign Office. This 'monument of clumsiness', as Chamberlain called the draft, warned Mussolini that conflict between Italy and France might, sadly, lead to war between Britain and Italy. Chamberlain deleted the warning – 'out of place in the letter' – and he and Wilson worked out an appeal to Mussolini for him to restrain Hitler. At the Cabinet meeting on 20 March Chamberlain overrode a mild protest from Halifax who wished to avoid giving Mussolini the 'impression that the Democracies were alarmed at the position and wanted him to get them out of a difficulty'. Halifax, subjected to the influence of the Foreign Office, had become more sceptical of the value of appeals to dictators than Chamberlain.[8]

Neither move prospered. Chamberlain told the Cabinet on Wednesday 22 March that 'the impression left on his mind as to the probable attitude' to the Declaration 'of both Poland and Russia was somewhat disagreeable'. The day before, the Polish Vice-Minister for Foreign Affairs told the British ambassador in Warsaw that he feared the declaration might provoke German anger and that Poland did not wish to co-operate with the USSR. The two objections were linked: Polish co-operation with the Soviet Union could provoke German hostility to Poland. Meanwhile in Moscow, Litvinov, the Foreign Minister, showed resentment because the British preferred their declaration to the Soviet suggestion of a six-power conference including Poland, Romania and Turkey. However, the Soviet government accepted the declaration, but only provided Poland did so first. These themes, the reluctance of the Polish government to join the USSR in an anti-German coalition and the mistrust of British policy shown by the Soviet government, dogged British international efforts from then until the middle of August 1939. As for Mussolini, he replied in a leisurely way to Chamberlain on 31 March. Pompous circumlocution wrapped up a simple message. He would do nothing to keep Hitler quiet unless France made concessions to Italy.[9]

The week beginning with his seventieth birthday on 18 March 1939 was heavy for the Prime Minister. The President of the French Republic, Albert Lebrun, came to London on Tuesday 21 March for a formal state visit. That day Chamberlain ordered the defence services to take precautions against Hitler because he 'was very much worried over the possibility of a surprise air attack. It didn't seem to me in the least probable but with this fanatic you can't exclude entirely the conception.' At 10 a.m. Chatfield presided over a meeting of the service ministers, the Chiefs of Staff, the commanders of the anti-aircraft units and of RAF Fighter Command. Horace Wilson told them, 'that owing to a series of rebuffs over the last few days [presumably the general outcry over the German occupation of Prague], Herr Hitler was now in a towering rage, and we could not disregard the possibility, however remote, that in his present mood he might embark upon some "mad dog" act.' He concluded by emphasising a central tenet of the Prime Minister's approach to the international scene after

March 1939: 'it would have to be borne in mind that if we took a major step to accelerate our readiness for war, this would be certain to be interpreted as an earnest of our intentions to encircle Germany.' Precautions must be taken against the excitable fanatic, but calmly, quietly and inoffensively so that he should not be pushed over the edge into madness. The ministers met the Prime Minister at midday when they passed on the suggestion from the Chiefs of Staff that an exercise could be staged 'which would increase our preparedness without being provocative' and at 6.15 p.m. they met again to approve orders for bringing the regular anti-aircraft units to readiness. In the evening Chamberlain attended the state banquet at Buckingham Palace. Afterwards, he told his sister, he took a sleeping pill, no doubt to ensure some rest before he met the French Foreign Minister the next day.[10]

High-handed German bullying continued. On 20 March Ribbentrop told the Lithuanian Foreign Minister that the Memel region, largely inhabited by Germans, must be restored to Germany at once. The Lithuanian government was given forty-eight hours to agree. If not, the German armed forces would seize the Memelland and then, once they started moving 'there was no means of knowing or telling where they would stop'. On 23 March Hitler, accompanied by cinecamera men, sailed into Memel harbour on the bridge of a German warship. On 22 March a message from Ogilvie-Forbes, in charge of the British embassy in Berlin, warned that reports of the British proposal for a four-power declaration were being attacked as 'encirclement'. 'It constitutes the best anti-British propaganda which the German Government could desire ... I am apprehensive of the effect of such a measure on Herr Hitler in his present state of mind, excited and elated as he is by his successes in Czecho-Slovakia and Memel.'

The state visit of President Lebrun, though mainly involving parades and formal sociabilities, also brought Bonnet, the French Foreign Minister, to London. On 22 March after the Cabinet meeting, before the lavish gala performance at Covent Garden, Bonnet, Halifax and Chamberlain discussed what to do if Poland declined to join the declaration. Bonnet vigorously insisted that Poland must be brought into any scheme of resistance. Germany must be made to feel that she would meet resistance in the east of Europe. To do this Poland and Romania must be induced to oppose German aggression. Poland should be brought in and then, perhaps, Poland, although opposed to any public agreement with the Soviet Union, might accept indirect assistance from the Soviet Union in the form of war material. 'If Poland did not participate, Russian assistance would be worth very little, but if Poland did participate, Russian assistance would be important.' Without Poland a two-front war could not be forced on Germany. 'It would, Monsieur Bonnet thought, be an advantage if Soviet help could be accepted by both Poland and Roumania. The important thing, however, was not to give Poland (or, indeed, Roumania) a pretext for running out on account of Russia.' Halifax did not want 'to give the Soviet Government the idea that we were pushing her to one side'. That, however, was what they decided to do. The British and French would ensure resistance to German aggression on the part of Poland and Romania; only later would the Soviet Union be asked to participate in such resistance. Bonnet, Halifax and Chamberlain agreed that when the expected Polish rejection of the four-power declaration arrived they would try for a Polish guarantee of Romania as a counterpart to a British and French promise that they would join Poland in assisting Romania.[11] Next morning at the Cabinet Chamberlain squashed a suggestion that Turkey might be brought into the peace front; to do so would worry Italy and he 'pointed out the supreme importance of bearing in mind Italy's point of view'. That day Sir Joseph Ball passed to Horace Wilson information from Dingli, his contact in the Italian embassy, to the effect that 'Mussolini is still very anxious to avoid war'.[12]

On 23 March Chamberlain spoke to representatives of the Labour Party who had asked to see him. He explained to them that the Poles would not sign the original declaration and that the Soviet Union must be kept in the background to win Polish co-operation; he suggested that Britain might eventually secure a promise from the USSR to aid Poland and Romania if the latter countries agreed. That afternoon he made a statement in the House of Commons explaining that he could not say yet what would emerge from consultations with other governments. He included reassuring messages to Germany. The

British would not 'stand in the way of any reasonable efforts on the part of Germany to expand their export trade ... Nor is this government anxious to set up in Europe opposing blocks of countries with different ideas about the forms of their internal administration.' That was a disguised way of saying that the government would avoid close association with the Soviet Union. In these days, Mr Chamberlain found a view to which he subsequently clung with all his characteristic tenacity, that the Soviet Union should be kept at arm's length and Poland embraced. He applauded Polish distaste for the Soviet Union and began to form a list of countries who might dislike association with the USSR or be alienated by British association with the USSR. Over the weekend this list had become, in addition to Poland and Romania, Finland, Yugoslavia, Italy, Spain, Portugal and 'certain South American republics'.[13]

Colonel Beck, the Polish Foreign Minister, tried to avoid either accepting or rejecting the British proposal for the four-power declaration by presenting a counter-proposal of a secret Polish-British agreement to consult together as under the declaration. This proposal met neither of the two urgent British requirements. The government wanted to warn Hitler and wanted the British public to know that it had done so. Beck puzzled the British. They did not know whether he hoped for protection for Poland against Hitler or whether he hoped to keep Poland's position as a partner of the Third Reich. In January 1934 the Polish-German non-aggression pact (and the ending of co-operation between the German army and the Soviet Union) marked a new era of Polish-German friendship. In 1938 Poland joined in the dismemberment of Czechoslovakia. Outwardly friendly Polish-German contacts took place in the winter of 1938–9. Early in January 1939 Beck visited Hitler at Berchtesgaden and later that month Ribbentrop came to Warsaw for the anniversary of the Polish-German agreement and, in public, the two Foreign Ministers exchanged the most cordial assurances of mutual good will. In the Foreign Office, Strang assessed the available evidence and decided that the Germans wanted to change the status of Danzig and wanted a motor road across the Polish Corridor. In his minute of mid-January he argued that Hitler might well be seeking a stable friendship with Poland to secure Germany's eastern front before attacking westwards.[14]

Signs of strain in German-Polish relations appeared in February 1939. The Polish ambassador in London told Strang that Beck had no intention of giving Germany something for nothing and the German ambassador to Poland remarked that the Germans insisted on the incorporation of Danzig into Germany, and a road across the Corridor under German sovereignty, but added that there could be no question of the use of force. In March things got rapidly worse. Poles expressed alarm at the German destruction of Czechoslovakia, and at the appearance of a German puppet-state in Slovakia and at the casual seizure of Memel. All these German actions were carried out without consulting the Polish government. On 21 March Ribbentrop summoned Lipski, the Polish ambassador. The German Foreign Minister threatened and bullied. 'The Führer', he told Lipski, 'had always worked for a settlement and an understanding with Poland. Even now the Führer was still pursuing this aim. However the Führer was becoming increasingly amazed at Poland's attitude.' Lipski went to Warsaw to report in a state of 'extreme pessimism' and Beck, the Polish Foreign Minister, found the situation 'very grave'. Poland would not accept German dictation.[15]

Both British and French officials noticed that Beck concealed from them what was happening between Poland and Germany. The French ambassador in Warsaw found the Polish foreign ministry 'extremely reticent' and the British ambassador found it 'extremely difficult to get straightforward answers'. The obvious conclusion was that Beck hoped to make some new bargain and restore German-Polish amity; evidently he thought that bringing outsiders into the German-Polish relationship would make it worse. This fitted his suggestion that any British guarantee to Poland should be secret, which would leave him free to reveal it to the Germans if it seemed useful to do so. The French were convinced that Beck hoped to reach a new Polish-German understanding. Leon Noël, the French ambassador to Poland, described such a policy as 'the law of his destiny' [la loi de son destin]. Léger, the Secretary-General of the French foreign ministry, thought Beck 'entirely cynical and false'. Indeed Léger believed that Beck hoped that Britain would refuse to promise to help Poland if attacked so that he could justify co-operation with Germany to his Polish colleagues. When there came reports of heightened tension between Germany and Poland these assumptions lay behind British assessments of Colonel Beck's likely response.[16]

On Friday 24 March the Polish ambassador in London accompanied Beck's proposal for a secret understanding with a rejection of the proposed four-power declaration: the Polish government objected to public association with the Soviet Union. Hitler might regard 'any strengthening of Poland's relations with the Soviet Union as the last straw' and so precipitate a 'catastrophe'. On Monday, after the weekend, the Foreign Office asked French approval for instructions to the British missions in Warsaw and Bucharest to promise British and French help in case Poland and Romania were attacked, provided that Poland would help Britain or France or Romania if any of those countries became involved in countering German aggression. Romania was to be asked if she would be prepared to help Poland. The French agreed, on 29 March, and that evening Sir H. Kennard in Warsaw and Sir R. Hoare in Bucharest were told to give the proposal to the two governments. The Foreign Ministers of Poland and Romania both replied evasively, each making objection to promises to help the other. British ministers evidently felt comparatively unhurried in making this proposal although the Parliamentary opposition persistently pressed for some action to follow the Prime Minister's apparent change of attitude in his Birmingham speech. A long-standing arrangement would bring Beck to London in a few days' time and, it seems, the government felt able to wait until then. Excitement soon replaced their calm.[17]

On Tuesday Joseph Kennedy, the United States ambassador in London, passed on the belief of the American embassy in Warsaw that Ribbentrop was demanding a German attack on Poland. American opinion would criticise British and French failure to help Poland. On Wednesday a 'most secret report' indicated that Germany had decided to seize Danzig and that action was 'imminent'. That evening, Ian Colvin, the Berlin correspondent of the *News Chronicle*, arrived in London and told Halifax and Chamberlain that Hitler would attack Poland very shortly unless it was made quite certain that Britain would then attack Germany. Ominously, German newspapers began to complain of 'anti-German agitation' and insulting and persecution of Germans in Poland. Halifax asked for an emergency meeting of the Cabinet, which assembled on Thursday morning. He feared an imminent move by Hitler and since 'the best means of stopping German aggression was almost certainly to make clear that we should resist it by force', he proposed 'a clear declaration of our intention to support Poland if Poland was attacked by Germany'. Given 'the view he took' of Beck he thought it worth discussing whether or not the Polish government should be informed in advance.

Here, the Prime Minister pointed out, 'was the actual crossing of the stream' beyond which lay British commitment to war against German attacks in eastern Europe. However, if Germany now forcefully seized more territory, the policy of securing peaceful change by discussion, in which Britain would play its part, would suffer another humiliating reverse and Britain's vulnerability would increase. Equally threatening was the prospect of Polish-German agreement. Chamberlain felt 'uneasy at the fact that our ambassador in Warsaw could obtain no information as to the progress of the negotiations between Germany and Poland. One possible, but very distasteful, explanation of this was that Polish negotiators were, in fact, giving way to Germany.' Another minister, Walter Elliot, put this view more bluntly: 'we ought to take steps to ensure that Poland did resist German aggression'. Chamberlain told his sister that 'the thought that we might wake up on Sunday or Monday morning to find Poland surrendering to an ultimatum was certainly alarming'.[18]

For the government, and especially for Chamberlain, both a German attack on Poland and a German agreement with Poland would be disastrous. Either event would mean a new failure in Chamberlain's 'positive policy of peace'. Both involved another German advance towards supremacy over continental Europe which British policy aimed to prevent. If either of these events took place a politically weakened Chamberlain would, assuming he could remain Prime Minister, be compelled at least to remodel his government. That week several Conservative critics again emphasised this point by supporting a House of Commons motion calling for a national government with powers to direct industry, capital and labour.

On Friday the Cabinet met again at midday in the Prime Minister's room in the House of Commons. It became even clearer that the guarantee to Poland was designed to prevent Polish-German agreement rather than a Polish-German war: 'further enquiries', Chamberlain explained, 'had failed to confirm the alleged German troop movements' and, he said, 'the French Government did not apprehend any immediate *coup* on the part of Germany.' Most of the discussion dealt with probable complaints from the Labour and Liberal Parties that 'Russia was being left on one side'. Chamberlain had talked on Thursday afternoon to the leaders of the Labour and Liberal Parties and he also talked to Lloyd George, by now in effect a one-man party, for fifteen minutes. Then he saw the Labour leaders again later in the evening. As usual confrontation with Lloyd George upset Chamberlain but, as he told his sister, 'all my bitterness seemed to pass away for I despised him and felt myself the better man'. He found the deputy leader of the Labour Party, Arthur Greenwood, to be helpful, but the other two Labour leaders who saw him, Hugh Dalton and A. V. Alexander, 'represented the pro-Russian section of the Labour Party'. Halifax was not worried. He intended to see Maisky, the Russian ambassador, that afternoon and expected him to be 'perfectly satisfied' and to say 'that the Russians were willing to help us if they were allowed to do so'. Thus some hint of the approval of the Soviet government could be given to the House of Commons.

Cabinet ministers raised little objection to the proposal to guarantee Polish independence against aggression, a guarantee that provided the occasion which brought Britain into war five months later.

The guarantee to Poland was a political not a military event. It warned Germany that armed attack eastwards would cause war with the British Empire. It made it clear that the line German forces must not cross lay somewhere close to the Polish-German frontier. It did not mean that the British authorities had worked out any mechanism for holding such a line if Germany went to war. The Foreign Office, in a paper drawn up on Wednesday for the Chiefs of Staff, observed that 'Poland has reached the parting of the ways, and will quickly have to choose between resistance to German expansion in co-operation with other States, or an agreement with Germany which would give her no guarantee against future dismemberment.' The military, through Admiral Chatfield, the new Minister for Co-ordination of Defence, told the Cabinet that it would be better to have Poland as an ally but made it clear that there had been no discussion with the French about a possible attack by the French army on the western frontier of Germany and, indeed, Chatfield thought that Poland would be overrun within two or three months after war broke out. The point of the guarantee was that Germany, it was hoped, would not risk war with the British Empire in addition to France. Hitler would not risk it, or, if he did, more prudent Germans would restrain him. It was not a matter of foiling a German military offensive but of preventing its ever being begun.

Just before 3 p.m. on Friday 31 March, the Prime Minister rose in the Commons to make his statement.[19] Certain consultations, he said, are continuing with other governments and, meanwhile, before they are concluded:

> I now have to inform the House that during that period, in the event of any action which clearly threatened Polish independence, and which the Polish Government accordingly considered it vital to resist with their national forces, His Majesty's Government would feel themselves bound at once to lend the Polish Government all support in their power. They have given the Polish Government an assurance to that effect.

11 Making a 'Peace Front': April–August 1939

With his enviable capacity for self-satisfaction, Chamberlain was delighted by his announcement of the guarantee to Poland on 31 March 1939. He congratulated himself not on an abrupt reversal of policy, in committing Britain to join a war provoked by an eastern European conflict, but on the limits on the scope of the commitment he put into the statement. 'It was, of course, mostly my own and when it was finished I was well satisfied with it. It was unprovocative in tone [i.e. Germany was not mentioned] but firm; clear, but stressing the important point (perceived alone by *The Times*) that what we are concerned with is not the boundaries of states but their independence. And it is we who will judge whether their independence is threatened or not.'[1]

Chamberlain, once again, was out of step with most of his ministerial colleagues, those MPs who concerned themselves with foreign affairs and the articulate section of public opinion. He wanted to make possible renewed negotiation with Germany while the others wanted to restrain Germany by threats. Chamberlain meant the guarantee to Poland to compel renewed Anglo-German discussions to secure European peace; the remainder hoped to join with other countries to impose peaceful conduct on Germany. Chamberlain found himself driven to apply his interpretation of British policy by quiet manoeuvre rather than by public proclamation.

To Chamberlain, the guarantee meant that the British government would decide whether or not Poland should be helped to resist German attempts to force territorial change. He could not maintain this view in public. On the evening the guarantee was announced, the London *Evening Standard* and, next morning, *The Times* newspaper reported obviously inspired comment. *The Times* explained that the guarantee committed the British government to 'fair and free negotiation'. It did not

bind Great Britain to 'defend every inch of the present frontiers of Poland ... Mr Chamberlain's statement involves no
blind acceptance of the *status quo*. On the contrary, his repeated
references to free negotiation imply that he thinks that there
are problems in which adjustments are still necessary.' It was
not, *The Times* leader explained, a political challenge to Germans. 'It is, on the contrary, an appeal to their better nature,
and an invitation to enter into closer relations if they will
conform to more normal practices in their intercourse with
foreign nations.' Halifax, until the Poles complained, thought
the article 'just right'.

All this suggested to the Polish ambassador in London,
Count Raczynski, the prospect of a new Munich over Poland.
He called at the Foreign Office and secured publication of a
communiqué expressing the surprise 'in official circles that
attempts should have been made in London to minimise the
Prime Minister's statement'. In the House of Commons debate
on the following morning, 3 April, Chamberlain claimed that
the only limitation he had in mind was that his declaration did
not concern 'some minor little frontier incident' and he did not
dispute the general opinion that only the Polish government
could decide what threatened the independence of Poland.
John Simon, replying for the government, claimed that the
limiting comment 'was entirely unofficial and in no sense inspired from any Government source whatever', remarks which
point to the Prime Minister's press secretary or Sir Joseph Ball
at Conservative Central Office.[2]

The reader, however, should not exaggerate the difference
between Chamberlain's personal view and the policy he was
compelled to follow. Certainly Chamberlain intended to maintain the United Kingdom as an independent great power, the
centre of the British Empire. Certainly he did not intend to
tolerate German threats to this independence or to allow Germany to reach a position in which such threats could be made.
He would never agree to German domination of continental
Europe. The special feature of his own view lay in his belief
that German, even Nazi, acceptance of the continued power of
the United Kingdom could be won by flexibility and readiness
to compromise. Chamberlain intended nothing less than to
arrange that the satisfaction of German aspirations should be

compatible with British power and independence. This ambition required moderation from Germany and from Britain. It involved British interference to quieten European conflicts and to maintain the balance of power. His policy was arrogant, not weak or timid.

Chamberlain's critics in 1939 thought this attempt to work with Germany doomed to failure. German expansion, they believed, could only be curbed by war or the threat of overwhelming strength. British military power must be maximised. Alliances must be made. Other peoples must be encouraged to resist Germany. They must not be made to fear that they might be employed as bargaining counters in an Anglo-German diplomatic search for reconciliation and compromise. Chamberlain's critics considered that his policy of appealing to the better nature of potential enemies might alienate potential friends. In one respect Chamberlain's critics felt uncertain: obviously those Germans who might restrain Hitler and moderate German policy should be encouraged to do so. Was this best done by blunt intimidation from outside or by tactful restraint? In the Commons debate Harold Nicolson, usually a critic of Chamberlain's attitude, argued that the British government should not seem to be 'encircling' Germany. He wanted, though, only to deny 'encirclement' in public discussion; Chamberlain might try to avoid the reality itself. Whenever Chamberlain could choose between threatening combativeness and careful moderation towards Germany, he chose the latter.[3]

The House of Commons discussed the guarantee on Monday 3 April. Apart from Sir Stafford Cripps, who eloquently set out the full left-wing view that the government, as a set of pro-Fascist defenders of capitalist privileges, insincerely threatened Germany only to deceive true democrats, the speakers applauded Chamberlain's new course. In addition to the usual praise for the Prime Minister from the small pacifist minority or from sycophantic Conservatives, the great men of the House spoke in support – Greenwood, the bibulous right-wing deputy leader of Labour; the Liberal leader, the verbose but elegant Sinclair; and Eden, Lloyd George and Churchill. Churchill expressed 'the most complete agreement with the Prime Minister'. But a constant theme preoccupied the most important speakers: Russia. Russian co-operation and support must be assured. Lloyd George put the point most vigorously: 'Without the help of Russia we are walking into a trap.'[4]

Making sure of the Soviet Union became the principal preoccupation of British diplomacy for the next five months. On many occasions in the past Chamberlain had shown reluctance to co-operate with the USSR. The new British promise to join in a German-Polish war did not change his mind. On 4 April, Beck, the Polish Foreign Minister, conferred with Halifax and Chamberlain in London during a visit arranged long before. The talks greatly pleased both British ministers. Beck readily agreed to a reciprocal guarantee, indeed he insisted that Polish dignity required that Poland should promise support in case of a German attack on the United Kingdom. However, he evaded the principal object of the British, to secure a Polish promise to support Romania against Germany, explaining that to do so would alienate Hungary. What seems to have impressed Chamberlain and Halifax most and caused them to tolerate this evasion was Beck's emphatic rejection of the USSR. Chamberlain openly put his position to Beck: 'His Majesty's Government were constantly being attacked in the House of Commons because they did not get onto better terms with Russia ... would it be embarrassing to Poland if His Majesty's Government now tried to improve their relations with the Soviet Government? This would not mean that they would make an agreement with the Soviet Government, but that they would try to establish such relations as would enable them to expect help from Soviet Russia in case of war.' Beck uttered 'the warning that, if Russia were brought in, this might well precipitate a conflict'. He felt convinced that 'a decision to open a war against Poland would be a very difficult one for Germany to take. Any association between Poland and Russia would bring that decision nearer.' Chamberlain applauded – 'I very much agree with him' he wrote.[5]

After the Polish guarantee Chamberlain continued eagerly to court the Italian dictator. For the Prime Minister, Mussolini's role was to help to tranquillise Hitler. He had taken some trouble to give Mussolini advance information of the Polish guarantee, 'having regard', he explained, 'to the cordial relations which exist between us'. A week later, however, as Chamberlain put it in an outburst of schoolboy fury, Mussolini behaved towards him 'like a sneak and a cad. He has not made the least effort to preserve my friendly feelings.' He had invaded and occupied Albania. The British and French foreign offices thought Mussolini was seeking prestige by showing that he could be as violent as Hitler and that he too could send his armed forces into another country, although Albania was, in any case, already effectively controlled by Italy. Indeed Italian forces had outdone Hitler's by shelling Durazzo. Menacingly, moreover, the strength the Italians employed suggested targets beyond Albania. At midnight on 8 April the Greek Prime Minister (and dictator), General Metaxas, 'deeply moved', sent for the British minister in Athens and told him that the Italians would soon attack Corfu. Greece would 'resist to the utmost and at the cost of all sacrifices'. That, the British minister commented, 'would mean that Italian action would be extended to the whole of Greece'. Next day, Easter Sunday, Halifax told the Italian chargé in London that the occupation of Corfu 'must be a matter of gravest concern' to the British government. British desire to dominate the eastern Mediterranean, Middle Eastern oilfields and the Suez Canal made a friendly Greece a 'vital interest'.[6]

The symptoms of crisis appeared. Halifax gave up his plans for Easter in Yorkshire and, after the three-hour service on Good Friday, the new crisis filled all his time. Chamberlain reluctantly returned from fishing in Scotland on Saturday, after Churchill had been 'at the telephone all day' urging the recall of Parliament. Churchill also spoke to Halifax on Friday, and met Chamberlain on Monday. On Sunday he wrote to Halifax demanding that the navy seize Corfu: 'What is now at stake is nothing less than the whole of the Balkan peninsula. If these states remain exposed to German and Italian pressure while we appear, as they may deem it, incapable of action, they will be forced to make the best terms possible with Berlin and Rome. How forlorn then will our position become!' Churchill telephoned the next day to Halifax to report, wrongly, that Metaxas had gone over to the Axis already. In this new crisis Chamberlain's reputation was once more at stake. Italian action made absurd the Prime Minister's belief in Mussolini's moderation and his sustained attempt, in spite of noisy Italian intervention in Spain and wild anti-French rhetoric, to work for peace with him. Churchill's activity reinforced his claim to ministerial office, a claim which he made directly that week by inviting the Conservative chief whip to dine, when he told him of his strong desire to join the government. Chamberlain believed that Churchill and Eden would exploit any political mistake he made. Now Mussolini had joined Hitler in enabling 'my enemies to mock me publicly and to weaken my authority in this country'. Though he was assured that his political position was intact, which was, of course, true as far as voting strength in the Commons was concerned, he felt 'very dispirited and very lonely'.[7] In making policy he had to take unwelcome opinions into account.

Variously composed meetings of ministers took place over the weekend and the full Cabinet met on Easter Monday. The Cabinet agreed to support Greece and Turkey against possible Italian aggression and left the Foreign Policy Committee to work out the details which the Cabinet approved before Parliament reassembled in the afternoon of Thursday 13 April. Oliver Stanley and John Simon thought it would be impossible to face parliament unless something definite had been done. Nevertheless Chamberlain proposed only to announce that the British government would regard any forceful disturbance of the status quo in the Mediterranean as 'an unfriendly act'. Halifax, however, reported that, like the House of Commons, the Turkish government had no faith in British firmness and declined to promise to join in resistance to Germany and Italy unless the British acted with vigour. Hence the Cabinet agreed to a statement, similar to the Polish guarantee, promising to Greece all support in Britain's power if that country resisted a threat to its independence.[8] During the meeting the Cabinet agreed to add a guarantee to Romania. In Paris the government feared an imminent German attack on Romania and, having agreed to the British proposal on Greece, urged that to guarantee Poland and Greece would be to leave Romania as an obvious victim. The British replied that it was better to exploit the prospect of a British pledge to Romania to gain Polish and Turkish support for Romania also. However, a telegram from Paris was brought to the Cabinet. Daladier, somewhat excited, insisted that a guarantee of Romania was 'the only way of averting a general conflagration', otherwise a German ultimatum to Romania would be presented 'within a few hours'. Some British ministers, particularly Chatfield, agreed that Romania was under threat. Thus when Chamberlain opened the debate in the House of Commons that afternoon he announced British guarantees of both Greece and Romania.

The British government wanted Turkey to become not simply another beneficiary of a British guarantee but an ally who would help to resist aggression outside its own boundaries. They asked the Turks to take on new commitments and the Turks looked for assurances of British power and determination. In the first place, the guarantees to Greece and Romania provided reassurance. Four weeks later the two governments announced their intention of negotiating an alliance. Meanwhile they promised to co-operate and help each other 'in the event of an act of aggression leading to war in the Mediterranean area'. This declaration, it was claimed, was not directed against any country but the two governments obviously intended to deter Italy.[9]

The House of Commons met soon after the Cabinet meeting on Thursday 13 April. The Prime Minister seemed tired and, according to the French ambassador, 'gave the impression of moving forward only under the impulsion of the national will' and of lagging behind. Chamberlain did not enjoy the debate that followed his account of the Italian invasion of Albania and his announcement of the guarantees to Greece and Romania. He did not enjoy the interruption of his peroration: 'We have exercised patience over a long period, in spite of many disappointments, in our efforts to remove suspicions, to promote good will and to keep the peace ... Let us, therefore, not put patience aside. [Hon. Members: "What about Russia?"] It is a little difficult, perhaps, to avoid the exhibition of strong feelings, but I hope that Hon. Members will not assume that, if I have not mentioned Russia in what I have said this afternoon, that means we are not keeping in the closest touch with the representatives of that country.' Once again the most prominent speakers, Attlee and Dalton for the Labour Party, Sinclair for the Independent Liberals and Churchill, with his growing prestige, called for alliance with the Soviet Union and at least six other speakers supported them. The line taken by Chamberlain and Halifax, on the other hand, was effectively summarised in an instruction to the British ambassador to Turkey. 'His Majesty's Government have no intention of concluding a bilateral agreement of mutual assistance with the Soviet government.'[10]

On 5 April the Cabinet discussed what should be done about the Soviet Union. The Prime Minister spoke firmly. He did not trust Russia; Poland and Romania did not wish to co-operate with Russia; he did not believe that Russia could provide much assistance, 'except for defensive purposes . . . and if an arrangement which included Russia would be likely to cause an explosion', by provoking Germany, it needed prolonged thought. He suggested making a permanent arrangement with Poland and then considering what further steps could be taken. Thus, for the moment, he dealt with 'the absurd hysterical passion of the opposition egged on by Ll G who have a pathetic belief that Russia is the key to our salvation' – that is his parliamentary opponents spurred on by Lloyd George. However, Mussolini's Albanian action and Turkey's desire to make sure of Soviet co-operation, together with the agitation in the Commons in the debate on 13 April, made it difficult to delay. On 14 April Halifax sent instructions to the British ambassador in Moscow. He was to suggest that the Soviet government should declare 'on their own initiative' that if aggression took place against any European neighbour of the USSR, which was resisted by the country concerned, 'the assistance of the Soviet Union would be available, if desired, and would be afforded in such manner as would be found most convenient'. Thus the British would secure Soviet help but would keep the USSR at arm's length and would not join with the Soviet Union in a public document. Poland and Romania would not be committed to receiving any Soviet help unless they asked for it. The day before, the French Foreign Minister made a quite different proposal to Moscow through the Russian ambassador in Paris. If France went to war with Germany as a result of helping Poland or Romania, the Soviet Union would immediately help France. In turn, if the Soviet Union became involved in war with Germany through helping either of these countries, France would immediately help the USSR. The two governments would at once discuss how to make effective their mutual assistance. France felt able to work together with the USSR; fear of causing offence in Germany or Poland seemed not to worry the French government.[11]

On 18 April 1939, the British and French Foreign Ministers received a counter-proposal from the Soviet government, combining, the Russians said, the British and French suggestions. The USSR offered a triple alliance, complete with a military convention. Britain (referred to as 'England'), France and the USSR would assist each other in case of aggression in Europe against any one of them. These countries would help against aggression any eastern European state bordering on the USSR. They would, as quickly as possible, work out the extent and form of military assistance in resisting aggression. The Soviet government asked the British to explain that their guarantee to Poland applied only against Germany. Poland and Romania were to revoke their defensive treaty against the USSR or extend it against all aggression. The three powers, once involved in war, could make peace only by common agreement. The political treaty would be signed simultaneously with the military agreement. The three powers would make a special arrangement with Turkey.[12]

The negotiations that followed over the next four months proved arduous, complicated, and futile. They can be summarised, before they are analysed, by noting that Britain and France eventually accepted all those Soviet conditions set out on 18 April. Formally, the only points on which agreement was never reached were over who was to decide if aggression had taken place against the states bordering the USSR, and, in the military arrangements, with respect to whether or not Poland would agree to the advance of Soviet troops across its territory. That is not to say that these points explain the eventual failure of the alliance; at the time of writing these words, more than half a century later, it is impossible to be certain of the reasons for the actions of the Soviet government. Mr Chamberlain's sustained opposition to an alliance with the USSR and the support given to him by Lord Halifax, originally firm but later more hesitant, shifting, as usual, as the view of his chief adviser, Cadogan, changed, provide the reason for delays on the British side of the negotiations. The Prime Minister's opposition to an alliance and the motive for his opposition, the fear of alienating the Germans, may explain the eventual abandonment by the Soviet government of any attempts they were making in the summer of 1939 to secure the British alliance.

Cadogan drew up hostile, even contemptuous, comments on the Russian proposal. He described it as 'extremely inconvenient. What it really comes to is that we have to balance the advantage of a paper commitment by Russia to join in a war on our side against the disadvantage of associating ourselves openly with Russia.' The disadvantage would be to help enemy propaganda (directed at the 'Red danger'), to offend Portugal, Spain and Yugoslavia, frighten Romania and upset Poland. The advantage was 'to say the least, problematical' so enfeebled the purged Red Army, so weak the Soviet navy, so out-of-date Russian aviation. The inefficient transport system would inhibit supply. 'Russia may be good for defence of her territory' but could not offer 'useful active assistance outside her frontiers'. The main point in seeking Russian support had been 'to placate our left-wing in England, rather than to obtain any solid military advantage' – Cadogan perhaps thought it tactless to mention the eagerness for a Soviet alliance of Churchill, Eden and Lloyd George. The 'left' would 'make the most' of refusal of the Russian proposal. He ended with an important opinion: 'There is further the risk – though I should have thought it a very remote one – that, if we turn down this proposal, the Soviet might make some "non-intervention" agreement with the German government.' Here, of course, was an abject failure, even on the part of the person who was, in principle, the best informed in the country, to foretell the future. There are some assumptions so firmly made that evidence to the contrary presents itself in vain. Cadogan himself, for instance, had minuted earlier in the year, at the beginning of February 1939: 'We shall have to watch very carefully the development of any tendency towards a *rapprochement* between Germany and the Soviet.' Yet he could not bring himself to believe his own observation. Hints and more than hints of German-Soviet contacts often came in but the assumption that the Soviet Union and Nazi Germany were, and must remain, each other's worst enemies, could not easily be dispelled. Chamberlain himself believed that Soviet help, for what it was worth, could be had irrespective of the conduct of the western powers. According to Joseph Kennedy, the US ambassador in London, to whom Chamberlain habitually spoke with freedom, he felt at the time that 'he can make a deal with Russia at any time now, but is delaying until he definitely gets the Balkan situation straightened away'.[13]

Cadogan read his paper to Halifax who approved it and then Cadogan presented it to the Foreign Policy Committee of the Cabinet on 19 April. His advocacy, supported, in the absence of Halifax, by R. A. Butler, helped Chamberlain to persuade the Committee to reject the Soviet proposal or, as he put it, 'we shall endeavour to convey the impression that the time for a military alliance was not yet ripe'. The British, therefore, told the French government that they planned to try again to persuade the Soviet government to make the unilateral declaration that they would, without preconditions, help any eastern European country which asked for Soviet help. The French proposed instead a triple alliance of their own drafting; the British urged them to drop this and try for the declaration. The French Foreign Minister asserted that the Soviet government would insist on a British and French promise to make war on Germany if the USSR became involved in war with Germany; however, the French government would be delighted if the British succeeded, but they did not think they would. Disregarding British wishes, Bonnet gave the Russian ambassador in Paris the text of the French scheme for a triple alliance, allegedly in the 'heat of the moment', perhaps to try to encourage the Soviet authorities to believe that a real alliance was attainable. On 6 May the British Foreign Office sent their reply to the Russian proposal of 18 April. After four meetings of the Foreign Policy Committee of the Cabinet and three meetings of the full Cabinet, they repeated to Moscow their proposal that the Soviet government should make a unilateral declaration of support for the victims of aggression. These proposals Seeds put to Molotov on 8 May.[14]

In the middle of these leisurely deliberations, M. Gafencu, the Romanian Foreign Minister, came to London. He charmed and pleased those who met him, not least Halifax who found their minds 'worked very much alike'. He was 'much impressed by M. Gafencu's words – "If war was certain he would not care who helped him: but if there were a 5 per cent chance of peace, he did not wish to jeopardise it by associating with a country in whom he had no confidence".' Halifax himself declared that a tripartite alliance 'would make war inevitable' and he admitted only 'the bare possibility that a refusal of Russia's offer might even throw her into Germany's arms'.[15]

An event obviously important, but hard to assess, took place on 3 May 1939. In the morning Litvinov discussed with Sir William Seeds what the British promise to Poland in case of aggression of 'all support in their power' actually meant. Litvinov showed his normal fluency and self-possession. Seeds was surprised when next day's papers announced that he had been replaced as Commissar for Foreign Affairs by V. M. Molotov. This replaced a jovial, communicative advocate of collective security and, in public, of collaboration with the democratic west with one of the most important persons in the regime, a man whose attitudes to foreign policy were unknown. It obviously meant that the ruling group in the USSR intended to take over day-to-day handling of foreign affairs. Henceforward Molotov, one of the toughest negotiators of the twentieth century, consulting Stalin and probably personages such as Voroshilov, Zhdanov and Kaganovitch, devoted himself to extracting from the British a pledge to join with the USSR in any war with Germany, a pledge Chamberlain was determined to refuse. Chamberlain, backed by a less and less reliably sympathetic Cabinet, sought to extract a promise of as much Russian support in case of war as was convenient to the British, in a form that would not alarm Poles, or annoy Germans. Molotov's tenacity matched Chamberlain's obstinacy. Molotov wanted an unbreakable alliance covering every possibility of Soviet-German conflict; Chamberlain wanted the minimum Anglo-Russian association he could persuade his Cabinet and his party to regard as sufficient.

In arguing for the declaration and against an alliance, Chamberlain and Halifax encountered disagreement from only two or three of their colleagues. Samuel Hoare, Oliver Stanley and Malcolm MacDonald urged that the British must look for terms for co-operation acceptable to the Soviet government. They tried to persuade their colleagues to agree to the Russian suggestion that the three powers should each promise not to make a separate peace in case they went to war. Chamberlain and Halifax objected to 'changing the whole basis of our policy and risking the alienation of our friends' and Chatfield, the Minister for Co-ordination of Defence, helped them by observing that 'close relations with the Soviet would not justify alienating strategically important countries like Spain and Portugal'. In consequence Seeds again presented to Molotov on 8 May the suggestion that the Soviet government should declare 'on its own initiative' that it would help, if asked by them, any country in eastern Europe on behalf of which the British and French had already gone to war to assist against German aggression. Now the suggested declaration proposed a Soviet promise which would come into effect only after Britain and France had already fulfilled their pledges but the new proposal still avoided any direct British association with the USSR.[16]

Late on 15 May Molotov gave Seeds a firm rejection of the British proposals. He wanted an alliance: the British and French must promise help to the Soviet Union in case of direct attack, the three powers should guarantee all the countries to the west of the Soviet Union including Finland, Estonia and Latvia, and were to agree on how mutual assistance would be given. Even now Chamberlain and Halifax struggled against the alliance. In the evening of 16 May they found the Foreign Policy Committee difficult to manage. Chatfield, who remained in contact with the Chiefs of Staff, reversed his earlier opinion and began to argue that it would be dangerous to have the USSR neutral in a war and that it would be disastrous if the Soviet Union made an alliance with Germany. It seems he now took this possibility more seriously than did Halifax, who dismissed reports of the possibility of a Hitler–Stalin pact 'which might' he said 'be spread by persons who desired to drive us into making a pact with Russia'. Halifax yet again attempted to get an independent Russian declaration, this time by offering staff conversations. He did it through Vansittart who talked next day to Maisky, the Soviet ambassador, and told him, speaking 'personally', that he intended to submit certain proposals to Halifax if he could be assured in advance that they would be acceptable to Moscow. It was the declaration again, this time with an offer of military conversations. On 19 May Maisky reported Moscow's rejection and explained 'that the only basis on which the Soviet Government were prepared to proceed was that of a Triple Pact'.[17]

Now the question was inescapable: alliance or nothing? So far Mr Chamberlain had persuaded the Cabinet to ask the Soviet authorities to make their own separate, independent declaration of willingness to give help to any country that asked for it. The USSR demanded an alliance – a British promise of assistance to the Soviet Union against Germany. To Chamberlain's horror support for the alliance became overwhelming among his colleagues. An article in *Isvestya* on 11 May set out the Soviet requirements of three-power mutual assistance and shared obligations to defend each other and the countries on the western frontiers of the USSR: 'an odd way of carrying on negotiations', Chamberlain wrote, complaining of this publication, 'but they have . . . no manners and they are working hand-in-hand with our opposition' and with Churchill. On 19 May a Commons debate enabled Lloyd George to denounce 'a great desire, if possible, to do without Russia . . . For months we had been staring this powerful gift horse in the mouth.' The usual Parliamentary stars followed: Attlee, Churchill, Sinclair and Eden; only one comparatively obscure Conservative backbencher, Mr H. V. A. M. Raikes, supported the Prime Minister. Daladier, the French Prime Minister, could not understand why Halifax and Chamberlain made so much fuss. He insisted that an alliance with Russia would make war less likely rather than, as Halifax suggested to him, 'provoke Germany to violent action'. In spite of this, two days after he had talked to Daladier in Paris, Halifax tried in conversations in Geneva to persuade Maisky of the merit of a three-power agreement by Britain, France and the Soviet Union to help each other in case any of the three went to war to support a state guaranteed by them against German attack, but without their making a promise to help each other in case of direct attack on any one of them. Maisky insisted on a triple mutual guarantee against direct aggression by Germany against any of the three signatories. Halifax concluded his report from Geneva by gloomily explaining that the choice was plain – between breakdown of the negotiations or triple alliance.[18] The Soviet Union would not promise aid to its neighbours without receiving every possible guarantee from Britain and France that they would collaborate with the Soviet Union to protect the USSR from German attack.

The message gave Chamberlain a 'very tiresome week' as he faced 'the fateful decision'. Poland and Romania let him down by failing to object to the principle of an alliance. Cadogan and Halifax now thought alliance better than breakdown and circulated to the Cabinet a careful memorandum of this conclusion. No sign of opposition to an alliance appeared in the British press. 'Some of the members of the Cabinet who were most unwilling to agree to the alliance', Chamberlain grumbled, 'now appear to have swung round to the opposite view.' Admiral Chatfield, the Minister for Co-ordination of Defence, caused him particular distress when he reported that the Chiefs of Staff had changed their minds. He, and they, no longer thought it essential not to annoy Spain and decided that a full Anglo-Franco-Soviet alliance was necessary to block any Nazi-Soviet understanding. Moreover 'it was obvious', Chamberlain thought, 'that refusal would create immense difficulties in the House even if I could persuade my Cabinet.' In the Foreign Policy Committee 'the only support I could get for my view was from Rab Butler [the Under-Secretary for Foreign Affairs] and he was not a very influential ally.' The problem was his belief 'that the alliance would definitely be a lining up of opposing blocs and an association which would make any negotiation or discussion with the totalitarians difficult if not impossible.'[19]

He sent for Horace Wilson. They talked and an idea emerged: 'most ingenious' Chamberlain thought. He would avoid the 'idea of an alliance' and substitute 'a declaration of our *intentions* in certain circumstances in fulfilment of our obligation' under Article 16 of the Covenant of the League of Nations. He recovered his equanimity and found himself in 'a happier mood'. It remained, of course, to find out 'what the Russians have to say but I think they will find it difficult to refuse'. He would offer what the Russians would think to be an alliance and the Germans would not.

The Cabinet, at last, decided to go for the alliance on 24 May 1939. Halifax went so far as to say that the idea of a German-Russian understanding 'was not one which could be altogether disregarded'. Chamberlain managed to delude Sir Samuel Hoare, who was consistently in favour of alliance, into putting forward the League of Nations idea, first to the Foreign Policy Committee. Halifax, reversing his earlier opinions, asserted that an alliance with the USSR would make war less likely. He gave the encouraging news that Maisky, the Russian ambassador, had said that if the British agreed to a triple relationship the Russians would not prove difficult on other matters. That afternoon, after the Cabinet meeting, Chamberlain went down to the Commons and announced that the alliance was as good as made.[20]

The Soviet authorities soon administered a severe shock. Seeds and Payart, the French chargé, presented the new British proposals, which the French government agreed to support, to Molotov in the Kremlin on 27 May. If France and Britain were attacked by Germany (referred to as 'a European power'), or if they went to war to aid a European state which had asked for help to resist attack, or if they went to war to defend a state which they had promised to help against aggression 'in conformity with the wishes of that state', then the USSR would give France and the United Kingdom all the support and assistance in its power, acting in accordance with the principle of Article 16 of the League Covenant. Equally if the USSR were at war for those reasons, Britain and France, following the principles of the League, would go to its aid. The allies, therefore, would help only countries who wished to be helped. Molotov, sitting behind a large desk raised on a platform above his interlocutors, suggested that the British and French could not be serious; they merely wished to pass time in futile talk. Bringing in the League would mean, Molotov asserted, that Bolivia could block action while an aggressor bombed Moscow. The draft treaty suggested consultation on how to make mutual assistance effective; Molotov argued this was provision for talk rather than immediate and effective action. Another section aroused Molotov's contemptuous anger. The alliance would include this provision: 'the rendering of support and assistance in the above cases is without prejudice to the rights and position of other Powers'.

The Foreign Office immediately sent a telegram to Seeds in Moscow asking him to see Molotov again to explain that the British were indeed in earnest. Seeds acted at once – he received the telegram in the early evening of 30 May and immediately requested an interview. Molotov, evidently interested, received him at the Kremlin at 10.30 that evening and they talked until nearly midnight. Two types of difficulties were impeding the negotiations for an alliance. Chamberlain created one set of obstructions, trying, more and more alone, to frustrate the negotiations. There were other, real difficulties. Molotov emphasised one of them, which he declared to be a vital issue. How were eastern European states who did not wish Soviet aid to be protected from German occupation? Finland, Estonia and Latvia would not accept guarantees against Germany. What would happen if states bordering on the Soviet Union collapsed under German attack or, as in the case of Czechoslovakia in March, 'invited' German forces to enter in response to German threats? Seeds replied that an aggressor arriving on the Soviet border would have to reckon with immediate British assistance to the USSR if he went further. However, neither the British government nor British opinion would force guarantees of protection on countries which did not desire them. They would be menaces rather than guarantees. Molotov, indeed, clearly intended that 'assistance' to states bordering on the Soviet Union might be forced on them by the USSR. Next day he publicly exposed to the Supreme Soviet his concern to ensure the defence of the Baltic states and, ominously, announced that contacts could continue with countries like Germany and Italy and that, in particular, commercial negotiations with Germany were about to resume.[21]

On 2 June Molotov gave Naggiar and Seeds new Soviet proposals. They mentioned the League in the preamble but made no mention of Article 16, they listed countries the allies had agreed to defend: Belgium, Greece, Turkey, Romania, Poland, Latvia, Estonia and Finland. Thus Molotov removed the British provision that states would be given aid only if they wished for it. If any one of the allies detected a threat of aggression the three would consult at once and 'establish in common' the moment for putting mutual assistance into effect. The three were to agree not to make a separate armistice or peace. The British mechanism for reaching decisions restarted. The Foreign Policy Committee met three times and the full Cabinet discussed their conclusions. The French government repeatedly pressed for speedy conclusions but it could not

compel the British to be more yielding. Full British participation was indispensable to make convincing any deterrent
against German violence and so the British government took
the decisions rather than the French. Chamberlain's contribution to the discussion was to insist that the three allies must
consult and agree before any one of them did anything to
defend an unresisting state against aggression, although Halifax thought Russia might suspect this as a possible excuse for
inaction. Worrying about the slow pace of negotiations, Halifax
suggested sending the Foreign Office legal adviser to Moscow
to smooth the drafting. Instead Cadogan persuaded Halifax to
recall Seeds to brief him so that he could answer some of
Molotov's points on the spot. Illness prevented his return so
William Strang, head of the Central Department of the Foreign
Office, went to Moscow. The ambassador in Paris, Eric Phipps,
was also recalled. On 7 June Chamberlain gave the House of
Commons a brief statement on the negotiations and the 'one or
two difficulties to be resolved' especially the impossibility of
imposing 'a guarantee on states which do not desire it' and
announced that a 'Foreign Office official would go to Moscow'.
This aroused concern. William Strang, although an exceptionally able official, was, of course, unknown outside the
Foreign Office and many people immediately felt that some
well-known person might better smooth the way to
agreement.[22]

Chamberlain and his closest admirers showed a defensive
sense of isolation. That month, June 1939, one of the early
Gallup opinion polls gave 84 per cent 'yes' replies to the direct
question, 'Do you favour a military alliance between Britain,
France and Russia?' Uneasily, they thought themselves victims
of hostile plots. Sir Eric Phipps wrote from Paris to Horace
Wilson that he had asked Daladier whether it was the Soviet
embassy that had persuaded him that the failure to send an
important person to Moscow had caused offence there. He
suspected a false rumour deliberately spread to help Chamberlain's enemies. Phipps then asserted that Daladier had it from
Léger, the permanent head of the French Foreign Office, who
'is on the very closest terms of friendship' with Vansittart,
feared both by Phipps and Wilson. 'Please burn this letter',
Phipps requested – but he kept a copy himself. Wilson replied

with weary tolerance 'over these antics' but he added 'presently there may be a clear case', presumably to enable him to under-mine Vansittart. Chamberlain, showing his sense of loneliness, complained to his sister that Anthony Eden 'went to Halifax and suggested that we should send him as a special envoy to Moscow. He found a not unsympathetic hearer' but Chamber-lain quickly called Halifax to order. 'Nevertheless Lloyd George repeated it to Butler and even suggested that if we did not approve of Anthony, Winston should go! I have no doubt that the three of them talked it over together, and that they saw in it a means of entry into the Cabinet and perhaps later on the substitution of a more amenable P.M.!'[23]

Phipps supplied Chamberlain with a useful argument against concessions to Molotov. He reported from Paris the view of Bill Bullitt, the loquacious and opinionated American ambassador to France, who had once served as US ambassador in Moscow. 'He is convinced that an agreement with them [the USSR] is necessary, but still more convinced that we shall never reach it if we give them the impression that we are running after them.' Phipps' contribution to the Foreign Policy Committee meeting of 9 June, which took the main decisions, seems to have been to support the Prime Minister. Chamberlain thought that 'unless we showed that we were prepared to drive a hard bargain, we should necessarily get the worst of the bargain. He did not think that Russia could now afford to break off negotiations and we could therefore afford to take a fairly stiff line. Sir Eric Phipps confirmed that this was the view held by Mr Bullitt.' Halifax showed uncertainty and confusion. Britain needed an agreement with Russia to forestall 'what might be the most serious danger, namely an agreement between Germany and Russia', which seemed to be an argument for concession. Yet, admitting 'considerable distrust' of Bolshevik guarantees and undertakings', he argued that it was not worth making conces-sions to secure Soviet promises.[24]

Seeds, Strang and the French ambassador in Moscow spent nearly three hours with Molotov on 15 June. Seeds produced a memorandum, brought by Strang, for discussion together with newly drafted British proposals for the alliance. These re-quired consultation between the three powers before any of the allies intervened in a non-guaranteed state. Thus the British rejected Molotov's main demand and insisted that they must have the right to stop 'help' going to states that did not want it. Article 16 of the League reappeared in the British draft and the Soviet proposal for a pledge not to make a separate peace disappeared, though the British promised to concede this point if everything else were agreed. Next morning another of what Seeds called 'the thunderous Tass communiqués' appeared in the newspapers: the results of 'acquaintance with Anglo-French formulae are regarded in the circles of the People's Commissariat for Foreign Affairs as not being entirely favourable'. That afternoon Molotov called in Strang, Seeds and Naggiar and during a meeting of an hour and a half denounced the new proposals. If the British and French 'treated the Soviet government as being naïve or foolish people, he himself could afford to smile, but he could not guarantee that everyone else would take so calm a view'. He objected to consultation, as a substitute for automatic action to keep neighbouring states out of German power. If the western powers absolutely refused to guarantee Estonia, Latvia and Finland then it might be best, he said, for Britain, France and the USSR merely to agree to defend each other against direct attack.[25]

After leaving Molotov, the French ambassador urged that the British should accept the Soviet demands over the Baltic states. This, in substance, they proceeded to do. The Foreign Office returned to a French draft which M. Corbin had delivered, before the latest approach to Molotov, and which went further to meet Russian demands, and produced a new text which promised mutual aid against any aggression by Germany ('another European State') which 'constituted a menace to the security of one of the three countries' in addition to mutual aid in case of aggression against a country guaranteed in advance. Surprisingly, Article 16 reappeared. The Foreign Policy Committee considered it on 20 June, together with the crisis with Japan developing in Tientsin. At last the Committee agreed to accept, if necessary, the 'no separate peace' clause. Halifax warned, reversing his earlier attitude, 'that information from many different sources pointed to the necessity, after we had gone so far, of reaching an agreement with Russia, otherwise Hitler might well be encouraged to take some violent action'. Chamberlain insisted that the 'Russians had every intention of reaching agreement but wished to get the best possible terms by bargaining'. He began to favour the simple three-power alliance, without provision for aid to any other country than the three allies, but recognised that the public would then think negotiations had failed. Ministers agreed to try out the new draft on Molotov.[26]

On 21 June Strang, Seeds and Naggiar had another two-hour meeting with Molotov. Though 'genial in manner' he was discouraging in substance and next day Molotov sent for them again and rejected the proposals. He now insisted that all the states the USSR intended to aid should be listed in the treaty.

Halifax showed dismay and bewilderment. He asked Seeds to try to find out what Molotov really wanted. Seeds replied on 24 June. The Soviet rulers, he thought, wanted the British and French to allow them to intervene in the Baltic states if they decided that their governments and ruling classes were about to co-operate with Germany. With this reflection the Foreign Policy Committee, now including ten ministers in addition to the Prime Minister, about one-half of the whole Cabinet, reassembled on 26 June 1939 with R. A. Butler, Horace Wilson, Cadogan and Malkin, the legal adviser, in attendance as usual. Vansittart did not come in 1939 as he had to the special meetings in September 1938. Halifax asserted that the Soviet government were anxious to secure a treaty in spite of what Chamberlain called their 'bazaar haggling'. Once again, ministers retreated in face of Soviet demands; they would accept a list of states to be 'helped' against aggression, provided it included Switzerland and the Netherlands, which concerned the French and British; if not they would go for the simple tripartite mutual guarantee without any provisions for assisting other countries. Once again Halifax seemed confused. At one moment, he believed the simple treaty would block collusion between Germany and Russia and, at another moment, that it would not prevent their partitioning Poland between them. Chamberlain remained calm. As he wrote to Hilda: 'My colleagues are so desperately anxious for it [agreement with the USSR] and so nervous of the consequences of failure to achieve it that I have to go very warily but I am so sceptical of the value of Russian help that I should not feel that our position was greatly worsened if we had to do without them.'[27]

Three days later a long article appeared in *Pravda*. Zhdanov set out his coldly threatening 'personal opinion' on the negotiations; his 'friends', he wrote, did not agree with it. Stalin was known to confide in Zhdanov. 'It seems to me', he concluded, 'that the English and French do not want a real agreement or one acceptable to the USSR: the only thing they really want is to talk about an agreement and, by making play with the obstinacy of the Soviet Union, to prepare their own public opinion for an eventual deal with the aggressors. The next few days must show whether this is the case or not.' If Britain and France were planning a bargain with Germany, which, no doubt, the Soviet government must have assumed would be at its expense, then the USSR should obviously strike first with its own bargain with Germany.

On 20 May, Molotov asked, in a friendly talk with the German ambassador in Moscow, that a 'political basis' should be found for German-Soviet economic co-operation. Hitler ordered reticence in return – presumably he feared that Molotov would exploit German eagerness to bargain with the Soviet Union as a means of pressing Britain and France into full alliance on Russian terms. On 17 June, however, Schulenburg, the German ambassador in Moscow, then in Berlin to report, agreed with the Soviet chargé in Berlin that German-Soviet relations were improving. On 29 June, the day of the *Pravda* article, Molotov, in a friendly talk with Schulenburg, 'described a normalisation of relations with Germany as being desirable and possible'. The Germans continued cautious and Schulenburg approved this caution since, he thought, 'the Russians would not commit themselves before the critical moment'.[28]

The British and French ambassadors saw Molotov again on 1 July. Molotov objected to the inclusion of the Netherlands, Luxembourg and Switzerland in the list of states to be defended. Moreover, Molotov now demanded something new, that 'indirect aggression' in the sense of, for instance, the Czech surrender in March, should be included. At this stage he suggested only the insertion in the treaty of the words 'direct or indirect'. On 3 July he gave the ambassadors the formal Soviet reply. The Soviet rulers now wanted agreement on a definition of 'indirect aggression' to be put into a secret protocol together with the list of states. The Soviet government wanted assistance to be given automatically to one of the three allies which went to war because of 'direct or indirect aggression' by a 'European Power' 'against another European State whose independence or neutrality the contracting country concerned felt obliged to defend against such direct or indirect aggression'. Indirect aggression now meant 'an internal coup d'état or a reversal of policy in the interests of the aggressor'. Thus Molotov continued to seek clear and unequivocal British and French agreement to Soviet help to neighbouring states, whether wanted or not.

The Foreign Policy Committee met at once. Halifax and Chamberlain tried to stop 'this perpetual argument'. They wanted to fall back on the limited tripartite pact with provisions for consultation over cases not involving direct attack on any of the three. In effect, Halifax and Chamberlain wanted to give up the effort to secure a Soviet guarantee for Poland. Halifax argued that the Soviet authorities would do what they thought best if war came regardless of treaty promises, although he also argued that the three-power treaty against direct attack by Germany on Britain, France or the USSR would prevent Soviet co-operation with Germany. Hoare and Stanley, however, successfully opposed them. They agreed that 'indirect aggression' as defined gave the Soviet Union a free hand in neighbouring states but wanted to continue the search for agreement. In the end the Committee agreed to try for a bargain. The British and French would give up insistence on promises of aid for the Netherlands and Switzerland in return for the abandonment of the Soviet definition of indirect aggression. Failing that, they should fall back on the simple tripartite treaty, with possible extensions left for subsequent negotiation. Bonnet instantly telephoned a protest from Paris. He wanted every effort to be made to obtain a general agreement including, above all, provisions for the defence of Poland and Romania; only *in extremis* and only after reference to London and Paris, should Seeds and Naggiar fall back on the limited three-power pact.[29]

The British and French representatives talked again to Molotov from 6 p.m. to 8.30 pm. on 8 July and from 6 p.m. to 9 p.m. on 9 July. Three issues now remained: should the Netherlands, Switzerland and Luxembourg be included? How should

'indirect aggression' be covered? Should the agreement come
into force only after the conclusion of a military agreement?
Molotov included Holland and Switzerland but Soviet agreement to defend them against aggression would come into force
only when Turkey and Poland had concluded pacts of mutual
assistance with the USSR (an unlikely event as far as Poland
was concerned) and only when Holland and Switzerland had
recognised the Soviet Union. He insisted that the military and
political agreements must be signed simultaneously. Moreover
Molotov now redefined indirect aggression as an action
accepted by any of the named states (Turkey, Greece, Romania, Belgium, Poland, Estonia, Latvia and Finland) which involved the use of its territory or its armed forces for aggression. Any of these countries might allow this to happen under
threat of force. Then there followed the words which worried
the British ministers: 'or without any such threat'. The Soviet
government clearly intended to limit the independence of
neighbouring states.[30]

British ministers, eleven in the Foreign Policy Committee,
and another twelve at the Cabinet, looked for another concession to induce the Russians to give up their demand to intervene in any neighbouring state if they thought it to be moving
closer to the Germans. Chamberlain had soothing words for his
Cabinet colleagues: 'on the whole he was disposed to take the
view that the Soviet Government intended to make an Agreement with us but that they were probably in no hurry to do so.'
He passed on to the Committee Nevile Henderson's opinion
that 'it would be quite impossible for Germany and Soviet
Russia to come together'. Halifax thought 'it would be disastrous for us to accept any formula which allowed internal
interference in any form'. American opinion might find it
immoral and Britain might be dragged into an unnecessary war
on some specious pretext. He suggested agreeing to Molotov's
demand that a military agreement should be signed and come
into force at the same time as the political treaty; in return, he
hoped, Molotov would give up his definition of indirect
aggression.[31]

To Chamberlain's pleasure, Halifax was becoming irritated,
' "fed up" with Molotov whom he describes as maddening'. The
Prime Minister wrote to his sister: 'If we do get an agreement,

as I rather think we shall, I'm afraid I shall not regard it as a triumph. I put as little value on Russian military capacity as I believe the Germans do.' It is striking that Chamberlain showed surprise when the British ambassador to Warsaw told him, and air intelligence confirmed, that the Red Air Force was capable of bombing east Prussia. 'I would like', Chamberlain wrote, 'to have taken a much stronger line with them all through, but I could not have carried my colleagues with me.' Halifax looked forward to the military conversations when 'no great progress would be made. The conversations would drag on . . . In this way, we shall have gained time and made the best of a situation from which we could not now escape.' Neither Halifax nor Chamberlain cared what happened. The French, however, worried deeply about continued delay so the British agreed to try again to separate the political alliance from the military agreement and to get their way on indirect aggression. Hence a futile interview with Molotov on 17 July.[32]

Two days later the Cabinet agreed to try the bargain proposed the week before of trading military talks against the Soviet definition of indirect aggression. Halifax did not conceal his indifference, although he did take the trouble to explain the indirect aggression difficulty to the leaders of the Labour Party. Some members of the Cabinet became alarmed. Halifax admitted that 'it seemed that discussions of some kind were proceeding between the German Government and the Soviet Government. It was impossible to assess their real value, but it seemed likely that these discussions related to industrial matters.' Mr Chamberlain 'could not bring himself to believe that a real alliance between Germany and the Soviet Union was possible'. In this way Chamberlain and Halifax were suggesting that concessions were unnecessary. Now Daladier and Bonnet, by contrast, pleaded desperately for surrender, if necessary, to Molotov's terms both on indirect aggression and on the military agreement: the success of the Russian negotiations, they begged the British to believe, was a question of peace or war. Chamberlain and Halifax took part in a discussion in the Foreign Office. They rejected the French appeal; they would not, whatever happened, accept the Russian position on indirect aggression. Reluctantly the French gave way. Chamberlain was no longer afraid that the negotiations might succeed:

'We are only spinning out the time before the inevitable break comes and it is rather hard that I should have to bear the blame for dilatory action when if I wasn't hampered by others I would have closed the discussions one way or another long ago.'[33]

On 23 July the British and French ambassadors in Moscow told Molotov that their governments agreed that a military agreement must be signed before the political agreement came into effect. Molotov apparently softened. Indirect aggression, he claimed, would cease to be a problem once military conversations began. He insisted that staff talks must start at once. This demand the ambassadors telegraphed to London and Paris. The British and French governments agreed, the latter with eagerness. British ministers felt complacent. Halifax asserted that the military conversations would take 'a very long time'. They could therefore insist on the British view on 'indirect aggression', that is that the United Kingdom should refuse to agree to a Soviet right to intervene in the border states. Above all, Halifax believed, there was 'no danger now of an imminent breakdown during the next critical weeks', the weeks before autumn rains began, rains which would muddy the roads and make unlikely any German attack on Poland.[34]

Now the British and French statesmen and soldiers discussed how the military missions should travel to Moscow. Daladier and Bonnet demanded the quickest route: by direct train from Paris – non-stop flights were still impossible. Chamberlain and Halifax found convincing reasons for the slowest method, by chartered passenger ship to the Baltic and then by train to Moscow. The French were told that they could go by train if they wished but that they would travel alone: the military missions, headed by the modern-minded, able French general, Doumenc, and the British admiral, Plunkett-Ernle-Erle-Drax, whom many writers have unjustly mocked because of his name, embarked on the *City of Exeter* at Tilbury on 5 August.[35]

Two days earlier Count Schulenburg, the German ambassador in Moscow, had spent an hour with Molotov. Instead of opaque hints he now presented specific German offers. Germany recognised vital Soviet interests in the Baltic states. While striving for peaceful satisfaction of German demands on Poland, if this attempt went wrong, Germany would protect all

Soviet interests and reach an understanding with the Soviet government on Poland. Schulenburg found Molotov friendly and interested. He thought, however, that the Soviet government was determined to reach agreement with Britain and France if they fulfilled all Soviet wishes.[36] We do not yet know when Stalin and his associates decided to make a bargain with Hitler rather than to join Britain and France to fight him. Schulenburg's remarks made it clear that it was now urgent for the Soviet leaders to decide, assuming, as seems probable, that they had not yet done so. Evidently the Germans were about to attack Poland. British, French and German evidence makes it seem likely that the Soviet rulers, although their suspicions had been enlarged by British prevarication and what they learned of British approaches to Germany, still awaited the military talks before their verdict. Possibly they hoped to secure their objects through this new negotiating mechanism.

The Soviet authorities gave the British and French missions a warm welcome. The senior officers of the French mission, and the British general, stayed in a government guesthouse in considerable comfort, lavishly fed and carefully waited on. A brief encounter with Molotov caused the military delegates to pity the two ambassadors for what they had had to endure. Voroshilov, on the other hand, short, plump, with a round ruddy face, gave an impression of honesty and aroused more friendly feelings. The British and French thought he wanted agreement. The missions caught only a distant glimpse of Stalin at the annual air display. The newly arrived military found Seeds tired, disillusioned and unwell, feeling that Paris and London had delayed too long and given an impression of indecision. Naggiar, the French ambassador, concentrated on one issue. Speaking specially quietly inside the embassy, so that Russian listening devices could not pick up the conversation, or talking in the open air, he discussed the mission's instructions. 'Have you brought something precise on right of passage across Poland? Have you assurances on the subject?' Doumenc said 'No'. 'So they have neither read nor understood my dispatches; it is a capital point and cannot be dodged.' Voroshilov proved him right. Voroshilov was the head of the Russian team and apparently its only contact with Stalin and Molotov.

Shaposhnikov, the Red Army Chief of Staff, took the lead in technical discussions.

The talks began on 12 August 1939 in a house which once belonged to a rich Moscow industrialist. At first, cordiality and growing mutual confidence seemed to prevail and the delegations increasingly relaxed into those somewhat artificial outbreaks of laughter which briefly disperse the tensions of formal meetings. On the morning of the third day, however, the French delegation noticed that Voroshilov winced at one part of Doumenc's answer to his question of how the western staffs expected the Red Army to reply to aggression against Poland or Romania; it would be, Doumenc explained, for the Polish or Romanian armies to defend Polish or Romanian territory and the USSR would aid them on their request. There was laughter after Doumenc finished his exposition and asked Voroshilov if he had made himself clear, when the marshal replied 'No'. Then, when silence returned, 'Forgive me . . . I do not understand how the Soviet armies are to participate in the common effort.' Soon he put precise questions: 'Will Poland accept the entry of Soviet troops on its territory around Vilna to make contact with the enemy? Will Poland allow Soviet troops passage through southern Poland? Will Romania give passage to Soviet troops?' There was laughter, for the last time, when Voroshilov said he required a clear reply. The British and French missions tried, with mounting desperation, to evade these questions. The Red Army, they explained, should remain poised to enter Poland and Romania, whose governments would surely invite it in once war had begun. 'And suppose they do not?' asked Voroshilov. Without precise answers, he said, to his precise questions the talks could not succeed.[37]

That night, 14 August, Doumenc sent a telegram to Daladier, as Minister of War, and Naggiar to the French Foreign Office demanding the most urgent action in Warsaw, 'without waiting for the British Cabinet to consult', Naggiar added pointedly. In Paris Bonnet and Gamelin, and in Warsaw the French ambassador and the military attaché, supported by their British counterparts, demanded Polish consent to the entry of the Red Army in case of war. Beck and Stachiewicz, the Polish Chief of Staff, refused. If they agreed, they said, the

Russians would tell the Germans. Then war with Germany would become inevitable; the Russians did not intend to take part in a war against Germany; if they ever came to Polish territory, they would never leave it. The military talks went on for another three days in Moscow, and the Russians asked for Anglo-French warships to go to the Baltic, to be based, together with ships of the Red Navy, in harbours belonging to Finland, Estonia and Latvia: the British and French were to make these arrangements. On 18 August the western visitors lodged in the Russian guesthouse observed intense activity through the night in a neighbouring house, the former Austrian embassy, where preparations were in train for new visitors. They proved embarrassing neighbours.[38]

Meanwhile frenetic diplomatic activity broke out in Berlin. For some months cautious gestures towards détente had been exchanged between Germany and the USSR and mutual press attacks ceased in the spring. On 14 August Ribbentrop cast aside all reticence. He told Schulenburg to tell Molotov that he proposed to come to Moscow to open a 'new future' and to settle, to the complete satisfaction of Germany and the USSR, every issue from the Baltic to the Black Sea: that is, to partition eastern Europe. Polish-German relations, Ribbentrop explained, were deteriorating fast. Molotov remained coy; 'preparation' was needed. On 17 August, Schulenburg told Molotov that Ribbentrop would fly to Moscow any time from next day onwards. Serious events were on the way and German-Russian relations must be 'clarified'. Molotov suggested proceeding slowly, step by step, to a non-aggression pact. Ribbentrop replied with a message from Hitler to Stalin asking for Ribbentrop to be received on 22 August or 'at latest' on 23 August. Ribbentrop would come with the 'fullest powers'. At last, on 21 August, Stalin agreed to Ribbentrop's arrival on the next day but one. Just before midnight Berlin radio interrupted a musical programme with a triumphant announcement. Ribbentrop was going to Moscow to conclude a non-aggression pact. For most Europeans it was a message of misery: war was coming. For Hitler the neutrality and economic assistance of the Soviet Union made it possible to risk a second world war. The Soviet rulers evaded that risk for the time being and secured what the British and French had failed to offer – they advanced westwards their line of defence against the capitalistic world and gained more time to win the military benefits of Stalin's pitiless industrialisation.[39]

To many at the time, particularly in France, a military alliance between Great Britain, France and the USSR seemed the best hope, perhaps the only hope, of curbing Nazi Germany without war. It is probable that Chamberlain destroyed this hope. We cannot be certain of the intentions and assumptions of Stalin and his associates. We can be confident, however, that any government headed by Chamberlain needed to make extraordinary efforts to convince that group that it was prudent to ally with Britain against Germany. Even if it had succeeded, many difficulties stood in the way of alliance. We do not know how far these difficulties, above all that of bringing Poland and the Baltic states into collaboration with the USSR, might have become soluble with a British government that seemed eager to work with the Soviets to stop Germany. As it was, Chamberlain, sometimes almost alone, succeeded in providing a series of justifications, if not reasons, for Soviet rejection of alliance. Of course the Soviet government would have done better to join with Chamberlain in trying to persuade Hitler out of further adventure; probably Chamberlain made that choice seem too dangerous.

12 Confronting Italy, Japan and Germany: April–August 1939

Chamberlain's hopes for peace soon caused him, as usual, to overcome his irritation at Mussolini's caddish behaviour in Albania. He still thought Mussolini the most likely person to persuade Hitler to be moderate. Even when announcing the guarantee to Greece the Prime Minister, as Mussolini and Ciano were told in advance, was 'as little provocative as possible' in criticising the Italian invasion. Chamberlain tried hard to win Daladier to his view because he took seriously Mussolini's claim that he would try to restrain Hitler only if France made concessions to Italy, or, at least, discussed Italian claims. His attempts to persuade the French to do this secured support from Halifax, Phipps and Henderson, as well as the two successive British ambassadors in Rome, Perth and Loraine, and the acquiescence of the Foreign Office and the Cabinet while, among the French, François-Poncet, now French ambassador in Rome, and Bonnet enthusiastically agreed. Bonnet intrigued with the British to help them to persuade Daladier to overcome the hostility towards concession to Mussolini of Léger, the official head of the French Foreign Office, and, among French ministers, Reynaud, Sarraut, Campinchi and Mandel, and most of French opinion, both from the Left, opposed to Italian Fascist dictatorship and from the Right, concerned to maintain French power in North Africa. Italian demands in Tunisia aroused alarm. The Italian government objected to French supremacy in Tunisia. Among over 2 million natives, there were about 200,000 from elsewhere, half French citizens, half Italians. The French believed that the ruling classes should all become French citizens. The Italian government wanted to prolong the convention of 1896 giving equal rights to Italian as to French citizens.[1]

Chamberlain and Halifax took no interest in the details. 'I don't know the rights and wrongs . . . but I do feel in my bones

. . . that Musso wants to play in with us and curb Hitler, but that he won't do this unless and until he can get going with France', Halifax wrote in a personal letter to Phipps. Egged on by Bonnet, they pressed Paris with persistence. On 22 April 1939 Phipps passed half an hour with Daladier and told him that 'Franco-Italian relations were the key to peace or war'. On 20 May Halifax, visiting Paris, told Daladier 'that an improvement in Franco-Italian relations was vital for the world'. In June Phipps wrote to Chamberlain and Halifax. Bonnet had asked him to suggest that Chamberlain should himself write to Daladier. Horace Wilson and the Prime Minister drafted a letter, but in the end it was a draft from Vansittart that was thought least likely to ruffle Daladier. In it Chamberlain, however, included a paragraph he wrote himself. It embodied his line of thought in the summer of 1939. Now, he believed, 'some sort of precarious balance of power exists. But that position cannot be permanently maintained and if a real peace is to be established we must make some positive efforts of a constructive character to ease the tension and restore confidence to Europe.' Presenting the letter to Daladier, Phipps said Chamberlain thought that war or peace probably depended on Daladier's response.[2]

Daladier remained unmoved, contradicting the belief that French governments always did what the British told them to do. Daladier made indirect and furtive approaches to the Italian government, but publicly, and to the British, firmly refused any discussion of Italian claims. Mussolini, Daladier believed, would think any French eagerness for discussion to be a sign of weakness and firmness was, he claimed, the best way of securing Italian moderation. Muslim opinion in French North Africa would dislike any French weakness against the Fascist Italians who claimed, implausibly, to stand for Islam, while French colonists there would not tolerate it. Daladier thought the Italian government to be 'gangsters' who were 'in with Herr Hitler up to the hilt'. He had received 'countless messages and telegrams from North African Chieftains expressing intense loyalty to France, hatred of Italy and calling upon the French government to show utmost firmness'. In Paris Daladier told a politely persistent Halifax that 'Italy seemed to think that France was on the point of disintegration and was coveting French possessions. The worst thing France could do would be to yield to this campaign of violence and blackmail.'[3]

No Franco-Italian détente followed the British appeals. On 22 May the 'Pact of Steel' formalised a military alliance between Italy and Germany. In spite of these setbacks Chamberlain tried a direct appeal in a personal message presented to Mussolini on 5 July. He asked Mussolini to restrain Hitler from a coup in Danzig. In reply Mussolini lectured Loraine, the British ambassador in Rome, about his fidelity to the German alliance and blamed Poland for the problem of Danzig. This rebuff did not stop Chamberlain and Halifax from the wish to try again. This time the suggestion came from the High Commissioners of Australia and South Africa that Mussolini should be asked once more to restrain Hitler. Cadogan was away on holiday; perhaps his absence explains Halifax's approval. Chamberlain, of course, agreed. 'I think it a good thing that the Dominions feel that their suggestions are appreciated and the idea itself seems worth exploring further.' Loraine, less inclined to deferential treatment of Mussolini than Lord Perth, his predecessor as ambassador in Rome, criticised the suggestion: 'I am not at all easy in my mind that an approach to Signor Mussolini in the sense suggested to you . . . might not be interpreted as weakening of our attitude of support for Poland.' Halifax withdrew the idea with a typical double negative: 'I do not disagree with your judgement of the situation.'[4]

All this made no difference. Mussolini, perhaps reluctantly, and Ciano, the Italian Foreign Minister, tried to influence Hitler to stop the war, and kept Italy out of it in 1939. They studied the balance of forces in and around the Mediterranean. Their conclusions overrode the alliance signed in May 1939 between Italy and Germany, the 'Pact of Steel'; on 19 August the British ambassador in Rome reported that Italy would not encourage Hitler into war and the next day that Italy would probably remain neutral.[5]

Confronting Japan brought a clear-cut, theatrically vivid crisis. The scene was Tientsin, in north China, about 80 miles from Peking. There, in part of the city, about 3000 British lived in the British concession, applying British law in British courts and enforcing it by British-officered police and half a battalion of British infantry. With them lived 2000 other foreigners and 45,000 Chinese. The Japanese army occupied and controlled the ports and cities of north China outside the foreign concessions. On 14 June 1939 Japanese soldiers and Chinese police under their direction blockaded the British area of Tientsin. Wire fences, soon electrified, prevented entry and departure except at carefully controlled check-points. There the Japanese restricted the entry of all goods except food, and the supplies of ice needed to deal with the baking heat of summer, but even these were delayed and reduced. Most dramatically they restricted the passage of anyone going into the concession or leaving it. They singled out the British for specially harsh treatment: often they sent them back to the end of queues and forced them to wait as long as four hours in the glare of the sun. Searches, accompanied by contemptuous bullying, caused much shock to British newspaper readers. The assistant secretary of the Tientsin race club, *The Times* reported, had been stripped naked in full view of passing Chinese women and children and his British passport thrust down his mouth. British women endured obscene gibes from Japanese-controlled police and a few were strip-searched.[6]

The principal British authority in Tientsin, the consul-general, Jamieson, had amply warned London in advance and the British ambassador in Tokyo, Sir Robert Craigie, added emphasis. The occasion of the crisis began with the murder in the Grand Theatre, in the British concession, of the manager of the Federal Reserve Bank. This Federal Reserve Bank was a Japanese-sponsored alternative to the banks employing Chinese government currency and its local manager was a Japanese protégé. Four Chinese, suspected of joining in the murder, sought sanctuary in the British concession from trial by courts of the Japanese puppet-Chinese government. The Japanese military commanders argued that in general British concessions should cease to give refuge to anti-Japanese terrorists and, in particular, that these four men should be handed over. During several weeks before the Japanese blockade began the British consul-general in Tientsin pleaded in repeated telegrams to be authorised to hand over the four accused and warned that the Japanese would take drastic and hostile action if he did not. Sir Robert Craigie, the British ambassador in Tokyo, earnestly supported him. A formidable group of experts opposed these advocates of deference to Japanese wishes. The eloquent British ambassador to Chiang Kai-Shek's internationally recognised Chinese government in Chungking, Sir Archibald Clark-Kerr, insisted that Chiang's resistance prevented Japanese victory in China and that the British should do nothing to discourage him. Moreover concessions to the Japanese, Clark-Kerr believed, led only to further Japanese demands so that co-operation with the Japanese military, so far from securing British influence and property in China, would make their destruction more likely.[7]

Before the crisis those who made decisions in London about the Far East and who replied to the increasingly urgent messages from Japan and China were the members of the Far Eastern Department in the Foreign Office. Most of them knew China well and among them was a leading authority on Japanese history and culture, Sir George Sansom. It was only when the crisis broke in mid-June that Cadogan, the chief Foreign Office official, Halifax, Chamberlain and the Cabinet and its committees took control of the Tientsin problem. Until then the increasingly alarmed messages from Japan and China did not, it seems from the relevant files, get beyond the head of department or Sir George Mounsey, the superintending assistant under-secretary. From Tientsin, on 11 June, Jamieson made a desperate final appeal to the Foreign Office against the instructions to refuse to hand over the four accused Chinese: 'Unless altered instructions are given the innocent British community of Tientsin will be faced with hardship, loss and danger to life.' On this Sir John Brenan, who had been consul-general in Shanghai until 1937, attached his departmental minute: 'In deference to Sir A. Clark-Kerr, who has fervently espoused the Chinese cause, we have taken a stand in defence of these four men from which it will be difficult to withdraw with dignity.' The Foreign Office told Jamieson that only if 'independent evidence' against the four alleged murderers other than that from Japanese sources, became available, 'we might then reconsider our attitude'.[8]

Two days later, the Japanese blockade shocked Cadogan and Halifax into dismayed attention. 'I think we've bungled this. I blame myself – and I am of course responsible', Cadogan wrote, 'for not taking more interest in it.' Chamberlain, as usual, readily blamed the Foreign Office and wrote 'of this mess into which our Foreign Office has so rashly landed us' and of its 'anti-Japanese bias'. The crisis touched every British preoccupation in the summer of 1939. Should the British government try to preserve British trade and investment in China by collaboration with Japan against the nationalist government of Chiang Kai-Shek in Chungking or should it seek to weaken Japan by supporting Chiang? Would policies sympathetic to Japan make more, or less, probable a future Japanese threat to imperial and dominion territories in Hong Kong, Malaya, Singapore, Burma, India, Australia, or New Zealand? Could naval forces sufficient to deter, intimidate or challenge Japan be despatched to Singapore? To do so would mean withdrawing the fleet from the eastern Mediterranean. That might increase Italian unreliability and alter the balance of power in the Mediterranean and cause the French navy to bring their two modern battle cruisers from the Atlantic to protect French sea routes to North Africa. The Royal Navy would then find it difficult to find enough capital ships to counter the German battle cruisers and 'pocket battleships' in the Atlantic.[9] If Britain quarrelled with Japan, German belligerence might be increased or, as some argued, it might be increased if Britain reacted weakly to Japanese provocation. Equally Mussolini's hostility might be deterred, or encouraged, by British actions in China. The United Kingdom could confidently risk war against Japan only with the assured help of the United States. Without that help should the British government defer to Japan? Or should it resist Japanese pretensions as a means of winning support from American public opinion and so making help from the United States more likely in the future? An alliance with Germany was known to be tempting Japanese leaders; indeed the British ambassador in Tokyo believed that the Japanese army in China set off the Tientsin crisis to worsen relations with Britain and so overcome the reluctance of more cautious Japanese to ally with Germany. British attempts to win Soviet support might be jeopardised by a quarrel with Japan – or, alternatively, by British failure to be firm. The Tientsin crisis, therefore, involved the general balance of power, the strength of the coalition that Britain and France could assemble compared to that led by Germany.[10]

The crisis came in mid-June 1939. At that stage in the summer, ministers and their advisers were all in London and the mechanism of decision by the Cabinet and its committees and sub-committees ran smoothly. The crisis and the seriousness with which the Japanese set about humiliating the British, came as a surprise. Presumably calmed by the confidently pro-Chinese Far Eastern Department in the Foreign Office, Halifax informed the Cabinet on 7 June that his officials had told him that the refusal to give way to Japanese demands for the handing over of the four Chinese in Tientsin was unlikely to lead to 'any serious development'. Thus his mild warning of the 'possibility' of trouble led to no discussion. Even a week later when the Japanese had announced the blockade, Halifax treated it as a Japanese 'attempt to save face' and he thought it 'unlikely that there would be any catastrophic events in Tientsin'. Chamberlain, on the contrary, felt apprehensive. Looking back on Jamieson's warnings from Tientsin he did not feel complacent. At once he spoke in anticipation of a crisis: 'The situation in Europe was not such that it would be easy for us to send a fleet to the Far East.'[11]

Soon the Japanese made clear their intention to harass and humiliate. Chamberlain asked the Chiefs of Staff to report on what could be done. At first they insisted that only two capital ships could be spared for the Far East from home waters and the Mediterranean. Then, pushed into a calculation based on the withdrawal of battleships and battle cruisers from the Mediterranean, they reported a figure of seven, assuming the need for six to be kept to hold the Germans, a need emphasised by French determination to withdraw two battle cruisers from the Atlantic to the Mediterranean in case the British fleet went east. The Japanese might be able to send nine capital ships south towards Singapore. Even this extreme measure, therefore, gave no secure margin without United States help. Before the Foreign Policy Committee meeting on Monday morning 19 June Halifax telephoned Joe Kennedy to point out that 'there seemed little we could do in the Far East unless the United States joined in with us'. Kennedy promised to speak to President Roosevelt.

The record of the Foreign Policy Committee meeting on Monday 19 June 1939 evokes memories of the great days of Chamberlainite appeasement. The Prime Minister set the tone. To retaliate against Japan by imposing economic sanctions would either be ineffective or might drive Japan to war. Hence the government should not impose sanctions unless ready to fight a war. For that the United Kingdom was too weak. Craigie in Tokyo should be instructed to try to negotiate a settlement. Halifax set out a narrative and a balanced analysis. Oliver Stanley, the familiar member of the 'weaker brethren', queried Chamberlain's approach. He worried about the effect on American opinion of immediately opening negotiations with Japan which 'might involve us in a very humiliating surrender': the Prime Minister 'did not see why we need be driven into a very humiliating surrender'. After the meeting, at which he was present but silent, an old friend and supporter, Lord Runciman, sent his thoughts to the Prime Minister – 'In the absence of a certain promise of active naval and military help from the USA my view is emphatically against any step calculated to lead to war.' That evening Kennedy brought a reply from Washington, coming from Hull, the Secretary of State, rather than from the President. Kennedy telephoned to Halifax that 'he did not think the United States Government would take any further action at the moment beyond Mr. Cordell Hull's statement' which was to the effect that the US government was 'observing with special interest' the events in China. While adopting a menacing attitude towards Japanese expansion in general Roosevelt and Hull could not allow themselves to show concern for specifically British interests. Halifax telegraphed immediately to Craigie instructing him to open talks with the Japanese Foreign Minister, Arita.[12]

Once the Japanese 'arrow' was 'off the bow', as the Japanese military spokesman in Tientsin put it, their demands widened beyond the handing over of the Chinese suspected of murder. They asked that Britain co-operate in the construction of the Japanese 'new order' in the east and cease to support Chiang Kai-Shek, and they wanted the British to stop supporting Chungking government currency and to accept the notes of the Japanese-controlled Federal Reserve Bank. After a month of discussion Craigie and Arita initialled a document issued in

London and Tokyo on 24 July 1939. Craigie did his best to make it seem that the Japanese gained nothing by insisting that the British government was only confirming its usual attitude and not changing it under pressure from Japan. In the Craigie–Arita accord, however, the British explicitly promised to do nothing to interfere with or diminish Japanese control in the areas of China occupied by Japan.[13]

The British had morally surrendered. Yet within another month they rejected further Japanese demands and suspended negotiations. This surprising reversal derived from pride, built on past British power, and on prudent calculation of how to defend the fruits of past British power through a twentieth century of growing weakness in comparison with developing competitors. The pride, the arrogance of an imperial nation, many divergent groups of people expressed; the cautious calculation of how to react with limited strength was quieter and more private, a matter for ministers and Foreign Office officials. Japanese tactics at Tientsin aimed to humiliate and therefore roused anger. At Tientsin, Jamieson, the consul-general, who had pleaded with London to give way to the Japanese army before the crisis, demanded firmness after it had begun: the 'Japanese, who have tacit respect for the white races and for British in particular, will realise for [the] first time that they can with impunity humiliate British people . . . Our future in North China and perhaps elsewhere in the east also depends therefore on strong action being taken in the present situation to maintain our prestige.' At Hong Kong, which the British could not defend against any serious Japanese assault, the GOC, General Grasett, signalled to Major-General Pownall, the DMO in the War Office, who passed on his 'admirable appreciation' to the Foreign Office: 'Method and outlook displayed by Japanese [are] typically oriental and reaction to strong action may be expected to be oriental . . . in my opinion we have nothing to lose by a strong policy in Far East even though our means of expressing it may appear to be slender.'

Even *The Times*, not notable in those days for reckless belligerence, wrote that 'passive submission to the blockade of the Settlement will not satisfy the British public'. Eden won applause in the House of Commons when he asked if Craigie had made it plain to the Japanese that the British government 'are not prepared to acquiesce in this blockade'. Chamberlain spoke to the House of 'these intolerable insults' and told a rally of government supporters in Cardiff: 'No government can tolerate that its nationals should be subjected to such treatment [applause] as we read of in Tientsin.' Chatfield, fully aware of British naval problems, wrote that: 'War may be thrust on us by the Japanese . . . by reason of a succession of further insults to which, as a great Imperial Power, we could not submit.' Another Admiral of the Fleet, Sir Roger Keyes, told the Commons, 'I know the Japanese so well; they will not stand up to a firm front.' According to Sumner Welles in Washington Sir Ronald Lindsay, the British ambassador, spoke with 'ill-concealed impatience and even indignation of the foreign policy pursued by his own government' and 'with considerable vehemence . . . said that there came a time in the affairs of any country when, if it had any self-respect, it had to fight even if it had to fight alone'. In London Kennedy reported Halifax as realising that 'British public opinion is being aroused frightfully and he is only afraid that they are finally going to get mad and demand that something be done'. Among Liberals and on the left these emotions were shared and reinforced by the perception of China as a member of the League wronged by aggressive militarists. For example, Labour Party representatives (Citrine, Dalton and Morrison) met Chamberlain and Halifax on 28 June. They urged that the Prime Minister's reference to 'intolerable insults' was 'the least that should be said' and 'that action must be taken to stop the indignities inflicted upon British people'.[14]

On 26 July 1939 President Roosevelt unexpectedly gave notice of the abrogation of the Japanese-American commercial treaty 'in order' he told a British official, 'that the dictators should not imagine that they could get away with it'. By this time Roosevelt had begun to act to strengthen Britain and France so far, and only so far, as he could maintain the support of public and Congressional opinion. He had just been defeated in his attempt to revise the neutrality laws. Now he felt able to go ahead because Senator Vandenburg had presented a resolution calling for denunciation. Roosevelt's action increased pressure on the British to be firm towards Japan. Craigie, the

British ambassador in Tokyo, involved in detailed negotiation, insisted that it made no difference or made things worse: 'the effect here . . . is one of irritation at lack of manners rather than apprehension that United States really means business this time' and impetus had been given to the pro-German alliance movement. The Far Eastern Department in the Foreign Office thought differently. Its head believed 'that the denunciation by the United States of the commercial treaty has got the Japanese "completely guessing" '. Craigie's arguments for conciliation towards Japan lost some of their force: resistance seemed more promising and the fear of losing American good-will by 'appeasing' Japan and of offending American supporters of China grew more urgent.[15]

At the beginning of August 1939 Craigie's negotiations were moving towards agreement on the policing of Tientsin but there loomed over them the main Japanese aim, to force British co-operation in the weakening of Chinese resistance to Japanese control of China. The Japanese, sensibly from their point of view, devoted themselves to undermining the value of the currency of the Chinese government, the dollar or 'fapi', for what distinguishes armies from bands of brigands is their capacity to pay for their needs. In August the issue was the fate of the silver deposited in the vaults of the Bank of Communications in the British concession in Tientsin, about 14 million dollars, perhaps one million pounds sterling in value. The transfer of the silver would, of course, lessen the metallic backing for Chinese government paper. Craigie suggested that the silver should be transferred to Japanese control in return for a pledge to keep it under seal until the end of the war between Japan and China. Craigie again pleaded for concession to Japanese wishes. Otherwise 'the military extremists and all the worst elements in Japanese politics' would get their way, force through an alliance with Germany and encourage Hitler to risk a world war. The British should encourage the moderates in Japan, well represented in the Tokyo government of Hiranuma and Araki who were 'definitely working for improvements in relations with the United States and Great Britain'. A long telegram ended: 'I can only urge with all emphasis at my command that we should not miss the chance which, with a full sense of responsibility, I maintain now exists of removing Japan finally from German orbit.'[16]

Craigie encountered scepticism in the Foreign Office. Sir George Sansom, a recognised authority on Japan, denied any fundamental difference between Japanese extremists and moderates. 'All Japanese want a "new order" in Asia, and a "new order" involves the ultimate displacement of Great Britain in the Far East. The difference between the extremists and the moderates is not one of destination, but of the road by which that destination is to be reached and the speed at which it is to be travelled.' Cadogan, who had experience in China, noted 'I agree'. Sansom was sympathetic to Japan and believed that there must eventually be 'some "new order" in Eastern Asia in which Japan plays a dominant part' but his memorandum helped the Far Eastern Department in the Foreign Office to set off a reaction to Craigie's eagerness to win the favour of Japanese ministers. Halifax gloomily worried. He told Cadogan, just back from two weeks' leave, that he could not allow himself a real holiday, unlike Chamberlain, who, more imperturbable, went to Scotland for salmon-fishing. Halifax and Cadogan feared any possibility of a break with Japan while crisis with Germany came closer. In the end, however, the Far Eastern Department, supported by Sir George Mounsey, persuaded them to take a firm line.[17]

On 16 August Syers, the Prime Minister's private secretary, sent to Scotland a file containing Foreign Office comments, draft telegrams to Craigie rejecting his proposals, and a covering letter from Halifax. Halifax wrote to Chamberlain objecting to Craigie's proposal which, he thought, would not end Anglo-Japanese discord while 'worsening our present position vis-à-vis of the United States and of China'. On the other hand, to refuse to transfer silver from British-controlled territory might 'get us into trouble with the Japanese'. Halifax felt he needed Chamberlain's approval. The choice was clear. The British could avoid trouble by making sufficient concession to Japanese wishes at the expense of those Chinese who were resisting Japanese domination. To fit in with Japanese wishes, however, must, it seemed, lead to diminished hope of eventual American support for British power and independence. The United States government, or so it seemed, could eventually support Britain only if the British seemed active in the defence of their own independent power and influence and so active in defence of a world congenial to Americans: including the 'open door' to world trade and investment in China, as part of a world in which aggressive dictators were contained. When (false) rumours reached Roosevelt that the British contemplated closing the Burma Road, the only effective supply line to China other than from the Soviet Union, he commented, so Welles reported, to the British and French and also to the Soviet representative in Washington, that the position of the United States would become one of 'trying to lend its moral support to a power which is deliberately intent on suicide'. President Roosevelt dared not give the impression to that large number of American citizens who objected to involvement in the outside world that he hoped to help Britain to defend positions that the British themselves would not defend and so rescue the British from perils created by their own selfish weaknesses. With difficulty he might slowly persuade American opinion to accept American action parallel with that of the British against aggressors but not action consequent on British scheming or evasiveness. British rejection of compromises with the aggressor states offered the best chance of eventual United States support for British resistance to them.[18]

Syers also sent a copy of Halifax's letter, and the draft instructions for Craigie, to Horace Wilson in Cheltenham. Next morning Wilson telephoned his approval of the instructions to Craigie and rejected a suggestion from Simon that the decision should be put off to enable Cabinet ministers to consider it. When Chamberlain telephoned Syers at midday, Syers 'told him what Sir Horace Wilson had said and he then authorised me to tell Lord Halifax that he agreed with the course proposed' – a note which suggests Wilson's influence was greater than he admitted. Chamberlain wrote down his reasons for Halifax. He was 'particularly impressed' by a memorandum from Mounsey. This paper twice emphasised the importance of the support of 'American and world opinion' as an argument against bilateral negotiations with Japan.

The telegrams went out that evening. To Craigie went regret 'that in spite of every natural desire to follow the line of compromise that you have suggested, His Majesty's Government have not found it possible to do so'. To Paris the Foreign

Office explained 'that if there is to be a real chance of American co-operation, the United States Government will only offer such co-operation at some stage when they see we have made a stand ourselves'. Craigie's talks with Kato, the Japanese government's negotiator, were adjourned. Chamberlain expected 'fresh anxieties'. They came, but not, for the moment, from Japan. Within a few days the announcement of the German-Soviet non-aggression pact, first made in Berlin late on 21 August, transformed the outlook for Japan. The Soviet Union and Japan fought several severe frontier battles on the disputed frontiers between Mongolia and Manchuria. In July Japanese attacks gained no marked successes. The assumption that Germany would maintain a threat to the USSR in Europe lay behind Japanese strategic calculations. Suddenly this assumption collapsed. Soon the bewildered Japanese government resigned. In August 1939 the possibility of a German-Japanese alliance directed against Britain and the Soviet Union vanished.[19]

Japanese ambitions revived in 1940 when the Germans defeated France and occupied the Netherlands. With the United Kingdom threatened by invasion the British Empire became desperately vulnerable. The threat the USSR presented to Japan, however, remained until the Germans attacked the Soviet Union in June 1941. After the summer of 1940, the United States administration, in order to make the world balance of forces less unfavourable to the British Empire, took a series of steps to restrain Japan from southwards expansion by cutting off essential supplies to Japan, steps which eventually caused the Japanese to attack Pearl Harbor in December 1941 rather than surrender to American demands that Japan should reverse its aggressive policies begun in the 1930s. The British did not make or direct this policy, they followed the lead of Roosevelt and Hull.

The rejection by Chamberlain and Halifax in August 1939 of Craigie's attempt to restore Anglo-Japanese friendship was the result of their desire to win the help of the United States in the preservation of British wealth and power. Their foreign policy was designed to preserve British independence by responding to foreign threats either with conciliation or by resistance. In 1939, in the Far East, weakness paradoxically dictated a policy of resistance designed to win United States support for the pursuit of British ends. Thereafter, except when British desperation in the summer of 1940 induced an important but temporary concession to Japan in the form of the closing of the Burma Road to supplies for nationalist-controlled China, British policy towards Japan followed, and so tried to encourage, American initiatives. The Tientsin crisis, therefore, brought the first statement of the theme that came to dominate British foreign policy in the second half of the twentieth century: the subordination of British policy to that of the United States in attempts to exploit American resources for British purposes.

In 1939, however, the problem of Hitler pervaded everything. If that were solved, and German peacefulness secured, the British Empire need not fear Italy or Japan. Chamberlain's self-confidence recovered even from the shock of the destruction of Czechoslovakia. He managed, albeit with doubts and hesitations, to convince himself that peace by agreement, even with Hitler's Germany, remained possible and that a policy of coercion and threats, aimed at forceful restraint of Germany, should not be pursued so vigorously as to jeopardise that possibility. Flashes of hope illuminate his private correspondence, and even his recorded remarks to ministerial colleagues, though he knew that they, for the most part, did not share his dogged optimism.

The Duke of Buccleuch and Lord Brocket, both keen partisans of Anglo-German understanding, went over to Berlin in April to join in celebrating Hitler's fiftieth birthday, an event marked by a military display formidable even by the standards of the Third Reich. Chamberlain thought it worth recording that Germans they spoke to assured them that the Munich agreement remained intact – 'Hitler still considered himself bound by the declaration he signed with me . . . Perhaps Hitler has realised that he has now reached the limit' though 'we won't take any chances'. In the same letter, Chamberlain commented on the suggestion that he should signal his determination to resist German aggressiveness by bringing Churchill into his government. He told his sister: 'If there is any possibility of easing the tension and getting back to normal relations with the Dictators I wouldn't risk it by what would certainly be regarded by them as a challenge.' Churchill remained outside the government until war was declared. A week later, Chamberlain reflected, 'I can't see Hitler starting a world war for Danzig.'[20]

In May Chamberlain showed hesitant confidence in the 'moderates' in Germany. He feared a coup in Danzig: 'We are therefore still in the danger zone, but I myself still believe that Hitler missed the bus last September and that his generals won't let him risk a major war now. But', he added with a bleak outbreak of humour, 'I can't see how the détente is to come about as long as the Jews obstinately go on refusing to shoot Hitler!' A few weeks later he wrote that 'I can't help thinking that he [Hitler] is not such a fool as some hysterical people make out and that he would not be sorry to compromise if he could do so without what he would feel to be humiliation. I have got one or two ideas which I am exploring though once again it is difficult to proceed when there are so many ready to say "Nous sommes trahis" at any suggestion of a peaceful solution.' In mid-July, the Prime Minister told the Cabinet 'that the Foreign Secretary's view, which he shared, was that the present international situation was best left to cool down, and that a reasonable solution of the Danzig problem should not be impossible if the temperature dropped.' That weekend he wrote to sister Hilda that it was important not to frighten Hitler into the belief that the British might grow strong and attack Germany. Hitler could be satisfied if he were patient. He intended to persuade Mussolini to calm Hitler, and he was trying to get Daladier to co-operate. 'I believe that if I am now allowed I can steer this country through the next few years out of the war-zone into peace and reconstruction.' Next week he wrote to sister Ida that the Germans would soon understand that they could not win a war at any reasonable cost and then 'we can talk'. Leo Amery's observation after hearing the Prime Minister in the House may well be justified: 'He is being pushed all the time into a policy which he does not like and hates abandoning the last bridges which might still enable him to resume his former policy.'[21]

At the end of the month Chamberlain complained of the conduct of Robert Hudson, the junior minister in charge of the Department of Overseas Trade, in letting contacts with Germans become known to the suspicious public but:

In the meantime there are other and discreeter channels by which contact can be maintained for it is important that those in Germany who would like to see us come to an understanding should not be discouraged. My critics of course think it would be a frightful thing to come to any arrangement with Germany without first having given her a thorough thrashing to larn her to be a toad. But I don't share that view. Let us convince her that the chances of winning a war without getting thoroughly exhausted in the process are too remote to make it worthwhile. But the corollary to that must be that she has a chance of getting fair and reasonable consideration and treatment from us and others if she will give up the idea that she can force it from us and convince us that she has given it up.[22]

In August, having arranged that Parliament should go into long recess on the 4th, he went off to Scotland, leaving Halifax to worry in London. He arrived back in Downing Street on Monday 21 August in time for the immediate preliminaries to war. His attempts to win an amenable Hitler by direct persuasion, or by appealing to 'moderates', had not come to much. He was conscious that he could not openly advocate discussion or negotiation with Hitler. Almost everyone now rejected the notion of appeasement. However, he went to Scotland in reasonably tranquil spirits. He told his sister, Ida, 'I see no reason to change the views I recently expressed to you on the outlook': that is 'talk' with the Germans should soon be possible. Chamberlain looked forward to an autumn General Election with confidence, mingled with some uncertainty as he studied by-election returns. In May 1939 he thought that 'apathy' at by-elections did not indicate lack of support for the government and comforted himself with information that the Labour Party executive felt an election now would be a disaster. Yet in July he felt 'pretty sick of the perpetual personal attacks on me at home'. He had been told that feeling in his favour was unmistakable in Cornwall yet 'it hasn't shown itself in the by-election and sometimes I wonder what *would* happen in a general election'. Apparently the Germans learned from Sir Joseph Ball (of Conservative Central Office) that the election was planned for November 1939. Dirksen, the German ambassador, pointed out that Chamberlain would have to fight the election either on the programme of 'readiness for the coming (inevitable) war' or 'safeguarding world peace with Chamberlain'. Was Chamberlain's political position strong enough, the ambassador speculated, to enable him to make a gesture which his opponents would denounce as a relapse into 'the proscribed policy of "appeasement" '? Samuel Hoare wrote to Chamberlain on the day he went to Scotland, suggesting Chamberlain come shooting in Norfolk in September 'in case Hitler and politics make it possible'. He thought 'all the prospects seemed to be good' for an election in November. Chamberlain himself wrote to his sister 'at present I should be quite confident of the result but I should warn you that the C.O. [the Conservative Central Office] says we shall certainly lose seats'.[23]

Chamberlain endured a campaign in much of the press, led by the *Daily Telegraph*, demanding Churchill's appointment to the government. As Hoare put it early in July, 'the papers of the Left and the important papers of the Right' were 'shouting with one voice for his inclusion'. Oliver Stanley suggested to the Prime Minister that he should bring in Churchill and offered to give up his own office as a Cabinet minister. Churchill certainly wanted office. In April he even said so directly to the Conservative chief whip. Chamberlain commented on Churchill 'the nearer we get to war the more his chances improve and vice versa'. What Chamberlain needed for his own political security was evidence of conciliatory intentions from the dictators. Only then could he have risked a cautious public resumption of 'appeasement' in the sense of finding out what the dictators wanted and attempting to satisfy their more reasonable wishes by peaceful means. The foreign policy of 10 Downing Street, that is to say Chamberlain's and Horace Wilson's, was somehow to secure gestures of good will from Hitler, which they usually spoke of as 'steps to restore confidence'. Public demand for Churchill and the almost universal anxiety to secure an alliance with the USSR expressed support for a policy of demonstrative firmness towards Hitler, to deter him, by threats of force, from further acts of aggression. Foreign Office officials, and Halifax, used a phrase attributed to Weizsäcker, the official head of the German foreign ministry, who, with prudence, played the role of a non-Nazi moderate: the

British should practise 'un silence menaçant'. Across that threatening silence, Chamberlain, however, whispered tentative
promises of good-will to accompany international confidence
restored by some Hitlerian gesture.[24]

These must be private whispers; Chamberlain dared not
publicly break silence because too many journalists and MPs
would accuse him of weakening coercive deterrence. He conveyed them through German visitors to London or through
British travellers to Germany. The most important German
visitor was Dr Helmuth Wohlthat, a senior German official
closely connected with Göring. Horace Wilson saw Wohlthat,
who visited London on questions relating to fleecing refugees
from Germany and whaling, on 6 and 7 June, 18 July and 31
July 1939. Wilson sent the Foreign Office his record of only
one of these conversations. Wohlthat's report to Göring on the
July conversations shows that one, at least, took place at the
Duke of Westminster's London house, presumably to keep it
secret. Wilson seems to have insisted that Hitler must make
clear that he intended to renounce aggression. Then benefits
would flow from co-operation. Wohlthat's report specified the
benefits, especially easier access to world markets, through
colonial development and joint economic planning. German-
Polish issues would become easy of solution once Polish independence was no longer at issue. In his conversation Robert
Hudson, secretary to the Department of Overseas trade,
offered Wohlthat the prospect of an immense loan to strength-
en the German balance of payments until the export trade of
a newly pacified Germany revived. It was this conversation that,
to Chamberlain's dismay, the newspapers made public. Questions in Parliament forced him into the evasive admission that
'Sir Horace Wilson, as Chief Industrial Adviser to the Government' (a function now eclipsed by Wilson's other activities), 'has
frequently seen Herr Wohlthat when he has been over here on
a visit. He saw him again on his recent visit.'[25]

After this embarrassment Chamberlain and Wilson returned
to 'discreeter channels'. They had found one when they entrusted Henry Drummond-Wolff with messages for the German government setting out the economic benefits, including a
possible loan, that peace would enable the British government
to secure for Germany. Drummond-Wolff went to Berlin on 10

May having had a 'long conversation' with Sir Horace Wilson. (It was perhaps in connection with this visit that Cadogan, following a telephone intercept, went to see Horace Wilson on 3 May to complain that No. 10 seemed to be 'talking "appeasement" again'.) In Berlin Drummond-Wolff talked to Wohlthat and another official of Göring's department. About the same time *The Times* began to print a series of letters advocating discussions to settle international difficulties, including German-Polish disputes, from an ex-minister, Lord Rushcliffe, a Labour pacifist, Lord Ponsonby, two Oxford historians, Lord Elton and J. A. R. Marriott, and a prosy Cambridge exponent of political theories, Sir Ernest Barker. Two well-informed observers, Oliver Harvey, Halifax's official private secretary and Corbin, the French ambassador, believed that some of these letters were encouraged, or even drafted, by Sir Horace Wilson.[26]

Now Downing Street reinforced these signals. A member of the old-established and substantial firm in Mincing Lane, which belonged to his family, and which had interests in materials used for special steels, E. W. D. Tennant, as a result of employing a long-standing Nazi as an agent in Germany, had become something very unusual, an admirer and friend of Ribbentrop. Tennant offered to go to see Ribbentrop and Wilson briefed him carefully in two meetings on 10 July and just before his departure to Germany on 24 July. Wilson told Tennant 'that, in no circumstances, was he to mention to anybody the fact that he had had this conversation with me or that he had been in any way in touch with the Prime Minister'. While making it clear to Ribbentrop that Britain was determined 'to assist any state whose independence is threatened' there was also, Tennant should explain, 'willingness to reason with reasonable people'. On 26 July, Tennant visited Ribbentrop at his recently acquired lakeside country house at Fuschl, near Salzburg, and shared with him the eleven-hour train journey to Berlin the next day. At the end of July Tennant sent a long report to Wilson and, which cannot have pleased Wilson, sent a copy to Sir Robert Vansittart in the Foreign Office.

In the train Tennant had a long conversation with Hewel, Ribbentrop's liaison officer with Hitler. Hewel gave him what seems an accurate account of Hitler's thinking. The Führer was 'convinced that the Jews have now so much power in the government of Britain that he has come to the conclusion that probably there is nothing to be done but fight it out' since 'he has a definite programme in view which he is determined to fulfil during his lifetime which will make Germany healthy, rich, self-supporting and impregnable'.[27]

In July 1939, Arthur Bryant, the widely read 'patriotic' historian, who specialised in inspiring accounts of the stirring English past, joined in. He too spoke, apparently without prompting, to Hewel, and then submitted to Downing Street notes that he proposed to send to Hewel, on the assumption that they might be passed on to Hitler. Chamberlain regarded his efforts with condescension. Noting that if Hitler should declare a three-year period of peace, as Bryant suggested, the result would be 'incredulity and derision', he thought, however, that Bryant's 'naïvety' might lend force to his pleas for moderation. Soon Bryant provided concealment for another and more important contact, this time with Hitler himself. Lord Kemsley the press proprietor, owner of the *Sunday Times* and the *Daily Sketch*, arranged with Otto Dietrich, Hitler's press secretary, for an exchange of articles, one, on German attitudes and policies, to be published in Britain, the other, from Britain, to be published in Germany. Bryant was put to work on the latter article.

Kemsley visited Germany ostensibly to discuss the articles; in fact he hoped to meet Hitler. He did, at Bayreuth, on 27 July 1939. Hitler spoke amiably and vaguely. He wanted colonies and 'the cancellation of the Versailles Treaty'. Kemsley, however, extracted from Hitler the suggestion 'that each country should put its demands on paper, and that this might lead to a discussion'. Hence a flurry of excitement at Downing Street after Kemsley called there, with his notes, on 31 July. Horace Wilson discussed with Kemsley how to secure compete secrecy, and agreed that his conversation with Hitler should be talked of only as a courtesy call linked with the exchange of articles. That evening Halifax came over to Downing Street. He and Chamberlain agreed to take up Hitler's 'suggestion' and Wilson drafted a letter which Kemsley would send to Dietrich. Halifax agreed that, apart from Cadogan, no one in the Foreign Office should be told. Next day Wilson modified the draft in consultation with Kemsley, Chamberlain himself added a sentence to emphasise the need for Hitler to do something to restore confidence, Kemsley promised secrecy and said he would have the letter to Dietrich typed in his private office and taken to Dietrich by his own secretary. These furtive promptings were vain: Hitler did not respond. Dietrich belatedly sent an unimportant article to Kemsley on 17 August which, he wrote, might help to restore confidence. The interest of these attempts at contact lies not in their effectiveness as British attempts to prevent war but in the evidence they provide of the state of mind of Chamberlain and Halifax: if anything their effect on the international scene was to make Anglo-German war more likely.[28]

Other, equally futile, contacts came from Swedes who believed, correctly, that Göring wished to avoid war with Britain and, wrongly, that the British might be persuaded to take his word for it that such a war was unnecessary. Wenner-Gren, a Swedish manufacturer (of electrical goods under the Electrolux brand) and Dahlerus, another Swedish magnate, passed Göring's thoughts on to the British and conveyed back what they supposed to be British thinking, helped by several British businessmen whom they introduced to Göring. The Prime Minister himself talked to Wenner-Gren on 6 June and Halifax talked to Dahlerus on 25 July. Chamberlain declared that discussions could only come after German action to restore confidence. Halifax expressed interest in what Göring might say but insisted that 'I should know nothing about it officially . . . if any official connection were ever to be established, it would only do mischief and create quite unnecessary and undesirable misunderstanding'. When Dirksen, the German ambassador, met Horace Wilson on 3 August, Wilson insisted that Hitler must help to restore confidence. He pointed to 'the very militant character of public opinion . . . it was quite out of the question for the Government to think of any general discussions until steps had been taken of a kind that would not merely alter public opinion but be acceptable to public opinion as justifiable.' As late as 20 August, however, when the formidable German war machine was clanking and hissing, Wilson still agreed with another German go-between 'that it was a great mistake to go on asserting our determination to fulfil our obligations; the only effect of this is to irritate and annoy Hitler'.[29]

The futility of these conversations lay in the incompatibility between British and German aims. Hitler employed his own special channel to the British and French, Karl Burckhardt, the League of Nations high commissioner to Danzig, to whom he sent his personal aircraft to bring him to Berchtesgaden. Through Burckhardt he set out what he wanted. Hitler, from his mental vision of inevitable conflict and international struggle, explained that he must make his people safe from war-time blockade. 'Shall I not do better to leave 2,000,000 on the battlefield than to lose many more from hunger?' His demands were, he thought, modest: 'I have no romantic aspirations; I have no desire to dominate. Above all I want nothing from the West. Not today and not tomorrow. I look for nothing there, once and for all, nothing. All the ideas which people ascribe to me are inventions. But I must have a free hand in the East.' Hitler would 'guarantee all the English possessions in the world'; Burckhardt put into his mind the idea of a discussion with a German-speaking Englishman. Halifax summed it up when he passed it all on to Chamberlain and remarked that he could not imagine what the 'Englishman' would say 'inasmuch as Hitler's whole line of thought seems to be the familiar one of the free hand in the East, and, if he really wants to annex land in the East on which he can settle Germans to grow wheat, I confess I don't see any way of accommodating him'. One communicative visitor to London Chamberlain and Halifax did not see: Lieutenant-Colonel Count von Schwerin of the German war ministry. Schwerin told those he met that war was certain unless Hitler personally were convinced of British strength and determination. Churchill should join the government for, at the moment, Hitler believed British foreign policy to be 'thoroughly flabby' and Churchill's advent 'would convince Hitler that we really meant to stand up to him'.[30]

Chamberlain's conciliatory contacts might, on the other hand, weaken Hitler's belief in British resolve to fight for the European balance of power and so make him more likely to upset it. Much evidence, however, suggests Hitler had decided, that, as he grew older (he seems to have felt old at 50), he could not wait much longer. If Britain chose to interfere in his remodelling of Poland, in spite of all his assurances of good intentions towards the British Empire, then it showed the need of force to compel Britain to leave continental Europe alone. Moreover the issue of the Polish-German frontier was the one on which Hitler could expect most German support for a war with Britain. A more likely effect of British gestures of conciliation may have been to convince German moderates, especially sceptical soldiers, that Hitler could avoid a long and hazardous war, yet continue German expansion. In August 1939, strengthened by the prospective neutrality of the USSR, Hitler could reassure German doubters.

Chamberlain and Halifax worried most about the reaction of British Members of Parliament and the public if they heard of their conciliatory gestures. Chamberlain, indelibly, permanently, stood out as the unique man of Munich, the bold advocate of concession, the opponent of resistance. Halifax had often disagreed in private, but to the world outside Westminster he remained Chamberlain's loyal assistant. Nearly everyone took for granted their dislike of their newly proclaimed policy of guarantees and of the 'peace front' against Nazi aggression. Many people suspected them of eagerness to return to 'appeasement'. T. L. Horabin, elected, to Chamberlain's dismay, at the North Cornwall by-election, spoke in his maiden speech of the 'infirmity of purpose' that 'many people in this country and many people in neutral and allied countries, and certainly I believe, the leaders of the Axis powers' saw in the British government. This theme was taken up by foreign ambassadors: Corbin reported to Paris that other foreign missions had noted rumours of Anglo-German contacts and he reported himself as startled by a British under-secretary, presumably R. A. Butler, a keen 'appeaser', who had told him that some sort of Anglo-German bargain was inevitable. The French embassy in Berlin noted how Ribbentrop and Goebbels, for instance, used the Hudson–Wohlthat contacts to argue that Chamberlain's 'intransigence' towards Germany would soon pass. Maisky, the Soviet ambassador in London, told Moscow, early in May, of his belief in Chamberlain's continued pursuit of the Munich policy although he maintained that British public opinion would prevent a return to appeasement. Some weeks later Lloyd George explained to Maisky his view of

Chamberlain's plans. He would press moderation on Poland and Germany, by persuasion and threats, and then 'try once more to reach an agreement with the aggressors, or at least delay for a long time the signing of a treaty with the Soviet government'. Near the end of July 1939 Maisky sent a telegram to Moscow pointing to corroboration of Lloyd George's warnings. Maisky referred to the Hudson–Wohlthat conversations and, he wrote, 'it has been learned from reliable sources that through unofficial emissaries Chamberlain is now sounding Hitler to see whether it might not be possible to "settle" or at least to postpone the aggravation of the Danzig problem'.[31]

British policy towards Germany in the spring and summer of 1939 offered no hope of Anglo-German understandings. Chamberlain and his government, warmly supported, it seems, by British opinion, intended to prevent German dominance in Europe. Germany could be prosperous and powerful. German trade and interest in eastern Europe could be encouraged and the British Empire made still more accessible to German enterprise. But Hitler, it is certain, wanted more. He had in mind the creation of a powerful German empire militarily unbeatable by any possible combination of adversaries. To this the British government and the majority of the British people would not voluntarily assent. That made conciliatory efforts pointless. Nor did British policy deter. It is probable that Chamberlain encouraged Germans, who might otherwise have restrained Hitler, to believe that British threats to resist German aggression were empty. Today, moreover, one great interpretative question still remains open. We do not know what caused the rulers of the USSR to make the Soviet-German agreement. It is possible, even probable, that doubts of British reliability as an ally against Germany influenced their calculations. Chamberlain, given his record, and that of his government, invited such doubts and, to overcome them, he had to compensate for his past by special vigour in pursuit of peace by deterrence. This he did not supply. As a result Chamberlain may have misled the Soviet government. Probably they supposed he aimed for a bargain with Hitler at the expense of the Soviet Union. It was not true; Chamberlain hoped to find ways of limiting German power. To do so by persuasion, if it had been possible, rather than by force was as desirable for the Soviet Union as for the United Kingdom. Chamberlain did not give the impression, even if it was the truth, that his object was to limit the growth of German power.

13 Arms and the Economy

British foreign policy could have been much simpler if Britain had been militarily stronger than Germany. Three factors determined British armed strength in the 1930s. First, Great Britain began to prepare for war later than Germany. Second, the population and industrial resources of the United Kingdom were less than Germany's and, thirdly, a smaller proportion of British resources was devoted to rearmament.

In the Anglo-German arms race, the British team ran under a self-imposed handicap. Hitler fired the starting-gun in February 1933: only the Germans moved. As early as October 1933 Chamberlain thought that 'common prudence would seem to indicate some strengthening of our defences' but it was not until July 1934 that the Cabinet agreed to a programme 'for meeting our worst deficiencies'. It was only in February 1936 that the Cabinet approved a programme for a possible war, a programme to be carried out in three to five years. One set of figures demonstrates the advantage of starting early. In that year, 1936, Germany produced 5112 aircraft, the United Kingdom 1877. Only in 1940 did British aircraft production, with the highest priority, overtake German.[1]

The total population of Germany in 1935 was about 67 million, while, in 1938, German Austrians and German Czechoslovaks added another 10 million; the United Kingdom contained about 47 million. In some other critical respects Germany had more resources for arms production than Britain. In 1937 German steel production, at about 20 million tonnes, was well ahead of the British figure, in that boom year, of 13 million. In 1938 capital goods production in Germany exceeded that of Britain and France combined. In one essential sector, Britain lagged badly: machine-tools. Germany produced more than twice as many as Britain.[2]

Population size and industrial capacity set the limit to British military strength. How close to that limit the United Kingdom came depended on public attitudes and on decisions made by the government, which determined how many men and women and how much of the available resources would be employed in making weapons or in training to use them. The government made the most important decisions early in 1936. Preparations for war must not interfere with ordinary production. Rearmament was to be added to existing production and not substituted for any of it.

After the General Election of November 1935, which maintained a safe Conservative majority, the Baldwin–Chamberlain government set itself to consider what the navy, army and air force required to be ready for war. At the election both Baldwin and Chamberlain emphasised in their speeches the need for Britain to arm. Chamberlain gave himself the credit for 'the wisdom of the conclusion at which I was the first to arrive, viz. that we ought to fight the election on a defence programme'. He claimed that Britain should be strong: 'In that way only can she fulfil what I believe to be her mission – the mission of peace-maker of Europe.' Baldwin pledged that: 'In no conceivable circumstances ... must we feel that we are inferior in the air to any nation within striking distance of this country and in no conceivable circumstances should it be impossible for our people, whatever may happen, to be secured in the supplies of their food from overseas.' Neither suggested building up the army; both insisted on the moderation of their plans. Chamberlain claimed to be 'the very last person to agree to any greater expenditure on defence than is absolutely necessary'. And Baldwin put it categorically: 'There has not been, there is not, and there will not be any question of huge armaments or materially increased forces.'[3]

They had won a 'mandate', but of a restricted kind. With it the government prepared for war. In February 1936 Chamberlain suggested to Baldwin that Lord Weir should be added to the committee of ministers that considered the rearmament plan put forward by the armed services. He was the head of his family's engineering firm in Glasgow, where he had worked since the age of 16, and he knew the ways of government as an adviser and as one of the founding fathers of the RAF; he had been Secretary for Air at the end of the First World War. Since March 1935 he had been advising the Air Ministry on increasing aircraft production. Now he spoke with authority and confidence and worked with Chamberlain. The services' report to the Cabinet committee remarked that their programme could not be carried out in full in three years. Weir asserted to the ministerial committee that the programme could not be completed even in five years unless a 'semi-war organisation was introduced or, alternatively, a reduction was effected in normal civilian activity and our export trade'. Later Weir explained that 'semi-war conditions' would involve direction of business and 'would necessitate interference with existing civil and export trade'. Instead, he urged the need to work out priorities. That was done: the navy was allowed as many warships as it could procure and man, the needs of the air force would be met, but most of the requirements of the army were to be deferred. There should be no interference with civilian production. The full Cabinet approved on 25 February 1936.[4]

This decision fixed the scale of British manufacture of weapons. 'Finance', that is, the limits to government spending on armaments which the Treasury persuaded the Cabinet to accept, mattered less. The only successful attempt by the Treasury to force a reduction in defence expenditure, in the second half of 1937, was designed to check inflation, and, therefore, derived from the scarcity of the resources needed for arms production, that is to say from inability to produce more whatever the availability of money. Usually manufacturers attempting to increase arms production found the first check to their efforts came from shortage of labour. The problem was skill. Above all, manufacturers needed workers who could make or use machine-tools or supervise their use. This required training and experience. Unemployment levels among skilled workers in the engineering industry were well below the levels among the working population as a whole and, among these relatively few skilled unemployed, the skills of many were outmoded or insufficient. Repeatedly ministers responsible for arms production, especially Inskip, appointed in the spring of 1936 to 'co-ordinate' defence, a role which, in practice, involved deputising for the Prime Minister in supervising defence production, and Swinton, the Secretary for Air, told the Cabinet that more arms could be made more quickly if they agreed to compel the transfer of skilled workers from civilian production. This the government did not do and Chamberlain took his share in their refusal.[5]

The reasons given by the ministers who considered the rearmament scheme in their report to the full Cabinet seem so casual as to suggest that they believed their assertion that 'we must aim at securing our service needs without interference with or reduction of production for civil and export trade' was so obviously correct that it needed no careful defence. They produced one dubious economic argument and then added a political objection: 'Any such interference would adversely affect the general prosperity of the country and so reduce our capacity to find the necessary funds for the Service programmes. It would undoubtedly attract Parliamentary criticism.' In practice the government seems to have feared a public dislike of interference and of the tax increases necessary to contain inflation. Fear of public hostility to rearmament was shown in the desire of ministers to make the rearmament programme seem to be small in scale. Chamberlain thought that 'it would probably be advisable to avoid figures which could be added up to a larger amount than public opinion was anticipating'.[6]

A few months later a paper which Chamberlain circulated to the Cabinet pointed out that 'already there are signs of impending shortages of skilled labour; already, too, there are signs that our exports are slackening . . . and it is only too clear that overseas trade once lost will not be easy to recover'. That was a powerful argument against diversion: no one could deny that exports should be encouraged. British strategy for military victory called for a long war. In war-time increased imports would be wanted and exports must fall. Loans from abroad, if available at all, would be easier to secure if the British peace-time balance of payments were strong and, if loans (or gifts) could not be had, then gold reserves built up by peace-time surpluses would be the only financial alternative to liquidation of British capital assets abroad. A strong balance of payments had the leading role in reinforcing what the Treasury and Inskip called the 'fourth arm of defence'.[7]

More difficult to explain on economic grounds is the government's decision not to interfere with civilian production for the home market. Reduction in volume of output for the home market might, it is true, increase the costs of production per unit of output in firms active in manufacture both for home and export trade and so weaken competitiveness in export markets. Political reasons probably counted more. Arms production usually required a higher proportion of skilled labour than civilian products. To turn over civilian producers to arms would therefore often increase unemployment among the mass of the unskilled. To take some skilled labourers away from civilian firms and transfer them to armaments factories would sacrifice the jobs of a larger number of unskilled workers. Swinton told the Cabinet in November 1936 'that if we could "pick the eyes out of", say, Singer's Sewing Machine works and certain other engineering firms we should in a comparatively short time get improved production' but, he added, 'the immediate result would be to throw out of employment in such a factory a number of the residue of the workers'. The future of the Conservative Party seemed to depend on the success of the 'National Government' in persuading voters to believe that economic recovery since 1931 was its work and that Conservative government brought safely growing prosperity, falling unemployment, and improved conditions of life, in contrast to the alleged follies of Labour in power. About that time, for instance, the Council of the Federation of Building Trades Employers noted 'that the government dare not let it be assumed that housing activity would be severely curtailed in favour of war preparation'. In 1936 and 1937 rearmament remained unpopular particularly among the liberal-minded. This political atmosphere changed only later, in 1938.[8]

Neville Chamberlain never denied the need to equip the United Kingdom with anything needed to ensure safe defence. He wanted effective defence and he wanted it to be sustained until general arms limitation could be secured, however long that might take. At the same time he hoped to keep going the steady rise in average British standards of living since 1932. That meant reluctance to increase taxation and a continued effort to keep interest rates low and to avoid diversion of industry. Both Hitler and Attlee could then be kept at bay, and the successes of Chamberlain's Chancellorship of the Exchequer protracted into his Prime Ministership.

Chamberlain virtually dictated the rearmament plan that the Cabinet eventually approved. He recorded privately that the policy of the ministerial committee whose report determined the Cabinet's decision 'has been guided by me'. He went on to explain that he had 'got S.B. [Baldwin] to add Weir' to the committee and then he arranged that Weir should press for the solution that Chamberlain favoured. Without direction of industry the whole scheme of strengthening all three services could not be carried out even in five years let alone in three. Weir put forward 'a view which', wrote Chamberlain, 'I have long been urging on some of my colleagues' that a 'fighting Air Force' should be substituted for an expeditionary force of ground troops. What was 'vitally important' was to find a 'deterrent' against a rapidly rearming Germany. Eden supported Chamberlain: 'From that point of view the air would assume first place.' Chamberlain, worried that 'it would be thought that I was merely advocating the cheapest way of defence instead of the best' later set out his case. By the time a British field force had been dispatched to the Continent, which he put, optimistically, at two weeks after the outbreak of war, the decisive encounter might already have taken place in a German onslaught on France: 'It was for consideration whether, from the point of view of a deterrent, a strong offensive air force was not more effective than a field force which could not be put in the field for two weeks.' If the Germans, on the other hand, attacked eastwards 'it would appear again that the most effective deterrent to Germany's aggression might take the form of an air offensive'.[9]

Starting from the fact that British industrial capacity did not permit the full demands of the navy, army and air force to be met in the time required without diversion of resources from civilian products, and from the assumption that such diversion must not be allowed, Chamberlain evolved a set of priorities for production which laid down a strategy for war. The navy must defend British trade and destroy that of the enemy. To carry out this role seven new capital ships were to be begun in the next three years (only the first two were to be announced in 1936) with appropriate flotillas, to make the British battle fleet equal to the totals of Japan's and Germany's. (The Admiralty asked for more than that but agreed that its higher target for a 'new standard fleet' could only be for a longer term.) The air force was to complete its existing programme of 1500 first-line machines by April 1937, but 'it may be necessary to reconsider this figure' to match German increases. Meanwhile, 'the Air Ministry should have latitude to vary the Royal Air Force programme so as to improve its offensive power and constitute the most effective deterrent against German aggression ... This will involve some increase in numbers in addition to the substitution of larger and more efficient machines.' Now, early 1936, designs were requested for new heavy bombers and thus were laid the foundations of the heavy bomber force which devastated German towns after 1942, but before then the strategic bombing force was unimpressive. In 1938 German bombers deterred the British rather than the other way round.[10]

The army suffered the most from lack of productive resources. The General Staff asked for a five-division regular army to be reinforced in war by a twelve-division Territorial Army, the whole to be equipped and trained for continental war. Ministers decided to postpone decision on whether or not to modernise the twelve Territorial divisions. In October 1936 Chamberlain began a campaign to stop the creation of this substantial field force for possible continental intervention. On 19 October, Chamberlain, nursing an attack of gout, summoned Inskip to his bedside to tell him his reasons. He recorded that Deverell, the Chief of the Imperial General Staff, said that on the outbreak of war the French would retire southwards to their fortifications and the Belgians northwards to theirs 'leaving a gap through which the Germans will pour and seize the Channel Ports. I said', Chamberlain's record continues, ' "Tell that to the Marines". That is what might happen if we don't warn the French. If we do they can't afford to leave a gap or their own rear would be turned.'[11]

However, a few weeks later Duff Cooper, as Secretary for War, circulated to the Cabinet a paper from the army staff calling for seventeen fully-equipped divisions to be ready to be dispatched from the United Kingdom for overseas service as soon as possible after the outbreak of war. After a few days Chamberlain put in his riposte. Already industry was strained which 'tends to indicate that the execution of the programme approved in February which included the re-equipment of five regular divisions only is as much as our resources can at present stand; and that to add to the programme any substantial degree of re-equipment of the Territorial Force would only result in the breakdown of the whole scheme.' If British resources were used for the navy and air force they would have more impact. Moreover 'the political temper of people in this country is strongly opposed to continental adventures', they will feel preparations for large-scale military operations on the Continent to be 'likely to result in our being entangled in disputes which do not concern us'.

The Cabinet asked the three Chiefs of Staff to consider the issue; the other two supported the army. 'Dog wouldn't eat dog', Chamberlain commented. He won just the same. Early in February 1937 he wrote a jaunty letter to Ida. He had had a good week. He had heard Schnabel play Beethoven's last piano sonata: 'As I get older I seem to get more out of music.' Then: 'Secondly I have at last got a decision about the Army and it practically gives me all I want. The Regular Army is to be armed cap-à-pie with the most modern equipment, and is to be ready to go anywhere anytime. But we are not committed to sending it anywhere anywhen. The Territorials are to have similar equipment but only in sufficient quantity to enable them to train . . . The War Office have renounced all idea of a continental army on the scale of 1914–18 and have, with a certain amount of grumbling, accepted the above.' Hoare and Swinton told him that the Chiefs of Staff of the Navy and Air Force really agreed: 'It is satisfactory to know that the seadog and the airdog think the wardog ought to be eaten – by some other dog.'[12]

A defensive strategy lay behind these armament priorities. When he became Prime Minister, Chamberlain pushed matters further. He shifted Duff Cooper, who too readily responded to the generals' pressure for a large, balanced, army, and substituted Hore-Belisha at the War Office. Hore-Belisha, an ambitious minister, who aroused the contempt of his military staff by his love of publicity and his instinct for 'photo opportunities', kept in touch with the latest theories of war. In particular, he was much influenced by Liddell Hart, another *bête-noire* of the generals. Basil Liddell Hart, a fluent self-confident writer, eventually encapsulated his views in his *Defence of Britain*, published in 1939, which Chamberlain's diary shows him to have read. Liddell Hart's pre-war views were not at all what he, later, after the war, made them out to have been. He asserted that the First World War showed that ground armies on the defensive were heavily superior to attacking armies. An attacking army needed a three to one superiority to have any hope of victory, not only at the decisive point, but, it seemed, all along the line. Thus the French army alone should be able to make France, and Belgium, secure from German invasion. The British need not, therefore, join in the direct defence of France. Their real contribution to an Anglo-French war with Germany would be blockade, supported by increasing aerial bombardment, and the defence of Britain required, above all, a counter to the new threat from the air.[13]

In July 1937 the Treasury expressed alarm about the increasing cost of the armaments programme and its effect on 'economic stability', an alarm apparently provoked by fear of inflation, as armaments orders supplemented boom conditions in industry and led to mounting shortages of skilled labour, with 'poaching' of labour and increasing wages. Moreover the Treasury urged that, if peace were preserved, substantial armed forces would still have to be maintained so that the question of the size of the resources that could, politically and economically, be devoted to the armed services might be a long-lasting problem. In November 1937, the Treasury, through Sir Richard Hopkins, produced the crippling argument that spending on armaments could not be increased because if it were financed by more borrowing it would risk added inflation, while if it were financed by extra taxation it might deepen a possible depression. At that moment Hopkins' indecision on whether to fear inflation or depression was justified by uncertainty as to whether or not fiscal and monetary policy in the United States would be sufficiently relaxed to check the recession now beginning there. Only if the United States financial authorities managed to set the American economy growing again would the United Kingdom escape the depressing effects of a contraction in export markets.

Armaments spending, the Treasury therefore insisted, must be limited. The government decided yet again to curtail projected spending on the army, a process smoothed by the still amenable Hore-Belisha. The Cabinet reduced intervention in ground battles in western Europe to a still lower priority. As Inskip's paper put it: 'the continental hypothesis ranks fourth in order of priority and the primary role of the Regular Army becomes the defence of Imperial commitments, including anti-aircraft defence at home.' From the Territorial Army there should be drawn more anti-aircraft units and the rest 'should be regarded as available to support the Regular Army in their primary role of Imperial defence overseas as soon after the outbreak of war as their training and equipment permits'. The army had been planning for a Field Force of five divisions capable of disembarking on the Continent within fifteen days from mobilisation. Now the Field Force was to 'operate in an Eastern campaign', apparently in Egypt. Thus, early in 1938, preparations for land fighting against the German army were pushed to so low a priority that, in practice, they could not be carried out at all because, in fact, planned arms production was not being attained. In 1937 the programme was not fulfilled. Chamberlain remarked to the Cabinet in February 1938 that 'we were seriously behind hand already'.

Chamberlain drew attention to one way of accelerating armaments production: 'An improvement might be obtained, however, by action to secure skilled labour, which might be effected by putting pressure on manufacturers to release it for armament work.' He then argued against his own suggestion, 'That was a possibility that ought to be kept in mind. That would mean that we should meet our short-range difficulties and chance the long-range ones, for the course proposed would involve throwing away a great deal of goodwill. He thought it only right to say, however, that that was a possibility which could be considered if necessary.'[14]

After the Anschluss, and the open use of armed violence by Hitler's government, British attitudes perceptibly changed. Now rapid rearmament, especially in the air, became generally popular – that the Royal Navy should be strong had always been taken for granted. Chamberlain adapted himself to the new atmosphere. He changed his Air Minister and accepted Inskip's suggestion that the Cabinet should abandon, in public, the assumption that the course of normal trade should not be impeded. On 24 March 1938 Chamberlain announced the new doctrine in the Commons, without suggesting any means to enforce it: 'Rearmament work must have first priority in the national effort.' Then he reaffirmed the policy of appeasement: 'to employ ourselves, and to urge others to employ, the methods of reason and diplomacy rather than those of menace and force.' Of course the statement that normal trade should not necessarily have priority made it easier to persuade manufacturers to give priority to work for defence but it fell far short of Churchill's suggestion that legislation should give the government 'necessary powers to divert industry . . . from the ordinary demands of commerce so as to fit our rearmament in with the needs of our export trade and yet make sure that rearmament has supreme priority'.[15]

In 1938 military chickens came home to roost. Asked to consider the military implications of war in support of France, if France helped Czechoslovakia against a German attack, the Chiefs of Staff replied in March 1938 that French land forces could not prevent the defeat of Czechoslovakia and that a long war would be needed to liberate it; in that war British and French naval superiority would steadily erode German strength, though a hostile combination of Germany, Italy and Japan would be perilous for the Empire. The Chiefs of Staff feared that the German air force might win a short war by striking a 'knock-out blow' on the United Kingdom through a bombing attack continued for two months or more. They calculated that the combined Franco-British air striking force could deliver less than one-third of the German bomb load. The Germans would have more than 1500 bombers and 540 fighters against a combined Franco-British total of 836 bombers and 675 fighters. Most British fighter aircraft were actually slower than the majority of the German bombers they would try to intercept. Only four radar stations would be ready. In September 1938 the secretary of the Committee of Imperial Defence, Hastings Ismay, produced a short and lucid paper arguing that British defences would be much better able to parry a German knock-out blow after 6 or 12 months' delay. These consequences of the belated nature of British rearmament and of the attempt to add armaments production to existing manufacture rather than to curtail civilian production did not explain Chamberlain's policy. However, they helped to justify it.[16]

Changes came in 1938. Naval production continued, inhibited principally by the difficulties of making gun-mountings, optical instruments and armour plate; priority for the production of anti-aircraft guns began to show effects; above all production for the air force began steadily to grow. Numerical increase followed a Cabinet decision: priority should no longer be given to the offensive bomber strike force to deter a German air attack by threatening massive retaliation. Instead a serious attempt should be made to create a defence against the German attack. This followed from the development of new, fast, single-seat monoplane fighters, the Hurricane and Spitfire, and from the prospective extension of radar stations for early warning of the approach of enemy aircraft. In April and November 1938 the Cabinet agreed to increase and accelerate aircraft production; in November they insisted on giving priority to fighters. Thus British strategy became strictly defensive: the idea of countering a German knock-out blow with an immediate British riposte, the strategy of massive retaliation, was dropped, at least for the immediate future. In a war with Germany, the French would look after themselves (and help to keep Italy quiet) while the United Kingdom would ward off the German knock-out, and, in a long war, slowly sap German strength by naval blockade and, eventually, by strategic bombing.[17]

Arms production increased in 1939, especially of aircraft. In the first six months of 1938, industry delivered 1045 aircraft; in the same months in 1939, 3753 aircraft. Recession had set in in the USA, insufficiently checked by the authorities, and British exports fell. That, while making worse the problem of finding foreign exchange, had a helpful consequence: the falling off in economic activity in Britain released skilled labour and machine-tools. Among members of the AEU, the Amalgamated Engineering Union, the main trade union in aircraft manufacture, unemployment rose from November 1937 (1.88 per cent) to the end of 1938 (3.07 per cent). In September 1938 a special enquiry found 11,232 unemployed skilled engineering workers, 5028 more than in May 1937. Of the unemployed, 8282 were thought suitable for immediate employment, without retraining, though only about 2600 were 'able to work to fine limits'. (The survey carefully noted the places in which these 2600 were to be found.) Here was an opportunity for increased manufacture. Moreover the Air Ministry took trouble to exploit the resources released by recession. In the summer of 1938 it began to insist that its contractors should undertake to sub-contract at least 35 per cent of the total man hours involved. In that way the work would go to the labour rather than the labour be transferred to aircraft factories. By September 1939, the Luftwaffe had about 3000 first-line aircraft ready for combat, the British about 1400 (and the French about 800) but the RAF was catching up at last (and, early in 1940, British production overtook the German).[18]

The fall in British exports caused by the economic turndown in the USA freed resources for arms manufacture. However, in another way, it weakened British preparation for war. Exports fell; imports were greater than they would have been without rearmament. Hence the British balance of payments suffered. This supplied a possible explanation for the financial phenomenon that caused most worry to the well-informed: the weakness of sterling in the foreign exchange markets. Capital outflows began in the spring of 1938 as holders of sterling moved into dollars and, later on, into francs. The reaction of the British authorities was to feel that the pound was overvalued and should be allowed to fall; the American authorities believed the British were seeking an under-valued pound which would check exports from the United States by making them more expensive in countries that used sterling or whose currencies were linked to sterling. The depression in the United States, they feared, would be protracted and deepened, and American exporters turn nasty. More or less emphatically, sometimes very emphatically, the US Treasury, and the President himself, pressed the British to keep sterling at a high level. They threatened to make it futile for the British to allow sterling to depreciate by reducing the gold price of the dollar, that is by an American devaluation.

In consequence the British government were compelled either to engage in stiff deflation, which was politically difficult, especially with an election in prospect, or to use the Bank of England's gold holdings to prop up the value of sterling. Sales of gold reduced British reserves by one-quarter in 1938 and by the same proportion in the first half of 1939. The problem this posed, as the Treasury pointed out, was that, in the probable absence in war-time of foreign loans, reserves accumulated in peace-time would be needed to pay for imports of food, raw materials and munitions during the long war which British strategy required. In July 1939 the Treasury argued that the moment was already in sight when financial weakness would make victory in war impossible.

This brought two responses. One, from Oliver Stanley, was that there would 'come a moment which, on a balance of our financial strength and our strength in armaments, was the best time for war to break out. It might be desirable to consider whether at such a period we should apply strong pressure to Germany to relax the international tension.' Since Hitler, at nearly the same time, cited economic difficulties, which for Germany also meant shortage of foreign exchange, as a reason for going to war soon, it is possible to suggest that economic constraints forced both Britain and Germany into mutual defiance in 1939. A more relaxed reaction came from Lord Halifax. He thought the Treasury made too much fuss and that in war the United States would provide what might be needed: a shrewd prediction which had little definite evidence at that time to support it.[19]

One episode illustrates British weaknesses. In April 1939, Sir Arthur Robinson wrote to Horace Wilson discussing compulsory powers to direct industry. Robinson 'was a good deal shaken by what the Treasury told me . . . about the difficulty of purchases in America because of the gold situation. I said to them that we must have a clear statement about that, because if it is so bad that we cannot draw heavily on the U.S.A. for machine-tools, I think it will almost certainly be necessary at once to take priority powers over the U.K. output, whether we do or do not have to face the voiding of running contracts for export.' It is interesting that Robinson seemed surprised. He was the civil servant who co-operated with the Minister for Co-ordination of Defence, first with Inskip and then Chatfield. Even after three years on the job he evidently retained illusions about British strength, not perhaps with respect to the machine-tool industry but in international finance.[20]

In 1939 the army began to be re-created. Halifax told ministers that refusal to equip an army for continental war might alienate the French 'if they were left with the impression that it was they who must bear the brunt of the fighting and slaughter on land'. The Chiefs of Staff feared that France, threatened by Germany and Italy, 'might well give up the unequal struggle unless supported with the assurance that we should assist them to our utmost'. French policy provided other new preoccupations for the British Cabinet. The January war-scare suggested that Hitler was considering a direct attack on Britain, or on the Netherlands, or both. What would the French do? The visit of Ribbentrop to Paris in December 1938 implied that the French might become as unreliable in support of the British as the British had often been in support of the French. Moreover Chamberlain had his own reasons for seeking French good-will; he wished to persuade Daladier to conciliate Mussolini.

British army chiefs complained that in war they would have no more than five divisions available in the first year 'equipped, it will be observed, on a scale suitable for a Second Class theatre of operations'. In February 1939 the Cabinet agreed that the regular divisions should be fully equipped, and four Territorial divisions given full equipment and reserves for embarkation six months after the outbreak of war.[21] After the German seizure of Prague two measures further transformed the British army. First the Territorial Army was to be brought up to full strength, then it was to be doubled. This was another response to the French demands for a British land contribution. Alarmed by the numerical superiority a fully mobilised German army must possess over the French, the French general staff called for an increased British expeditionary force. The British response, of course, represented only a promise for the more or less remote future, given the need for time to train and equip larger numbers than the existing body of untrained and ill-equipped volunteers. The planned increase in the size of the British army would either be no more than a gesture or it would require urgent acceleration of production.

Ambiguity at the top level surrounds the origins of conscription, the second great measure. French opinion complained of British self-exemption from peace-time military service; at home Conservative critics asked for organised 'national service' to demonstrate defiant resolve. Chamberlain, correctly, pointed out that Labour would object, so that compulsory service would demonstrate domestic discord. In any case voluntary recruitment for the air force and navy was comparatively easy and the army had low priority. The doubling of the Territorials needed more part-time volunteers rather than full-time conscripts. The introduction of conscription was, in fact, carried out not to fulfil the new priority of bringing help to the French army but to support the old priority of defence against German air attack. The limitation to six months' service in the new 'militia' shows that only comparatively simple training could be given to the recruits if the conscripts were to be of any military use for any part of that short period.

Fear of the surprise German air attack brought conscription. Chamberlain, however strong his hopes of friendship with the Third Reich, never failed in vigilance for the defence of Britain. In 1939 he wanted anti-aircraft and searchlight sites to be ready to go into instant action round the clock every day. The only way of doing so was to call out Territorials or Reservists. Legally this could only be done by formal proclamation of a 'state of emergency' and Chamberlain asked Halifax what effect 'the Declaration of Emergency would have in Germany'. To this tense and alarming measure Chamberlain persuaded his Cabinet to prefer conscription. Chatfield, the Minister for Co-ordination of Defence, whose professional standing as Admiral of the Fleet gave him an independent position in the government, labelled this device as 'using a sledge hammer to crack a nut'.[22]

Since Munich the advocates of alternatives to appeasement had called even more energetically for a Ministry of Supply to accelerate the making of munitions. Such a ministry (headed, perhaps, by that famous ex-Minister of Munitions, Winston Churchill) would be given powers to direct industry or, even if such powers were not taken, could more effectively co-ordinate production than, it was alleged, the Minister for Co-ordination of Defence, and his henchman Sir Arthur Robinson, without a department at their disposal, could hope to do. Finally Chamberlain gave way and on 20 April 1939 proposed the creation of a Ministry of Supply. Legislation, followed by orders in council, gave the government power to compel acceptance of its contracts and from August 1939, just before the war broke out, the government, at last, could direct the diversion of civilian production to rearmament.

Chamberlain had fought long and hard to defend civilian industry from interference. He aimed for peace, but peace combined with prosperity. He did not want an all-out arms race. The recession of 1938 involuntarily freed resources, of skilled labour and machines, for armaments. In 1939 rearmament and recovery made skilled labour scarce once more and once more wage-rates began to climb. The addition of the army as an effective claimant for other weapons beside anti-aircraft guns made the agitation for control of industry irresistible. As usual the compelling impact on Chamberlain came from his supporters and allies. Hore-Belisha, as War Minister, told the CID on 6 October 1938 that production of anti-aircraft guns 'could only get substantial acceleration if skilled labour was provided and if powers were taken which would give army orders in private factories effective priority over civilian orders'. Then in a public speech at Cardiff he asserted that 'under our present system nothing can guarantee' acceleration of the armament programme and suggested a ministry with 'full powers to allot orders, to assign priorities, to control the supply of raw materials and to make arrangements for the diversion of skilled labour'.[23] Chamberlain firmly rejected such thoughts. Horace Wilson helpfully talked to some industrialists who reported that 'there has as yet been no failure on the part of industry to provide the supplies required by the Departments', but then they gave the game away, 'except insofar as there has been lack of the necessary equipment or the necessary very highly skilled labour'; deficiencies which it was the precise purpose of a Ministry of Supply to prevent. Chamberlain noted irritably on Wilson's record that one of Wilson's interlocutors, Sir A. Roger, the industrialist, had written a letter to The Times which 'is not altogether helpful and was taken as support for a M. of Supply'. Alexander Roger wrote: 'Only a few of the scores of efficient factories in the country are today working at full strength.' Chamberlain told Wilson that he would see Dawson of The Times, and had already warned the editor of the Sunday Times against the proposal for a Ministry of Supply but, Chamberlain went on, Sam Hoare as well as Hore-Belisha, 'are very anxious for it – I believe purely on political grounds'.[24] Chamberlain understood that Hoare and Hore-Belisha wished to meet public demand. He did not.

The government survived a demand for a Ministry of Supply mounted by the Liberals in November 1938, the occasion on which Churchill, vainly, asked for 50 Conservatives to join him in voting against the government, and only Brendan Bracken and Harold Macmillan responded. After the German occupation of Prague in March 1939, the pressure on the Prime Minister became irresistible. In April Chatfield wrote to him explaining that both he and W. S. Morrison, who helped with the production side of his job as Minister for Co-ordination of Defence, wanted a Ministry of Supply with powers of direction; Hore-Belisha now pointed out that machine-tool makers were quoting delivery in 50 to 60 weeks; Buck de la Warr also wrote to Chamberlain. Even Chamberlain's old ally, William Weir, wrote from his Glasgow works, surprised that there were no 'new domestic steps': 'I would like to have you declare an Emergency State . . . nothing has yet been done effectively in regard to industrial production. Normality is still the keynote and a new note should be struck.' The Advisory Panel of Industrialists, set up in December 1938 to deflect criticism from the government, summed up the position of the supporters of a Ministry of Supply in a letter from their chairman, Greenly, to Sir Arthur Robinson, written in a style of embarrassed pomposity: 'From the evidence we have had in the course of our examination of Supply problems, we have come to the conclusion that industry has given very real proof of its readiness to co-operate with the government but without such powers . . . (for example, to enforce priorities) ordinary trade commitments have prevented the productive capacity of the country being utilised to the fullest extent.'[25]

What effects did the scale and efficiency of British rearmament have on foreign policy? It is worth asking first what effects foreign policy had on the British rearmament effort.

The Labour and Liberal oppositions regularly complained that the government's arms programmes were narrowly 'national' and did not fit into a policy of 'collective security'. They were correct; there was no question of discussion with any other states about possible military collaboration. The basis of any military collaboration must have been Anglo-French. No comprehensive discussions about a combined Anglo-French strategy against Germany took place before 1939. British governments carefully avoided anything that might imply a new commitment to join France in a war with Germany. To do so might offend the Germans and might encourage France to reject conciliation towards Germany and so run counter to 'appeasement'. 'Staff talks' seemed especially dangerous. Before 1914, many writers claimed, staff talks with the French had morally pledged Britain to intervene in a Franco-German war. So, though French security from invasion was essential to British security, yet the British government left it to the French to arrange the defence of France. British rearmament concentrated on the defence of the United Kingdom. The navy should defend British merchant ships; the air force counter a German air strike against Britain. Apart from anti-aircraft batteries, the army was neglected until 1939. An Anglo-French strategy worked out in 1936 or 1937 would have reflected the French desire for a small but highly equipped, mobile British armoured corps. French wishes, in practice, had no effect on British rearmament. Where foreign policy did influence British rearmament, it delayed it. British rearmament started late because the main purpose of policy was to win agreement to prevent an arms race, not to win the race. Mr Chamberlain, when Chancellor of the Exchequer, led the way in making up for lost time within the limits set by respect for non-military manufacture. The programme the Cabinet approved early in 1936 probably went as far as was politically possible before 1938 – it was as much as public opinion was likely to accept, and, in public, ministers understated its size. After the Anschluss, and, more markedly still after Munich, opinion changed: the public wanted increased and accelerated production and Chamberlain began to lag behind. For him September 1938 was a stage on the way to peace; for most others, even among Chamberlain's Cabinet, it was a month of narrowly averted war, a crisis which could easily recur. After Munich, Chamberlain continued to believe that all-out arms production might reduce hope of a détente with Germany.

At the first Cabinet meeting after Munich, on 3 October 1938, Chamberlain emotionally expressed his hope for an agreement to stop the arms race and opposed any great increase in the British armaments programme. At the end of that month he told the Cabinet that 'a great deal of false emphasis had been placed on rearmament, as though one result of the Munich Agreement had been that it would be necessary for us to add to our rearmament programme'. In November Chamberlain worried about laying down 20 new escort vessels for the navy and insisted that the decision should be reconsidered if it involved problems in foreign policy because of the possible 'effect on Germany'. Later in the same Cabinet he opposed building the heavy long-range bombers asked for by the RAF, prefacing his remarks by noting: 'In our foreign policy we were doing our best to drive two horses abreast, conciliation and rearmament. It was a very nice art to keep these two steeds in step.' His tone contrasted with his call for a bomber strike force as a deterrent two and a half years before. Now it seemed, efforts for conciliation required restraint in rearmament. Chamberlain, however, supported the building of more fighters as a defence against German air attack.[26]

Mr Chamberlain's objections to provocatively dramatic crisis measures survived 15 March 1939 and Hitler's triumphant arrival in Prague. His hesitation over the Ministry of Supply and its powers and his reluctance to declare a state of emergency went with his tenacious hope for 'talk' with Germany. Chamberlain's refusal to defend peace by preparing as if for imminent war restricted production by its effects on the skilled engineering workers' union, the AEU. The union's membership included most of the skilled labour whose co-operation would accelerate arms production. Employers pressed for their agreement to 'dilution' and 'deskilling', changes in manufacturing routines which would make it possible to reduce the proportion of fully skilled men needed for production processes. The union thought it should defend the key positions and the pay differentials of its members by resisting such pressures. The foreign policy of the government gave trade unions an excuse for resisting appeals to their patriotism, which invocations of a great national, and international, effort, to resist fascism might have made overwhelming.

In April 1938 the AEU President, Mr J. C. Little, in a meeting with Inskip to discuss relaxation of union rules, explained that the government had failed to honour its promises to the union made during the First World War. Then he went on:

> 'Up to now we see very little reason for recommending any kind of relaxation to our members, because frankly we are not satisfied with your policy.'
> Sir Thomas Inskip: 'You mean our foreign policy.'
> Mr Little: 'Your foreign policy, if you can call it a policy.'

It was only in August 1939 that the Engineering Employers' Federation secured an agreement with the AEU.[27]

Foreign policy dictated the scale and speed of British rearmament rather than the other way round. However, in 1938 and 1939 British preparation for war, or the lack of it, did influence policy towards Germany. In 1938 British vulnerability to German air attack, exaggerated as it perhaps was, helped Chamberlain to win support for his policy, though it was not the reason he adopted it; in 1939 British air defence was stronger. Radar, or RDF, as it was then known, covered most of the south and east coasts. Few knew of its existence but members of the government were aware that it had somehow become easier to detect approaching aircraft. The government gave ample publicity to the new fast single-seater fighters, the Hurricane and the Spitfire. In consequence more people became ready to resist Germany and compelled Chamberlain to pursue by stealth his last attempts at appeasement. Indeed he even, in public, abandoned the very word. Chatfield, his Defence Minister, preparing a speech in June 1939, was told that 'the Prime Minister himself wishes to use as little as possible in political speeches the word "appeasement" which is now open to considerable misconstruction'.[28]

The final question about British military preparations concerns the strategy they implied and the extent to which they made that strategy workable. British strategy became defensive. In 1936 Chamberlain demanded a bomber striking force ready to attack Germany as soon as war broke out; by 1938 he was urging reliance on defence to foil a German strike. Germany would be forced into a long war to defeat Britain. British armed strength could then be built up, after the outbreak of war, so making German victory less and less practicable.

Rational calculation would stop Germany going to war at all. Chamberlain explained in July 1939 'what Winston and Co. never seem to realise. You don't need offensive forces sufficient to win a smashing victory. What you need are defensive forces sufficiently strong to make it impossible for the other side to win except at such a cost as to make it not worthwhile.'[29] Hitler and the Nazis, unfortunately, specialised in unreason. Chamberlain's hopeful foreign policy caused him to restrain armaments production. Before 1938 most people approved his caution in rearmament; after Munich he acted as a brake on his less sanguine colleagues.

Chamberlain's strategy called for a successful and protracted defence. After war had begun, Britain would, at last, go over to a war economy. Eventually Anglo-French resources should be able, if necessary, to destroy an enfeebled Germany. Provided that the French army held France and the Low Countries, aided by the distraction of German attention from the Western Front by the Red Army, provided that the menace of the United States Pacific fleet intimidated Japan, provided that America gave economic help, Anglo-French strategy in the summer of 1939 made sense. Most of these conditions were not fulfilled. The failure of Chamberlain's foreign policy and of the strategy that went with it justified those who had demanded all-out rearmament.

14 Resources for War: the British Dominions and the United States

In a long war the British hoped for help in material, men and munitions from the four British Dominions, Canada, South Africa, Australia and New Zealand, and tools and weapons from the United States. How safely the United Kingdom could count on them set problems of varied intensity. Only one could be relied on without any doubt: New Zealand. Paradoxically New Zealand criticised British foreign policy with more vigour than any of the others, joining British anti-appeasers in vehement support for the League of Nations, yet at the Imperial Conference in 1937, the Prime Minister of New Zealand, the British Cabinet was told, 'said roundly one day that if the United Kingdom was at war New Zealand would be at war, whether the issue was right or wrong'. Among the Dominions, Australia came next in degree of commitment; Canada and South Africa were much less sure. (The Irish Free State or Eire, it was wisest to regard as only technically a Dominion and to treat as a probable neutral.) British opinion assumed that the Dominions could be relied on. In January 1938, a Gallup survey asked: 'Do you think that the Dominions will fight with the British people in the case of another war?' 'Yes' replies amounted to 71 per cent, 'No' to only 4 per cent (the remainder had no opinion). Cabinet ministers were told the same in September 1938 by Malcolm MacDonald, the Secretary of State, who spoke to the High Commissioners, the London representatives of the Dominions, at the height of the Munich crisis. They favoured peace but he thought 'that if we were involved in war, all the Dominions would sooner or later come in with us'.[1]

British culture, the English language and family links with many people in the United Kingdom explained Dominion attitudes. In South Africa these links did not exist among the

Afrikaans speakers (nor among the suppressed non-white populations), nor in Canada among the French-speaking section of the population; France was not a source of migration in the nineteenth and twentieth centuries and recent Canadian connections with France were tenuous. The international security of Australia and New Zealand, moreover, still depended on British strength, until the USA was ready to take over that British role. For white South Africans, the colonial power of the United Kingdom in Africa contributed to the stability of their society. For Canadians, apart from sentiment, the British connection remained an element in national identity, a mark of difference from the United States. For all the Dominions, however, their independent status mattered most: it was impossible for the United Kingdom government to control their policies. Whatever the Dominions did they intended to do of their own volition, as free and equal associates of the United Kingdom.

From the British point of view, therefore, they made up a friendly but awkward group. In 1937 their representatives assembled in London at the Imperial Conference. British ministers lectured them on circumstances and policy and they exchanged opinions. Malcolm MacDonald, as Secretary for the Dominions, gave a summary to the Cabinet of their views, modified at the Conference, as he put it, by 'education and patient communication of the facts'. Mackenzie King, the Canadian Prime Minister, a man alarmingly attached to mysticism, spoke 'in a slightly isolationist spirit'. Then, expressing his League point of view, the New Zealand Prime Minister made 'a polite but rather comprehensive attack on the United Kingdom's foreign policy'. For South Africa, General Hertzog, the rival within the United Party of the more imperially minded ex-Boer, Smuts, 'had intimated the view that our attitude to the French was too warm, and towards the Germans too cold'. Then 'even the Australian Delegation had roundly criticised our opposition to the Anschluss'. They all favoured appeasement, except New Zealand.

Including New Zealand, they all disliked and feared British commitments to intervene in European conflicts. Mackenzie King, for instance, told the Conference that he was about to visit Hitler. He would tell him of 'the sympathy which was felt with Germany in England' although 'if Germany should ever turn her mind from constructive to destructive efforts against the United Kingdom all the Dominions would come to her aid'. And 'there would be great numbers of Canadians anxious to swim the Atlantic!' On another occasion, however, he explained to MacDonald that 'he was nervous lest, if Great Britain became involved in a European war, Canadian public opinion might not be willing to follow Great Britain. When he was leaving Canada many people had told him to give a message to us to the effect that we should keep out of the quarrel between Germany and France, wash our hands of it and "leave the Germans and French to kill each other if they wanted to".'[2]

The Dominions regularly intervened to oppose British entanglement in Europe. At the time of the Rhineland crisis, in 1936, they said Britain should not replace even the Locarno guarantees to France. The Cabinet, in effect, agreed that the Dominions would have to be told not to be silly and Chamberlain even suggested that they should have the 'French view' explained to them. In 1937 Mackenzie King told the Conference that 'no issue raised with Canada could have so serious an effect as one arising from any suspicion of a commitment'. In early 1938 when the Cabinet agreed to Chamberlain's policy towards Czechoslovakia, not to promise support against Germany, Malcolm MacDonald backed the Prime Minister by remarking that 'while there was no suggestion the foreign policy of his country could be subordinated to the view of the Dominions . . . a policy of further commitments would be very unpopular in all the Dominions, except possibly New Zealand'. Even after Godesberg, the Dominion High Commissioners in London favoured acceptance of Hitler's terms. In the final crisis of August 1939 all of them, except the New Zealand representative, wanted, in the words of Inskip, now Dominions Secretary, 'to meet Hitler halfway, to put the most favourable interpretation on his words and to offer to discuss everything'.[3]

The Dominions had little or no influence on British policy except in supplying added justification to policies that Chamberlain and his supporters would have wished to pursue anyway. Apart from New Zealand their views tended to correspond to those of the Conservative isolationists, many of whom, indeed, put imperial interests at the top of their list of strategic priorities. In 1939 the Dominions, particularly South Africa and Canada, at first helped Chamberlain in opposing the Soviet alliance but then deserted him.[4]

The United States, of course, were yet more important as a potential source of strength for Britain at war. No one doubted that if the United States ever chose sides in a British conflict with any of the dictators they would be aligned with Britain. But would Americans, mostly uninterested in world affairs, and, in so far as some cared, mostly convinced that intervention in the First World War was a damaging mistake organised by a handful of financiers and arms merchants in league with scheming, clever, unscrupulous Europeans, among whom perhaps the most amiable, but certainly the most plausible and insinuating, were the British, permit Congress or the President to emerge from rigid neutrality? Whatever the British people thought, and Gallup discovered that the USA was their favourite foreign country, followed, at some distance, by France (Germany was the most disliked), most ministers and officials viewed the conduct of American administrations with irritation and resentment. As Chamberlain put it, tetchily, 'the Americans are chiefly anxious to convince their people that they are not going to be drawn into doing anything helpful for the rest of the world'.[5] That was written early in Roosevelt's presidency.

American administrations, British ministers believed, had precipitated Europe into the crisis of the 1930s. They blocked a solution of the problem of reparations by refusing to cancel war debts and made the problem worse by high tariffs and by selfishly frustrating the smooth working of the gold standard. Roosevelt, the British claimed, destroyed the World Economic Conference of 1933 by declining to stabilise the gold price of the dollar at a rate convenient for London. The Roosevelt administration, indeed, showed less interest than Hoover's in the smooth workings of the international financial system. Partly as a consequence, British governments in the 1930s felt better equipped to solve European problems and to pacify the Third Reich without American intervention, which, in any case, isolationism inhibited.

The United States, therefore, had surprisingly little influence on British policy in Europe, where 'appeasement' flourished.

Matters were very different with respect to policy in China in the 1930s. There the British had a choice between compromise with Japan or, alternatively, opposition to the expansion of Japanese control, together with the defence of the open door for international trade. The United States authorities, and that section of the American public, small but vocal, which concerned itself with China, regarded concession to Japan as a betrayal of international rectitude. On the other hand American opinion opposed war with Japan or, more accurately, never thought of it as possible. If the British failed to conciliate Japan, they could not count on military help from the United States in warding off the consequent threat to British investments, trade or settlements in China.

In the end, British policy rejected compromise with Japan. The protracted fuss made by the USA, repeated by League enthusiasts in Britain, at the failure of the British to show the amount of hostility to Japanese actions in 1931–2 demanded by Stimson, the Secretary of State, made the makers of British policy hesitate to risk renewed accusations of weakness. There were other reasons, particularly the difficulty in finding any basis for Anglo-Japanese understanding, and the scepticism among Far Eastern experts in the Foreign Office about whether permanent understanding was possible at all; most of them took the view that 'moderates' in the Japanese regime of the 1930s only differed from 'extremists' in the speed with which they hoped to expel Europeans from participation in the Chinese economy. If this were so then there would come a time when Japan must be confronted and it might be impossible to do so without American support. American opinion would be unlikely even to tolerate support for a Britain that sought refuge in compromise and retreat. Chamberlain, among British ministers, pursued most persistently the possibility of an entente with Japan, and, therefore, fully explored the obstacles that blocked it, and the problems caused by the American insistence that Britain should oppose Japan in China without offering any immediate hope of tangible American support.

American attitudes towards Europe, on the other hand, did not inconvenience Chamberlain once his 'appeasement' was fully launched. President Roosevelt, in his deceptively relaxed manner, kept a shifting balance between isolationists, on the one hand, and anti-Nazi involvement on the other. The result fitted Chamberlain's needs. He found that Roosevelt left the British government undisturbed in its search for peace and security except by the helpful gesture, easily squashed, of January 1938. The anti-appeasers would have preferred more American involvement in European affairs; Chamberlain did not want it. Later, in 1938, after the horrors of the attack on the German Jews in November, the United States administration became readier at least to condemn. Roosevelt's careful avoidance of any suggestion of Anglo-American co-operation in foreign policy meant that British independence in deciding policy remained intact.

Chamberlain became eager for American good-will. In 1938 and 1939 his attitude to Roosevelt and America differed from that of five years earlier. Irritation remained but Chamberlain could not fail to recognise that Roosevelt meant to help and that Congress, and American opinion, posed problems to the American President and were not, as Chamberlain once thought, merely a pretext for presidential inaction. A friendly United States provided a reserve of productive strength in case his policies failed; whatever his hopes and expectations he never intended to let British security and independence depend on German good-will. Moreover isolationist opinion limited Roosevelt to covert hints of support concealed by public protestations of steady neutrality in all armed conflicts. This suited Chamberlain very well because it gave no offence to Germans. Chamberlain rejected a chance of visiting Roosevelt in Washington or Hyde Park; he did not care much for leisurely unfocused discussion nor, as an active, interfering Prime Minister, could he afford the long time still needed to cross the Atlantic. However, he worked hard to forward the Anglo-American trade treaty of 1938. Cordell Hull, the American Secretary of State, held old-fashioned Cobdenite views, and believed that free trade would bring peace. The United Kingdom and the British Empire were still much the most important trading bloc in the world. If Hull were to succeed in his mission of lowering tariff barriers he must not fail in this treaty. He was prosy and sententious but he commanded unusual respect in Congress and from American political commentators. British negotiators thought the American proposals, on balance, damaging to British interests and likely to undermine the recently developed structure of Imperial Preference, which, it was thought, helped to unite the Dominions with Britain. Chamberlain particularly prized the new British tariff system and Imperial Preference, partly through family piety. Yet he argued for their weakening to please Hull. When extension of Imperial Preference to Nigerian exports was considered by the Cabinet in March 1937, Chamberlain declared that 'in relation to the proposed commercial treaty, he saw some glimmerings of hope of bringing the United States of America to a more reasonable frame of mind in matters of vast importance, such as their attitude in the event of hostilities and co-operation in the Far East. It was important that nothing in the nature of preference to a colony should be allowed to cut across such important considerations.'[6]

Chamberlain stuck to his position and persuaded the Cabinet to overrule departmental objection to, arguably, excessive concessions to American demands. According to the record he told the Cabinet in October 1938, in the final crisis of the negotiations, 'that he had taken great interest in these negotiations and much hoped that we should reach an Agreement. He had never hoped that we should obtain any great economic or political support. The advantages to be derived were of a somewhat negative kind. It was clear that if after months of negotiation no Agreement was reached, hard things would be said.' Chamberlain had come to recognise, after some years' experience, that Congress and the opinion that could carry its members, were forces much less easy for even a strong President to control as compared with a Prime Minister in relation to Parliament. Like many British politicians he had found it difficult to understand the limitations on what an American President can do. Now he seems to have understood that Roosevelt could, in the end, do what he might wish to do to support the United Kingdom only if the British government avoided giving political ammunition to his Congressional opponents. Chamberlain was supported by a passionate plea from the British ambassador in Washington, Sir Ronald Lindsay, in a telegram circulated as a Cabinet paper. He summarised familiar British reactions:

The protracted negotiations which have led to this [the final US requests on which they would sign] have brought me personally to that state of bitterness and exasperation which usually results from dealings with United States Government. Their delays and tergiversations have been intolerable, they concede no point of view but their own and their demands cause His Majesty's Government loss of revenue and administrative difficulties out of all proportion to the benefits likely to accrue from American trade. We are being put through the mangle of American politics.

Sir Ronald supplied Chamberlain with his 'somewhat negative arguments':

I have never said that even complete surrender by us would secure whole-hearted friendship of United States Government but it is certain, in case of failure, that blame will be laid on us in American eyes and we shall alienate the sympathy we can ill afford to lose.[7]

Soon Roosevelt, perhaps less hopeful after Munich than Chamberlain, began to give word of his intentions. He did so with careful secretiveness, bypassing the State Department and Joe Kennedy, the American ambassador in London, whose appointment, as usual, had been made to a rich and lavish party supporter rather than to a discreet career diplomatist. Roosevelt spoke to Arthur Murray, a Scottish friend (the heir to the Master of Elibank) who passed on his remarks to Chamberlain in December 1938. Roosevelt told Murray 'that he wished the Prime Minister to feel that he had, insofar as he, the President, was able to achieve it "the industrial resources of the American nation behind him in the event of war with the dictatorships".' Murray also explained Roosevelt's suggestions about ways in which 'outwith the Neutrality Law' he might assist British air production. Chamberlain asked Murray to talk to Kingsley Wood, Air Minister. After a surprisingly long delay Kingsley Wood told Murray to ask Roosevelt for a war-time supply of light alloys and for aircraft instruments. Roosevelt responded, rather vaguely, 'Things along that line are going much better both in England and in the United States.'[8]

Early in 1939 Roosevelt publicised his opposition to the dictators. Halifax thought it so important that he told the Cabinet; it coincided with the war-scare of January 1939 and was obviously meant to help deter Hitler from the attack on the Netherlands he allegedly had in mind, rumours of which the British passed on in full to Washington. Newspaper reports showed that Roosevelt had declared to the Military Affairs Committee of the Senate 'that the United States were prepared to give the Democracies, in any conflict with the Dictatorships, every possible assistance short of declaring war and sending American troops to Europe'. A week later, however, Halifax reported to the Cabinet that the American embassy had telephoned to him 'urging that it was undesirable that any public statement should be made in this country as to Mr. Roosevelt's recent utterance'.[9]

In April 1939 Roosevelt appeared on radio and film to challenge Hitler. The President demanded that Hitler promise not to attack a long list of European states (Hitler replied by a public display of his own, assembling his puppet-Reichstag for a sustained outburst of powerful sarcasm). The British government knew its role: to keep quiet to prevent any suspicion that Roosevelt was responding to British wishes, as distinct from independently assessed American needs. This role suited Chamberlain. In the House of Commons he spoke only of 'the great satisfaction' with which the government 'have welcomed the recent initiative'. At the time he was due to speak to a rally of 7000 Conservative women in the Albert Hall. Sir Joseph Ball, from Conservative Central Office, sent his suggestions: 'I suppose it will be necessary to refer to Roosevelt's initiative, but I understand this is unpopular in Germany, and it might, perhaps, therefore be unwise to lay emphasis on it!' Chamberlain solved the problem without difficulty; he did not mention Roosevelt's speech at all and so avoided embarrassment to his friend or irritation to his enemy.[10]

During the last pre-war display of Roosevelt's desire to strengthen the democracies, which ended ignominiously when he failed to get Congress to change the neutrality laws, the British government stood by, refraining from public comment.

Once again the British government found itself blackmailed into economic concession. Hull briefed Kennedy in London in June 1939, pointing out that 'conclusion of this deal would I think have good general effect on American opinion in regard to various other matters likely to come before Congress in the near future'.[11] This type of bribe, or threat, came several times again over other issues in the next few years from Washington to London. On this occasion Hull wanted to swap wheat and cotton for British tin and rubber for the US stockpile, funds allocated for the purpose having run out.

The British got no immediate reward for the forced barter of their tin and rubber, yet the United States in the months before the war more and more fulfilled British requirements. On 19 March 1939 Halifax sent off a cautiously worded but far-reaching suggestion to Washington. The British government 'cannot leave out of account the fact that, if they are involved in European conflict, they might not be able at once to reinforce on a large scale their naval forces in the Far East, and that might affect U.S. naval dispositions.' Two days later Halifax put it more clearly to the American ambassador, Kennedy: 'He said that in 1936 . . . Great Britain had promised Australia that, in the event of any trouble, they would send a fleet to Singapore. Under present conditions they do not feel they can spare a fleet for Singapore and they wonder if the United States would consider, at the psychological moment, transferring the American fleet back to the Pacific. This would be perfectly satisfactory to Australia and would permit the British Navy to function in the Mediterranean, where they planned to start operations.' The President responded amiably that this request was 'perfectly natural in the circumstances' and a few days later Kennedy told Halifax that Roosevelt would announce in mid-April that the US fleet would return to the Pacific in May.[12] Silently, with the minimum of fuss, an Anglo-American grand strategy thus evolved to counter the threat to the British Empire of a simultaneous war against Japan, Italy and Germany. It provided British and French military planners with a choice between keeping Italy neutral in war or defeating Italy at the start by making it impossibly risky for the Japanese fleet to operate in the south Pacific without first destroying the United States main fleet. It guaranteed unchallengeable Anglo-

French naval supremacy in the Atlantic and Mediterranean. A little later Commander Hampton, RN, secretly went to see the heads of the US navy and confirmed this grand strategy and requested the stationing of some American cruiser forces in the Atlantic. In the early summer of 1939 Roosevelt thought further about shouldering British burdens when he conveyed a message to Lord Stanhope, the First Lord of the Admiralty, that Britain should perhaps transfer to the USA a site for a naval base in the West Indies. Stanhope informed King George VI, but not the Foreign Office – the king assured Stanhope that he would not pass on the news. However, at the end of June Roosevelt called Lindsay, the British ambassador, to the White House, and put the suggestion to him as part of a secret plan for American naval patrols to keep belligerent warships out of American waters. Halifax and Chamberlain immediately agreed. (Roosevelt endeavoured to enforce his 'neutrality zone' after war broke out.)[13]

There was no question in 1939 of some kind of financial or trade war between Britain and the USA. The idea, which some historians have floated, that Chamberlain tried to improve Anglo-German relations in order to be able more effectively to resist American economic demands distorts the Anglo-American relationship in 1938–9. Economic approaches to the German government were political in aim, designed to secure peace and disarmament, which in the end, of course, would also bring economic advantages. The same is true of approaches to German industry to arrange market-sharing and price-fixing; for the government their object was to pacify Germany rather than to secure direct economic benefits, although, of course, the banking interests involved were looking for secure and profitable markets.

In March 1939 Roosevelt spoke to Sir Arthur Willert, an old British acquaintance. Willert reported the conversation to the Foreign Office. The President hoped to persuade Congress to modify the neutrality laws which forbade exports of munitions to countries at war so as to permit them instead to collect such exports from US ports for cash. He spoke with insouciant ignorance, whether real or affected, of the British problem of dwindling gold reserves. He thought the proposed cash-and-carry provisions for exporting munitions of war 'ought to be enough for us', Willert reported. 'We had ample funds in the United States and, anyhow', Roosevelt went on more comfortingly, if vaguely, 'money had odd but sure ways of getting to where it was most wanted.'[14]

In July 1939 Congress, however, inflicted a severe and well-publicised political defeat on President Roosevelt. As he had told Willert, Roosevelt wished Congress to remove the prohibition on the sale of arms to war-time belligerents so that Britain and France, at war, could buy and ship munitions from the United States. He hoped, in this way, to help to deter Hitler from aggressive war. The House of Representatives voted instead for an arms embargo and the Senate Foreign Affairs Committee then blocked reconsideration until the beginning of 1940. Hull and the President were openly snubbed. In London, though, the American department in the Foreign Office reassured angry ministers, disgusted by what they saw as the ignorance and stupidity of Congress. Its experts insisted that Roosevelt's defeat principally expressed hostility to his domestic political manoeuvres and that most American opinion outside Congress supported Roosevelt's opposition to the dictators and that, if war broke out, the President would prevail. At the end of August Roosevelt personally told the new British ambassador that 'he hoped and expected that in the event of war Congress would revoke the Act' but he added cautiously he 'could not be certain'.[15] At least there could no longer be any doubt where Franklin Roosevelt stood. His position suited Chamberlain very well; he provided an unprovocative reserve of strength to the United Kingdom. Roosevelt had become an asset in the Prime Minister's struggle for peace.

Roosevelt's pledges that he would try to provide all aid short of war supported the view expressed by Halifax that when Britain could no longer pay for imports from the United States, American finance would somehow be found, in spite of Roosevelt's assumption that the United Kingdom had enough money to pay for them. From London prospects looked uncertain. In the last complete year of peace, 1938, United Kingdom importers purchased 521 million dollars' worth of goods from the United States while Americans purchased only 118 million dollars' worth from Britain. Apart from food and raw materials any acceleration of British rearmament required imported machine-tools. Before the war broke out strictly military purchases by Britain from the United States and the Dominions remained small. From the United States they were limited by lack of foreign exchange; from the Dominions by their industrial weakness. From Canada there came anti-aircraft shells, but it was not until February 1940 that the first aircraft came to Britain from the Dominions – a Canadian-built Hurricane. During the first fifteen months of the war, Canada supplied 2.6 per cent of the weapons and ammunition issued to British Commonwealth forces and the other Dominions supplied 1.1 per cent. By the time war broke out the Royal Air Force had taken delivery of 278 aircraft from the United States: 228 North American Harvard machines, advanced training aircraft, and 50 Lockheed Hudsons, mostly used by Coastal Command for reconnaissance. During the first fifteen months of the war, the United States supplied 5.6 per cent of the weapons issued to British forces. During the whole course of the Second World War, however, the United States and the British Dominions produced nearly one-third of the munitions used by British Commonwealth forces, most of it financed by loan or gift.[16]

15 Alternatives to Appeasement

British governments in the 1930s, with Chamberlain increasingly in the lead, sought the 'appeasement of Europe' by looking for limited concessions to aggressive dictators sufficient to win their consent to agreed limitations on armaments. What alternative policies did rivals, opponents and critics propose?

One theme stands out. Above all, these critics spoke and wrote in favour of 'support for the League of Nations'. It was a phrase which had many different meanings. Some thought of the League as a means of organising armed resistance to aggressors, others saw it as a substitute for military defence, a means for negotiation and conciliation. The League, set up by the treaties ending the First World War, embodied the new belief that humanity could abolish war. That belief served to justify the First World War, and the catastrophic nature of the war made even stronger the conviction that it must be the 'war to end wars'. Somehow, its supporters thought, the League must stop war, and could do so if only it were energetically and sincerely upheld. In the later 1930s, the League as an organisation for coercion became the more widely favoured version; at first, however, the League as a means of conciliation, strengthened, at most, by economic pressure, but more often only by the force of world opinion, had the greatest appeal. In July 1934 the leader of the independent liberals, Sir Herbert Samuel, attacked those who were sceptical towards the League. 'In the Government, among Members of this House, among active members of the Conservative Party throughout the country, there are vast numbers of people who regard the whole idea of the League of Nations as merely the vision of amiable idealists, who have never expected any measure of general disarmament and have taken no interest in the whole subject ... There are great numbers of people in the world who take no interest in liberty, equality and fraternity, but put all their faith in infantry, cavalry and artillery.'

Samuel favoured 'the continuous strengthening of the collective system of control – the active participation in international affairs through the League of Nations and the strengthening of the collective system.' It turned out, however, that he did not suggest British support for Article 16 of the League Covenant. This pledged all members to treat any resort to war against any other member as an attack on themselves, immediately to sever 'all trade or financial relations' with the offending state, as soon as the League Council decided, and to contribute whatever 'effective military, naval or air force' the Council thought necessary 'to protect the Covenants of the League'. Samuel's speech showed no eagerness in this respect, indeed, it was isolationist in rejecting the idea of any British military action. His speech went on, 'we do not favour any further automatic commitments in Europe or elsewhere . . . Public opinion would not endorse any obligation undertaken by our Government which might result in our being obliged to send military or naval forces to take part in what was some purely local dispute, say, in the Balkans or in Central or South America which had not been found possible of solution through the machinery of the League of Nations . . . The collective system must be really collective, and there is no reason why this country alone, or even with one or two sympathetic allies, should undertake obligations which really devolve upon humanity at large.' Support for the League became a disguise for isolation when its Covenant was to be enforced by 'humanity at large'. Samuel, and the Liberals, seemed then to suppose that Britain could leave international problems to the League to solve.

Early in the 1930s, the Labour Party held similar views. The party conference in October 1933 carried unanimously a resolution supporting the League, but pledging the party 'to take no part in war and to resist it with the whole force of the Labour movment'. In 1934 Clement Attlee, then deputy leader of the Labour Party, wrote to his brother that the party 'has not really made up its mind as to whether it wants to take up an extreme disarmament and isolation attitude' or whether 'it will take the risks of standing for the enforcement of the decisions of a world organisation against individual aggressor states'.[1] Only in October 1934 did the party conference accept that armed force might perhaps be needed to back up economic sanctions against an aggressor: 'There might be circumstances under which the Government of Great Britain might have to use its military and naval forces in support of the League in restraining an aggressor nation which declined to submit to the authority of the League.' This view was carried in a card vote by about 1,500,000 to 673,000: a vote demonstrating the large number of dissenters among party activists from a policy carried forward mainly by the support of the big trade unions.

In 1935, as the League rallied against Mussolini, the Labour Party conference recorded only 100,000 votes against sanctions. Herbert Morrison, for the executive, made it clear that 'military sanctions cannot, in honesty, be ruled out'. Even so he minimised the warlike, coercive aspects of the League. 'Sanctions are not the only things mentioned in the Covenant . . . It indicates that this League may consider a peaceful revision of Treaties – all Treaties, including the Treaty of Versailles . . . The Covenant also contemplates that steps should be taken for disarmament and for the control of international aviation.' For Labour, even a coercive League, moreover, remained an alternative to British rearmament, not a justification for it. It should not bring an 'arms race' with all its provocative perils. Morrison accused Chamberlain of using Abyssinia as an excuse for arming. 'Already Mr Neville Chamberlain says that the moral of the present experience is more armaments' – this was in 1935 – 'that ought not to be the moral. The great purpose of collective peace and collective security should be that each nation requires less armaments to deal with potential aggressors.'[2]

Among Labour's supporters two minority groups dissented from the party's acceptance of a potentially coercive League. One was made up of pacifists. George Lansbury became leader in 1931, after Ramsay MacDonald had gone into coalition with the Conservatives. His claims to political influence lay entirely in home affairs; in foreign policy he advocated unconditional non-violence and so made himself increasingly irrelevant in debate, attracting from Conservative MPs patronising and dismissive tributes to his personal integrity and deep convictions. In 1935 Ernest Bevin, wielding his influence over the powerful block vote of the Transport and General Workers' Union, and exploiting his own harsh oratory, brutally told Lansbury to stop 'taking your conscience round from body to body' and so precipitated his resignation.

Lansbury's conscience continued to travel. In 1937 Lansbury, now 78 years old, took it to Paris, Berlin, Rome, Warsaw and Prague. He had a scheme for peace. There should be a world economic conference to secure the international control of colonies and a just distribution of the world's resources and so remove the cause of war. Hitler, 'one of the great men of our time', Lansbury thought, showed sympathy in a two-hour talk, promising that he would attend such a conference if it were called by a leading non-German such as Roosevelt. Lansbury believed that 'to live, Germany needs peace as much as any nation in the world. No one understands this better than Herr Hitler . . . When I came away it was my sincere belief that if negotiations could be started at once accommodation might be found. The threat of war was only a silly illusion which would soon dissipate if I could arrange a meeting between Stalin, Mussolini and Hitler with somebody as chairman with a sense of humour . . . I feel that a pleasant day's conversation in a villa on the Riviera might bring these three statesmen to realise that they have . . . a world of peace and security to gain.'[3]

The other dissenting minority within the Labour Party deduced its foreign policy from the theory of imperialism elaborated by J. A. Hobson and Lenin. A diminishing number of increasingly rich and powerful capitalists in advanced and industrialised countries extracted profits by holding down wages. The inadequate demand of the population of industrialised countries, reduced by the insufficient growth in their living standards that the search for capitalist profits necessarily dictated, caused a struggle for new markets, and also for new areas for investment, with populations whose living standards were low enough to make possible an increase in the return on capital. Thus capitalism necessarily produced 'imperialism', the search for territory with populations enjoying even lower standards than those prevailing at home, for owners of capital to exploit. In the twentieth century less and less of such territory was left. Struggles to seize and exploit such under-developed territories or to evict the present exploiters were inevitable and must inevitably lead to war. Under such circumstances the rational redistribution of the world's resources, called for by

Lansbury, was thought to be simply impossible. Only one way remained to win permanent peace. Socialism must spread to all the industrial countries. Only then could planning bring abundance to the masses.

Within the Labour Party these views had a brilliant advocate: Sir Stafford Cripps. In 1936, after the Rhineland occupation, he published this conclusion: 'Though wars may be delayed for a period by joining in the supremely dangerous game of power politics, a workers' Government must come by democratic methods or revolution before we in this country can start to build up a true world peace.' Cripps combined charm, kindness and generosity with his talents as a barrister. He favoured democratic, peaceful, change, with full compensation to the victims of social evolution, and abhorred violent class conflict: 'Reaction in Germany and revolution in Russia have both been marked by excesses which no normal human being could do other than loathe.' Only early and determined action, however, could avoid eventual domestic strife. With a workers' government in power in Britain the world would be told that: 'A new method of world development must be worked out by the co-operative effort of those countries which are convinced equally with our Government of the necessity for laying a new economic foundation for peace. This announcement, coming from a country which had been the pioneer of industrial imperialism and which is today the greatest imperialist power, would have a very marked effect upon world psychology. The thoughts of Governments and peoples would begin to turn away from the competitive antagonism that led to war and into the channels of reasoned co-operation.' To Cripps, of course, imperialist powers at present used the League 'to guard their own possessions and their own economic status'. Support for the League might imply no more than supporting a strong Anglo-French alliance. 'Under this guise the anti-German power grouping would earn the good will of many who would otherwise be against it, and rearmament, professedly for collective security, would be accepted by those who would never consent to such a step for imperialist purposes.' 'It was', Cripps explained, 'Mr Winston Churchill who first appreciated the value of this phrase to reactionary Conservatism.'[4]

Cripps and Lansbury, although steadily voted down by the

party, influenced Labour's public statements on foreign policy. The speeches given by official spokesmen at the House of Commons invariably asked for some way of improving access to raw materials and markets. Even more carefully the Labour opposition denounced 'the arms race' and insisted that its support for the League did not mean support for the steps to rearmament undertaken by the government. In March 1935 Attlee divided the House of Commons against the government's White Paper on defence, which set out the need for reinforcing British military strength; the Labour motion complained that the government policy 'is completely at variance with the spirit in which the League of Nations was created . . . gravely jeopardises the prospect of any Disarmament Convention, and so far from ensuring national safety will lead to international competition'. Labour also voted against the separate army, air and naval estimates. Even after the German announcement of conscription and of the creation of a military air force, Labour opposed increases in the RAF, 'in view of the reasonable speech made by Herr Hitler on May 21', in which Hitler declared himself ready to accept such limitations of armaments as are accepted by other powers. In 1936, shocked by the conduct of the government over the Hoare–Laval scheme but apparently unshaken by the German seizure of the Rhineland, the Labour Party again voted against the service estimates. At the party conference in October 1936, the executive set out 'the policy of the Labour Party to maintain such defence forces as are consistent with our country's responsibility as a Member of the League of Nations' but it declined 'to accept responsibility for a purely competitive armaments policy'. Labour said 'Yes' to armaments for 'collective security', 'No' to armed forces for national defence.[5]

In March 1937 they voted against the Defence Loans Bill, partly, it is true, because of the inflationary pressure their spokesman claimed it would create, but largely because it represented a 'vital blow aimed at the League of Nations' and because 'the Government have completely abandoned the League and collective security . . . their armament programme is based upon no plan whatsoever, except to build everything we can afford, and then to throw our weight as and when it suits our own interest to do so'. Separately, on the left, Cripps accused the government of 'planning death and destruction for millions of the world's workers'. Labour also voted against the individual service estimates, which, a party spokesman complained, were 'apparently based upon unilateral defence, which cannot of itself succeed, and which will go far to ruin the finances of the nation', and which neglected 'the ideal of a combination of nations which would pool their resources in order to deal with any aggressor who might seek to break the peace of the world'. In July 1937, however, Labour Members of Parliament decided only to abstain on the final vote of the total appropriation for defence. One of them defended their abstention at the party conference in October: it 'was not a vote in support of the Government; it was a method of making our position clear to the country as a whole, of making the country understand that while we condemn the Government we do not believe in unilateral disarmament. It was a way of making Hitler and Mussolini understand that a democratic nation will not leave the world at the mercy of lawless force.' Speaking for the party executive, Clynes asked the conference to support a call for a new government which must 'be strongly equipped to defend this country, to play its full part in Collective Security and to resist any intimidation by the Fascist Powers'. Sidney Silverman, from the left of the party, proposed more active opposition to the government and its arms estimates but, in spite of this hostility to the government's arms programmes, he spoke up for collective coercion and he demanded that the executive should 'restate clearly the Party's policy of rebuilding the League on the basis of a strong group of peaceful nations in Europe, firmly pledged to non-aggression and mutual assistance against any aggressor, and to a policy of close political and economic co-operation'. His proposal was heavily defeated, not, it seems, because he suggested a virtual triple alliance against Germany, but because he might allow Chamberlain's supporters to continue to accuse Labour of willing the end, collective force, and not the means, men and weapons. Lansbury's renewed demand for a world conference to secure 'collective equity and justice between the nations' as a substitute for armaments, secured 260,000 votes against over 2 million.[6]

Labour policy committed itself to an armed coercive League of Nations to resist the dictators. Card votes, with the disproportionate influence they gave to trade union delegations, produced misleading numbers yet support for an armed and active League had certainly at last come out on top. Labour speakers soon back-dated their support for an active League, ready, if need be, to resort to arms and increasingly blamed the government's conduct towards the League since 1931 for the perilous prospects of 1938 and 1939. A list of evasions featured regularly in their speeches. 'A long process of disorderly retreat' began in 1931 when Simon 'made the first great surrender' to Japan; then he helped to wreck the disarmament conference and Hitler began to arm. 'He armed without let or hindrance' and the government 'allowed Germany to outbuild us in the air'. Then Abyssinia, and the Hoare–Laval Pact and finally 'Spain and the farce of non-intervention'. It was at the end of 1937 that Hugh Dalton, having thus rewritten recent history, boomed across the House at the government an injunction to build through the League a combination of powers to counter Germany, Italy and Japan. Labour thus offered their alternative to the policy implicit in the impending visit by Halifax to Germany which Chamberlain was eagerly sponsoring.[7]

Among Liberals there took place a less complicated version of the same evolution. The British voting system meant that the 1,500,000 or so votes they secured in 1935 gave them only twenty MPs. Their attitudes mattered more than their numbers suggested. Since the First World War British politics have been decisively influenced by competition between the Left and Right for the old Liberal vote. In 1929 it numbered nearly 5,500,000 against the figures of somewhat over 8 million for Conservatives or Labour. In 1931 and 1935, partly because of the support for the Conservatives of the 'National Liberals', that figure fell to about 1,500,000. The Conservatives would be endangered if the opposition Liberals successfully reclaimed their old supporters. The opinion of Liberals, therefore, was something the Conservative leadership wished to win to its own side. On foreign policy, the most effective pressure group, the League of Nations Union, which most politicians felt obliged to 'support', was disproportionately influenced by Liberals. Their views, therefore, mattered and they unreservedly backed the League.

At first that meant opposing rearmament; the Liberals voted

against the service estimates in March 1935 and Archibald Sinclair, their spokesman, lamented the absence of a 'minister who will denounce the international nightmare of rearmament'. A year later, in 1936, just after the reoccupation of the Rhineland, Liberals voted for the service estimates, though taking a line in debate close to that of Labour. 'We are concerned . . . to base our policy on the Covenant of the League of Nations and measure our armaments by the requirement of collective security', while, on the air force estimates, they moved an amendment calling for the abolition of air forces and the internationalisation of civil aviation. In 1937 they voted against the Defence Loan but only because they favoured a capital levy. They voted for the service estimates and Sinclair reaffirmed their support for full collective security: 'we regard neutrality in the event of aggression in Southern or Eastern Europe as much as in the West, as inconsistent with the obligations of the Covenant.' The opposition Liberals had an explanation of the economic difficulties of the world, the absence of free trade, and 'the disease of economic nationalism with all its symptoms of quotas, tariffs and exchange restrictions'.[8]

Lloyd George needs analysis separate from other Liberals. He acted as an independent force in the manner of an eighteenth-century political potentate, relying on his prestige, his local political strength and his oratorical skill. Baldwin's position depended on his rejection of Lloyd George as an associate of the Conservative Party; Chamberlain, in his turn, equally detested Lloyd George whom he thought capable of employing any weapon to destabilise his government. Lloyd George could certainly be counted upon to find alternatives to the policies of any government which excluded him from office. In 1936 he tried to vary what was then the generally accepted line, of exploiting Hitler's post-Rhineland 'offers', by a more active pursuit of settlement with Germany than the Baldwin–Eden government seemed to be attempting. Lloyd George visited Hitler on 4 and 5 September 1936. The great men impressed each other and exchanged successful flatteries. For a while Lloyd George stressed the chances of Anglo-German entente. In March 1937 he urged a 'definite lead' from Britain to maintain 'the influence which it naturally possesses because of its enormous resources'. 'I say without any hesitation that I would come to an arrangement as far as Herr Hitler is prepared to go.' Lloyd George would accept, that is, a pact of mutual guarantee in the west leaving out eastern Europe. Lloyd George, however, seldom limited his political manoeuvres to one line. Moreover to support agreement with Hitler increasingly meant supporting Mr Chamberlain, which was not Lloyd George's intention. Soon he changed his tone. In June 1937 he explained that: 'I would have liked to have seen an arrangement come to with Germany for a Western European Pact. I think it was a mistake when Herr Hitler proposed it a year ago that we did not proceed immediately and take him at his word. But I am bound to say that the difficulties, which used to come from France, in the way of any scheme which gave justice and fair treatment to Germany – those difficulties now are made by Germany herself ... There is a lack of straightforwardness ... which I frankly say I would not have expected from the present head of the German Government. It was not the impression, at any rate, which he created upon my mind.' But Hitler had lost a friend: 'If the great Powers, France and Russia ... and ourselves talked quite frankly, brutally if you like, these three great Powers have such a force that there is no one in Europe could stand up against them' but the dictators 'are taking at the present moment rather a low view of the intelligence and courage of our Government – very low. I wish to God I could say it was too low'. Lloyd George, like the ex-Asquithian Liberals with whom he was loosely associated, moved towards a League to restrain aggression and, as he put it eloquently in 1938, impose disarmament on Germany.[9]

Conservatives, and their 'National' hangers-on, were, of course, under no obligation to find alternative policies to those of the government which they had been elected to support. Most Conservative MPs dutifully supported Baldwin and Chamberlain without open complaint. What Conservative dissent from the government there was took one of three forms: that British policy was too isolationist or, alternatively, insufficiently isolationist, or that British rearmament was inadequate. The third view can be found combined with either view about isolation. Some Conservatives thought that isolation from Europe should be complete, that there was no reason to interfere and that Britain should concern itself with the Empire. Quarrels with Germany were totally unnecessary and, if arrangements for mutual tolerance could be secured with Japan and Italy, enmity with those countries could be avoided. Armed strength would facilitate imperial tranquillity. The sentiments of Sir Arnold Wilson MP must have made a change for the British Universities League of Nations Society, which met at Oxford in January 1937. Having dismissed collective security he attacked the idea of alliances with 'countries in whose wisdom and stability he had no confidence whatever' before going on to urge the way 'of isolation' to be studied 'not merely as a practicable policy for Great Britain but for all Great Powers ... The policy of isolation required armaments if it were to succeed but not more than other policies required'. (Having worked for conciliation towards dictators until war broke out, he volunteered, though greatly over-age, for service as an air gunner and, predictably, lost his life in combat, in May 1940.) Mr Lambert, a Liberal National, responded to the Anschluss as a good isolationist: 'I do not want commitments on the Continent. I want to keep out of them. I believe in being strong and a good neighbour. Good neighbours are not always interfering in the affairs of their neighbours.'[10] Like other isolationists he soon became a 'warm supporter' of Chamberlain.

Others, although admitting that Britain should intervene in western Europe, if necessary, to help to maintain the independence of France and the Low Countries, rejected any intervention in eastern Europe. Their attitude commended them to Hitler's government: they would give Germany a free hand in the east. Their views easily harmonised with the almost universal belief that France was to blame for the dangerous state of Europe. If France were restrained by a firm British refusal to become involved in any French adventure in eastern Europe then the risks of war sharply diminished. Thus they believed France must be kept safe while working to weaken France and to destroy French alliances in eastern Europe. A sensible, unprovocative France, they argued, would be safe. A good example is Arthur Bryant, the 'patriotic' historian, who wrote to Baldwin, in April 1936, that Britain should not join France in opposing Germany because to do so would weaken 'the foundations of civilisation'. Another was Henry 'Chips' Chan-non, the rich, gossipy MP, whom Harold Nicolson encountered in an Austrian castle that autumn, asserting, as Nicolson put it, 'that we should let gallant little Germany glut her fill of the Reds in the East and keep decadent France quiet while she does so'.[11] (In 1938 R. A. Butler, Under-Secretary for Foreign Affairs, selected Chips as his Parliamentary Private Secretary.) Important ministers thought the same. Simon wrote to Baldwin and Eden shortly after the Rhineland occupation, worrying that the proposed staff talks with France and the reaffirmation of Locarno commitments would make the French feel 'they have got us so tied that they can safely wait for the breakdown of discussions with Germany. In such circumstances France will be as selfish and as pig-headed as France has always been and the prospect of agreement with Germany will grow dimmer and dimmer.' A few weeks later Baldwin asked a delegation of senior Conservative politicians: 'Supposing the Russians and Germans got fighting and the French went in as the allies of Russia owing to that appalling pact they made, you would not feel you were obliged to go and help France would you? If there is any fighting in Europe to be done, I should like to see the Bolshies and the Nazis doing it.' The isolationism of Cabinet ministers, however, can be distinguished from that of private individuals: the government never openly declared that Britain would disinterest itself in eastern Europe.

Admirals readily became isolationists. Admiral Domvile thought it 'quite certain that the man in the street is not going to be led into any wild business in which his own country's interests are not directly concerned'. He found himself in prison in 1940, as a potential collaborator with the Germans. Admiral Chatfield, then First Sea Lord, informed Vansittart in September 1936 that Britain should only go to war for France, Belgium or Holland. 'If Germany, realising this, tries to ex-pand to the South-East, we must accept it. Europe must work out its own salvation in that quarter.' He, as Chamberlain's Defence Minister, advocated alliance with the USSR in 1939. Admiral Drax went further. He feared that some believed that 'if a war starts between Germany and France we shall almost certainly fight on the side of France. That means, of course, that we ally ourselves with Bolshevik Russia (of all people!) for a war in which half Europe would be shattered.' In 1939 Drax led the British military mission to Moscow to try to conclude the alliance with the USSR.[12]

Easily the most forceful, effective and interesting dissident was Churchill. In British politics, he had placed himself, about the time of Hitler's coming to power, on the furthest right of the Conservative Party, the more effectively to challenge Baldwin's leadership, and his own exclusion from office, by sustained opposition to the National Government's India reforms. So he became the most articulate and distinguished of the 'die-hards', the associate of many isolationists, for whom the League of Nations represented an unlovely association of British pacifist disarmers and shifty, self-seeking, foreigners. Churchill's first reactions to Hitler's advent were entirely suitable. He opposed disarmament, indeed he claimed to have been 'saying for several years "Thank God for the French army"'. Now it would be quite unreasonable to try to reduce it; if the French army were reduced, then Britain's obligation under the Locarno treaty, to help France against German attack, would become more onerous. He rejected the interfering internationalist principles of the League: 'I sincerely believe this country has a very important part to play in Europe, but it is not so large a part as we have been attempting to play and I advocate for us in future a more modest role than many of our peace preservers and peace lovers have sought to impose upon us.' On the air estimates in March 1933 Churchill spoke at brilliant length, earning a tribute from a later speaker: 'whenever he makes a speech, whenever he writes a book, and, I am told, whenever he paints a picture, he is always able to produce a work of art and not infrequently a masterpiece.' Churchill mocked proposals for disarmament which 'would give great satisfaction to the League of Nations Union' and produce a 'warm sentimental, generous feeling that we were doing a great, wise, fundamental, eternal thing'. He hoped and trusted that the French 'will look after their own safety, and that we should be permitted to live our life in our island without being again drawn into the perils of the Continent of Europe. But I want to say that if we wish to detach ourselves, if we wish to lead a life of independence from European entanglements, we have to be strong enough to defend our neutrality ... I am strongly of opinion that we require to strengthen our armaments by air and upon the seas in order to make sure that we are still judges of our own fortunes, our own destiny and our own actions.'[13]

A year later Churchill proposed a four-fold increase in the strength of the air force to counter secret German rearmament. Sir Herbert Samuel, the Liberal leader, and, of course, a League of Nations enthusiast, denounced Churchill's demand as 'the language of a Malay running amok . . . the language of blind and causeless panic'. After the General Election of 1935, when the Ethiopian crisis whipped up 'support for the League', *The Economist*, then a liberal weekly, discussed the possibility of Baldwin's bringing Churchill back into the government. However, his inclusion, it thought, posing a significant pair of alternatives, would be 'regarded both at home and abroad as an indication that the government was likely to be more concerned with rearmament than with the League'. In fact, Churchill had already begun to link together concern for the League and for rearmament: 'Some people say "Put your trust in the League of Nations". Others say, "Put your trust in British rearmament." I say we want both. I put my trust in both.'[14]

In the first months of 1936 Churchill could reasonably hope, even expect, to return to office, at last, to supervise the carrying out of the government's defence programme. The unexpected appearance in March 1936 of Inskip, the lawyer, as Minister for Co-ordination of Defence signified an open rejection of Churchill, whose qualifications for the post were overwhelming. The return to the government of Hoare, as First Lord, in June, repeated and emphasised the rejection.

So, in 1936, Churchill, finding himself forced into independence, responded by violent and well-informed criticism of the government's measures to rearm, coupled with increasingly emphatic advocacy of collective security and the League, an advocacy which widened the appeal of his original theme of urgent rearmament. In November he argued that France and Britain alone could not equal German strength: 'It will be necessary for the western democracies, even at some extension of their risks, to gather round them all the elements of collective security or, if you prefer to call it so, combined defensive strength against aggression – the phrase which I prefer – which can be assembled on the basis of the Covenant of the League of Nations.' Evidently he still handled the language of the League with hesitation. He went on in carefully crafted phrases, to complain of the government's failure to set up a Ministry of Supply to organise arms production and took up Hoare's defence that the government were always 'reviewing the position': 'Anyone can see what the position is. The Government simply cannot make up their mind, or they cannot get the Prime Minister to make up his mind, so they go on in strange paradox, decided only to be undecided, resolved to be irresolute, adamant for drift, solid for fluidity, all-powerful to be impotent. So we go on preparing more months and years – precious, perhaps vital to the greatness of Britain – for the locusts to eat.' In 1936 Churchill became increasingly involved with all-party associations concerned to halt German aggression: especially the Anti-Nazi League and the 'Focus', from which emerged the movement for 'Defence of Freedom and Peace', which attached itself to the League of Nations Union. Thus, in the autumn of 1936, Churchill linked himself to the partisans of the League and they accepted this eloquent ally.

In the early 1930s, on the left and in the centre of British politics, everyone supported the League. Then that meant support for disarmament and international conciliation. Most of these League enthusiasts, as the perils of the 1930s grew more evident, came to think that the League should act as a coercive mechanism to restrain aggressors, using armed forces, if need be, to compel obedience to its verdicts. Some of the early supporters of the League, on the other hand, pursued a different path. They rejected armed coercion and stuck to disarmament and conciliation. In consequence, they became ardent supporters of Chamberlain and appeasement. Lansbury and the Independent Labour Party MPs followed this course. Herbert Samuel, unlike most of the Liberal supporters of the League, gave such enthusiastic support to Munich that Chamberlain offered him a place in his Cabinet.[15]

On the political Right, those who, in the early 1930s, advocated both armaments and isolation now also faced a choice. As Hitler's Germany grew stronger they either became more ardent isolationists or grew more afraid of German power. The former became zealous supporters of Chamberlainite appeasement, indeed often more determined Chamberlainites than Chamberlain himself. Sir Henry Page Croft, for instance, though unshakably determined to surrender no inch of British territory, went in with Chamberlain rather than Churchill. On the other hand some former isolationists supported Churchill's campaign for armaments *and* allies. L. S. Amery is an example.

Two combinations, each drawn from every part of the political nation, stood opposed on policy towards Hitler in 1938 and 1939. Chamberlain's supporters included crypto-Fascists on the Right and extreme pacifists on the Left. Churchill appealed to men and women drawn from every shade of the political spectrum, from Lord Lloyd to Stafford Cripps. Churchill boasted that 'all the Left Wing intelligentsia are coming to look to me for protection of their ideas and I will give it whole heartedly in return for their aid in the rearmament of Britain'.

Churchill's movement, under the aegis of the League of Nations Union, staged a public display in December 1936. At the Albert Hall, Conservatives, Liberals and Labour leaders demonstrated their newly created unity after the Right had taken up the League and the Left had taken up armaments. Sir Walter Citrine, the general secretary of the Trades Union Congress, Sir Archibald Sinclair, the leader of the Liberals, and Churchill appeared together on the platform. On 1 January 1937 a press statement appeared signed by twelve eminent personages: three Conservative, three Liberal, three Labour and three non-party. Churchill and Lloyd George signed, together with Sinclair and Gilbert Murray for the Liberals, and Attlee, Dalton and Noel-Baker for Labour. It affirmed the need for an active League to smooth international change but forcefully to frustrate aggressors. *The Times*, in an unfriendly leading article, complained that it 'puts too much of its emphasis on restraint and too little on reform', which was, of course, its intention.[16]

A combined campaign seemed well launched for 1937. Yet it stumbled. The start was overshadowed by excitement over the abdication of King Edward VIII. In 1937 Eden's skill in invoking the League protected the government from criticism. Spain embarrassed Churchill, the only possible leader of a cross-party alliance. So far as he had a political following, as distinct from commanding almost universal awe by his abilities, it came from the further right of the Conservative Party. For Labour and most Liberals, government-held Spain represented right and reason. For most of Churchill's associates it was simply 'red', a catspaw of the Bolsheviks. It was difficult for him, even without the Spanish complication, to include the Soviet Union as part of the coercive mechanism of the League, although without doing so the campaign made little sense. Moreover, in 1937 Churchill seems to have hoped for office once Baldwin had gone; Margesson, the chief whip, certainly discussed the possibility with a coldly disinclined Chamberlain, understandably fearful of Churchill's domineering ways. Later in the year, at the time of the government's successful challenge at Nyon to Mussolini's outrages, Churchill offered to the Conservative Party Conference lavish praise for the foreign policy of the government: 'His Majesty's Ministers possessed the confidence of the Empire in the sober and resolute policy which they were pursuing.'[17] Then towards the end of 1937, preoccupied by the publishers' deadline for the final volume of his enjoyable (and valuable) defence of his ancestor, the great Duke of Marlborough, he relapsed into an unusual silence.

It was very different in 1938. In February Hitler bullied Schuschnigg, Eden resigned and in March Hitler ordered Schuschnigg out and seized Austria. In two portentous speeches in the Commons, on 14 March and 24 March, Churchill relaunched his alternative: 'If a number of States were assembled around Great Britain and France in a solemn treaty for mutual defence against aggression; if they had their forces marshalled in what you may call a grand alliance; if they had their staff arrangements concerted; if all this rested, as it can honourably rest, upon the Covenant of the League of Nations, agreeable with all the purposes and ideals of the League of Nations; if that were sustained, as it would be, by the moral sense of the world; and if it were done in the year 1938 – and, believe me, it may be the last chance there will be for doing it – then I say that you might even now arrest this approaching war.'[18]

That spring and summer he stumped the country in what he called 'my all-party campaign' addressing 'a series of great meetings in the larger cities' deploying his full rhetorical panoply: 'On the rock of the Covenant of the League of

Nations alone can we build high and enduring the temple and the towers of peace.' During the crisis over Czechoslovakia, Labour, the Liberals and Churchill said very much the same things. On 8 September 1938 the National Council of Labour, uniting the trade unions and the party, issued a statement 'on the brink of war': 'The British Government must leave no doubt in the mind of the German Government that they will unite with the French and the Soviet Governments to resist any attack upon Czechoslovakia.' Three times Churchill urged Halifax and Chamberlain to warn Germany that Britain would join in resisting aggression in Czechoslovakia. On 21 September he protested in the press against the partition of Czechoslovakia and on the 26th called for a solemn warning to Germany by Britain, France and Russia. On 20 September the National Council of Labour denounced the proposed dismemberment of Czechoslovakia as 'a shameful betrayal'. In the Commons debate after Munich, Churchill used his most powerful rhetoric in an all-out attack on the government's foreign policy.[19]

At the end of the debate thirty Conservative MPs abstained on a Labour motion criticising the government. Most of these, however, although sympathetic to Churchill's ideas, preferred to attach themselves to Anthony Eden. After his resignation early in 1938 Eden took up the heritage of Baldwin in preaching the need for national unity and for a broad-based government. He did not wish to set himself up as a hostile rival to Chamberlain. Moreover his speeches became dull and empty after he resigned and lost the well-informed and able draftsmen of the Foreign Office. Conservative Central Office, however, which apparently felt its loyalty to be to the party leader, noted that although Eden 'always failed to crystallise his ideas into sufficiently concrete form' it might, just the same, be valuable for the Prime Minister to counter Eden, not on foreign issues, but by showing interest in, for example, 'higher old age pensions' to meet Eden's appeal to 'idealism'.[20]

In 1938 and early 1939, then, there was a clearly stated alternative to the government's policy towards Germany. Where the government stressed conciliation towards Hitler, 'the language of sweet reasonableness' as Duff Cooper dismissively put it in his resignation speech after Munich, Chamberlain's opponents preferred 'the language of the mailed fist'.[21]

They wanted military alliances to encircle Germany, alliances dressed up in the language, and cloaked by the procedures, of the League of Nations. Opposition to Chamberlainite appeasement was widely spread by September 1938. From Churchill and a few friends on the remote right, like Lord Wolmer, through the Eden group of progressively-minded Tories, taking in Lloyd George and the Sinclair Liberals, including the Labour Party together with a chastened Stafford Cripps, who had, at last, decided that resistance to fascism had to be attempted without first destroying capitalism, the ranks of opponents stretched to the Communists. Support for Chamberlain came from some of the old isolationists on the right, including a very few Nazi sympathisers, the mass of the Conservatives and a few Liberal and Labour pacifists. The almost complete agreement on policy towards Germany of 1936 had gone.

An intense and well-matched political struggle replaced it. Chamberlain's opponents were superior to his supporters in talent and eloquence. On the other hand they were dispersed and did not form a unified campaign front, a strategy consistently advocated only by the new-model Cripps. Churchill's natural friends were on the right of the Tories and likely to be alienated by intimacy with Labour. There is some evidence, mainly from Dalton, of abortive moves towards a common front. He reports a telephone conversation in which Churchill, in characteristic language, told Attlee that the Labour protest against the 'shameful betrayal' of Czechoslovakia 'does honour to the British nation' and that Attlee merely replied 'I am glad you think so' thus, according to Dalton, snubbing a possible offer of concerted action. Harold Macmillan, it seems, suggested a 1931-in-reverse in which, presumably, Churchill and whatever Conservatives he could carry with him would join with Labour and the Liberals in a new national government. It soon became clear that Eden, who had no intention of voluntarily subordinating himself to Churchill, would have none of it and, without him, the prospect of a substantial Conservative secession disappeared. The Labour leadership, on its side, when it came to the point, was afraid of upsetting its own supporters by mingling with Tories.[22]

Chamberlain did not intend to change his policies. After

September 1938 his Cabinet became difficult for him to manage especially because he could no longer count on the unconditional support of Halifax. If he brought Eden back, and still more if he let in Churchill, he would completely lose control of foreign policy. He would be compelled to abandon his hopes that he could revive the 'Munich spirit' and rediscover a conciliatory, compromising Germany, and perhaps even a cautious, moderate Hitler; he would have to renounce his effort to win Mussolini's help in fulfilling his hopes. War, Chamberlain thought, would inevitably follow his own political defeat.

The stakes were high and Churchill a glamorous and serious opponent. Churchill is now described as if he were, in the 1930s, a disregarded irrelevance, a 'failure' wandering in a 'wilderness'. He was, on the contrary, a highly successful, well-publicised writer and speaker. He showed as much confidence in his own abilities and insight as Chamberlain himself. Chamberlain, too, is written down, above all by the Churchillians, as a parochial, narrow-minded, dreary nonentity. In truth he was a hard-working, clear-headed and efficient statesman whose public speeches were well-composed and good to hear. Their duel of 1938–9 can be compared with those of Pitt and Fox or Gladstone and Disraeli.

Chamberlain had the advantage of a twentieth-century British Prime Minister to add to his workmanlike debating skill and his careful preparation: a well-drilled and obedient majority in the Commons, made up of Conservative or 'National' Members elected to support the Conservative Prime Minister. Chamberlain had about 400 of them to vote their confidence in his leadership. Anyone outside the government attempting to disturb this political herd must persuade them that the 'country' wanted a change and that many of them risked losing their seats at the next election unless they secured a change in the policy or personnel of the government. About 30 Conservative MPs showed themselves mutinous towards Chamberlain at the time of Munich. If Chamberlain allowed himself to seem out of touch with the opinions of potential Conservative voters, this sort of mutiny could expand very fast. Apart from the power and patronage of the Prime Minister, Chamberlain had some unpredictable advantages in that the politicians most likely to appeal to centre, respectable, liberal views were not determined opponents. Halifax, in public, suppressed his doubts and hesitations. Eden, in the role of political heir to Baldwin, did not attack Chamberlain, but preached national unity and the softening of political dispute. Dissident Conservatives were much influenced by Eden, who led them away from any Churchill-inspired mutiny.[23]

Chamberlain, however great his political assets, was compelled, after Godesberg, and, still more after the German occupation of Prague in March 1939, to accept, in appearance, much of the alternative policy pressed on his government. The public did not share Chamberlain's hopes. In an opinion poll in February 1939, only 28 per cent thought his policy would ultimately lead to enduring peace in Europe. However, he believed it his duty to serve his country by remaining in office and so to prevent reckless statesmen from ensuring a disaster; he tried until the last minute to avoid it by tireless application of the policy he believed to be correct and clung to appeasement until the end.

16 Outbreak of War

The British public sensed that the Nazi-Soviet pact made war certain. Most of the British people, however gloomily, accepted its approach with surprising resignation. It was not that they expected it to be painless; on the contrary they anticipated, first, violent attack from the air, then growing and protracted slaughter on a sombre Western Front. Human beings often find reserves of courage when danger is prospective rather than immediate. Reacting differently to the news from Berlin and Moscow, Chamberlain's government reinforced that public bravery by its own calm confidence. Chamberlain and Halifax, who set its tone, were less worried by the Nazi-Soviet pact than most of their fellow citizens. They had never shared the public belief that alliance with the USSR would deter Germany. They believed that it was the certainty of Anglo-French resistance that would do that. They reiterated British determination to go to war if Germany attacked Poland with less fear of provocation now that the Germans had somehow bought off their ideological foes. Paradoxically, therefore, for the leaders of the government, the Russo-German non-aggression pact encouraged firmness and made conciliatory gestures less necessary. The Nazi-Soviet pact caused the government immediately to reaffirm the British pledge to Poland. They thought their words would make it less likely that they would be called upon to fulfil that pledge.

Urgent anxiety struck the government a few days earlier than the announcement of the Nazi-Soviet pact. Throughout August 1939 reports flowed in of German army reservists recalled, of units brought to war strength and of troop concentrations. Danzig itself had turned into a German armed camp with numerous tough-looking 'tourists', including advance parties of the Gestapo. By the third week in August the Polish general staff had information of 21 German infantry divisions and 13 mobile divisions already concentrated or moving towards the German-Polish frontier. All this threatening activity could be regarded as part of a 'war of nerves' designed to give rise to a state of mind known to contemporaries as 'the jitters', a condition of fright which might lead the victim into offers of excessive concession or, alternatively, might stimulate demands for provocative counter-threats.[1]

The Prime Minister attempted to reinforce his immunity from 'jitters' by disposing of Parliament and departing for the remotest part of Scotland, in Caithness, to attack salmon. He arrived on 7 August 1939 at a lodge belonging to the Duke of Sutherland, near Loch More, a shallow lake, renowned among fishermen, although Chamberlain found the river much more rewarding than the loch itself. There he caught six salmon, but the weather was not good and he thought his catch meagre, not enough to take his mind off business. It was 'something to get away from London and into the open air', but he 'never enjoyed a carefree mind'. The Tientsin problem pursued him to Scotland but it was Hitler who brought him back, on Sunday 20 August, a day earlier than he had intended, and wrecked his plan to return to the north almost immediately and to stay in Scotland until September. On Friday Vansittart received reliable information that the Germans were about to attack Poland. Halifax reluctantly returned to London from Yorkshire and on Saturday 19 August sent off a letter to Chamberlain with the news of an expected German attack on Poland between 25 and 28 August. The crisis had begun.[2]

Parliament was recalled for Thursday to rush through the Emergency Powers Act, the Cabinet summoned for Tuesday and letters drafted for the Prime Minister to send to Hitler and Mussolini. Cadogan, Vansittart, Halifax and Horace Wilson agreed on the appeal to Mussolini. It began with a warning that if war should once start it would not 'be brought to an early conclusion by the defeat of Poland' and went on to invite Mussolini to restrain Hitler and to work with Great Britain to secure 'an agreed solution reached through free negotiation on equal terms between Germany and Poland'. With all this arranged, Halifax passed a typical, if crowded Sunday: early church, a flight to Yorkshire for the 'tail end of the Cricket Week' in his village, a 'little farming' and then to York for the night train back to London. Next day, Chamberlain and Halifax considered a bizarre message passed through the head of

MI6. Göring wished to fly secretly to England to see the Prime Minister. They agreed that he should arrive at a discreet airfield and go direct to Chequers where the staff would be sent away and the telephone disconnected; he never came.[3]

On Tuesday news of the Soviet-German pact met the immediate reaction of a Foreign Office press release that it did not affect British policy or the British guarantee to defend Polish independence. In France the news inspired deeper gloom. Without a long-sustained eastern front, the French government felt less confidence in the ability of the French army to hold off a German attack than did the British. In Paris soldiers and politicians reconsidered the Polish alliance. The Foreign Minister wished to renounce it; Daladier, the French Prime Minister, defeated him. He followed the advice of Gamelin, the French supreme commander designate. If France were ever to challenge German supremacy in Europe, now was the time because British support was, for once, assured. On the British government, therefore, with the USSR gone over from 'anti-fascism' to the German side, with France hesitant, and the USA a remote spectator, rested the decision of August 1939: should Hitler's attempt to build an impregnable thousand-year German Reich by threat and conquest be tolerated or resisted? So strong was the British sense of power and the corresponding assumption of obligation that British opinion adopted without discussion the task of defeating Hitler. The Cabinet met on Tuesday afternoon and approved a revised letter to Hitler which Henderson took by air to Salzburg and thence to Berchtesgaden. It stressed that the German-Soviet agreement did not alter Britain's obligation to Poland which the government 'are determined to fulfil': 'if the case should arise, they are resolved, and prepared, to employ without delay all the forces at their command, and it is impossible to foresee the end of hostilities once engaged'.[4]

Hitler spoke to Henderson on Wednesday with excitable violence. His written reply also denounced the 'wave of appalling terrorism' which British encouragement had allegedly caused the Poles to let loose on the Germans living in Poland. He was, he told Henderson, 50 years old and preferred war now to when he would be 55 or 60. Chamberlain reported Hitler when Parliament met next day as demanding once again a free hand in eastern Europe. In reply he proclaimed that Britain if necessary would fight to defend 'an international order based upon mutual understanding and mutual confidence' which should rest on 'the observance of international undertakings when they have once been entered into, and the renunciation of force in the settlement of differences'. Thus he claimed that British defence of a European balance of power coincided with high moral purpose.[5]

Next morning, Friday 25 August, Hitler tried again to persuade the British to act reasonably. Now back in Berlin, he summoned Henderson, the British ambassador, to see him at 1.30 p.m. The summons frightened Chamberlain who feared an immediate ultimatum. 'By bad fortune my people could find me nothing to do and I sat with Annie in the drawing room unable to read, unable to talk, just sitting with folded hands and a gnawing pain in the stomach.' As time passed, with no message of catastrophe, he recovered and even put on a display of calm. He received the first news of Hitler's words at dinner. Henderson's record and fuller telegram he refused to sit up for and went to bed and to sleep (in his account he congratulated himself here with an exclamation mark). 'Next morning it was on the breakfast table but I had my breakfast and read the papers before opening the box.'

The box contained Hitler's attempt to prevent the Second World War. He must solve the Polish problem. Once he had done that he would settle down and take up art. Then he would 'approach England once more with a large comprehensive offer'. He would accept a reasonable limitation of armaments. He was ready to pledge himself personally to secure the continued existence of the British Empire and to place the power of the German Reich at its disposal. He asked nothing more in return than limited colonial concessions negotiated by peaceful methods with the longest time limit. Hitler, therefore, promised an Anglo-German alliance in return for a free hand against Poland. He urged Henderson to fly to London 'to put the case'.[6]

Hitler's move aroused excitement among British ministers and their advisers. They came to the conclusion in these final days of August 1939, that Hitler was trying to avoid war. 'The German Government are wobbling.' Hitler had called off an attack on Poland fixed for dawn on 26 August. Dahlerus, the loquacious Swede, having talked again to Göring, told the British that 'there is a desire to get to terms'. Horace Wilson became 'very optimistic'. Halifax wrote hopefully a Foreign Office minute 'if Hitler is led to accept a moderate solution now, it is perhaps not altogether wishful thinking to believe that his position will suffer a certain diminution of prestige within Germany'. Chamberlain found himself repeatedly told when Germany would march. 'Yet they haven't marched yet and, as always, I count every hour that passes without a catastrophe as adding its weight to the slowly accumulating anti-war forces.'[7]

They failed to grasp the suicidal irrationality in Hitlerite Nazism. Hitler was engaged in a struggle for German survival in a world of conflicting nations and races, a struggle which had no logical end other than world domination or total defeat. In August 1939 he gave Britain the choice of war or acquiescence in the next stage of expansion towards German economic and military self-sufficiency. Very few showed signs of choosing a free hand for Hitler, only Nevile Henderson argued that Polish obstinacy was the problem and that the Poles should be coerced into a settlement and Horace Wilson and R. A. Butler favoured a gentle approach to Hitler. Chamberlain never accepted the free hand: the only settlement he would, or could, accept would be one that appeared compatible with Polish independence. Only, therefore, misplaced optimism made possible the extraordinary effort devoted to the reply to Hitler's offer. To some of those involved, conciliatory, tactful handling of Hitler might bring peace, to most the only way was firm, clear pledges to resist attack.

On Friday after leaving the Prime Minister at 11 p.m., Halifax returned to the Foreign Office and dictated what Cadogan described as a bad draft reply. It casts light on their relationship that Cadogan felt unable to interrupt because of the 'large audience' present. According to Oliver Harvey, Halifax believed 'something can be made' of Hitler's message. But Cadogan got his way and when Halifax finished, Cadogan read out some notes of his own. They adjourned at 1 a.m. On Saturday morning Cadogan elaborated his draft with Foreign Office officials and then went over to No. 10 and gave it to

Horace Wilson. Halifax, Chamberlain, Wilson and R. A. Butler discussed this draft until 1 p.m. when Nevile Henderson arrived from Berlin. In the afternoon Horace Wilson and R. A. Butler went to produce a revised draft ('*What* a party', commented Cadogan in his diary; 'What a pair!' Harvey wrote in his). Cadogan thought their draft '*quite* awful'. Harvey found it '*very* flabby'. Cadogan 'corrected worst errors' and then the Cabinet met, and, as Cadogan expected, objected to the Wilson–Butler draft. The Cabinet met at 6.30 p.m. 'It was suggested that the tone of the opening paragraph was somewhat too deferential and appeared to treat Herr Hitler's suggestions with somewhat too much respect.' Later the Cabinet agreed that ministers should send their individual comments to Simon. At 10 p.m. that Saturday Chamberlain, Halifax, Simon, Butler and Cadogan discussed the draft yet again until well after midnight. On Sunday morning Halifax and Cadogan started work once more and Makins and Strang, from the Foreign Office, joined in. The Cabinet met again in the afternoon. Before it met Simon went through the draft with some ministers. At the Cabinet it was agreed that other ministers should send their comments to Simon. Simon, Horace Wilson and Cadogan got down to it again. Vansittart commented on the draft at a late stage, and approved it, but the deletion followed of an 'appeasing' paragraph: this had made the statement that the British government 'wished to emphasise once more their earnest desire to join, if that be possible, with Germany in an attempt to build up a better order in Europe'.[8]

On Monday 28 August a third Cabinet reconsidered this well-worked draft of the Prime Minister's reply and at last it was ready. Henderson returned to Berlin that afternoon. The letter suggested direct discussions between the German and Polish governments to which Polish agreement had meanwhile been secured. However, it included a flat rejection of Hitler's hopes: the British government 'have obligations to Poland by which they are bound and which they intend to honour. They could not, for any advantage offered to Great Britain, acquiesce in a settlement which put in jeopardy the independence of the State to whom they had given their guarantee.' That position made war certain since Hitler was about to conquer some living space. British determination would make sure that

France would go to war and Italy remain neutral.

Soon after Nevile Henderson got back to his embassy in Berlin Hitler summoned him. 'Fortified by half a bottle of champagne', Henderson met Hitler and Ribbentrop at 10.30 p.m. and remained with them until nearly midnight, commenting on the British reply. Hitler became excited only when Henderson told him that it was not a question of Danzig and the Corridor but of British determination to resist force by force. Henderson saw Hitler again next day at 7.30 p.m. to receive the German reply to Chamberlain's much redrafted letter. This time Hitler became violent and he and Henderson shouted at each other, or so Henderson claimed. Hitler now launched a new manoeuvre to isolate Poland, after the failure of the Nazi-Soviet pact and his offer to guarantee the British Empire to do so. He planned to make proposals to Poland, which would be rejected by Poland but, he hoped, accepted by the British. He did not have much time: the Germans must finish Poland before autumn rain clogged their mobile divisions. On the other hand he did not, it seems, care very much: if the British insisted on intervention in the east of Europe this was a good moment for Hitler to use armed strength to dissuade them. At this interview Hitler agreed to do what the British asked and discuss his differences with Poland. However, he demanded that a Polish representative, equipped with full authority to accept any terms, should arrive in Berlin the next day. Halifax and Cadogan stayed up until 2.30 a.m. on 30 August to consider Hitler's latest message and at 2 a.m. sent a telegram to insist that it was 'unreasonable' to expect them to produce a Polish representative during the day which had just begun, 30 August. The British authorities remained surprisingly cheerful, however, encouraged by Dahlerus, who talked to Chamberlain and Halifax that morning. They imagined Hitler to be seeking to save face while retreating. Corbin put to Cadogan the opposite view, that Hitler was trying to get France and Britain to accept Poland's strangulation. Cadogan refused to give up his hypothesis. In the afternoon Chamberlain sent a new message to Hitler in which he welcomed evidence of 'a desire for Anglo-German understanding': this followed a telephone conversation between Göring and the ever-reassuring Dahlerus. Halifax and Cadogan worked out a reply to Hitler and a message to Beck, the Polish Foreign Minister, to press both sides to arrange Polish-German negotiations and took the telegrams to Chamberlain for approval. Meanwhile general mobilisation went forward in Poland and Germany. Eventually Halifax went to bed at 5 p.m. to recover lost sleep and the telegrams went out. In Berlin Henderson asked to see Hitler but instead faced Ribbentrop at midnight.[9]

Their dialogue was stormy. Ribbentrop declared that Poland had rejected German terms for a settlement by failing to send a plenipotentiary during the day. He read aloud 'at top speed' a list of those terms, then repeated that they were no longer on offer and refused to let Henderson have a copy. That night Henderson remained active until 4 a.m. Leaving Ribbentrop in the early hours of 31 August he asked the Polish ambassador in Berlin to come to see him and despite the obvious lack of interest in negotiation which both Hitler and Ribbentrop had shown, bullied him to go to Ribbentrop and ask for the 'terms'. After a telephone call from Dahlerus, who, after spending most of the night with Göring, explained to Horace Wilson that the German 'terms' were liberal, Cadogan, Halifax and Chamberlain sent a telegram to Warsaw urging the Polish government to tell the Polish ambassador in Berlin to ask Ribbentrop for the terms. That was as close as the directors of British policy came before war began to subjecting the Poles to a new Munich. It did not amount to much. There was no suggestion that the British and Germans, or the European great powers, would get together and impose a solution on Poland.[10]

That day, however, 31 August 1939, a suggestion for a new Munich came from the only government that wanted that outcome: the Italian. At 12.50 Ciano, the Italian Foreign Minister, who detested the idea of being dragged into a German-inspired European war, telephoned to Halifax and suggested, on behalf of Mussolini, a conference on 5 September to revise 'the clauses of the Treaty of Versailles which are the cause of the present grave troubles in the life of Europe'. The proposal was put to the British and French governments and Ciano sought their assent before asking Hitler. Immediately Halifax crossed Downing Street to No. 10 and arranged for Corbin, the French ambassador, to come there. In No. 10, Corbin found the usual foreign policy directorate: Chamberlain, Halifax,

Cadogan and Horace Wilson. He telephoned to Paris where Bonnet explained that he had received the same proposals. The British group wanted demobilisation before any conference.[11] Then, if Euan Wallace, a recently promoted Cabinet minister, is to be believed, Halifax and Cadogan joined him for a late lunch at his table in the Carlton restaurant. Apparently they said nothing about Mussolini's proposal. Halifax, however, radiated confidence. Hitler was providing him with 'the first sight of a beaten fox'. With extraordinary hopefulness, they discussed the need to overthrow Nazism as a preliminary to a new European settlement. Even the news that German radio reported the alleged Polish rejection of the German 'offer' failed to shake Cadogan's optimism as he wrote up his diary at midnight, a few hours before the Wehrmacht opened the attack on Poland: 'It *does* seem to me Hitler is hesitant and trying all sorts of dodges, including last-minute bluff. We have got to stand firm.' He and Halifax had been firm all afternoon and evening as Corbin kept them up to date with French reactions to Mussolini's proposed conference. Daladier declared that he would rather resign than accept a second Munich. Halifax agreed, though he wished not to seem to be missing a chance of peace.[12]

At dawn on Friday 1 September 1939 the German air force began to bomb Poland and the German army smashed forward. It was a day of national unity in Britain. Against the background of the steady and well-planned evacuation of children from the large towns and military zones, the Cabinet and Houses of Parliament showed virtual unanimity and, so far as their opinions can be judged, the public accepted without enthusiasm, but without much hesitation or doubt, that German action required the United Kingdom to go to war. The French embassy telephoned emphatic words to Paris: 'The British people is united as it has, perhaps, never been in all its history, in its determination to oppose any German attempt at domination and to safeguard the essential principles of international morality. It knows that it is engaging in an ordeal which will undoubtedly be long and which will require the heaviest sacrifices but it is determined to carry out to the end what it considers to be at once a duty and a mission, not only to its own country but also towards all civilised nations.'[13]

The Cabinet met at 11.30 a.m. The record gives Chamberlain's opening words: 'The Cabinet met under the gravest possible conditions. The event against which we had fought so long and so earnestly had come upon us. But our consciences were clear and there should be no possible question now where our duty lay.' Halifax referred to the Italian proposal for a conference which had now 'been overtaken by the course of events'. The Cabinet agreed on a message to the German government. Unless the aggression against Poland was stopped and German troops promptly withdrawn from Poland the British 'will without hesitation fulfil their obligation to Poland'. There was no time limit, but Cabinet ministers evidently thought of this as equivalent to an ultimatum and that a limit would soon be fixed with the French government. The Cabinet authorised Chamberlain and Halifax to work out the procedure for putting the guarantee to Poland into effect. Chamberlain made a statement to the House of Commons at 6 p.m. He expressed solemn determination: 'It now only remains for us to set our teeth and enter upon this struggle.' For the Labour Party Arthur Greenwood, and Sinclair, the Liberal leader, supported him, and both provided eloquent and uplifting perorations suitable for the last moments of peace. Determination to go to war dominated most outlets of opinion in reaction to the German attack on Poland. Partly it was because the obvious alternative was another 'Munich'. The evident uselessness of the first Munich made a second Munich seem futile as well as disreputable: 'Munich' meant working with the ostentatiously bullying government of Germany against its victim. The Polish guarantee made the possibility of any such collaboration seem dishonourable in the highest degree. Behind this determination, too, lay an attitude which is, in some ways, difficult to appreciate at the end of the twentieth century, a belief that British power, once mobilised, would unfailingly decide the outcome of a European war.

Discordant intrusions came from Paris. Georges Bonnet, the French Foreign Minister, felt far from sure that war was wise; Hitler had not been deterred by Franco-British measures and their failure should perhaps be accepted. He manoeuvred to defeat Daladier, who opposed any attempt at a new Munich. In the morning the Foreign Office learned that the French government had given a 'favourable reply' to the Italian suggestion of a conference, though insisting that Poland must be represented. Halifax, the French ambassador reported, thought the conference hardly a viable proposition and that it was 'holy water sprinkled on a condemned man with a rope round his neck' [c'était de l'eau bénite sur un homme qui a la corde au cou]. Bonnet telephoned Corbin that he 'did not share this sentiment'. He wished to 'neglect no effort to try to restore peace'. (He even put the suggestion of a conference to the Polish Foreign Minister.)[14]

Early on Tuesday 2 September Count Ciano, encouraged by Bonnet's reaction, told the Italian ambassador in Berlin to inform Hitler that he could secure everything he wanted without war by agreeing to a cease-fire, leaving the Germans in occupation of the Polish territory they had so far overrun, and a conference to follow in two or three days' time. Hitler reacted by enquiring if the warnings he had been given the day before were in the nature of an ultimatum. Assured they were not, he promised a reply in a day or two and Ribbentrop promised to give the outline reply by noon on Sunday 3 September. At 2.30 p.m. on Saturday 2 September, Ciano telephoned to Halifax to explain that he had revived the idea of a conference and to say that Germany wished to have until noon the next day to consider the conference. Halifax said he thought Hitler must first withdraw German troops from Poland. Ciano thought Hitler would refuse. Halifax, however, took the conference proposal seriously. He stopped John Simon from making a statement in the House of Commons on behalf of the government. Simon was about to tell the House that Nevile Henderson in Berlin would soon present the ultimatum to Germany that everyone expected. Instead he announced that Mr Chamberlain would make a statement later on that day.

Saturday 2 September now proved an unusual day in British politics. The Cabinet met twice, the second time at midnight, determined to override the Prime Minister and the Foreign Secretary. An infuriated House of Commons nearly overthrew the government. They all suspected the Prime Minister of falling into the temptation offered by Mussolini's conference. They feared he (and Halifax) might delay the British declaration of war so long that the German withdrawal they stipulated as a precondition of any conference might take place after Poland had already been crushed. Were their suspicions well-founded?[15]

During a few hours in the afternoon of 2 September the answer is 'yes'. That morning a telegram went to Paris asking the British ambassador to hurry the French ultimatum to Germany. The tone changed after a telephone call from Ciano to Halifax at 2.30 p.m. revived the conference idea which Halifax and Chamberlain had assumed the German invasion of Poland to have destroyed. They faced the hastily summoned Cabinet with a proposal to give the Germans extra time to think about the conference. Sir John Simon recorded 'the plan which these two provisionally favoured', an armistice in Poland with the forces halted where they were, while Hitler thought about a conference. The conference could then take place only if Hitler agreed to withdraw German troops from Poland. Hoare noted that Halifax was 'inclined to agree' to a conference on Tuesday 5 September if Hitler promised to withdraw. Halifax set out conclusions he and the Prime Minister had 'provisionally' arrived at. He suggested waiting for a reply to the British warning of 1 September until 12 noon on the next day, Sunday, which was the time Hitler had specified for his meditation on the conference proposal, or even 12 midnight at the end of Sunday. Chamberlain supported Halifax by stressing the French desire for delay.[16]

The Cabinet swept all this aside, led by Hoare. Ministers did not want delays or conferences. They wanted to carry out their promises to Poland. They insisted that war should begin at midnight that night, 2 September. The Prime Minister closed the meeting by repeating that he must consult the French government. As soon as the Cabinet meeting ended, Cadogan telephoned Bonnet, who refused to declare war at midnight and explained that French ministers would decide on their timing by 8 or 9 p.m. At 6.30 p.m. Halifax telephoned to Ciano in Rome. Halifax tried to keep the conference proposal alive. He asked Ciano 'to do his best with Berlin' to secure acceptance of the condition of German withdrawal from Poland. As yet he could not say how long Hitler would have to think about the conference because 'we were still in discussion with the French'. Halifax thus accepted French objections to the midnight declaration of war to give Hitler more time to make peace and made French agreement a pre-condition of British action. There were other good reasons for doing this; to declare war ahead of the French would imply, dangerously, that Britain was dragging France into war. Chamberlain and Halifax therefore felt able to override the Cabinet's decision and, instead of sending an ultimatum to expire at midnight, decided to fall in with French delays and give the conference another chance. Mussolini himself soon abandoned the conference as hopeless, but the news came after Chamberlain had given his tensely awaited statement to the House of Commons, when he still had hopes for the conference.[17]

About 6.30 the Speaker of the House of Commons told the House that the Prime Minister would soon make a statement. The Speaker suspended the sitting and arranged that the division bells should be rung when the House was to reassemble. A crowded, excited House watched Mr Chamberlain rise to speak about an hour later. Everyone knew, or thought they knew, that he would say that war would soon begin. Cabinet ministers awaited the announcement of their decision that war should begin at midnight. Chamberlain's first words reported that Hitler had not yet replied to the warning given the day before. His next remarks startled the House: 'It may be that delay is caused by consideration of a proposal which, meanwhile, had been put forward by the Italian Government, that hostilities should cease and that there should immediately be a conference between the five powers, Great Britain, France, Poland, Germany and Italy.' He insisted on German agreement to withdraw their forces from Poland as a condition of the conference and on negotiation between Poland and Germany but spoke as if he were discussing real possibilities. He ended with legalistic bathos: 'His Majesty's Government did not recognise the validity of the unilateral incorporation of Danzig into Germany.' There was no ultimatum, no announcement of war at midnight, only the statement that the government was 'in communication with the French Government as to the limit of time' within which the Germans must agree to withdraw from Poland. Talk of Italian proposals and of a conference evoked memories of Munich.

The House showed such hostility and anger that Chamberlain, as he told Halifax, believed that the government would fall next day. Halifax 'had never seen the Prime Minister so disturbed'. The Commons, apparently representative of opinion outside, was insisting on war to fulfil the guarantee to Poland. They did not think the war would be easy, they expected London and other towns to be bombed, they supposed the war might be long. Yet they were determined to go ahead. Moreover Cabinet ministers showed their feelings and wondered why their decision in the afternoon had not been put into effect; they suspected that Chamberlain was tempted by Mussolini's conference. When the House adjourned, several ministers assembled in Simon's room. 'The language and feelings of some of my colleagues were so strong and deep that I thought it right at once to inform the Prime Minister', Simon wrote. Then he took the protesting ministers to see Chamberlain. Returning to Simon's room the dozen or so ministers continued restless and made Simon write a letter to Chamberlain 'that our view was that in no circumstances should the expiry of the ultimatum go beyond 12 noon tomorrow, and even this extension of twelve hours beyond the Cabinet's earlier decision would only be acceptable if it was the necessary price of French co-operation'. Chamberlain then called Simon round to No. 10 – it was 10 p.m. – and joined in trying to persuade the French government to adapt itself to British urgency. Some of the anger of the House of Commons began to descend on the French. Corbin, the French ambassador, spent most of the evening in 10 Downing Street telephoning to Paris about the timing of the ultimatum, pressed by Sir John Simon, who warned him that unless the British government changed its language it would 'infallibly' be overthrown. Returning to the French embassy while the Cabinet assembled, before returning to Downing Street after midnight to hear its conclusions, Corbin received a telephone call from an infuriated and combative Churchill whose voice 'made the telephone vibrate'. If France failed England, Churchill shouted, he would never again take any interest in European affairs.[18]

Meanwhile Hitler and Ribbentrop tried a last-minute manoeuvre to keep Britain out of war. They ordered Hesse, press attaché at the German embassy in London, to go to see Horace Wilson and suggest that Wilson should go to Berlin to meet

Ribbentrop and Hitler 'to discuss the whole position, heart to heart'. Hesse saw Wilson at 10 p.m. Wilson responded 'in a friendly but negative manner' and reported the 'most violent indignation in the House of Commons and in the Cabinet' which, he explained, made it impossible for him to agree. The German suggestion came too late. Chamberlain and Simon agreed that the Cabinet must be got together again at once and it met just before midnight. A violent thunderstorm suitably concluded this fraught day. Parliament had adjourned until 12 noon on Sunday 3 September. The Cabinet all agreed that war on Germany must begin by then. In the end the Cabinet decided that the British ultimatum should be presented at 9 a.m. and expire at 11 a.m. even though the French government still refused to act then, and eventually went to war at 5 p.m.[19]

Chamberlain broadcast to the nation at 11.15 a.m.: 'We are now at war.' He spoke with dignity and in a manner suitably subdued and sad. The United Kingdom fought to safeguard British independence by opposing the use of force in Europe and by maintaining a balance of power. The Prime Minister ended his speech in words which gave another reason for war: 'It is evil things that we shall be fighting against, brute force, bad faith, injustice, oppression and persecution and against them I am certain that the right will prevail.'[20]

17 Conclusion

Study of documentary evidence has dangers. The abundant, well-arranged, lucid documentation accumulated by British governments and their advisers in the 1930s has sometimes overwhelmed historians into interpretative surrender. Ministers and civil servants, some historians conclude, could have done only what they did. They had no choice or, when they had, made the only choice that the information before them rationally dictated. Since the public records became available to historians at the end of the 1960s, judgements of Neville Chamberlain and his associates have become steadily more benign. In the circumstances he found, scholars suggest, he managed public affairs as well as anyone could have done.

Yet the sequel to his work was disaster. In 1940 Germany conquered France and directly imperilled the United Kingdom. From 1941 a great armed struggle decided whether Nazi Germany or the Soviet Union under Stalin should be the greatest power on the European continent: an unappetising prospect whoever won. This book does not try to explain what might have happened if Chamberlain and his policies had not existed. It does suggest that Chamberlain and his colleagues made choices among alternative possibilities and that so far as Chamberlain decided them, and he had great power within the government, they were choices for conciliation rather than resistance.

Moderation in the exercise of German military and industrial power was the object; the method was considerate politeness and the search for negotiated solutions to German grievances. Chamberlain hoped to persuade the Third Reich to limit its aims and to pursue them peacefully. He gave persuasion priority over coercion. Whenever the British government had to decide between resistance to German ambitions and compromise with them, Chamberlain led the way to compromise. Until 1938 this made him a vigorous exponent of a line of action favoured by ministers, officials, MPs and outside opinion. Until then policy towards Japan and Italy, especially over Ethiopia and Spain, aroused greater dissension than policy towards Germany. Outside Europe, the government showed more reluctance to involve the League of Nations than its critics, but the supporters of the League regarded it, at that time, as a means of avoiding coercive combinations, not of legitimising them. The policy of European 'appeasement', if necessary bypassing the League and French influence there, had general support in Britain. Chamberlain expressed widely shared opinions.

As time passed Chamberlain distinguished himself from most of his colleagues and most of British opinion by his growing conviction of the success of conciliation in turning Germany peaceful. In the spring of 1938, even after the Anschluss, his views still had much support. In September 1938, especially after Godesberg, his faith in his own success began to isolate him. He succumbed to the temptation to believe that actions which were specifically and evidently his own were triumphing: successful politicians must have faith in themselves and in this respect Chamberlain excelled. Hitler helped. He directly appealed to Chamberlain's vanity. He encouraged Chamberlain to claim special influence over him. In public speeches he made Chamberlain's hold on office a condition of peace. Sir Nevile Henderson, the British ambassador in Berlin, encouraged Chamberlain's hopes; he lost the confidence of the Foreign Office but kept his influence across the road in Downing Street.

In 1938, as Prime Minister, Chamberlain could have secured sufficient support either for the policies he pursued or for an anti-German alliance. After Munich he could, had he thought it right, have given up 'appeasement' and, as Halifax, for instance, sometimes hoped he would do, have based a policy of resistance to Hitler on a restored national consensus. At the end of 1938 and in the first months of 1939 Chamberlain, indeed, was uneasily aware that his opinions had lost support.

In December 1938 he confided to Baldwin: 'I have decided to encourage immediate formation of an organisation whose objectives would be to provide accurate and unbiased information about foreign affairs, and, at the same time, to promote friendly intercourse with other countries.' He complained that 'there is now no hope whatever of the League of Nations Union supplying the crying need for a central source of popular information upon the whole sphere of foreign relations'. He passed on memoranda from Sir Joseph Ball, at Conservative Central Office, pointing out that the League of Nations Union publications were now controlled by a company 'formed to popularise Mr Churchill and his policy'. He proposed as 'the best way of diverting the central body of British opinion from the special pleading of left-wing propaganda' to arrange for the setting up of the 'British Association for International Understanding'.[1]

Chamberlainite appeasement, it is true, was not a feeble policy of surrender and unlimited retreat. Chamberlain thought war futile and rejected it but never pursued 'peace at any price'. His policy meant intervention in continental Europe to induce Hitler's Germany to insist only on expansion so limited that it would not threaten the safety or independence of the United Kingdom. In retrospect this appears a bold, venturesome policy, certain, given the ambitions of Hitler, to lead to an Anglo-German war. As Prime Minister, Chamberlain struggled to impose his system of orderly conduct on continental Europe. He thought that he could do it in co-operation with Hitler. When Hitler proved difficult, he hoped to exploit the restraining influences of Mussolini and German moderates.

Chamberlain's purposes commanded general support. Moreover he did not intend to surrender the liberties and prosperity of the British people or to jeopardise their safety. He worked for a peaceful Europe beside which Britain would prosper. Critics, however, complained that his methods made war more likely; he believed that those critics would make war certain. Critics thought conciliation helped Hitler to make aggression seem rewarding; Chamberlain thought the opponents of his appeasement policy would provoke Hitler, or those who might otherwise restrain him, into violence. Both sides thought the other unimaginative and crude. Both hoped to restrain Hitler, or to influence other Germans to restrain him. Chamberlain believed conciliation the best method; others demanded firmness and threats. Hence the rising anger of disputes over British foreign policy in 1938 and 1939.

Chamberlain, for all his hopes, never intended to take risks with British safety by relying on German good-will. His aim was agreed limitation of armaments and until that took place he intended to keep Britain sufficiently strong to be capable of self-defence. The thesis of the famous pamphlet of 1940, *Guilty Men*, written by journalists who subjected Chamberlain and his ministers to violent condemnation, but left Beaverbrook out of their list, consisted to a large extent of denunciations of the weaknesses of the British expeditionary force that retreated to Dunkirk in 1940. The efficiency of the air force and navy in 1940 refutes their denunciation of Chamberlain as irresponsibly reckless. Still, it is clear that he did not think the threat from Germany made it necessary to push military production to the maximum politically and economically possible; the productive capacity freed by the recession of 1938 may be said to have prevented defeat in 1940, and not the efforts of the government.

After the Anschluss in March 1938 Chamberlain could, the evidence suggests, have secured sufficient support in Britain for a close alliance with France and a policy of containing and encircling Germany, more or less shrouded under the League covenant. After Munich, it even appears that it would have been politically easier for him to abandon appeasement, and to treat the Munich settlement, as many historians incorrectly claim he did, only as a means of deferring, rather than avoiding, an eventual confrontation of the Third Reich. He could even perhaps have denied Churchill the increase in political prestige that his denunciation of Munich eventually won for him. He did not do so and, on the contrary, expectantly awaited the negotiation with Nazi Germany of a definitive détente. Even after the German occupation of Prague in March 1939 he futilely tried to keep alive such hopes.

These hopes rested on a reasonable but incorrect interpretation of the way the Third Reich worked. Hitler, this view assumed, must be interested in keeping power and the policies that set off the Second World War did not seem a sound method; if he were foolish enough to follow them, however, sensible Germans would stop him. The Chamberlainites relied on sympathetic treatment of German grievances to win Hitler, or failing him, influential Germans, to peaceful ways. They did not succeed for, it seems, their conduct strengthened both

Hitler's ambitions and his internal authority. A linked error loomed large: western association with the USSR would annoy and provoke, rather than restrain, the Nazis and non-Nazi Germans. Chamberlain, therefore, shunned co-operation with the Soviet Union on any terms and tried to prevent it. Another mistake was his assumption that the USSR and Nazi Germany could never combine, so that he thought some approximate balance of power existed in Europe without any British effort to secure it.

This book argues that Chamberlain and his colleagues made choices among alternative policies. Those historians who have revised the earlier interpretation of Chamberlain, in which he was written off as an ignorant coward, imply that his foreign policy was dictated by realistic assessment of economic and military weakness and by British opinion. This book suggests that Chamberlain led the government in 1938 and 1939, particularly in the months after Munich, into rejecting the option of a close Franco-British alliance, which might have dealt firmly with Mussolini's pretensions, and might have acted as a nucleus round which those states with reason to fear the Third Reich could assemble to resist it. We still do not know whether or not it was possible to induce the Soviet Union to hinder rather than help Hitler's attempt in 1939 and 1940 forcibly to prevent the western powers from interfering in eastern Europe. Chamberlain refused to try; he thought collaboration with the Soviet Union undesirable and unnecessary. Yet Chamberlain had no intention of agreeing to a free hand for Germany in eastern Europe. This book suggests that he could have tried to build a barrier to Hitler's expansion. After March 1939 British attempts to do so were either half-hearted or too late. Academically, therefore, this study proposes that the balance of evidence points to counter-revisionist interpretations. Led by Chamberlain, the government rejected effective deterrence. Chamberlain's powerful, obstinate personality and his skill in debate probably stifled serious chances of preventing the Second World War.

References

ABBREVIATIONS

AC	Austen Chamberlain's Papers in Birmingham University Library
CAB	Cabinet Office Papers in the Public Record Office, Kew
DBFP	Documents on British Foreign Policy, followed by series number and volume number. References are given to document or page numbers, whichever is more convenient
DDF	Documents Diplomatiques Français. References as for DBFP
DGFP	Documents on German Foreign Policy, followed by series letter and volume number
FO	Foreign Office Papers in the Public Record Office, Kew
FRUS	Foreign Relations of the United States
HC Deb 5s	Parliamentary Debates, Official Report (Hansard) 5th series, preceded by volume number and followed by column number
NC	Neville Chamberlain Papers in Birmingham University Library
PREM	Prime Minister's Office Papers in the Public Record Office, Kew
PRO	PRO series of miscellaneous papers in the Public Record Office, Kew
T	Treasury Papers in the Public Record Office, Kew

1. NEVILLE CHAMBERLAIN: PERSONALITY AND POLICY

1. 351 HC Deb 5s, col. 292.
2. NC 2/26; NC 18/1/941, 948.
3. NC 18/1/870, 908; *The Times*, 5 May 1934, p. 14.
4. NC 18/1/908, 897, 874, 1105.
5. NC 18/1/940, 943, 948, 910.
6. NC 18/1/803, 874, 910, 911, 929, 952, 992.

7. FO 800/328, Hal 39/29; PRO 30/69/1752/2, diary, 7 Apr. 1936, 11 June 1936.

8. Kent Archives U1590, C658(c); John Colville, *The Fringes of Power* (London, 1985), pp. 35–6, 79; Trinity College, Cambridge, MSS RAB G8 (99), copy; R.R. James (ed.), *Chips. The Diaries of Sir Henry Channon* (London, 1967), p. 162.

9. NC 18/1/962, 1100; NC 8/24/1; R. Cockett, *Twilight of Truth* (London, 1989), p. 115.

10. NC 2/29/36; NC 18/1/948, 1107, 1108, 1110; NC 12/9/2,3; *The Countryman*, Idbury, Kingham, Oxon, Oct. 1937, pp. 45–6.

11. NC 2/29/36; NC 18/1/1104, 1105.

12. NC 18/1/950, 940, 948; *The Times*, 7 Nov. 1935, p. 12, 18 Dec. 1935, p. 18.

13. K. Feiling, *Life of Neville Chamberlain* (London, 1946), p. 360; NC 18/1/891.

14. NC 18/1/1121, 939, 1043; Colville, *The Fringes of Power*, p. 406: W.S. Churchill, *The Gathering Storm* (London, 1948), pp. 173, 199; *Chips. The Diaries of Sir Henry Channon*, p. 196.

2.   REARMAMENT AND REPARATIONS

1. R.A.C. Parker, *Europe 1918–45* (New York, 1970), p. 224.

2. Bruce Kent, *The Spoils of War* (Oxford, 1991), Table 12, p. 263; R.A.C. Parker, *Europe 1918–45*, pp. 212–27, 241–4.

3. D. Lloyd George, *The Truth about Reparations and War Debts* (London, 1932), p. 57; Elizabeth Johnson (ed.), *The Collected Writings of John Maynard Keynes*, vol. 18 (London, 1978), p. 364.

4. Bodleian Library, Simon MS 70, fols 86, 132; René Girault and Robert Frank, *Turbulente Europe et nouveaux mondes* (Paris, 1988), p. 164; League of Nations, *Statistical Yearbook 1937–8* (Geneva, 1938), p. 247.

5. Bodleian Library, Simon MS 70, fols 81–9; PRO 30/69/8/1 cit. in R.A.C. Parker, 'Probleme Britischer Aussenpolitik Wahrend der Weltwirtschaftskrise', in J. Becker and K. Hildebrand (eds), *Internationale Beziehungen in der Weltwirtschaftskrise 1929–33* (Munich, 1980).

6. D. Lloyd George, *The Truth about Reparations and War Debts*, p. 56.

7. DBFP 2, 4 nos 89, 220; 2, 5 no. 454 fn 6; 2, 6 nos 304, 305 pp. 461–2; no. 322 pp. 488–9.

8. DBFP 2, 6 nos 206, 324, 325.

9. DDF 1, 6, nos 104–5; DBFP 2, 15 App.4b, p. 773; FO 371/18847, C5004/55/18; FO 371/18734, A5573/22/45.

10. CAB 27/510, DC(M)(32) 101, fol. 168; CAB 27/507, DC(M)(32) 46, fols 168, 170; 292 HC Deb 5s, col. 2339.

11. CAB 27/507, DC(M)(32)45; 292 HC Deb 5s, col. 698.

12. NC 18/1/865, 870.

13. DBFP 2, 6 no. 488 p. 814, no. 489 p. 822.

14. DGFP C, 3 nos 190, 200; DBFP 2, 6 nos 473, 498 App. 2, no. 3 p. 967.

15. 295 HC Deb 5s, cols 877, 872, 981; Bodleian Library, Simon MS 7, 21 Dec. 1934, cit. R.A.C. Parker, 'Great Britain, France and the Ethiopian Crisis', *English Historical Review* (*EHR*) (Apr. 1974), 293.

16. DBFP 2, 12 nos 311, 359, 365–6, 362.

17. 299 HC Deb 5s, col. 89, 301 HC Deb 5s, col. 632.

18. DBFP 2, 12 nos 476–7, 524–7, 562, 570–1, 584; NC 18/1/910.

19. DDF 1, 9 no. 486; NC 18/1/910; CAB 23/81, fol. 228.

20. Bodleian Library, Simon MS 7, 27 Mar. 1935; NC 18/1/911; DBFP 2, 12 no. 651 p. 727; p. 744.

21. CAB 23/81, fol. 247.

22. DBFP 2, 12 no. 701; DDF 1, 10 no. 140; CAB 23/81, 20 and 21(35)1, 8 Apr. 1935, cit. Parker, 'Great Britain, France and the Ethiopian Crisis', *EHR* (Apr. 1974), 295.

23. NC 18/1/912; 301 HC Deb 5s, cols 570, 572, 577.

24. DBFP 2, 12 nos 678, 496, 651 pp. 739–40; 2, 13 nos 289–90, 304–5, 453; CAB 29/147, NCM (35) 11, 6 June 1935.

25. DBFP 2, 13 no. 348 p. 427, no. 289 pp. 342, 340, nos 305, 403. DGFP C 4 no. 275; FO 371/18848, C5280/55/18; NC 18/1/923.

26. DBFP 2, 15 no. 383 and fn 1, no. 404 and fn 5, nos 241, 271.

3. BRITISH POLICY AND THE LEAGUE: MANCHURIA AND ETHIOPIA

1. DBFP 2, 9 p. 288, fn 8.

2. Ibid., nos 655, 659, 663.

3. Ibid., nos 636 fn 8, 238 fn 2.

4. DBFP 2, 10 no. 228.

5. NC 18/1/918.

6. Bodleian Library, Simon MS 75, fol. 25; DBFP 2, 9 nos 583, 21 fn 9, 153 fn 12, 655.

7. DBFP 2, 10 no. 639; DBFP 2, 11 no. 415; DBFP 2, 9 no. 21.

8. 259 HC Deb 5s, cols 1189, 45, 60, 201–2.

9. 275 HC Deb 5s, cols 49, 66, 68, 71, 77, 88–9.

10. 292 HC Deb 5s, cols 2351, 2362–3, 2425.

11. 299 HC Deb 5s, cols 299, 915, 1404; DBFP 2, 13 App. I, no. 8 fn 2.

12. NC 18/1/882, 884–5, 889, 891, 881.

13. NC 18/1/892–3; DBFP 2, 13 no. 590.

14. D.S. Birn, *The League of Nations Union 1918–1945* (Oxford, 1981), pp. 150–1.

15. 292 HC Deb 5s, col. 675; *The Times*, 24 Nov. 1934, p. 7; 307 HC Deb 5s, col. 2036.

16. NC 18/1/929, 932; 292 HC Deb 5s, col. 2328.

17. FO 371/19158, J 7452/1/1; DBFP 2, 14 no. 230, 273.

18. DBFP 2, 14 App. II; nos 427, 431; NC 18/1/929.

19. DBFP 2, 14 nos 481, 476; DDF 1, 13 no. 150; FO 371/19123 fols 177–8; CAB 23/82 fol. 157.

20. NC 18/1/929; DBFP 2, 14 no. 493.
21. CAB 23/82 fol. 210; FO 800/295 fol. 199; DBFP 2, 14 no. 650.
22. DDF 1, 11, no. 179.
23. DDF 1, 13, nos 59, 308; 307 HC Deb 5s, cols 79, 354; DBFP 2, 15 nos 172, 274, 293; FO 371/19156, J6988/1/1; CAB 23/82, 50(35)2.
24. DBFP 2, 15 nos 323, 330, 336–8; CAB 23/82.
25. 307 HC Deb 5s, cols 718, 818, 821–7, 856.
26. Cambridge Univ. Library, Templewood MSS VIII-1.
27. CAB 23/90B Cabinet 56(35); A.J.P. Taylor, *Beaverbrook* (London, 1972), p. 360; Birmingham Univ. Library AC 41/1/67–8.
28. 309 HC Deb 5s, cols 85, 169.
29. CAB 23/83 Cabinet 11(36)5.
30. DBFP 2, 16 no. 20 and annex.
31. *The Times*, 11 June 1936, p. 10; CAB 23/84 fols 288–95.
32. DBFP 2, 15 nos 537 fn, 539 fn 6.

4. THE RHINELAND CRISIS AND COLONIES 1936–1937

1. DBFP 2, 15 no. 383 fn 7, App. 1(a) esp. paras 17, 25, 30, App. 4(b) esp. paras 28, 42.
2. Ibid., nos 509, 522.
3. DBFP 2, 16 nos 10, 20.
4. CAB 23/83 fols 233, 236–7, 240; DBFP 2, 16 no. 29 and fn 5.
5. DBFP 2, 16 nos 42, 37.
6. DDF 2, 1 no. 316.
7. DBFP 2, 16 p. 63, nos 61, 78, 98, 111, 119, 121 fn 1.
8. CAB 23/83, Cabinet 16(36); 309 HC Deb 5s, cols 1812; 1840–1, 1926–7.
9. CAB 23/83 fols 286, 289, 291–2, 295; DBFP 2, 16 nos 70, 74, 115, 131, 109.
10. DBFP 2, 16 no. 144; 310 HC Deb 5s, cols 848, 1435–49, 1496, 1498–9, 1523, 1461, 1482, 1538, 1540, 2555.
11. DBFP 2, 16 no. 262; DDF 2, 2 no. 2.
12. 310 HC Deb 5s, col. 2303; DBFP 2, 17 p. 791; DBFP 2, 16 nos 307, 336.
13. DBFP 2, 16 no. 508; DBFP 2, 17 nos 186, 258, 286, 321, 524.
14. DBFP 2, 17 no. 132, App. 2 p. 794.
15. 313 HC Deb 5s, col. 1223; DBFP 2, 16 App. 2 p. 756, no. 42 p. 55.
16. 310 HC Deb 5s, col. 2415; DBFP 2, 16 App. 10, no. 484; App. 3; 315 HC Deb 5s, col. 1132; FO 371/20475, W10243/79/98; *The Times*, 2 Oct. 1936, p. 8.
17. DBFP 2, 17 nos 342, 504, 506, 519; NC 18/1/991; DBFP 2, 18 no. 148.
18. DBFP 2, 18 no. 289, paras 20–1, nos 307, 366, 445, 462.
19. Ibid., no. 671; NC 18/1/971; DBFP 2, 18 no. 575.
20. DBFP 2, 18 no. 639.
21. FO 371/21127, R 839/188/12 fols 179–92.

5. THE SPANISH CIVIL WAR: BRITISH OPINION AND POLICY

1. DBFP 2, 17 nos 1, 19, 25, 44–5, 51–2.
2. Ibid., no. 56.
3. Ibid., no. 178.
4. CAB 23/87 fols 2–12; CAB 24/267 fols 26–34.
5. CAB 23/87 fols 299–303, 326, 360.
6. CAB 23/88 fol. 39; DBFP 2, 18 no. 393 fn 1.
7. CAB 23/88 fols 73–4; 322 HC Deb 5s, cols 598–9.
8. 322 HC Deb 5s, cols 1030, 1032, 1043–6, 1063, 1067, 1084–5.
9. *The Times*, 15 Apr. 1937, p. 18, 17 Apr. p. 14, 20 Apr. p. 17, 21 Apr. p. 16, 24 Apr. p. 12.
10. A. Bryant, *Humanity in Politics* (London n.d. [?1938]), p. 324; Bodleian Library, Conservative Party Archives NUA 2/1/51–2; CAB 23/88 fol. 66; H.P. Croft, *Spain, The Truth at Last* (Bournemouth, 1937).
11. India Office Library, MS Eur D 609/7 fol. 66; Duchess of Atholl, *Searchlight on Spain* (Harmondsworth n.d. [1938]); G.H. Gallup (ed.), *Gallup International Public Opinion Polls, Great Britain 1937–75*, vol. 1 (New York, 1976), pp. 1, 10–11.
12. *Report of the 36th Annual Conference of the Labour Party, Edinburgh 1936* (under 1936), pp. 169, 179–81, 213, 258; Churchill Coll. Archives LSPC 1/2 fols 11–13; *Report of the 37th Annual Conference of the Labour Party, Bournemouth 1937* (London, 1937), pp. 15, 212–15.
13. 328 HC Deb 5s, col. 310.
14. R.A.C. Parker, 'British Rearmament 1936–9: Treasury, trade unions and skilled labour', *English Historical Review* (Apr. 1981), 336, 342.

6. CHAMBERLAIN AND EDEN

1. NC 2/23A, 19 Jan. 1936; NC 18/1/1009, 1029.
2. CAB 127/158 fols 13–14.
3. CAB 23/87 fol. 33; DBFP 2, 19 p. 723; PREM 1/276 fol. 118.
4. PREM 1/276 fol. 215.
5. DBFP 2, 18 pp. 808–9.
6. NC 18/1/1014, 1025.
7. FO 371/20751, C7324/7324/18; PREM 1/330, Copy Halifax–Eden fol. 190.
8. Churchill College, Cambridge, Halifax microfilm Reel 1.3.2(ii) 29 Oct. 1937, 4 Nov. 1937; PREM 1/330 fols 174–5; PREM 1/210, Eden–Chamberlain, 3 Nov. 1937.
9. NC 7/11/30/67; PREM 1/330 fols 176–87; FO 371/20751, C7866/7324/18.
10. FO 371/20757 fols 98–9; DBFP 2, 19 pp. 493–4; PREM 1/330 fols 169–170.
11. Churchill College, Halifax microfilm A4.410.3.2. Halifax to Ormsby-Gore; DBFP 2, 19 pp. 540–55, 573.

12. DBFP 2, 19 pp. 579–81, 494–6.

13. Ibid., pp. 572, 601; DDF 2, 7 p. 576.

14. John Harvey (ed.), *The Diplomatic Diaries of Oliver Harvey* (London, 1970), p. 63; NC 18/1/103, NC 7/11/31/100.

15. DBFP 2, 19 pp. 580–1; CAB 4/26 fol. 335; DBFP 2, 21 pp. 611, 590, 497, 466.

16. DBFP 2, 21 pp. 262–3, 377, 470, 184–5, 630, 355–6, 363, 455–61, 469, 588 fn 4.

17. Ibid., pp. 529–30, 543, 581, 589–92, 598–603, 638, 645–7.

18. DBFP 2, 18 p. 896; DBFP 2, 19 pp. 22–30.

19. DBFP 2, 19 pp. 44–5, 107–8, 112, 118–20.

20. Ibid., p. 141; CAB 23/89, fol. 75; FO 800/328, Hal/37/1–3; DBFP 2, 19 pp. 155–66, 181–3, 200, 202; P. Gretton, 'The Nyon Conference: The Naval Aspect', *English Historical Review* (Jan. 1975), 103–12; DDF 2, 6 pp. 148–9.

21. CAB 23/89, fols 167–72; T273/410 Hankey–Wilson, 4 and 5 Nov. 1937, Tyrell to Wilson, 27 Oct. 1937; DBFP 2, 19 pp. 259, 603–5, 639–43.

22. DBFP 2, 19 pp. 679, 698, 709–11.

23. Cambridge Univ. Library, Baldwin Papers 97 fols 185–6; DBFP 2, 19 pp. 774, 725–32.

24. D. Dilks, (ed.), *The Diaries of Sir Alexander Cadogan, 1938–45* (London, 1971), pp. 36–7; FO 371/21526, A2127/64/45; DBFP 2, 19 pp. 739–40, 754–5, 759–61; CAB 23/92 fols 6–14.

25. DBFP 2, 19 pp. 760, 767, 776, 833, 902, 965.

26. W.S. Churchill, *The Gathering Storm*, p. 199.

27. DDF 2, 8 p. 517.

28. NC 18/1/1039; PREM 1/276 fol. 99; DBFP 2, 19 pp. 1140–1.

29. DBFP 2, 19 pp. 898, 912, 915; T273/410; PREM 1/276 fols 83–4.

30. CAB 127/158; PREM 1/276 fols 80–2; M. Muggeridge (ed.), *Ciano's Diplomatic Papers* (London, 1948), p. 183; DBFP 2, 19 pp. 1142–3.

31. CAB 23/92 fols 227, 262–3; DBFP 2, 19 pp. 956, 854; DDF 2, 8 pp. 470, 502, 519; 332 HC Deb 5s, cols 226–7, 253–62.

32. DBFP 2, 19 p. 1144.

7. CHAMBERLAIN AND HALIFAX: MARCH–AUGUST 1938

1. NC 18/1/1053.

2. DBFP 2, 21 pp. 666–80, 687, 819–22.

3. K. Feiling, *Life of Neville Chamberlain*, p. 338; DBFP 2, 19 pp. 1084–124, 1137.

4. DBFP 2, 19 pp. 658, 631, 686, 695, 630; Churchill College, Cambridge, Halifax microfilm Reel 1.3.2(ii).

5. R. Cockett, *Twilight of Truth. Chamberlain, Appeasement and the Manipulation of the Press* (London, 1989), p. 41; Churchill College, Cambridge, Halifax microfilm A4.410.3; D.C. Watt, *1939: How War*

Came. The Immediate Origins of the Second World War, 1938–9 (London, 1989), p. 35.

6. DBFP 2, 19 pp. 853–7.
7. Ibid., pp. 926–7, 970.
8. Ibid., p. 860.
9. Ibid., pp. 748, 771–91, 838, 843, 845.
10. Ibid., p. 993; CAB 24/275, fols 256–8.
11. CAB 23/92, Cabinet 11(38)4.
12. NC 18/1/1041, 1042; CAB 27/623 fol. 139.
13. FO 800/313 fol 45; NC 18/1/1041, 1043.
14. FO 371/21674 fols 114–25.
15. CAB 27/623 fols 153–95, 211–12; NC 18/1/1042.
16. CAB 27/627 fols 35–42; CAB 23/93 fols 32–44.
17. A. Duff Cooper, *Old Men Forget* (London, 1953), p. 218; J. Harvey (ed.), *The Diplomatic Diaries of Oliver Harvey* (London, 1970), p. 51; NC 2/23A, 10 Feb. 1936.
18. DBFP 3, 1 pp. 97, 62–4, 101.
19. CAB 27/623 fols 157, 169, 193; FO 800/309 fol. 184; G.L. Weinberg, *The Foreign Policy of Hitler's Germany. Starting World War II 1937–1939* (Chicago, 1980), pp. 361–2; DGFP, D, 2 nos 244, 247.
20. FO 800/311 fols 27–8, 3–10, 16–17.
21. D. Dilks (ed.), *The Diaries of Sir Alexander Cadogan*, p. 71.
22. Ibid., p. 73; NC 18/1/1049; A. Duff Cooper, *Old Men Forget*, p. 220; DBFP 3, 1 pp. 198–234.
23. DGFP, D, 2 nos 143, 147.
24. Fondation nationale des sciences politiques, Paris, Daladier papers 2DA1, Dr2, sdr b.
25. DGFP, D, 1 no. 19; D, 2 nos 151, 23, 221.
26. DGFP, D, 2 no. 107; J.W. Bruegel, *Czechoslovakia Before Munich* (Cambridge, 1973), pp. 138–9, 212; CAB 23/93 fols 194, 297; DBFP 3, 1 App. 2.
27. FO 371/21724, C5686/1941/18, C5989/1941/18; FO 800/309, H/VI/20.
28. DBFP 3, 1 nos 232–3, 238, 240, 249–50, 264.
29. DBFP 3, 1 no. 271, pp. 346–7; FO 371/21140, R7303/770/67; CAB 29/93, fol. 379; CAB 23/94 fols 44, 64, 137.
30. DBFP 3, 1 no. 510; CAB 23/94 fols 163–6; 338 HC Deb 5s, col. 2963.
31. CAB 23/94 fols 220–1; DBFP 3, 2 no. 546.
32. DBFP 3, 2 nos 551, 587.
33. DBFP 3, 2 no. 575; NC 18/1/1062.
34. DBFP 3, 2 nos 539, 608; T273/403, Notes by Wilson, 12 Aug. 1938.
35. NC 18/1/1064; DBFP 3, 2 App. 4 (i)(ii).
36. DBFP 3, 2 App. 4 (i)(ii); NC 7/11/31/123.
37. DBFP 3, 2 nos 686, 695; CAB 127/158 fol. 26; NC 18/1/1066.

8. MUNICH

1. CAB 23/94 fols 285–317.
2. CAB 127/158 fol. 28; Churchill College, Cambridge INSP, Diary Pt 1, fols 4, 7.
3. DBFP 3, 2 nos 819, 823; Cambridge Univ. Library, Templewood MSS X, 5, notes on crisis, Sept. 1938.
4. CAB 23/95 fols 14–15.
5. DBFP 3, 2 nos 844, 848–9, 861.
6. PREM 1/266 fol. 316; DBFP 3, 2 nos 862, 866, 883, 894.
7. CAB 23/95 fols 34–6.
8. DDF 2, 11 no. 151.
9. NC 18/1/1069; DBFP 3, 2 nos 895–6.
10. CAB 27/646, CS (38)5 fols 25–38; CAB 23/95 fols 64–111; DBFP 3, 2 nos 908, 911.
11. DBFP 3, 2 no. 928; CAB 27/646, fols 41–4; CAB 23/95 fols 114–35.
12. DBFP 3, 2 pp. 404–6, 416–17, 424–5, 444, 438–40; DDF 2, 11 pp. 340–1, 347–8, 358–9, 361, 397–8, 394.
13. *The Times*, 23 Sept. 1938, p. 16; DBFP 3, 2 pp. 463–73.
14. DBFP 3, 2 pp. 477, 480–9, 499–508; PREM 1/266A fol. 175; CAB 27/646. App. 2 to Mtg 3 p.m., 23 Sept., fol. 84.
15. DGFP, D, 2 no. 583; CAB 27/646.
16. CAB 23/95 fols 178–90; DBFP 3, 2 nos 1078, 1081 pp. 511–12.
17. DBFP 3, 2 no. 1081 p. 490; DGFP, D, 2 no. 589.
18. CAB 23/95 fols 195–233; Borthwick Institute, York, Halifax papers A4.410.3.7; Earl of Birkenhead, *Halifax. The Life of Lord Halifax* (London, 1965), p. 400.
19. DBFP 3, 2 pp. 510, 518–19, 525; CAB 23/95 fols 220, 230–1, 235–45.
20. CAB 23/95 fols 288–9; A. Duff Cooper: *Old Men Forget*, p. 237; DGFP, D, 2 no. 610.
21. DDF, 2, 11 no. 405 pp. 612–13; DBFP 3, 2 no. 1096 p. 536 fn 1; no. 1111 p. 550; M. Gilbert, *Winston S. Churchill*, vol. V *Companion*, Part 3, p. 1182.
22. DBFP 3, 2 nos 1115–16, 1118 pp. 552–7, no. 1121 pp. 559–60; PREM 1/266 fol. 77; DGFP, D, 2 no. 634.
23. DBFP 3, 2 no. 1121, p. 559; A. Duff Cooper, *Old Men Forget*, pp. 238–40; BBC sound archives.
24. CAB 23/95 fols 273–4; *The Times*, 26 Sept. 1938, p. 14, 27 Sept. p. 9, 28 Sept. pp. 14–15; BBC sound archives; DBFP 3, 2 no. 1125 p. 561, nos 1158–9 pp. 587–8; Cambridge Univ. Library, Templewood MSS X, 5 Notes on crisis, Sept. 1938.
25. 339 HC Deb 5s, cols 5–28; Bodleian Library, Simon MS 10, fols 12–13; D. Dilks (ed.), *The Diaries of Sir Alexander Cadogan*, p. 109 and photograph opp. p. 245.
26. Duff Cooper, *Old Men Forget*, p. 241; Gaumont British News film 'Munich'; DGFP, D, 2 no. 670; DBFP 3, 2 pp. 630–5.

27. DBFP 3, 2 pp. 635–40; Gaumont British News 'Munich'; BBC sound archives; K. Feiling, *Life of Neville Chamberlain*, p. 382; *The Times*, 28 Oct. 1948, p. 5.

9. FROM MUNICH TO PRAGUE

1. 339 HC Deb 5s, col. 545; NC 18/1/1072; FO 800/328, Copy Halifax to Chamberlain 11 Oct. 1938, Hal/38/88; Churchill College, Cambridge, HNKY 4/30.
2. PREM 1/266A fols 19–25; NC 18/1/1071; CAB 23/95 fol. 304.
3. 339 HC Deb 5s, col. 39, 551; DDF 2, 12 no. 41; PREM 1/318, Halifax to Chamberlain, 15 Oct. 1938.
4. 339 HC Deb 5s, col. 88; FO 800/328, Hal 38/88; NC 18/1/1072.
5. NC 18/1/1071; DGFP, D, 4 no. 251; 339 HC Deb 5s, col. 558; 341 HC Deb 5s, cols 1129, 1209–14; CAB 23/96 fols 92, 141–2.
6. N.H. Baynes (ed.), *The Speeches of Adolf Hitler*, vol. 2 (London, 1942), pp. 1534–6, 1544–8, 1555–7.
7. DBFP 3, 3 pp. 275–7.
8. Bodleian Library, Conservative Party Archives CRD 1/7/35/15; Churchill Coll. Archives MRGN 1/3, 23 Dec. 1938.
9. DBFP 3, 3 pp. 282, 585, 608–9; CAB 23/97 fols 12, 53–64, 109–17; CAB 24/282, CP 3(39) and annex; DBFP 3, 3 nos 189, 325.
10. CAB 23/96 fols 291–2, 428–34; DBFP 3, 3 pp. 356, 458–9.
11. DDF 2, 13 nos 26, 28, 283 and note, pp. 45, 50, 513; 342 HC Deb 5s, cols 852–3; DBFP 3, 3 p. 513; CAB 23/96 fol. 433; PREM 1/327, Chamberlain to the King, 17 Jan. 1939.
12. NC 18/1/1079, 1080, 1082; PREM 1/318 fols 3–11.
13. BBC sound archives; Churchill Coll. Archives PHPP 3/5 fols 47–8; CAB 23/87 fol. 254; NC 18/1/1086; *Anglo-German Review* (Mar. 1939), 119; DBFP 3, 4 p. 591; *The Times*, 31 Jan. 1939, p. 14.
14. BBC sound archives, Chamberlain's speech, 28 Jan. 1939; DBFP 3, 4 App. 2 pp. 597, 600, 174–7; FO 371/22951, C3938/8/18.
15. DBFP 3, 4 pp. 174–7, 589–96; K. Feiling, *Life of Neville Chamberlain*, pp. 396–7.
16. DBFP 3, 4 pp. 219–21, 231; DDF 2, 12 p. 810; 2, 14 p. 429.
17. DBFP 3, 4 pp. 250, 253, 260, 403–5.·

10. GUARANTEE TO POLAND

1. CAB 23/98 fols 7–15; D. Dilks (ed.), *The Diaries of Sir Alexander Cadogan* (London, 1971), p. 157; 345 HC Deb 5s, cols 440, 559.
2. BBC sound archives.
3. DBFP 3, 4 pp. 360–1, 366–7, 369–70.
4. CAB 23/98 fols 44–7, 50–1.
5. 345 HC Deb 5s. cols 731, 697–8, 2587; NC 18/1/1105.
6. CAB 23/98 fols 129–30; DGFP, D, 6 no. 35 p. 39.
7. NC 18/1/1090; DBFP 3, 3 pp. 427, 486–7; D. Dilks (ed.), *Cadogan Diaries*, p. 161; DDF 2, 15 p. 109–10.

8. PREM 1/327, fol. 32; CAB 23/98, Cabinet 13(39)2; DBFP 3, 4 p. 402–3.
9. CAB 23/98, fol. 95; DBFP 3, 4 pp. 428–9, 467, 572–3.
10. NC 18/1/1091; CAB 21/592.
11. DBFP 3, 4 pp. 455–63, 475–6, 482.
12. CAB 23/98 fol. 96; PREM 1/329 fols 68–9.
13. FO 371/22967, C4317/15/18; 345 HC Deb 5s, col. 1462; CAB 27/624 fols 200–1.
14. DBFP 3, 3 pp. 580–1, 4 pp. 15–16, 31–2.
15. DBFP 3, 4 pp. 112, 147; DDF 2, 15 pp. 125–8, 252–4; DGFP D, 6 no. 61; Jean Szembek, *Journal 1933–1939* (Paris, 1952), pp. 433–5.
16. DDF 2, 15 pp. 215, 263–4; DBFP 3, 4 p. 497, no. 515.
17. DBFP 3, 4 pp. 514–17, 540–1, 555–6.
18. CAB 23/98 fols 156–67; *The Times*, 28 Mar. 1939, p. 14, 29 Mar., p. 16; NC 18/1/1092.
19. DDF 2, 15 pp. 261–2; NC 18/1/1092; CAB 23/98 fols 187–94; 345 HC Deb 5s, col. 2415.

11. MAKING A 'PEACE FRONT': APRIL–AUGUST 1939

1. NC 18/1/1092, 2 Apr. 1939.
2. *The Times*, 1 Apr. 1939, p. 15, 3 Apr., p. 14; Bodleian Library, MS Dawson 43, Diary 3 Apr. 1939; Edward Raczynski, *In Allied London* (London, 1962), pp. 13–14; 345 HC Deb 5s, cols 2481–6, 2581–8.
3. 345 HC Deb 5s, cols 2527–9.
4. Ibid., cols 2497, 2509.
5. DBFP 3, 5 no. 2, pp. 12–13; NC 18/1/1093.
6. DBFP 3, 4 no. 518; NC 18/1/1094; DBFP 3, 5 nos 97, 101.
7. D. Dilks (ed.), *Diaries of Sir Alexander Cadogan*, p. 170; J. Harvey (ed.), *The Diplomatic Diaries of Oliver Harvey* (London, 1970), pp. 275–6; FO 800/318, fols 100–2; NC 18/1/1091, 1094.
8. CAB 23/98 fols 289–90; CAB 27/624 fols 238, 244, 261; DBFP 3, 5 nos 48, 53.
9. DBFP 3, 5 nos 311, 393; 347 HC Deb 5s, col. 953.
10. DDF 2, 15 no. 415 p. 671; 346 HC Deb 5s, cols 5–140 esp. col. 15; DBFP 3, 5 no. 310.
11. CAB 23/98 fols 213–14; NC 18/1/1093; DBFP 3, 5 nos 199, 170; DDF 2, 15 no. 387.
12. DBFP 3, 5 no. 201.
13. CAB 27/624 fols 309–12; DBFP 3, 4 no. 76; FRUS 1939, 1, pp. 139–40.
14. D. Dilks (ed.), *Cadogan Diaries*, p. 175; CAB 27/624 fols 295–300; DBFP 3, 5 nos 247, 277, 318, 350, 351.
15. Phipps Papers, Churchill College, Cambridge PHPP 1/22 fol. 47; CAB 27/624 fol. 340; CAB 23/99 fol. 129.
16. DBFP 3, 5 nos 344, 353, 421, 520; CAB 27/624 fols 962–5.
17. CAB 27/625 fols 24–55; CAB 23/99 fol. 156; DBFP 3, 5 nos 527, 589.

18. DBFP 3, 5 nos 481, 581–2; 347 HC Deb 5s, col. 1815; NC 18/1/1099, 1100.

19. DBFP 3, 5 nos 556, 595, 589; NC 18/1/1100.

20. NC 18/1/1101; CAB 23/99 fols 267–85; 347 HC Deb 5s, col. 2267.

21. DBFP 3, 5 nos 624–5, 648, 657, 665, 670; DDF 2, 16 no. 364.

22. DBFP 3, 5 no. 697; CAB 27/625 fols 75–140; CAB 23/99 fols 269–85; D. Dilks (ed.), *Cadogan Diaries*, pp. 785–6; 348 HC Deb 5s, cols 400–1.

23. G.H. Gallup (ed.), *Gallup International Public Opinion Polls, Great Britain 1937–75*, vol. 1, p. 20; Churchill College, Cambridge, Phipps Papers PHPP 3/5 fols 50–2; NC 18/1/1102.

24. DBFP 3, 5 no. 719; CAB 27/625 fols 100–1, 109.

25. DBFP 3, 6 nos 60, 66, 73, 74.

26. Ibid., no. 20; CAB 27/625 fols 183–6.

27. DBFP 3, 6 nos 126–7, 139; CAB 27/625 fols 193–200; NC 18/1/1105.

28. DBFP 3, 6 nos 193, 424; DGFP, D, 6 nos 582, 540, 579, 648.

29. DBFP 3, 6 nos 207, 227; CAB 27/625 fols 235–49; CAB 23/100 fols 76–8.

30. DDF 2, 17 nos 112, 154; DBFP 3, 6 nos 279, 281–2.

31. CAB 23/100 fols 135–8; CAB 27/625 fols 269, 258.

32. NC 18/1/1107; FO 371/23070, C 9612/3356/18; CAB 27/625 fol. 268; DBFP 3, 6 no. 338.

33. CAB 23/100 fols 185–7; DBFP 3, 6 nos 357–8; DDF 2, 17 no. 243; NC 18/1/1108.

34. CAB 23/100 fol. 224.

35. DBFP 3, 6 nos 464, 474, 489, 500, 520; CAB 27/625 fols 332–4.

36. DGFP, D, 6 no. 766.

37. DDF 2, 18 Addenda.

38. Ibid., nos 23–4, 113–14; DBFP 3, 7 nos 87–8, 90.

39. DGFP, D, 7 nos 56, 70, 75, 105, 113, 125, 132, 142, 158.

12. CONFRONTING ITALY, JAPAN AND GERMANY: APRIL–AUGUST 1939

1. DBFP 3, 5 nos 139, 150, App. I iv, v; FO 371/23795, R3658/7/22.

2. Churchill College, Cambridge, Phipps Papers PHPP 1/22 fol. 47; DBFP 3, 5 nos 255, 570; 6 nos 48, 326; PREM 1/329.

3. DBFP 3, 5 nos 255, 570.

4. DBFP 3, 6 nos 234, 261, 593; FO 371/22974, C4997/15/18 fols 289–91; DBFP 3, 7 no. 47.

5. DBFP 3, 7 nos 71, 86.

6. *The Times*, 13 June 1939, p. 16, 14 June, p. 14, 16 June, p. 14, 23 June, p. 14.

7. DBFP 3, 9 nos 1, 2, 5, 29, 55, 64, 89, 114, 119, 132, 134, 138, 142–3, 147, 169, 176–7, 203, 321.

8. FO 371/23398, F5621/1/10.

9. D. Dilks (ed.), *The Diaries of Sir Alexander Cadogan*, p. 197; NC 18/1/1104, 18/1/1107; DBFP 3, 9 nos 203, 231, 331–2; CAB 2/9 Part 1 fols 28–31.

10. DBFP 3, 9 nos 221, 253, 264, 271, 277, 461, 473, 495, 505; FO 371/23529, F 8502/6457/10 f287; DDF 2, 16 no. 509.

11. CAB 23/99 fols 311, 339–42.

12. CAB 2/9 Part 1 fols 28–30; CAB 27/625 fols 144–58, 168–9; PREM 1/316 fol. 78; DBFP 3, 9 no. 232 fn 2.

13. DBFP 3, 9 nos 196, 365.

14. FO 371/23399, F 5993/1/10 fols 199–200, F 5914/1/10; *The Times*, 20 June 1939, p. 15, 22 June, p. 8, 24 June, p. 7; 348 HC Deb. 5s, cols 2201, 2610; 350 HC Deb 5s, col. 2871; British Movietone News, 29 June 1939; CAB 16/183A f258; FRUS 1939, vol. 4, pp. 194–5, 205–6; PREM 1/325.

15. DBFP 3, 9 nos 431, 441, 477; FRUS 1939, vol. 3 pp. 570–3.

16. DBFP 3, 9 no. 492, 473.

17. Ibid., App. 1 pp. 528–32; D. Dilks (ed.), *The Cadogan Diaries*, pp. 193–5.

18. PREM 1/316 fols 3–4, 7–9, 12–19; DBFP 3, 9 no. 459; DDF 2, 17 no. 437.

19. PREM 1/316 fols 3–4, 7–9, 12–19; DBFP 3, 9 nos 535, 541.

20. NC 18/1/1095, 1096.

21. NC 18/1/1101, 1105; CAB 23/100 fol. 150; J. Barnes and D. Nicholson (eds), *The Empire at Bay. The Leo Amery Diaries 1929–45* (London, 1988), p. 553; NC 18/1/1107, 1108.

22. NC 18/1/1110.

23. NC 18/1/1100, 1107, 1111; DGFP, D, 6 nos 564, 716; Cambridge Univ. Library, Templewood MSS X-4.

24. Cambridge Univ. Library, Templewood MSS X-4; NC 7/11/32/243; NC 18/1/1094, 1095; DBFP 3, 6 no. 36.

25. DGFP, D, 6 no. 716; DBFP 3, 6 no. 354; 350 HC Deb 5s, col. 1027.

26. DGFP, D, 6 nos 368, 380; D. Dilks (ed.), *Cadogan Diaries*, p. 178; *The Times*, May 3, p. 15, May 4, p. 17, May 5, p. 18, May 8, p. 19, May 6, p. 13; J. Harvey (ed.), *The Diplomatic Diaries of Oliver Harvey* (London, 1990), p. 286; DDF 2, 16, no. 168.

27. PREM 1/335; E.W.D. Tennant, *True Account* (London, 1957), pp. 215–26.

28. PREM 1/333; FO 800/316 fols 154–7; PREM 1/332.

29. DBFP 3, 6 nos 443, 533, App. IV (i) pp. 736–8; PREM 1/331A fols 157–8.

30. DBFP 3, 6 no. 659 pp. 692–3, 696; PREM 1/331A, 14 Aug. 1939; DBFP 3, 6 no. 269.

31. 350 HC Deb 5s, col. 2030; DDF 2, 17 no. 268, 331; V.M. Falin and others (eds), *Soviet Peace Efforts on the Eve of World War II*, Part 2 (Moscow, 1973), nos 284, 372, 381.

13. ARMS AND THE ECONOMY

1. NC 18/1/847; CAB 4/23 fol. 276; CAB 4/24 fol. 199; CNRS, *Français et Britanniques dans la drôle de guerre* (Paris, 1979), article by P. Masefield, 'La Royal Air Force et le production de guerre en Grande Bretagne', p. 437; R. Wagenfuhr, *Die deutsche Industrie im Kriege 1939–45*, 2nd edn (Berlin, 1963), p. 74.
2. *UN Demographic Yearbook 1955*, Table 3; B.R. Mitchell, *European Historical Statistics* (London, 1975), Table E9; A. Toynbee and F.T. Ashton-Gwatkin (eds), *The World in March 1939* (London, 1952), p. 452.
3. NC 18/1/932; *The Times*, 23 Sept. 1935, p. 14; 5 Oct., p. 17; 31 Oct., p. 8; 29 Oct., p. 8.
4. NC 7/11/32/294; CAB 4/24 fols 199, 228, 234; CAB 16/123 fols 87, 90.
5. R.A.C. Parker, 'British Rearmament 1936–9: Treasury, trade unions and skilled labour', *English Historical Review* (Apr. 1981), 306–11.
6. CAB 4/24 fols 200, 205; CAB 24/265 fol. 265v.
7. CAB 24/273 fol. 267.
8. CAB 23/86 fol. 87; Parker, 'British Rearmament 1936–9', *EHR* (Apr. 1981), 325–6.
9. NC 2/23, 19 Jan. 1936; CAB 16/123 fols 97, 103.
10. CAB 4/24 fols 202, 204.
11. NC 2/23, 25 Oct. 1936; CAB 23/96 fol. 142.
12. CAB 24/265 fols 265–6 paras 10, 14, 15; NC 18/1/993.
13. B.H. Liddell Hart, *The Defence of Britain* (London, 1939); NC 2/29/36.
14. CAB 24/270 fols 271–2; R.A.C. Parker, 'British Rearmament 1936–9', *EHR* (Apr. 1981), 311–12; T161/855/48431, 2 Dec. 1937, 25 Nov. 1937; CAB 24/273 fols 271–2, 323; CAB 23/92 fols 129, 145–6.
15. CAB 23/93 fols 43, 46; 333 HC Deb 5s, cols 1410, 1412, 1452.
16. CAB 27/627, col 698; CAB 21/544.
17. CAB 23/93 fols 215–21; CAB 23/96 fols 156–73.
18. M.M. Postan, *British War Production* (London and Nendeln, 1975), App. 4; CAB 21/1112; Parker, 'British Rearmament 1936–9', *EHR* (Apr. 1981), 319, 338–9; CNRS, *Français et Britanniques*, pp. 413, 443.
19. R.A.C. Parker, 'The Pound Sterling, the American Treasury and British preparations for war, 1938–1939', *English Historical Review* (Apr. 1983).
20. PREM 1/336 fol. 10v.
21. CAB 24/283 fol. 14; CAB 23/97 fols 306–7.
22. CAB 23/98 fols 98–100, 133, 277–8, 331–3; CAB 23/99 fols 8–9, 14–19.
23. R.J. Minney, *The Private Papers of Hore-Belisha* (London, 1960), pp. 158–9.
24. PREM 1/336 fols 25–7.

25. *The Times*, 22 Oct. 1938, p. 8; NC 7/11/294, 11 Apr. 1939; Copy, CAB 24/287 fols 60–1.

26. CAB 23/95 fols 304–5; CAB 23/96 fols 92, 141–2, 164.

27. R.A.C. Parker, 'British Rearmament 1936–9', *EHR* (Apr. 1981), 336, 340.

28. FO 371/22973, C8300/15/18.

29. NC 18/1/1108.

14. RESOURCES FOR WAR: THE BRITISH DOMINIONS AND THE UNITED STATES

1. DBFP 2, 18 p. 902; Gallup Polls, p. 7; CAB 23/95 fol. 262.

2. DBFP 2, 18 pp. 901–2; 2, 17 p. 292.

3. CAB 23/83 fols 313–14; CAB 32/130 fol. 50; CAB 23/93 fol. 41; CAB 23/95 fol. 210; Churchill College, Cambridge, Copy Inskip Diary, 2 fol. 19.

4. CAB 23/99 fol. 129; CAB 27/635 fol. 36.

5. NC 18/1/847.

6. CAB 23/87 fol. 338.

7. CAB 23/96 fol. 21; CAB 24/279, CP 225(38) fols 196–7.

8. PREM 1/367; FDR Library. Hyde Park, New York PSF Box 53, GB: Arthur Murray.

9. CAB 23/97 fols 404, 197.

10. 346 HC Deb 5s, col. 165; Bodleian Library, Oxford, CRD 1/24/3; *The Times*, 12 May 1939, p. 10.

11. FRUS 1939, 2, pp. 234–57 esp. p. 248.

12. FO 371/23560, F2879/456/23, F2880/456/23; F2963/2963/61.

13. FO 371/23561, F4962/456/23, F7010/456/23; Kent Archives U1590, C658 (Royal Family); FO 371/23901, W10081/9805/49.

14. FO 371/22892, A2907/1292/45.

15. Cordell Hull, *The Memoirs* (London, 1948), vol. 1, pp. 641–53; FO 371/22815, A4979/98/45.

16. N. Duncan Hall, *North American Supply* (London, 1955), pp. 3, 9, 35, 39, 67; CNRS: *Français et Britanniques dans la drôle de guerre*; P. Masefield, 'La RAF et le production de guerre en Grande Bretagne', p. 444.

15. ALTERNATIVES TO APPEASEMENT

1. 292 HC Deb 5s, cols 677–681; *Labour Party Conference*, Hastings, Oct. 1933 (London, 1933); Kenneth Harris, *Attlee* (London, 1982, pb edn 1984), p. 117.

2. *Labour Party Conference*, Southport, Oct. 1934 (London, 1934), p. 244; *Labour Party Conference*, Brighton, Oct. 1935 (London, 1935), pp. 192–3.

3. *Labour Party Conference*, Brighton, Oct. 1935, p. 178; George Lansbury, *My Quest for Peace* (London, 1938), pp. 138–63; DBFP 2, 18 no. 419.

4. Stafford Cripps, *The Struggle for Peace* (London, 1936), pp. 116, 154, 64, 60.

5. 299 HC Deb 5s, col. 35; *Labour Party Conference*, Oct. 1935, p. 88; *Labour Party Conference*, Oct. 1936, p. 182.

6. 321 HC Deb 5s, cols 568, 611, 1397, 1914; *The Times*, 22 Feb. 1937; *Labour Party Conference*, Bournemouth, Oct. 1937, pp. 203, 195–6; 328 HC Deb 5s, cols 570–7.

7. 328 HC Deb 5s, cols 572–4.

8. 299 HC Deb 5s, col. 622; 310 HC Deb 5s, cols 95, 330; 325 HC Deb 5s, col. 1541; 333 HC Deb 5s, col. 1432.

9. DBFP 2, 17 no. 295; 321 HC Deb 5s, cols 3161–2; 325 HC Deb 5s, cols 1592–3, 1599; 341 HC Deb 5s, cols 177–83.

10. *The Times*, 9 Jan. 1937, p. 14; 333 HC Deb 5s, col. 1433.

11. Cambridge Univ. Library, Baldwin MS 124 fol. 54; N. Nicholson (ed.), *Harold Nicolson, Diaries and Letters 1930–9* (London, 1966), p. 273.

12. Birmingham Univ. Library, Avon MS, AP 20/1/15; PREM 1/194; M. Gilbert: *Winston S. Churchill*, vol. V *Companion*, Part 3 (London, 1982), p. 291; Sir B. Domvile, *Look to your Moat* (London, 1937), p. 145; FO 800/394 fol. 16; Churchill Coll. MS DRAX 2/18.

13. 276 HC Deb 5s, cols 542–3, 545, 2793–4, 1833; 275 HC Deb 5s, cols 1817–20, 1833.

14. R. Churchill (ed.), *Winston S. Churchill, Arms and the Covenant* (London, 1938), pp. 152, 272; 292 HC Deb 5s, col. 675; *The Economist*, 23 Nov. 1935, p. 1005.

15. 317 HC Deb 5s, cols 1100–1, 1107; B. Wasserstein, *Herbert Samuel, A Political Life* (Oxford, 1992), pp. 391–2.

16. M. Gilbert, *Churchill*, vol. V *Companion*, Part 3, pp. 449–50; *The Times*, 1 Jan. 1937, pp. 12–13.

17. NC 8/24/1; Bodleian Library, Conservative Party Archives NUA 2/1/52 fol. 31.

18. 333 HC Deb 5s, cols 99–100.

19. M. Gilbert, *Churchill*, vol. V *Companion*, Part 3, pp. 990, 1171–2, 1177; *Headway*, vol. 20 no. 6 (June 1938), 102; *Labour Party Conference*, Southport, Apr. 1939 (London, 1939), pp. 13–15; M. Gilbert, *Churchill*, vol. V, pp. 966, 971–2; 339 HC Deb 5s, cols 359–73.

20. Bodleian Library, Conservative Party Archives, CRD 1/7/37 fol. 4, Clarke to Sir J. Ball, 27 Jan. 1939.

21. 339 HC Deb 5s, col. 34.

22. B. Pimlott (ed.), *The Political Diary of Hugh Dalton, 1918–40, 1945–6* (London, 1986), p. 242; H. Dalton, *The Fateful Years* (London, 1957), pp. 202–3.

23. R.R. James (ed.), *Chips. The Diaries of Sir Henry Channon* (London, 1967), p. 176; N. Nicolson (ed.), *Harold Nicolson Diaries and Letters 1930–9*, pp. 378, 397; G.H. Gallup (ed.), *Gallup International Public Opinion Polls, Great Britain*, vol. 1, p. 13.

16. OUTBREAK OF WAR

1. DBFP 3, 6 nos 325, 355; ibid., 7 no. 197.
2. NC 18/1/1114; D. Dilks (ed.), *Cadogan Diaries*, pp. 196–9; FO 800/317 fol. 82.
3. FO 800/317 fol. 82.
4. DBFP 3, 7 no. 137, 146; CAB 23/100, fols 325–32.
5. DBFP 3, 7 nos 200, 211, 248; 351 HC Deb 5s, cols 8–10.
6. NC 18/1/1115; DBFP 3, 7 nos 283–4.
7. DBFP 3, 7 nos 397, 399, 628–9, 402 fn 3, 445 fn 8; Cambridge Univ. Library, Templewood MSS X-5, 1939 Notes, 29 Aug.; NC 18/1/1115.
8. Dilks (ed.), *Cadogan Diaries*, pp. 201–3; J. Harvey (ed.), *Diplomatic Diaries of Oliver Harvey*, pp. 305–8; CAB 23/100 fol. 382, PREM 1/331A fols 118–19.
9. DBFP 3, 7 nos 426, 501, 455, 508, 490, 502, 504, 515, 525, 538, 543; Dilks (ed.), *Cadogan Diaries*, pp. 204–5.
10. DBFP 3, 7, nos 570–1, 574–5, 589, 596.
11. Ibid., 590; DDF 2, 19 Add. 2, pp. 455–6.
12. Bodleian MS Eng. Hist. c 495, Wallace Diary; Dilks (ed.), *Cadogan Diaries*, p. 206; DBFP 3, 7 no. 604; DDF 2, 19, Add. 2, p. 457.
13. DDF 2, 19 no. 371.
14. CAB 23/100 fols 443, 445, 448; 351 HC Deb 5s, cols 126–38; DBFP 3, 7 no. 644; DDF 2, 19 nos 320–1, 333.
15. Ministero Degli Affari Esteri, *I Documenti Diplomatici Italiani* (Rome, 1953), ser 8, vol. 13 no. 571; DGFP D, 7 no. 541; DBFP 3, 7 no. 710; 351 HC Deb 5s, col. 221; Bodleian Library, Simon MS 11, fols 2–7.
16. Bodleian Library, Simon MS 11, fols 2–17; Cambridge Univ. Library, Templewood MSS X-5, 2 Sept. 1939; CAB 23/100 fol. 464.
17. DBFP 3, 7 nos 713, 739; CAB 23/100 fol. 448.
18. 351 HC Deb 5s, cols 280–2; FO 800/317 fol. 84; DDF 2, 19, p. 471.
19. DGFP D, 7 no. 558; DBFP 3, 9 App. IV p. 539; Bodleian Library, Simon MS 11, fols 15–17.
20. BBC sound archives.

17. CONCLUSION

1. Cambridge Univ. Library, Baldwin MSS 174, fols 19–27.

Sources, Books and Articles

This book is based on primary sources. The most important are those in the Public Record Office in Kew and in the University of Birmingham library. The Public Record Office contains the carefully organised papers of the Cabinet Office with the records of the Cabinet and its Committees, of the Prime Minister's Office, and of the various government departments, including the Foreign Office. Many Foreign Office papers are in print and, in the volumes produced by later editors of the *Documents on British Foreign Policy*, notably W. N. Medlicott, there are some from the Cabinet and other sources. At Birmingham there are Neville Chamberlain's papers, of which the most revealing, as he obviously intended them to be, are the extraordinary series of letters to his sisters, continued over more than 25 years: they set out for the historian his own description of his intentions and his justification of his actions.

The writer of this book has formed his own view by studying the sources and seeking in that way to judge for himself how British policy was determined. On balance, it seems to him, the evidence shows that Chamberlain, first, became the most active exponent of an agreed policy towards Germany and, then, as others came to doubt and hesitate, argued and manoeuvred to continue it. The evidence, the author believes, shows Chamberlain's supremacy in the making of British policy in these years. Further, he suggests, Chamberlain consciously chose 'appeasement': the active search for agreements to limit armaments and to settle German grievances. Chamberlain followed that policy because he thought it correct; he chose the policy and he was not the mere puppet of circumstantial constraints.

Since writers have been able to study the records many have shown more sympathy than before towards Chamberlain and his colleagues. Until then, Churchill's condemnation, reinforced in 1963 by a lively book from Richard Gott and Martin Gilbert, overwhelmed the cautious defence of Feiling, Chamberlain's first biographer. After 1969, on the other hand, most historians have, with reason, denied that Chamberlain was cowardly, ignorant or incompetent, but scholars have analysed the factors influencing British policy so effectively as sometimes to make it seem that there was no possible alternative. The list of publications given below, though incomplete, includes several such studies. Most notably a concise, scholarly and elegantly persuasive statement of the case that Chamberlain, far from surrendering to illusions, advocated the best, or perhaps the only, policy towards Germany that circumstances allowed, was given in a masterly lecture by Chamberlain's biographer, David Dilks. The present book suggests that Chamberlain was wrong when he argued that no effective methods of securing British safety and prosperity were possible other than those he advocated: much recent writing represents a posthumous triumph for Chamberlain's argumentative skill.

Geoffrey Warner set this book going and provided enjoyable conversations. Gratitude is due to the Earl of Halifax, Viscount Simon, Viscount Margesson and Viscount Weir for access to their papers. The author is grateful to Conservative Central Office for the use of their records and to the Master and Fellows of Churchill College, the Master and Fellows of Trinity College, Cambridge, the Syndics of the Cambridge University Library, the Curators of the Bodleian Library and the Kent Record Office for opportunities to study papers in their care. Acknowledgements are also due to Birmingham University Library.

The most valuable collections of unpublished evidence are in the Public Record Office at Kew; the Special Collections Library at the University of Birmingham; Churchill College, Cambridge; the Cambridge University Library; and Room 132 in the Bodleian Library, Oxford. The author's thanks are especially due to their staffs and particularly to Dr B. S. Benedikz at Birmingham. Crown copyright material in the Public Record Office is reproduced by permission of the Controller of Her Majesty's Stationery Office. During nearly two decades Oxford students of this subject have given enjoyable opportunities for discussion of the evidence. Vanessa Graham, for the publishers, has shown extraordinary kindness and patience. Otherwise the author's special thanks are due to Patricia Lloyd, secretary at Queen's College, Oxford.

ALASTAIR PARKER

PUBLISHED COLLECTIONS OF DOCUMENTS

Documents on British Foreign Policy, 2nd series 1929–38, 21 vols, ed. R. Butler, W.N. Medlicott and others (London, 1946–85).

Documents on British Foreign Policy, 3rd series 1938–39, 9 vols, ed. E.L. Woodward and others (London, 1949–55).

Documents Diplomatiques Français, published by the Ministère des Affaires Etrangères. Série 1, 1932–5, 13 vols (Paris, 1964–84).

Documents Diplomatiques Français, Série 2, 1936–9, 19 vols (Paris, 1963–86).

Documents on German Foreign Policy (ed. M. Baumont and others), Series C, 1933–7, 7 vols (London, Washington and Paris, 1957–83).

Documents on German Foreign Policy, Series D, 1938–9, 7 vols (London, Washington and Paris, 1949–56).

Foreign Relations of the United States, published by the State Dept. (for 1919–39, Washington, 1934–56).

Documenti Diplomatici Italiani, published by the Ministero Degli Affari Esteri, Series 8, vols 12–13, 1939 (Rome, 1952–3).
Soviet Peace Efforts on the Eve of World War II, ed. V. Falin and others (Moscow, 1973).
Winston S. Churchill. Documents ed. M. Gilbert: *Churchill,* vol. V *Companion,* Part 3 (London, 1982).

DIARIES AND MEMOIRS

AMERY, LEO, *The Empire at Bay. The Leo Amery Diaries 1929–45,* ed. J. Barnes and D. Nicholson (London, 1988).
AMERY, L. S., *My Political Life III: The Unforgiving Years* (London, 1955).
BOOTHBY, R., *I Fight to Live* (London, 1947).
BUTLER, R. A., *The Art of the Possible* (London, 1971).
The Diaries of Sir Alexander Cadogan, 1938–45, ed. D. Dilks (London, 1971).
Chips. The Diaries of Sir Henry Channon, ed. R. R. James (London, 1967).
CHURCHILL, W. S., *The Gathering Storm* [Second World War, I] (London, 1948).
COLVILLE, J., *The Fringes of Power* (London, 1985).
DALTON, HUGH, *Memoirs II. The Fateful Years 1931–45* (London, 1957).
The Political Diary of Hugh Dalton, ed. B. Pimlott (London, 1986).
DUFF COOPER, A. (Lord Norwich), *Old Men Forget* (London, 1953).
EDEN, ANTHONY (Lord Avon), *The Eden Memoirs I: Facing the Dictators* (London, 1962).
The Diplomatic Diaries of Oliver Harvey 1937–40, ed. J. Harvey (London, 1970).
HENDERSON, H., *Failure of a Mission* (London, 1940).
HOARE, SIR SAMUEL (Lord Templewood), *Nine Troubled Years* (London, 1954).
JONES, T., *A Diary with Letters 1931–50* (London, 1954).
NICOLSON, HAROLD, *Diaries and Letters I 1930–39,* ed. N. Nicolson (London, 1967).
Chief of Staff: The Diaries of Lt. General Sir Henry Pownall, vol. I *1933–40,* ed. B. Bond (London, 1974).
SLESSOR, SIR JOHN, Marshal of the RAF, *The Central Blue* (London, 1956).
STRANG, WILLIAM (Lord Strang), *At Home and Abroad* (London, 1956).
STRANG, WILLIAM (Lord Strang), *The Moscow Negotiations* (Leeds, 1968).
TENNANT, E.W.D., *True Account* (London, 1957).

GENERAL STUDIES

ADAMTHWAITE, A., *Making of the Second World War* (London, 1979).

BELL, P.M.H., *The Origins of the Second World War in Europe* (London, 1986).
GIRAULT, R. and FRANK, R., *Turbulente Europe et nouveaux mondes 1914–41* (Paris, 1988).
GRENVILLE, J. A. S., *A World History of the Twentieth Century*, vol. I *1900–45* (London, 1980).
KITCHEN, M., *Europe Between the Wars* (London, 1988).
MOWAT, C. L., *Britain Between the Wars 1918–40* (London, 1955).
NORTHEDGE, F. S., *The Troubled Giant* (London, 1966).
OVERY, R. J. and WHEATCROFT, A., *Road to War* (London, 1989).
PARKER, R. A. C., *Europe 1918–39* (London, 1969).
ROBERTS, J. M., *Europe 1880–1945* (London, 1967).
TAYLOR, A. J. P., *English History 1914–45* (Oxford, 1965).
TAYLOR, A. J. P., *The Origins of the Second World War* (London, 1961).

BIOGRAPHIES

BIRKENHEAD, LORD, *Halifax. The Life of Lord Halifax* (London, 1965).
CARLTON, D., *Anthony Eden* (London, 1981).
CHARMLEY, J. D., *Duff Cooper* (London, 1986).
COLVILLE, J. R., *Man of Valour, The Life of Field Marshal the Viscount Gort* (London, 1972).
CROSS, J. A., *Sir Samuel Hoare* (London, 1977).
CROSS, J. A., *Lord Swinton* (Oxford, 1982).
DILKS, D., *Neville Chamberlain I, 1869–1929* (Cambridge, 1984).
DUTTON, D., *Simon* (London, 1992).
FEILING, K., *The Life of Neville Chamberlain* (London, 1946).
GILBERT, M., *Winston S. Churchill*, vol. V, *1922–39* (London, 1976).
HARRIS, K., *Attlee* (London, 1982).
HEUSTON, R. F. V., *Lives of the Lord Chancellors, 1885–1940* (Oxford, 1964).
LOUIS, W. R., *In the Name of God, Go! Leo Amery and the British Empire in the Age of Churchill* (New York and London, 1992).
MARQUAND, D., *Ramsay MacDonald* (London, 1977).
MIDDLEMAS, K. and BARNES, J., *Baldwin* (London, 1969).
MACLEOD, I., *Neville Chamberlain* (London, 1961).
MINNEY, R. J., *The Private Papers of Hore-Belisha* (London, 1960).
READER, W. J., *Architect of Air Power* [Weir] (London, 1968).
RHODES JAMES, R., *Churchill, A Study in Failure* (London, 1970).
RHODES JAMES, R., *Eden* (London, 1986).
ROBERTS, A., *The Holy Fox. A Biography of Lord Halifax* (London, 1991).
ROSE, N., *Vansittart, Study of a Diplomat* (London, 1978).
ROSKILL, S., *Hankey, Man of Secrets*, vol. III, *1931–63* (London, 1974).
TAYLOR, A. J. P., *Beaverbrook* (London, 1972).
WASSERSTEIN, B., *Herbert Samuel, A Political Life* (Oxford, 1992).

BRITISH POLICY

ANDREW, C. M., *Secret Service. The Making of the British Intelligence Community* (London, 1985).

ASTER, S., *1939, the Making of the Second World War* (London, 1973).

BIALER, U., *The Shadow of the Bomber: The Fear of Air Attack and British Politics 1932–1939* (London, 1980).

BIRN, D. S., *The League of Nations Union 1918–45* (Oxford, 1981).

CEADEL, M., *Pacifism in Britain* (Oxford, 1980).

CHARMLEY, J. D., *Neville Chamberlain and the Lost Peace* (London, 1989).

COCKETT, R., *Twilight of Truth: Chamberlain, Appeasement and the Manipulation of the Press* (London, 1989).

COLVIN, I., *The Chamberlain Cabinet* (London, 1971).

COWLING, M., *The Impact of Hitler* (Cambridge, 1975).

CROZIER, A. J., *Appeasement and Germany's Last Bid for Colonies* (London, 1988).

DOUGLAS, R., *In the Year of Munich* (London, 1977).

DOUGLAS, R., *The Advent of War 1939–40* (London, 1978).

EDWARDS, J., *The British Government and the Spanish Civil War* (London, 1979).

EMMERSON, J. T., *The Rhineland Crisis March 7, 1936* (London, 1977).

FUCHSER, L. W., *Neville Chamberlain and Appeasement, a Study in the Politics of History* (New York, 1982).

FURNIA, A., *The Diplomacy of Appeasement* (Washington, 1960).

GANNON, F. R., *The British Press and Nazi Germany 1936–39* (Oxford, 1971).

GILBERT, M., *The Roots of Appeasement* (London, 1966).

GILBERT, M. and GOTT, R., *The Appeasers* (London, 1963).

GRIFFITHS, R., *Fellow Travellers of the Right. Enthusiasts for Nazi Germany 1933–39* (London, 1980).

HILL, C., *Cabinet Decisions on Foreign Policy, October 1938–June 1941* (London, 1991).

LAMB, R., *The Drift to War 1922–39* (London, 1989).

LEE, BRADFORD, A., *Britain and the Sino-Japanese War* (Stanford, 1973).

LEUTZE, J. R., *Bargaining for Supremacy: Anglo-American Naval Collaboration 1937–41* (Chapel Hill, NC, 1977).

LOWE, P., *Great Britain and the Origins of the Pacific War, 1937–41* (Oxford, 1977).

LOUIS, W. R., *British Strategy in the Far East 1919–39* (Oxford, 1971).

MEDLICOTT, W. N., *Britain and Germany: The Search for Agreement 1930–7* (London, 1969). Also in D. Dilks (ed.), *Retreat from Power: Studies in Britain's Foreign Policy* (London, 1981).

MIDDLEMAS, K., *The Diplomacy of Illusion* (London, 1972).

NEWMAN, S., *March 1939, the British Guarantee to Poland* (Oxford, 1976).

PARKINSON, R., *Peace for our Time* (London, 1971).

PETERS, A. R., *Anthony Eden at the Foreign Office 1931–38* (Aldershot and New York, 1986).

PRATT, L. R., *East of Malta, West of Suez, Britain's Mediterranean Crisis* (Cambridge, 1975).

PRAZMOWSKA, A., *Britain, Poland and the Eastern Front, 1939* (Cambridge, 1987).

ROBBINS, K. G., *Munich 1938* (London, 1968).

ROCK, W. R., *British Appeasement in the 1930s* (London, 1977).

ROCK, W. R., *Chamberlain and Roosevelt 1937–40* (Columbus, Ohio, 1988).

ROSTOW, N., *Anglo-French Relations 1934–36* (London, 1984).

SCHMIDT, G., *The Politics and Economics of Appeasement* (Leamington, 1986).

TAYLOR, T., *Munich, the Price of Peace* (New York, 1979).

THOMPSON, N., *The Anti-Appeasers. Conservative Opposition to Appeasement in the 1930s* (Oxford, 1971).

TITMUSS, R. M., *Problems of Social Policy* (London, 1950).

WALEY, D., *British Public Opinion and the Abyssinian War* (London, 1975).

WATT, D. C., *Personalities and Policy* (London, 1965).

WATT, D. C., *How War Came: The Immediate Origins of the Second World War, 1938–9* (London, 1989).

WATT, D. C., 'Misinformation, Misconception, Mistrust – Episodes in British Policy and the Approach of War', in M. Bentley and J. Stevenson (eds), *High and Low Politics in Modern Britain* (Oxford, 1983).

WEBBER, G. C., *The Ideology of the British Right 1918–39* (London, 1986).

SOCIAL AND ECONOMIC STUDIES

Comité d'Histoire de la 2ᵉ guerre mondiale: *Français et Britanniques dans la drôle de guerre* (Paris, 1979).

FEINSTEIN, C. H., *National Income, Expenditure and Output of the U.K. 1855–1965* (Cambridge, 1976).

GORDON, G. A. H., *British Seapower and Procurement between the Wars* (London, 1988).

HANCOCK, W. K., and GOWING, M. M., *British War Economy* (London, 1949).

HOWSON, S., *Domestic Monetary Management in Britain 1919–38* (Cambridge, 1975).

HOWSON, S., *The Economic Advisory Council 1930–39* (Cambridge, 1977).

INMAN, P., *Labour in the Second World War* (London, 1957).

KAISER, D. E., *Economic Diplomacy and the Origins of the Second World War* (Princeton, 1980).

MIDDLETON, R., *Towards the Managed Economy: Keynes, the Treasury and the Fiscal Policy Debate of the 1930s* (London, 1985).

MOGGRIDGE, D. (ed.), *The Collected Works of John Maynard Keynes*, vol. IX and vol. XXI (London, 1972 and 1982).

OVERY, R. J., *The Air War 1939–45* (London, 1980).

PEDEN, G., *British Rearmament and the Treasury* (Edinburgh, 1979).

POSTAN, M. M., *British War Production* (London, 1952 and 1975).

RICHARDSON, H. W., *The Economic Recovery of Britain* (London, 1967).

SHAY, R. P., *British Rearmament in the Thirties: Politics and Profits* (Princeton, 1977).

TEICHOVA, A., *An Economic Background to Munich, International Business and Czechoslovakia* (Cambridge, 1974).

WENDT, B. J., *Economic Appeasement* (in German) (Dusseldorf, 1971).

MILITARY

BOND, B., *British Military Policy Between the Two World Wars* (Oxford, 1980).

BOND, B., *Liddell Hart. A Study of his Military Thought* (London, 1977).

GIBBS, N. H., *Grand Strategy, I, Rearmament Policy* (London, 1976).

HOWARD, MICHAEL, *The Continental Commitment* (London, 1972).

MURRAY, W., *The Change in the European Balance of Power 1938–9* (Princeton, 1984).

POST, G., *Dilemmas of Appeasement: British Deterrence and Defense, 1934–37* (Cornell, 1993).

ROSKILL, S., *Naval Policy Between the Wars*, vol. 2, *1930–9* (London, 1976).

SMITH, M., *British Air Strategy Between the Wars* (Oxford, 1984).

WARK, W. K., *The Ultimate Enemy – British Intelligence and Nazi Germany 1933–9* (London, 1985).

WATT, D. C., *Too Serious a Business* (Cambridge, 1975).

OTHER GREAT POWERS

ALEXANDER, M. S., *The Republic in Danger. General Maurice Gamelin and the Politics of French Defence 1933–40* (Cambridge, 1992).

ADAMTHWAITE, A., *France and the Coming of the Second World War* (London, 1977).

CARR, W., *Arms, Autarky, Aggression* (London, 1979).

DALLEK, R., *Franklin D. Roosevelt and American Foreign Policy 1932–1945* (New York, 1979).

DUROSELLE, J. B., *La Décadence 1932–1939. Politique etrangère de la France* (Paris, 1979)

HASLAM, J., *The Soviet Union and the Struggle for Collective Security in Europe 1933–39* (London, 1984).

HOCHMAN, J., *The Soviet Union and the Failure of Collective Security 1934–8* (Ithaca, 1984).

HOFFMAN, P., *The History of the German Resistance* (Cambridge, Mass., 1979).

IRIYE, A., *The Origins of the Second World War in Asia and the Pacific* (London, 1987).

JORDAN, N., *The Popular Front and Central Europe* (Cambridge, 1992).

KERSHAW, I., *The Nazi Dictatorship* (London, 1989).

KERSHAW, I., *Hitler* (London, 1991).

KLEMPERER, K. von, *German Resistance Against Hitler* (Oxford, 1992).

KNOX, M., *Mussolini Unleashed 1939–41* (Cambridge, 1982).

MACK SMITH, D., *Mussolini's Roman Empire* (London, 1977).

OFFNER, A. A., *American Appeasement 1933–38* (Cambridge, Mass., 1969).

OVENDALE, R., *Appeasement and the English Speaking World* (Cardiff, 1975).

MACDONALD, C. A., *The United States, Britain and Appeasement 1936–1939* (London, 1981).

REYNOLDS, D., *The Creation of the Anglo-American Alliance 1937–41* (London, 1981).

ROBERTS, G., *The Unholy Alliance: Stalin's Pact with Hitler* (London, 1989).

VAÏSSE, M., *Sécurité d'abord. La Politique française en matiére de désarmement, 1930–4* (Paris, 1981).

WARNER, G., *Pierre Laval and the Eclipse of France* (London, 1968).

WEINBERG, G. L., *The Foreign Policy of Hitler's Germany. Starting World War II, 1937–39* (Chicago, 1980).

YOUNG, R. J., *In Command of France: French Foreign Policy and Military Planning, 1933–40* (Cambridge, Mass., 1978).

COLLECTIONS OF ESSAYS

ANDREW, C. M. and DILKS, D. (eds), *The Missing Dimension. Governments and Intelligence Communities in the Twentieth Century* (London, 1984).

BOYCE, R. and ROBERTSON, E. M. (eds), *Paths to War. New Essays on the Origins of the Second World War* (London, 1989).

DILKS, D. (ed.), *Retreat from Power: Studies in Britain's Foreign Policy*, vol. I *1906–39* (London, 1981).

MARTEL, G. (ed.), *The Origins of the Second World War Reconsidered – the A. J. P. Taylor Debate after 25 Years* (Boston, Mass., 1986).

MOMMSEN, W. J. and KETTENACKER, L. (eds), *The Fascist Challenge and the Policy of Appeasement* (London, 1983).

NISH, IAN (ed.), *Anglo-Japanese Alienation 1919–52* (Cambridge, 1982).

ARTICLES

Abbreviations: *Eng. Hist. Rev.*   *English Historical Review*
                 Hist. J.   *Historical Journal*
                 Int. Hist. Rev.   *International History Review*
                 J. Contemp. Hist.   *Journal of Contemporary History*

ANDREWS, C. M., 'Secret Intelligence and British Foreign Policy 1900–1939', in C. M. Andrews and J. Noakes (eds), *Intelligence and International Relations 1900–45* (Exeter, 1987).

AULACH, H., 'Britain and the Sudeten Issue', *J. Contemp. Hist.* (1983).

BEICHMAN, A., 'The Origins of the Conservative Research Department', *J. Contemp. Hist.* (1978).

BIALER, U., '"Humanization" of Air Warfare in British Foreign Policy', *J. Contemp. Hist.* (1978).

BOADLE, D., 'Vansittart's administration of the Foreign Office in the 1930s', in R. T. A. Langhorne (ed.), *Diplomacy and Intelligence during the Second World War* (London, 1985).

CEADEL, M., 'The Peace Ballot 1934–5', *Eng. Hist. Rev.* (1980).

COCKETT, R. B., 'Ball, Chamberlain and *Truth*', *Hist. J.* (1990).

COGHLAN, F., 'Armaments, Economic Policy and Appeasement', *History* (1972).

DILKS, D., 'The British Foreign Office Between the Wars', in B. I. C. McKercher and D. J. Moss (eds), *Shadow and Substance in British Foreign Policy 1895–1939* (Edmonton, 1984).

DILKS, D., '"We must hope for the best and prepare for the worst." The Prime Minister, the Cabinet and Hitler's Germany 1937–9', *Proceedings of the British Academy* (1987).

DOUGLAS, R., 'Chamberlain and Eden 1937–8', *J. Contemp. Hist.* (1978).

DUNBABIN, J. P. D., 'British Rearmament in the 1930s', *Hist. J.* (1975).

EATWELL, R., 'Munich, Public Opinion and Popular Front', *J. Contemp. Hist.* (1971).

FEARON, P., 'The British Airframe Industry and the State 1918–35', *Economic History Review* (1974 and 1975).

HALL, H. H., 'The Origins of the Anglo-German Naval Agreement', *Hist. J.* (1976).

HARRISON, R. A., 'Testing the Water. A Secret Probe towards Anglo-American Military Cooperation in 1936', *Int. Hist. Rev.* (1985).

LAMMERS, D., 'Fascism, Communism and the Foreign Office', *J. Contemp. Hist.* (1971).

LAMMERS, D., 'From Whitehall after Munich: The Foreign Office and the Future Course of British Policy', *Hist. J.* (1973).

LITTLE, D., 'Anti-Bolshevism and British Non-intervention in the Spanish Civil War', *J. Contemp. Hist.* (1988).

LUNGU, D. B., 'The European Crisis of March–April 1939: The Romanian Dimension', *Int. Hist. Rev.* (1985).

MACDONALD, C. A., 'Britain, France and the April Crisis of 1939', *Review of European Studies* (April 1972).

MACDONALD, C. A., 'Economic Appeasement and the German "Moderates"', *Past and Present* (1972).

MANNE, R., 'The British Decision for Alliance with Russia May 1939', *J. Contemp. Hist.* (1974).

MANNE, R., 'The Foreign Office and the Failure of Anglo-Soviet Rapprochement', *J. Contemp. Hist.* (1981).

MARKS, F. W., 'America's Role in the Appeasement of Nazi Germany', *Hist. J.* (1985).

MURRAY, W., 'German Air Power and the Munich Crisis', in B. Bond and I. Roy (eds), *War and Society* (London, 1976), vol. I.

OVERY, R. J., 'German Air Strength 1933–9', *Hist. J.* (1984).

PARKER, R. A. C., 'Great Britain, France and the Ethiopian Crisis', *Eng. Hist. Rev.* (1974).

PARKER, R. A. C., 'Economics, Rearmament and Foreign Policy', *J. Contemp. Hist.* (1975).

PARKER, R. A. C., 'The British Government and the Coming of War with Germany', in M. R. D. Foot (ed.), *War and Society: Historical Essays in Honour and Memory of J. R. Western* (London, 1973).

PARKER, R. A. C., 'British Rearmament 1936–9: Treasury, Trade Unions and Skilled Labour', *Eng. Hist. Rev.* (1981).

PARKER, R. A. C., 'The Pound Sterling, the American Treasury and British Preparations for War, 1938–9', *Eng. Hist. Rev.* (1983).

PEDEN, G. C., 'Sir Warren Fisher and British Rearmament against Germany', *Eng. Hist. Rev.* (1979).

PEDEN, G. C., 'The Treasury View on Public Works and Employment in the Interwar Period', *Economic History Review* (1984).

PEDEN, G. C., 'The Burden of Imperial Defence and the Continental Commitment Reconsidered', *Hist. J.* (1984).

PEDEN, G. C., 'A Matter of Timing: The Economic Background to British Foreign Policy 1937–9', *History* (1984).

POST, G., 'The Machinery of British Policy', *Int. Hist. Rev.* (1979).

PRAZMOWSKA, A. J., 'Poland's Foreign Policy September 1938–September 1939, *Hist. J.* (1986).

PRAZMOWSKA, A. J. 'War over Danzig?', *Hist. J.* (1983).

PUGH, M., 'Pacifism and Politics in Britain 1931–5', *Hist. J.* (1980).

ROBERTS, G., 'The Fall of Litvinov: A Revisionist View', *J. Contemp. Hist.* (1992).

ROBERTS, G., 'The Soviet Decision for a Pact with Nazi Germany', *Soviet Studies* (1992).

ROBERTSON, J. C., 'The British General Election of 1935', *J. Contemp. Hist.* (1974).

ROSE, N., 'The Resignation of Anthony Eden', *Hist. J.* (1982).

SCHRÖDER, H. J., 'Economic Appeasement', *Vierteljahrshefte für Zeitgeschichte* (1982).

SCHRÖDER, P. W., 'Munich and the British Tradition', *Hist. J.* (1976).

SHAI, A., 'Was There a Far Eastern Munich?', *J. Contemp. Hist.* (1974).

STAFFORD, P., 'The Chamberlain–Halifax Visit to Rome: A Reappraisal', *Eng. Hist. Rev.* (1983).

STAFFORD, P., 'The French Government and the Danzig Crisis: The Italian Dimension', *Int. Hist. Rev.* (1984).

WATT, D. C., 'British Intelligence and the Coming of the Second World War in Europe', in E. R. May (ed.), *Knowing One's Enemies* (Princeton, 1986).

WEINBERG, G. L., ROCK, W. R. and CIENCIALA, A. M., 'The Munich Crisis Revisited', *Int. Hist. Rev.* (1989).

Index